ON WATERLOO

CLAUSEWITZ, WELLINGTON and the CAMPAIGN OF 1815

Translated and Edited
by
CHRISTOPHER BASSFORD
DANIEL MORAN
and
GREGORY W. PEDLOW

Published by
CLAUSEWITZ.COM
2010

Printed in the United States of America.

Third Printing

Copyright © 2010 by Christopher Bassford, Daniel Moran, Gregory W. Pedlow, and Clausewitz.com.

ALL RIGHTS RESERVED

ISBN 10: 1453701508
ISBN 13: 9781453701508

Carl von Clausewitz and Arthur Wellesley, 1st Duke of Wellington, *On Waterloo: Clausewitz, Wellington, and the Campaign of 1815*, ed./trans. Christopher Bassford, Daniel Moran, and Gregory W. Pedlow (Clausewitz.com, 2010).

Includes maps, index, and extensive documentation. Contains material from: Carl von Clausewitz, *Der Feldzug von 1815 in Frankreich*, in *Hinterlassene Werke des Generals Carl von Clausewitz über Krieg und Kriegsführung* (Berlin: Ferdinand Dümmler, 1835), volume 8; *The Dispatches of Field Marshal the Duke Of Wellington, During His Various Campaigns in India, Denmark, Portugal, Spain, the Low Countries, and France, from 1799 to 1815*, in 12 volumes, compiled by Lieut. Colonel Gurwood (London: John Murray, Albemarle Street), volume 12; "Memorandum on the Battle of Waterloo," 24 September 1842, from *Dispatches, Correspondence, and Memoranda of Field Marshal Arthur Duke of Wellington*, edited by his son, the Duke of Wellington (London: John Murray, 1863), v.10; various archives, including The British Library and the Papers of the First Duke of Wellington held by the University of Southampton; and various essays by the editors, Christopher Bassford, Daniel Moran, and Gregory W. Pedlow.

Subject classifications include:
1. Europe—history—18th century—19th century.
2. Europe—politics and government—1789-1900.
3. Military art and science—Great Britain—History.
4. Clausewitz, Carl von, 1789-1831.
5. Wellington, Arthur Wellesley, Duke of, 1769-1852.
6. Napoleon I, Emperor of the French, 1769-1821.
7. Waterloo, Battle of, 1815.
8. History—philosophy.

ON WATERLOO

What the layman gets to know of the course of military events is usually nondescript. One action resembles another, and from a mere recital of events it would be impossible to guess what obstacles were faced and overcome. Only now and then, in the memoirs of generals or of their confidants, or as the result of close historical study, are some of the countless threads of the tapestry revealed. Most of the arguments and clashes of opinion that precede a major operation are deliberately concealed because they touch political interests, or they are simply forgotten, being considered as scaffolding to be demolished when the building is complete.

Carl von Clausewitz
On War

CONTENTS

	Acknowledgments	xi
	A Note on Sources and Translations	xiii
	About the Editors	xvii
	Maps	xviii
I.	Introduction by Christopher Bassford	1
II.	The Waterloo Dispatch by the Duke of Wellington	15
III.	Letters Home by Carl von Clausewitz	23
IV.	Correspondence within Wellington's Circle	31
V.	The Campaign of 1815 by Carl von Clausewitz	55
	Chapter 1. French Forces. Creation of the Standing Army	55
	Chapter 2. Depots and the *Armée Extraordinaire*	57
	Chapter 3. Bonaparte's Boasting About His Resources	58
	Chapter 4. Dispositions of the Army	59
	Chapter 5. The National Guard	63
	Chapter 6. An Attack on the Allies in April	64
	Chapter 7. Defense	66
	Chapter 8. Attack on Wellington and Blücher	69
	Chapter 9. Allied Forces	70
	Chapter 10. Opposing Forces and Order of Battle	71
	Chapter 11. Reflections on Wellington's Dispositions: Assumptions That Must Be Made	73
	Chapter 12. Critique	77

CONTENTS

Chapter 13. Dispositions and Concentration of the Prussian Army ... 79
Chapter 14. Object of the French Attack ... 80
Chapter 15. The Point of Union of the Two Allied Armies ... 83
Chapter 16. Calculation of the Time Required for Concentration: The Prussian Army ... 84
Chapter 17. Wellington's Army ... 86
Chapter 18. Reflections ... 87
Chapter 19. Bonaparte Assembles His Army ... 88
Chapter 20. Blücher's Concentration at Sombreffe ... 89
Chapter 21. Wellington's Concentration ... 90
Chapter 22. Bonaparte's Thrust is Directed at Blücher ... 92
Chapter 23. The Action at Charleroi ... 94
Chapter 24. Situation the Morning of 16 June ... 97
Chapter 25. The Battle of Ligny ... 99
Chapter 26. Blücher's Dispositions ... 100
Chapter 27. Dispositions on the Front at Ligny ... 101
Chapter 28. Dispositions on the Front at Sombreffe ... 102
Chapter 29. Arrival of the Duke of Wellington ... 104
Chapter 30. Bonaparte's Plan of Attack ... 105
Chapter 31. Critical Analysis ... 107
Chapter 32. Principal Moments of the Battle ... 112
Chapter 33. Critical Observations on the Whole Battle: Blücher ... 120
Chapter 34. Bonaparte ... 124
Chapter 35. The Action at Quatre Bras ... 127
Chapter 36. Reflections ... 129
Chapter 37. Movements on 17 June: Blücher ... 132
Chapter 38. Wellington on 17 and 18 June ... 137
Chapter 39. The Battle of Belle-Alliance: Wellington's Deployment ... 138

CONTENTS

Chapter 40. Bonaparte's Plan of Attack	140
Chapter 41. Key Events of the Battle: Wellington's Defense	141
Chapter 42. The Attack of the Prussians	147
*Chapter 44. Combat at Wavre on the 18th and 19th: Grouchy's March	150
Chapter 45. General Thielmann's Dispositions	152
Chapter 46. Grouchy's Attack on 18 and 19 June	154
Chapter 47. Combat at Namur	157
Chapter 48. Reflections on the Battle: Bonaparte	159
Chapter 49. The Allies	178
Chapter 50. The Battle of Wavre	179
Chapter 51. A Second Battle against Blücher	182
Chapter 52. Consequences of the Battle	187
Chapter 53. The March on Paris: Initial Pursuit	192
Chapter 54. The March on Paris: Critical Comment	198
Chapter 55. Table of Marches	201
Chapter 56. The Condition of Paris	209
Chapter 57. Advance of the Remaining Armies into France	217
Chapter 58. The Conquest of the Fortresses	218
VI. Memorandum on the Battle of Waterloo by the Duke of Wellington	219
VII. Clausewitz on Waterloo: Napoleon at Bay by Daniel Moran	237
VIII. Wellington versus Clausewitz by Gregory W. Pedlow	257
Index	289

* There is no Chapter 43 in any version of Clausewitz's campaign study.

Acknowledgements

A project like this book is necessarily the product of many hands. The editors are exceedingly grateful to Mrs. Noran V. Stocks, who laboriously transcribed the Liverpool translation from the original in the Wellington papers held by the University of Southampton Library, and who provided many interesting insights concerning the manuscript collection. We are also grateful, of course, to Southampton University itself for the necessary permissions, and particularly to Dr. C.M. Woolgar, archivist, for his helpful guidance. Also very helpful was R.C. Snelling of the British Library in London; the Library granted us permission to publish items from the Liverpool papers. Ms. Toni Mortimer, of the Ohio State University, typed the German text of Clausewitz's published *Der Feldzug von 1815 in Frankreich* into our computers. Many thanks go to the late Gunther E. Rothenberg of Purdue University, who made available his encyclopedic knowledge of the Napoleonic wars, and to Donald D. Horward of Florida State University, who provided boundless encouragement and enthusiasm. The initial translation of Clausewitz's two post-battle letters to his wife Marie was provided by Ambassador Stanley A. Riveles, then on the faculty of the National War College. Patrick Maes of the Association Belge Napoleonienne and Philippe de Callataÿ of the Waterloo Committee of Belgium provided considerable advice as well as assistance with their extensive libraries on the Waterloo Campaign. The maps are reproduced with the kind permission of the curator of Special Collections, Florida State University Library, Dr. Lucy Patrick. Many thanks go to Napoleonic scholar John Hussey, whose sharp eye for detail helped us correct a number of errors.

A Note on Sources and Translations

The materials presented here stem from a variety of sources. Wellington's original 1815 battle report and his 1842 reply to Clausewitz's critique were both published in the 19th century. They are presented unedited, the only additions being a few notes by the present editors. Several items of correspondence between Wellington, his staff, and Lord Liverpool are reproduced with minor editing, based largely on the original manuscripts included among the Wellington papers in the Southampton University Library and in the British Library.

Our translation of Clausewitz's study of the campaign of 1815 is complete and is based on the first collected edition of his writings, published under the supervision of his wife shortly after Clausewitz's death. There it appeared as *Der Feldzug von 1815 in Frankreich*, in *Hinterlassene Werke des Generals Carl von Clausewitz über Krieg und Kriegsführung* (Berlin: Ferdinand Dümmler, 1835), volume 8. (Electronic versions of the 1862 edition, including a transcription into a more readable modern typeface, are included with the internet version of this book.) However, we have also made use of the more accurate text, based on Clausewitz's original manuscript, that Werner Hahlweg included in his critical edition of some of Clausewitz's writings. Hahlweg used the title that Clausewitz himself had proposed, *Feldzug von 1815: Strategische Uebersicht des Feldzugs von 1815*, in Carl von Clausewitz, *Schriften—Aufsätze—Studien—Briefe*, 2 volumes in 3, edited by Werner Hahlweg (Göttingen: Vandenhoeck & Ruprecht, 1966-90), volume 2, part 2: 936-1118. We therefore treat the title as *The Campaign of 1815: Strategic Overview of the Campaign of 1815*. We have not sought to reproduce Hahlweg's extensive notes, but we have relied on them to identify a few important textual variants, as well as some of Clausewitz's sources. On the whole, our aim has been to produce a readable rather than a critically exhaustive text, with sufficient scholarly apparatus to clarify Clausewitz's meaning without interrupting the flow of his argument. To this end we have silently corrected a number of incidental errors of spelling, formatting, and arithmetic, of the kind that Clausewitz himself would certainly have caught if he had sought to publish his history. More significant emendations are enclosed in square brackets or discussed in the notes. All footnotes are by the present editors, unless otherwise noted. The identities of most individuals that Clausewitz mentions, including full names, dates of birth and death, and the ranks they held in 1815, are included in the index if they are known.

Our text of Clausewitz's campaign study differs in significant respects from the one Wellington read. Lord Liverpool's text (which we have made available in full in the internet version of this book) was casual, incomplete, and never intended for publication. The result inevitably included many small errors and was often too literal to capture the true meaning of Clausewitz's sophisticated German. It omitted chapters 1 through 7 and 48 through 58, which Liverpool judged would be of no interest to the duke, presumably because they did not bear directly on the fighting at Waterloo or on events leading up to it. He also left passages in French untranslated, and sometimes softened Clausewitz's occasionally blunt language out of deference to the duke's feelings. Some of Liverpool's more significant editorial alterations, omissions, and errors are addressed in the notes, as are comments on the manuscript by Wellington and members of the circle.

We do not believe, however, that the deficiencies of Liverpool's translation were responsible for the duke's reaction to Clausewitz's work. These are attributable to Wellington's own sensitivities, predilections, and prejudices, and those of his correspondents.

Distances: In Clausewitz's original text the distances were given in Prussian miles [*Meilen*], an obsolete measurement that was equivalent to 4.6 English miles or 7.4 kilometers. We have converted all distances from Prussian miles into English miles.

Maps: In the 19th-century German editions of Clausewitz's history there are references to details of maps in an atlas prepared by the German General Staff in the 1820s: August Wagner, *Plane der Schlachten und Treffen welche von der preussischen Armee in den Feldzügen der Jahre 1813, 14 und 15 geliefert worden*, 4 volumes (Berlin: G. Reimer, 1825). The maps themselves were not included in the published version of Clausewitz's campaign study. As the Wagner atlas is now quite rare and difficult to find, we have included the relevant portions of Wagner's maps in the present publication, from copies in the possession of Special Collections,

Florida State University Library. Complete images of Wagner's maps of the battles of Ligny, Belle Alliance (Waterloo), and Wavre are provided with the internet version of this book. For the convenience of the reader, some additional maps of the relevant region have been provided. These, slightly modified, are from *The Cambridge Modern History Atlas*, eds. Sir Adolphus William Ward, G.W. Prothero, Sir Stanley Mordaunt Leathes, and E.A. Benians (London: Cambridge University Press, 1912).

Short Titles: The following short titles are used throughout the present book in referring to certain key sources:

Historical and Political Writings.	Carl von Clausewitz, *Historical and Political Writings*, edited and translated by Peter Paret and Daniel Moran (Princeton, New Jersey: Princeton University Press, 2003).
Mémoires.	Napoléon, *Mémoires pour servir à l'histoire de France en 1815* (Paris: Barrois, 1820).
On War.	Carl von Clausewitz, *On War*, edited and translated by Michael Howard and Peter Paret (Princeton, New Jersey: Princeton University Press, 1976/1984).
Schriften.	Werner Hahlweg, ed., Carl von Clausewitz, *Schriften—Aufsätze—Studien—Briefe*, 2 volumes in 3 (Göttingen: Vandenhoeck and Ruprecht, 1966-90).
Werke.	Carl von Clausewitz, *Hinterlassene Werke des Generals Carl von Clausewitz über Krieg und Kriegsführung*, 10 volumes (Berlin: Ferdinand Dümmler, 1832-37).

Internet Site: An electronic version of this book was posted to the internet in April 2010, at URL *http://www.clausewitz.com/readings/1815/*. In addition to the text and graphics of this printed version, it includes August Wagner's original maps of the battles of Ligny, Belle Alliance (Waterloo), and Wavre, electronic versions of Clausewitz's published book in German, and other enhancements.

About the Editors

CHRISTOPHER BASSFORD, a former U.S. Army artillery officer, is Professor of Strategy at the National War College in Washington, DC. He is the author of *Clausewitz in English: The Reception of Clausewitz in Britain and America, 1815-1945* (Oxford University Press, 1994) and *The Spit-Shine Syndrome: Organizational Irrationality in the American Field Army* (Westport, CT: Greenwood Press, 1988). He is also one of the editors of the Boston Consulting Group's business-oriented *Clausewitz On Strategy: Inspiration and Insight from a Master Strategist* (New York: Wiley, 2001). As a US Marine Corps doctrine writer, he authored MCDP 1-1, *Strategy* and MCDP 1-2, *Campaigning* (both 1997). He is the internet editor of *The Clausewitz Homepage*.

DANIEL MORAN is Professor of National Security Affairs at the Naval Postgraduate School in Monterey, California. He is co-editor with Peter Paret of Clausewitz's *Historical and Political Writings* (Princeton University Press, 1992). Recent works include *The People in Arms* (co-edited with Arthur Waldron, Cambridge, 2003) and *Wars of National Liberation* (Harper-Collins, 2006).

GREGORY W. PEDLOW has been Chief of the Historical Office at NATO's Supreme Headquarters Allied Powers Europe (SHAPE), near Mons, Belgium, since 1989. He is the author of *The Survival of the Hessian Nobility, 1770-1870* (Princeton University Press, 1988); *The CIA and the U-2 Program, 1956-1962* (Center for the Study of Intelligence, 1998); *NATO Strategy Documents, 1949-1969* (NATO, 1997); and articles on 19th-century Germany, NATO and the Cold War, and the Waterloo campaign of 1815. He serves on the Waterloo Committee of Belgium, which seeks to preserve and improve that historic battlefield, and has been named a Fellow in the International Napoleonic Society.

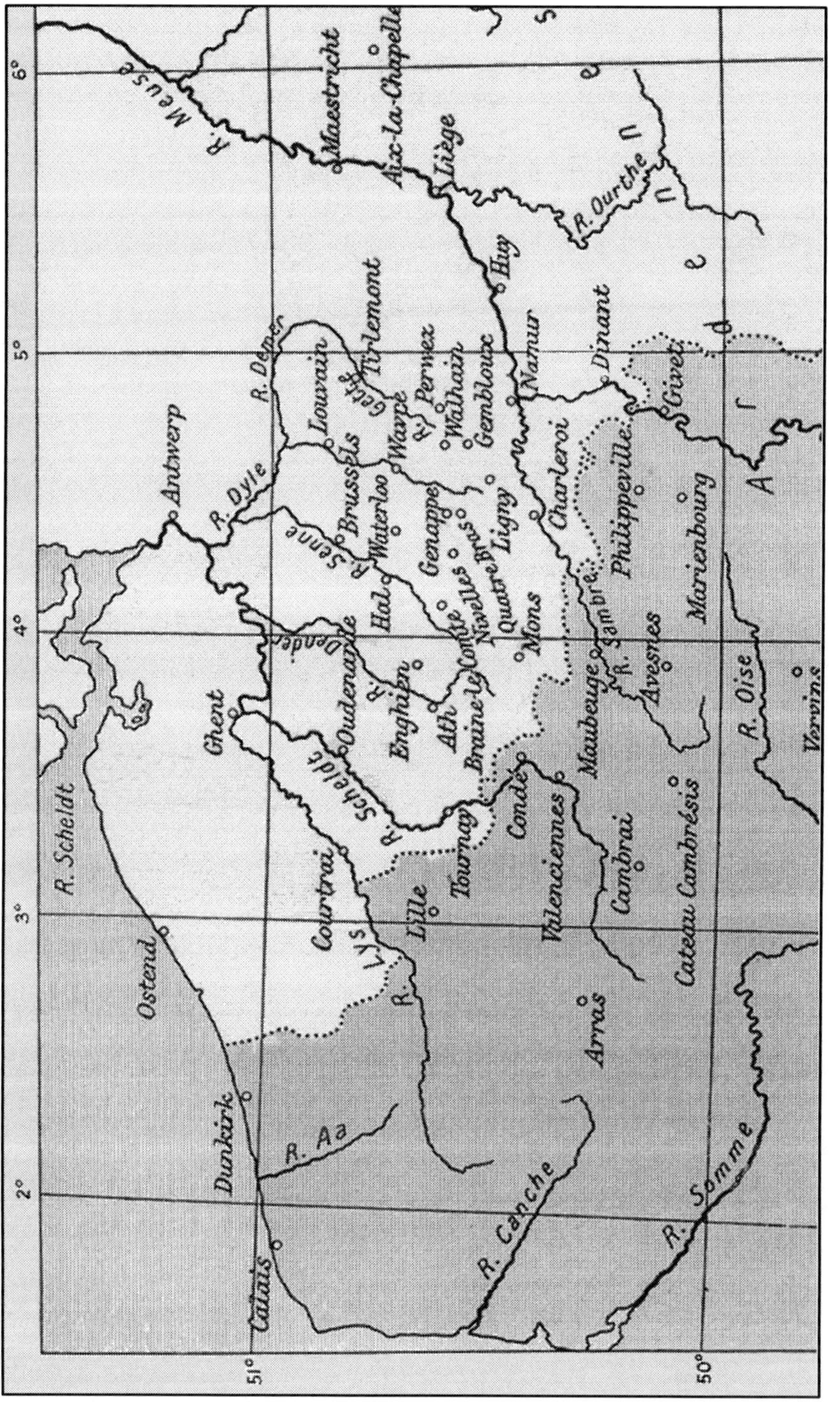

R. Meuse
Maestricht
Aix-la-Chapelle
Liège
R. Ourthe
Huy
Tirlemont
R. Demer
Antwerp
R. Dyle
Louvain
Gette
Perwez
Walhain
Wavre
Gembloux
Namur
Dinant
Givet
Brussels
R. Senne
Waterloo
Genappe
Ligny
Charleroi
Philippeville
Marienbourg
Hal
Quatre Bras
Nivelles
Mons
R. Sambre
Avesnes
Maubeuge
R. Dender
Enghien
Braine-le-Comte
Ath
Oudenarde
Ghent
R. Scheldt
R. Scheldt
Courtrai
Tournay
Condé
Valenciennes
Cambrai
Cateau Cambrésis
R. Oise
Vervins
Lille
R. Lys
Ostend
Arras
Dunkirk
R. Aa
Calais
R. Canche
R. Somme
Ardennes
6°
5°
4°
3°
2°
51°
50°

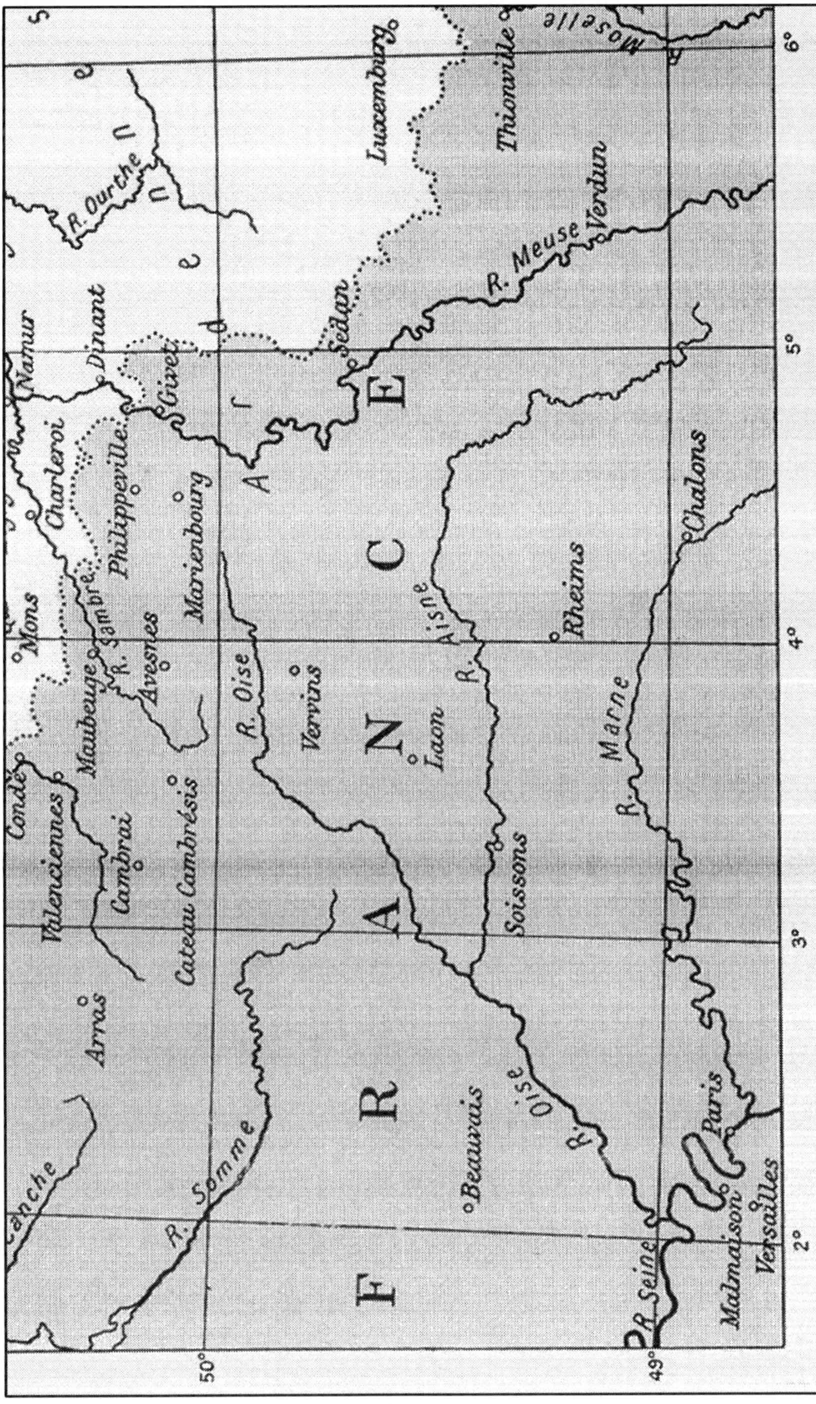

F R A N C E
Namur
Dinant
Charleroi
Philippeville
Givet
Sedan
Mons
Maubeuge
R. Sambre
Avesnes
Marienbourg
Condé
Valenciennes
Cambrai
Cateau Cambrésis
Arras
Canche
R. Somme
Beauvais
R. Oise
Vervins
Laon
R. Aisne
Soissons
Rheims
R. Marne
Chalons
Paris
Malmaison
Versailles
R. Seine
R. Meuse
Verdun
Luxemburg
Thionville
R. Moselle
R. Ourthe
50°
49°
2°
3°
4°
5°
6°

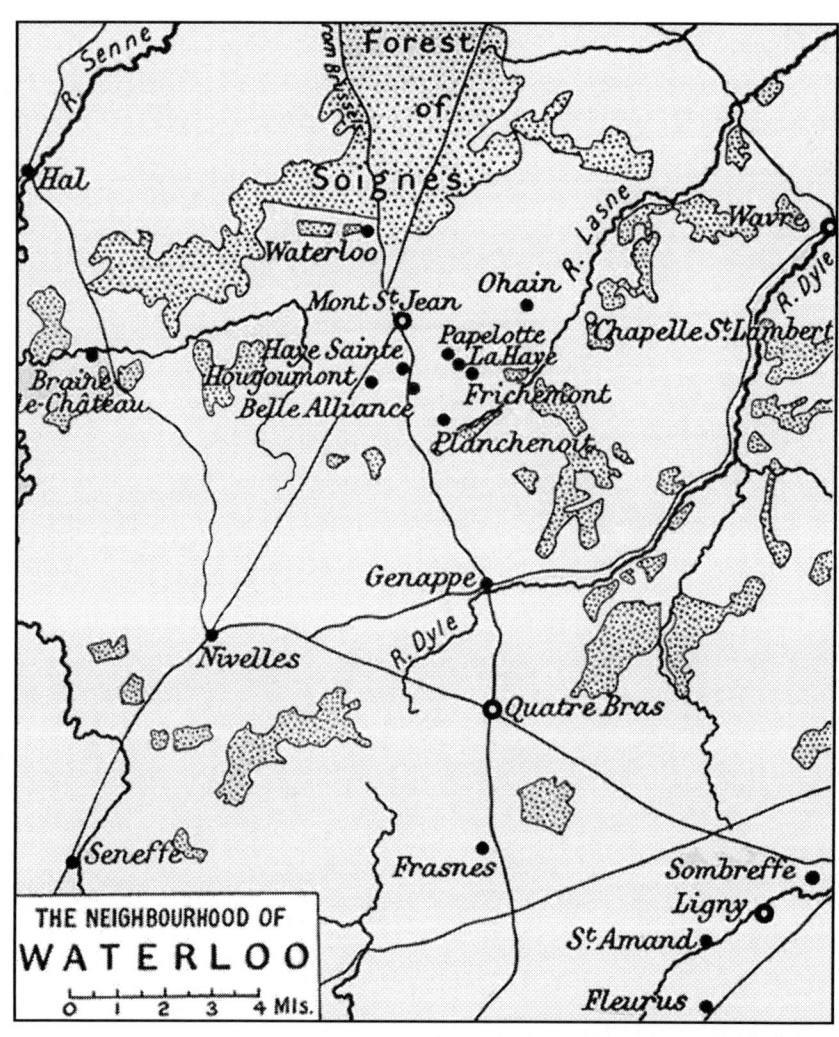

This map and those on the previous two pages are taken, slightly modified, from *The Cambridge Modern History Atlas*, eds. Sir Adolphus William Ward, G.W. Prothero, Sir Stanley Mordaunt Leathes, and E.A. Benians (London: Cambridge University Press, 1912), courtesy the map collection of the University of Texas at Austin. These maps are placed here for the convenience of the reader, and, unlike the maps on pp.103 and 146, have no direct connection to either Clausewitz's or Wellington's writings on Waterloo.

I.

INTRODUCTION[1]
by Christopher Bassford

"The battle of Waterloo is undoubtedly one of the most interesting events of modern times, but the Duke entertains no hopes of ever seeing an account of all its details which shall be true."[2] Thus wrote the Duke of Wellington to a friend in 1816. Along the same lines, Wellington once pointed out that a battle was a social event, rather like a ball: full of interesting incidents that none of the participants could later put into anything like a firm chronological order, much less reconstruct into a coherent story.[3]

As practical historians, the editors of the present work are, of course, in full agreement with the Duke on one point. It is indeed impossible to recapture past events, even those in which we ourselves have participated, with anything approaching perfect fidelity.

Nonetheless, it is interesting and sometimes even useful to try. Though Wellington obviously knew the inherent imperfections of the genre, he himself was an avid reader of military history. It was only with regard to his own battles that he complained of historians' futile attempts to capture events on paper. "Surely," he said, "the details of the battle might have been left in the original official reports. Historians and commentators were not necessary."[4] In accordance with this attitude, it was Wellington's official policy not to endorse or make public reply to any of

---

1 This introduction derives substantially from Chapter 3, "Clausewitz in Great Britain before 1873," in Christopher Bassford, *Clausewitz in English: The Reception of Clausewitz in Britain and America, 1815-1945* (New York: Oxford University Press, 1994), 37-50.
2 Wellington to Sir John Sinclair, 13 April 1816, *Supplementary Despatches, Correspondence, and Memoranda of Field Marshal Arthur Duke of Wellington*, edited by his son, the Duke of Wellington (London: John Murray, 1863), 10:507.
3 This line appears in a letter of 8 August 1815 from Wellington to an unidentified respondent. *The Dispatches of Field-Marshal The Duke of Wellington During his Campaigns in India, Denmark, Portugal, Spain, The Low Countries, and France, And Relating to America, from 1799 to 1815*, selected and arranged by Walter Wood (New York: E.P. Dutton & Co,, 1902), 461.
4 "Memorandum on the Battle of Waterloo," 24 September 1842. *Supplementary Despatches*, 10:530.

INTRODUCTION

the vast number of studies of Waterloo published between 1815 and his death in 1852.[5] He did, however, utilize anonymous literary agents to attack treatments he considered particularly scurrilous or bombastic. His private secretary, Colonel John Gurwood, and his younger friend Francis Egerton, the Earl of Ellesmere, were the authors of numerous book reviews reflecting the Duke's annoyance. One such review, for example, attacked the famous Swiss military writer Antoine-Henri Jomini for his "pompous charlatanerie,"[6] even though Jomini was taking Wellington's side in the debate over Waterloo.[7] Jomini's chief offense, it seems, was his claim to understand the eternal, underlying rules governing warfare. Such theories were, in Wellington's view, "mere reveries," inherently useless.

It is all the more surprising, therefore, that the single major exception to Wellington's refusal to enter personally into the debate over Waterloo came in response to another theorist's study of the Waterloo campaign. That theorist was the Prussian military philosopher, General Carl von Clausewitz.

Wellington and Clausewitz were men quite unalike in background and temperament. Arthur Wellesley (1769-1852) was born into a modestly influential if not particularly prosperous family, a younger son of an impoverished Irish lord. He was the consummate leader: a brilliant field commander with a taste for defensive tactics but a keen eye for offen-

---

5 Francis Egerton wrote that "The Duke had made it a rule never to read any work whatever bearing on his military career, He said that they would merely tempt and provoke him to comments which he could not make without offense to living men.... He did, however, although very rarely, make an exception to this rule, as when he wrote his famous memorandum in reply to Clausewitz's 'History of the Campaign.'" *Personal Reminiscences of the Duke of Wellington by Francis, the First Earl of Ellesmere*, edited by his daughter Alice, Countess of Strafford (London: John Murray, 1904), 82.

6 Unsigned, "Marmont, Siborne, and Alison," *Quarterly Review*, v.LXXVI (June and September 1845), 204-247. This article was apparently a joint venture of Gurwood, Egerton, and Wellington himself. See archives of the John Murray Company, manuscript index to v.LXXVI, *Quarterly Review*; J.H. Stocqueler, *The Life of Field Marshal the Duke of Wellington* (London: Ingram, Cooke, and Company, 1853), 2:330. Egerton's vociferous attacks on Alison, concerning his discussion of Waterloo, were made with the Duke's "approbation and assistance." Egerton, *Reminiscences*, 58.

7 In the debate in question, Jomini differed with Napoleon's criticism of Wellington's decision to fight where he did. See Baron de Jomini, trans. Capt. G.H. Mendell and Lieut. W.P. Craighill [USA], *The Art of War* (Philadelphia: J.B. Lippincott, 1862; reprinted, Westport, CT: Greenwood Press, 1971), 183.

sive opportunities; a charismatic personality; a masterful organizer and manager; and a far-sighted strategist who knew well how to capitalize on assets like the Royal Navy and British financial resources. He was adept in alliance diplomacy, in managing multinational forces, and in dealing with the home government while winning victories in the field. First gaining prominence as a "sepoy general" in India, he waged a victorious five-year campaign to drive the French out of Portugal and Spain (1808-14) and won more victories in France itself before Napoleon's first abdication. Unlike most other senior Allied commanders, however, prior to Waterloo he had never confronted Bonaparte himself on the field of battle. Created Duke of Wellington in 1814, he crowned his military career with his victory over Napoleon the following year. Wellington's later ventures into domestic politics, however, including a two-year stint as prime minister (1828-30), were not successful. With his natural conservatism growing increasingly hidebound, Wellington's impact on government and especially on the army—of which he was appointed commander-in-chief in 1842—was unfortunate. The army's poor showing in the Crimean War (1853-56) is often blamed on his lingering influence.

Carl Philipp Gottfried von Clausewitz (1780-1831) was the youngest son of a poorly paid minor Prussian official with dubious claims to nobility. In contrast to Wellington, Clausewitz was reserved, shy, and intensely intellectual, a consummate staff officer in the great tradition of the Prussian/German general staff. Clausewitz entered the Prussian army before his twelfth birthday. He first saw combat as a thirteen year-old ensign in 1793, at the siege of Mainz. After Prussia withdrew from the wars of the French Revolution in 1795, he applied himself to his own education: beyond strictly military subjects, Clausewitz developed a wide-ranging set of interests in art, science, and education. So successful were his efforts that in 1801 he was able to gain admission to the Institute for Young Officers in Berlin (which would eventually evolve into the famous *Kriegsakademie*—the German War College). He quickly came to the attention of the new director, Gerhard von Scharnhorst, a key figure in the Prussian state during the upheavals of the Napoleonic wars. Impressed by Clausewitz's ability, Scharnhorst became his sponsor, mentor, and close friend.[8] Clausewitz graduated at the top of his class in 1803 and was re-

---

8 On Scharnhorst's ideas and influence, see Charles Edward White, *The Enlightened Soldier: Scharnhorst and the Military Gesellschaft in Berlin, 1801-1805* (New York: Praeger, 1989).

INTRODUCTION

warded with the position of military adjutant to the young Prince August. This brought him into close contact with the royal family and with events at the very center of the Prussian state.

Unlike Wellington prior to Waterloo, Clausewitz saw battle—several times—against Napoleon himself. Prussia's forces were shattered in humiliating defeats at Jena and Auerstädt in 1806, and Clausewitz was captured. When he returned from a comfortable internment with his prince in 1808, he joined energetically with Scharnhorst and others in a reform movement aimed at restructuring both Prussian society and the army in preparation for what he felt to be an inevitable new struggle with the French. Though no revolutionary himself, he recognized that Prussia would have to modernize and liberalize its society if it were to compete with revolutionary France. He remained deeply involved in events in Berlin, becoming military tutor to the Crown Prince in 1810. In 1812, however, Prussia, by force of circumstances allied to France, agreed to provide an army corps to assist in the invasion of Russia. Along with a number of other officers, Clausewitz therefore resigned from the Prussian service and accepted a commission in the Russian army in order to continue the resistance to Napoleon. There, Clausewitz participated in the drawn-out Russian retreat and fought in the slaughterhouse battle at Borodino. He witnessed the disastrous French retreat from Moscow, including the catastrophic crossing of the Beresina river. Crossing behind the French lines on a covert mission, he then played a key role in negotiating the "Convention of Tauroggen." This negotiation brought about the defection of General H.D.L. Yorck von Wartenburg's Prussian corps from the French army. That action led eventually to the entry of Prussia into the anti-Napoleon coalition and, after some delay, to Clausewitz's reinstatement and promotion to colonel in the Prussian army. Clausewitz participated in many key events of the War of Liberation (1813-1814). However, bad luck, the King's lingering resentment over his actions in 1812-13, and suspicions concerning his political liberalism prevented him from obtaining any significant command.

During the Waterloo campaign, Clausewitz served as chief of staff of the Prussian 3rd Corps, commanded by General J.A. von Thielmann. The corps fought at Ligny, successfully extricating itself from the Prussian defeat there. Then—outnumbered two to one—it played a crucial if often uncelebrated rear-guard action at Wavre, which prevented Marshal Grouchy's detached forces from rejoining Napoleon at Waterloo.[9]

In 1818, Clausewitz was promoted to general and became administrative head of the war college in Berlin. He spent his abundant leisure time writing studies of various campaigns and preparing his *magnum opus* on military theory, *Vom Kriege* (in English, *On War*). In the emergency of 1830-31, when revolutions in Paris and Poland seemed to presage a new general European war, he was appointed chief of staff of the field army, which was sent to the Polish border under Field Marshal August Neidhardt von Gneisenau. Although war was averted, Clausewitz remained in the east, organizing a sanitary cordon to stop the spread of a cholera epidemic from Poland. When Gneisenau died of the disease in August 1831, Clausewitz took command of the army but, "once the danger of serious fighting had passed,"[10] he was replaced by the inexperienced but politically more palatable Field Marshal Karl Friedrich von dem Knesebeck. Somewhat depressed by this turn of events, he returned home, immediately fell ill with cholera himself, and died in November 1831. His many unfinished manuscripts, including those constituting *On War*, were later published in ten volumes of collected works. These were assembled and edited by his wife, Marie von Clausewitz. Marie considerably outranked her husband socially (she was born a Countess) and shared a famously deep intellectual partnership with her husband—accounting for the fact, extremely surprising in the 19th century, that a woman wrote the preface to the Western world's greatest work of military theory.

Clausewitz wrote his campaign studies, not as formal histories for publication, but rather as a means for developing, testing, and refining his ideas in the laboratory of actual events. *The Campaign of 1815*, though often referred to as a "history," does not attempt to provide a comprehensive narrative of events. Rather, it is a strategic analysis focusing on key strategic- and operational-level issues in the sequence in

---

9 Clausewitz's experience at Wavre is analyzed in Peter Paret, *Clausewitz and the State: The Man, His Theories, and His Times* (Princeton: Princeton University Press, 1976), 247-250; Roger Parkinson, *Clausewitz: A Biography* (New York: Stein and Day, 1971), chapters 13 and 14; Raymond Aron, trans. Christine Booker and Norman Stone, *Clausewitz: Philosopher of War* (Englewood Cliffs, N.J.: Prentice-Hall, 1985), 30-31. Paret's book is by far the best treatment of Clausewitz's life and intellectual evolution available in English.
10 Paret, *Clausewitz and the State*, 428.

INTRODUCTION

which they arose. It is subtitled "Strategic Overview of the Campaign of 1815" and treats the campaign as a whole—the Battle of Waterloo was simply one very prominent episode. It was probably the most sophisticated of Clausewitz's campaign studies in terms of its relationship to his maturing theories.[11] He wrote it between 1827 and 1830, and used material from it in teaching the Crown Prince.[12] It was published in 1835 as the eighth volume of Clausewitz's collected works.[13]

As a theorist, Clausewitz distinguished carefully between the role of the historian and that of the military critic, even though he recognized that the two roles often went together. He maintained that historical research proper has nothing to do with either theory or criticism; it is the discovery, interpretation, and arrangement of "equivocal facts," subject to differing interpretations. Interpretation is analysis, not research. Critical analysis is the tracing of effects back to their causes. Criticism proper is the investigation and evaluation of actions taken, the consideration of alternative courses of action (i.e., a counter-factual or alternative-history approach), the realm of praise and censure. In such evaluation, actions must be analyzed not only on their own level (i.e., tactical, strategic, political) but also as they interact at other levels. Theory provides the framework for analysis and judgement.

Clausewitz employed this approach in *The Campaign of 1815*. Despite the fact that he had participated in the campaign himself, his discussion is detached and impersonal. The only exception to this detachment is his obvious animosity towards Napoleon. This animosity stems not only from his personal political passions but also from his irritation as an analyst with what he regarded as the Emperor's systematic distortion of the record. In general, Clausewitz had great professional respect for Bonaparte's military skills, so much so that he has often been called—erroneously—the "high priest of Napoleon."[14] In reality, Clausewitz was the exponent not of Napoleon but rather of the most capable among the

---

11 This is the opinion of Paret, Werner Hahlweg (Clausewitz's modern German editor), Eberhard Kessel, and Daniel Moran. See Moran's essay in the present work; Paret, *Clausewitz and the State*, 340; Carl von Clausewitz, *Schriften—Aufsätze—Studien—Briefe*, ed. Werner Hahlweg (Göttingen: Vandenhoeck & Ruprecht, 1990), 2:924-935.
12 Hahlweg, 937.
13 Carl von Clausewitz, *Der Feldzug von 1815 in Frankreich* (Berlin: Ferdinand Dümmlers, 1835).
14 This term originated with British military historian J.F.C. Fuller.

men who defeated him, especially Scharnhorst. His professional respect for Napoleon is naturally not so evident in his discussion of a campaign marked by such serious mistakes on the Emperor's part.

Around 1839, Wellington's friend Cecil Cope Jenkinson, third Lord Liverpool, was introduced to Clausewitz's collected works by a German friend.[15] Liverpool (1784-1851) was the younger brother of the Tory prime minister in office between 1812 and 1827. He had spent time as a youth in the Royal Navy, served as attaché at Vienna, and fought in the Austrian army at Austerlitz. Afterwards he entered Parliament, joined the cabinet in 1807, and became under-secretary of state for war and the colonies in 1809. Liverpool was initially interested only in Clausewitz's study of the campaign of 1812 in Russia, especially in Clausewitz's role in General Yorck's defection. He then grew absorbed in the philosopher's other works, and became quite enthusiastic about the theoretical arguments contained in *On War*. Wellington, however, was concerned only with Clausewitz's discussion of the Waterloo campaign, particularly his analysis of Marshal Grouchy's operations.[16] It was Liverpool who provided the Duke with a rough, partial manuscript translation of *The Campaign of 1815*, which was never designed for publication but still exists in Southampton University Library's collection of Wellington's papers.[17] At the urging of Liverpool, Gurwood, and Ellesmere, Wellington formally replied to Clausewitz's analysis in a memorandum dated 24 September 1842. He did not intend that his memorandum be made public, but his son nonetheless published it in 1863.

It is difficult to characterize the Duke's personal attitude towards Clausewitz. He went into Liverpool's translation extremely skeptical of—even hostile to—historians in general and military theorists in particular. Despite his own interest in ascertaining the facts about Grouchy's activities, he abhorred the "critical morality" that leads historians like Clausewitz to pursue awkward truths when these might cause political frictions at home or inflame relations among allies. There's nothing particularly reprehensible in these attitudes. Wellington was, after all, a soldier and a

---

15 Liverpool to Wellington, 10 September 1840, Papers of the first Duke of Wellington, University of Southampton (WP2/71/28).
16 Wellington to Liverpool, 14 September 1840, Papers of the Third Earl of Liverpool (Add MSS 38196, f 143), The British Library.
17 Wellington Papers 8/1 contains Liverpool 's translation of Clausewitz's *Campaign of 1815*, together with correspondence and memoranda about it dating from 1842.

policy maker, not an academic. His values had to be essentially political in character. But he also overtly rejected Clausewitz's critical method, which involves not only establishing what actually did happen but also comparing it with alternative courses of action at various key points: "It is useless to speculate upon supposed military movements which were never made, and operations which never took place, or the objects of the several chiefs of Generals opposed to each other." That attitude cannot be explained by Wellington's professional role, because taking such alternatives into account is inherent in strategy making. On the other hand, Wellington's treatment of Clausewitz, while self-justifying and argumentative, is not disrespectful. His comments contain none of the vitriol that his literary agents routinely heaped on writers who offended him (and those agents sought actively to discourage Wellington from being too cantankerous in his treatment of Clausewitz). He credits Clausewitz with a good understanding of the relationship between politics and military operations, even while disputing his understanding of British policy in 1815. He grudgingly accepts Clausewitz's critical characterization of the Allied armies' dispositions prior to the start of operations—while pointing out that everything worked out well anyway.

In all likelihood, Wellington went on record in response to Clausewitz not because of any great personal interest or irritation, but because of the hectoring of his friends and assistants. More important than Wellington's own motives, therefore, are those of Ellesmere, Liverpool, and Gurwood in choosing Clausewitz as the catalyst for their efforts. These men were anxious to get the aging hero to leave some definitive public statement of his views on the battle. The group's interest in Clausewitz's ideas was positive, however, and deeper than merely in using him to prod Wellington to write. In June 1842, Egerton, reviewing a biography of Marshal Blücher, referred to "the remarks of a very able Prussian critic of the [1815] campaign, the late General Clausewitz."[18] As Gurwood made clear when urging the Duke to read Liverpool's translation, they felt that Clausewitz was also an honest writer seeking the truth, rather than one with a personal or national ax to grind. In September 1842, Egerton wrote that "He seems to me free from national prejudices & nonsense." Liverpool probably provided Wellington with Clausewitz's lengthy discussion of

---

18 [Egerton], "Life of Blücher," *The Quarterly Review*, v.LXX, no.CXL (June & September 1842), 462.

the Battle of Ligny in order to demonstrate to him, before he came to the remarks on the battle at Waterloo itself, that the Prussian writer was detached and as critical of his own army's operations as of the British and French. Liverpool was so intrigued by Clausewitz's great theoretical book, *On War*, that he offered to translate it for the Duke—an offer Wellington naturally refused. In 1843, Egerton went on to translate and anonymously publish Clausewitz's study *The Campaign of 1812 in Russia*.[19] Wellington himself remained sufficiently interested in Clausewitz's views to discuss the latter book in some detail with Egerton.[20] Overall, then, we must conclude that the whole group, Wellington included, found Clausewitz's work to be of very substantial merit.

Nonetheless, Wellington clearly misunderstood Clausewitz's arguments concerning Waterloo in at least one important respect, and that misunderstanding has had a lasting negative impact on Clausewitz's reputation in Britain. Wellington believed that Clausewitz's criticism of the disposition of his forces prior to the start of the campaign was rooted in the idea that the Allied armies, based on some general principle, should have sought a "great battle" with Napoleon. Wellington saw no value in seeking such a "great battle ... even under the hypothesis that the result would have been a great victory." His object was the preservation of the Allied forces in Belgium for use in crushing Napoleon through actions coordinated with the other Allied armies, most of which had not yet arrived in the theater of war. Because of the Alliance's sheer numerical superiority, this would have been a far more sure strategy—and less costly in its result. The moral effect of a defeat, on the other hand, might have imperiled the entire Allied cause. Despite what Wellington acknowledged as Clausewitz's political sophistication, his supposed desire for decisive battle did not, in this case, accord with the policy of the Alliance or of the British government.

Wellington's broad reasoning was sound, but he had missed Clausewitz's point. Rather than making a general principle of the need to seek decisive battle, Clausewitz was making a very specific point about Napoleon. His analysis was based both on the French emperor's habitual

---

19 Carl von Clausewitz, *The Campaign of 1812 in Russia* [trans. Francis Egerton] (London: J. Murray, 1843; reprinted, Hattiesburg, MS: Academic International, 1970; reprinted Westport, CT: Greenwood Press, 1977; reprinted, London: Greenhill Books, 1992).
20 Ellesmere, *Reminiscences*, 238-9.

INTRODUCTION

behavior and on the particular strategic situation in 1815. Napoleon did not orient his operations on the seizure of geographic points but on his enemy's army, which he characteristically sought to destroy in a decisive engagement. This was especially necessary in 1815, given Napoleon's political situation. In Clausewitz's view, therefore, Wellington need not have worried about being prepared to cover all of the various avenues on which Napoleon might advance: Wherever the Allied armies stood was where Napoleon would go. The Duke therefore should have sought to concentrate his forces in preparation for the "lightning bolt" that Napoleon would inevitably hurl against him, rather than scattering his forces to protect all key locations and potential avenues of advance. It was thus Napoleon, not Clausewitz, who sought to impose a decisive battle on the Allied armies. And, of course, he succeeded in doing precisely that.

The result of Wellington's misunderstanding has been an enduring belief among many British writers—most of them quite unaware of its origins with Wellington—that Clausewitz's theories about war are based on the quest for a "decisive battle." In fact, while Clausewitz argued that combat is what distinguishes war from politics in general, and he clearly preferred decisive strategies to aimless puttering about, there is no indication that he believed in fighting "great battles" for their own sake or that wars were likely to be resolved in a single great blow. Wellington and Clausewitz were simply talking past one another on this issue.

It is intriguing, however, that Wellington, who—along with most British soldiers of the 19th century and later—sneered at the very idea of a "theory of war," should nonetheless have made such a clear theoretical argument about the relationship between policy and military strategy: "The historian [i.e., Clausewitz] shows in more than one passage of his History that he is not insensible of the military and political value of good moral impressions resulting from military operations." Wellington's comments sound, in fact, very much like Clausewitz's famous line in *On War* that "War is the continuation of politics by other means." The great strength of Clausewitz's analytical approach is in fact to demonstrate the impact of political concerns at what many or most military historians would consider to be purely operational or even tactical levels. Wellington's response to his study of 1815 likewise engages political concerns, to great effect.

ON WATERLOO

It is also revealing that Wellington's circle should have been so interested in Clausewitz. In fact, 19th-century British writers on military affairs were quite respectful of Clausewitz, even when disputing his conclusions or complaining of the mental effort required to read his major work. It was only after the disasters of World War I that Clausewitz became the object of British hostility, largely because some writers came to blame the influence of Clausewitz's theories for the grotesque slaughter on the Western Front. That accusation was based on a misunderstanding of *On War*'s arguments—fostered in no small part by Wellington's misinterpretation of Clausewitz's *Campaign of 1815*—as well as on a great exaggeration of the degree to which Clausewitz's ideas had actually been accepted by pre-war European military thinkers.[21] Unfortunately, these misperceptions and others long made an unthinking (and unreading) hostility to Clausewitz common among many British military writers. This hostility resulted in a great deal of foolishness, well captured in a comment by the otherwise sensible Brigadier Peter Young: "For those who would perceive the art of war, the cool, historical analysis of past operations is a more reliable lantern than all the philosophizing of von Clausewitz and his disciples."[22] The "cool analysis of operations" is, in fact, and as the present work demonstrates, what Clausewitz's "philosophizing" is all about.

Wellington's exchange with Clausewitz was well known in the 19th century.[23] For some reason, however, it has fallen into obscurity in the 20th, so much so that some prominent British military historians expressed astonishment to us when informed of its existence. Even though Wellington's memorandum is one of only two major discussions by the battle's victor, and despite the fact that Clausewitz was a prominent witness and participant in the campaign, neither source is widely quoted

---

21 See Bassford, *Clausewitz in English*, 122-143.
22 Brigadier Peter Young, ed., *Great Battles of the World on Land, Sea, and Air* (New York: Bison Books, 1978), 9.
23 For example, it was discussed in G.R. Gleig's *The Life of Arthur Duke of Wellington* (London: Longmans, Green, Reader, and Dyer, 1865), 382. Lieut.-Colonel Charles C. Chesney, R.E., *Waterloo Lectures: A Study of the Campaign of 1815* (London: Longmans, Green, and Company, 1868) was extremely popular and influential. Chesney was an avid reader of Clausewitz's work and often accepted Clausewitz's analysis over Wellington's. E.L.S. Horsburgh, *Waterloo: A Narrative and a Criticism* (London: Methuen, 1895), appears to draw on both the Duke's response and Clausewitz's study; also, Horsburgh's general approach seems to have been influenced by the discussion of "critical analysis" in *On War*.

INTRODUCTION

in studies in the English language. For example, Jac Weller, *Wellington at Waterloo* (New York: Thomas Y. Crowell, 1967), makes an obscure reference to Clausewitz's assessment and the Duke's response, but does not discuss it. John Keegan's discussion of Waterloo in *The Face of Battle* (New York: Dorset, 1976) makes no reference to Clausewitz at all. Clausewitz is mentioned in David Chandler's *Waterloo: The Hundred Days* (London: Osprey, 1980), but only in vague general reference to the theories contained in *On War*. The same is true of Paddy Griffith, ed., *Wellington as Commander: The Iron Duke's Generalship* (Sussex: Antony Bird Publications, 1985). Neville Thompson, *Wellington after Waterloo* (London: Routledge and Kegan Paul, 1986) makes no reference to the exchange. In a remark that may reveal one cause for the exchange's eclipse, Weller noted in his bibliography that "Germans who have written about the campaign are too much interested in pleading their own causes." In fact, Clausewitz went out of his way to absolve Wellington of accusations that he had failed to honor his pledge to support the Prussians at Ligny. Egerton, as noted above, felt that Clausewitz lacked national prejudices.[24] Wellington, in turn, was happy to note the decisive Prussian contribution to his victory. It seems that many modern writers are not so accommodating—a legacy of 1914, not 1815.

While these larger theoretical and historical issues are important (in fact, profound), for most readers the value of the exchange between Wellington and Clausewitz will lie in its arguments about the battle itself. The present book offers readers the opportunity to understand for themselves the divergent views of two highly experienced Napoleonic-era soldiers, both of them participants—albeit at different levels of command—in one of the most famous and important military campaigns in history. The utterly pragmatic Wellington, victorious commander at Waterloo, is widely viewed as the greatest general in Britain's long history. The theoretically-inclined Clausewitz, at the time of Waterloo a well respected but relatively junior Prussian staff officer, is generally regarded today as the greatest of all Western military thinkers. Both were intimately familiar with the context and with key personalities and events of the Waterloo campaign. Each put much effort years afterwards into struggling to grasp the whole. Neither fully succeeded. By studying the

---

24 Egerton to Arbuthnot, 5 September 1842. WP 2/91/148. This letter is reproduced on p.42 below.

ON WATERLOO

exchange between them, we can become participants in their struggle for a fuller understanding of what remains, indeed, "undoubtedly one of the most interesting events of modern times."

Christopher Bassford
April 2010

II.

THE WATERLOO DISPATCH[1]
by the Duke of Wellington

To Earl Bathurst.

WATERLOO   June 19, 1815

My Lord,

Bonaparte, having collected the 1st, 2nd, 3rd, 4th, and 6th corps of the French army, and the Imperial Guards, and nearly all the cavalry, on the Sambre, and between that river and the Meuse, between the 10th and 14th of the month, advanced on the 15th and attacked the Prussian posts at Thuin and Lobbes, on the Sambre, at daylight in the morning.

I did not hear of these events till in the evening of the 15th; and I immediately ordered the troops to prepare to march, and afterwards to march to their left, as soon as I had intelligence from other quarters to prove that the enemy's movement upon Charleroi was the real attack.

The enemy drove the Prussian posts from the Sambre on that day; and General Ziethen, who commanded the corps which had been at Charleroi, retired upon Fleurus; and Marshal Prince Blücher concentrated the Prussian army upon Sombreffe, holding the villages in front of his position of St. Amand and Ligny.

The enemy continued his march along the road from Charleroi towards Brussels; and on the same evening, the 15th, attacked a brigade of the army of the Netherlands, under the Prince de Weimar, posted at

---

[1] *The Dispatches of Field Marshal the Duke Of Wellington, During His Various Campaigns in India, Denmark, Portugal, Spain, the Low Countries, and France, from 1799 to 1815*, in 12 volumes, compiled by Lieut. Colonel Gurwood (London: John Murray, Albemarle Street),12:478-484. The original dispatch is in the Public Record Office, WO 1/205, ff. 313-316. John Hussey, "Wellington's Draft of His Waterloo Dispatch and the Reports of the Allied Commissioners," *First Empire* no. 87 (2006), 12-17, contains an interesting and detailed analysis of the original draft, which is in the British Library, BL Add MS 69850.

Frasne, and forced it back to the farmhouse, on the same road, called Les Quatre Bras.

The Prince of Orange immediately reinforced this brigade with another of the same division, under General Perponcher, and, in the morning early, regained part of the ground which had been lost, so as to have the command of the communication leading from Nivelles and Brussels with Marshal Blücher's position.

In the meantime I had directed the whole army to march upon Les Quatre Bras; and the 5th Division, under Lieutenant-General Sir Thomas Picton, arrived at about half-past two in the day, followed by the corps of troops under the Duke of Brunswick, and afterwards by the contingent of Nassau.

At this time the enemy commenced an attack upon Prince Blücher with his whole force, excepting the 1st and 2nd Corps, and a corps of cavalry under General Kellermann, with which he attacked our post at Les Quatre Bras.

The Prussian army maintained their position with their usual gallantry and perseverance against a great disparity of numbers, as the 4th Corps of their army, under General Bülow, had not joined; and I was attacked myself, and the troops, the cavalry in particular, which had a long distance to march, had not arrived.

We maintained our position also, and completely defeated and repulsed all the enemy's attempts to get possession of it. The enemy repeatedly attacked us with a large body of infantry and cavalry, supported by a numerous and powerful artillery. He made several charges with the cavalry upon our infantry, but all were repulsed in the steadiest manner.

In this affair His Royal Highness the Prince of Orange, the Duke of Brunswick, and Lieutenant-General Sir Thomas Picton, and Major-Generals Sir James Kempt and Sir Denis Pack, who were engaged from the commencement of the enemy's attack, highly distinguished themselves, as well as Lieutenant-General Charles Baron Alten, Major-General Sir C. Halkett, Lieutenant-General Cooke, and Major-Generals Maitland and Byng, as they successively arrived. The troops of the 5th Division, and those of the Brunswick corps, were long and severely engaged, and conducted themselves with the utmost gallantry. I must particularly mention the 28th, 42nd, 79th, and 92nd Regiments, and the battalion of Hanoverians.

ON WATERLOO

Our loss was great, as your lordship will perceive by the enclosed return, and I have particularly to regret His Serene Highness the Duke of Brunswick, who fell fighting gallantly at the head of his troops.

Although Marshal Blücher had maintained his position at Sombreffe, he still found himself much weakened by the severity of the contest in which he had been engaged, and, as the 4th Corps had not arrived, he determined to fall back, and to concentrate his army upon Wavre; and he marched in the night, after the action was over.

This movement of the Marshal rendered necessary a corresponding one upon my part; and I retired from the farm of Quatre Bras upon Genappe, and thence upon Waterloo the next morning, the 17th, at ten o'clock.

The enemy made no effort to pursue Marshal Blücher. On the contrary, a patrol which I sent to Sombreffe in the morning found all quiet, and the enemy's vedettes fell back as the patrol advanced. Neither did he attempt to molest our march to the rear, although made in the middle of the day, excepting by following, with a large body of cavalry brought from his right, the cavalry under the Earl of Uxbridge.

This gave Lord Uxbridge an opportunity of charging them with the 1st Life Guards, upon their *débouché* from the village of Genappe, upon which occasion his lordship has declared himself to be well satisfied with that regiment.

The position which I took up in front of Waterloo crossed the highroads from Charleroi and Nivelles, and had its right thrown back to a ravine near Merke Braine, which was occupied, and its left extended to a height above the hamlet Ter la Haye, which was likewise occupied. In front of the right center, and near the Nivelles road, we occupied the house and gardens of Hougoumont, which covered the return of that flank; and in front of the left center we occupied the farm of La Haye Sainte. By our left we communicated with Marshal Prince Blücher at Wavre, through Ohain; and the Marshal had promised me that, in case we should be attacked, he would support me with one or more corps, as might be necessary.

The enemy collected his army, with the exception of the 3rd Corps, which had been sent to observe Marshal Blücher, on a range of heights in our front, in the course of the night of the 17th and yesterday morning, and at about ten o'clock he commenced a furious attack upon our post at Hougoumont. I had occupied that post with a detachment from General Byng's brigade of Guards, which was in position in its rear; and it was for some time under the command of Lieutenant-Colonel Macdonell, and afterwards of Colonel Home; and I am happy to add that it was maintained throughout the day with the utmost gallantry by these brave troops, notwithstanding the repeated efforts of large bodies of the enemy to obtain possession of it.

This attack upon the right of our center was accompanied by a very heavy cannonade upon our whole line, which was destined to support the repeated attacks of cavalry and infantry, occasionally mixed, but sometimes separate, which were made upon it. In one of these the enemy carried the farmhouse of La Haye Sainte, as the detachment of the light battalion of the German Legion, which occupied it, had expended all its ammunition; and the enemy occupied the only communication there was with them.

The enemy repeatedly charged our infantry with his cavalry, but these attacks were uniformly unsuccessful; and they afforded opportunities to our cavalry to charge, in one of which Lord E. Somerset's brigade, consisting of the Life Guards, the Royal Horse Guards, and 1st Dragoon Guards, highly distinguished themselves, as did that of Major-General Sir William Ponsonby, having taken many prisoners and an eagle.

These attacks were repeated till about seven in the evening, when the enemy made a desperate effort with cavalry and infantry, supported by the fire of artillery, to force our left center, near the farm of La Haye Sainte, which after a severe contest was defeated; and, having observed that the troops retired from this attack in great confusion, and that the march of General Bülow's corps, by Frischermont upon Planchenois and La Belle Alliance, had begun to take effect, and as I could perceive the fire of his cannon, and as Marshal Prince Blücher had joined in person with a corps of his army to the left of our line by Ohain, I determined to attack the enemy, and immediately advanced the whole line of infantry, supported by the cavalry and artillery. The attack succeeded in every point: the enemy was forced from his positions on the heights, and fled in the utmost confusion, leaving behind him, as far as I could judge, 150 pieces of cannon, with their ammunition, which fell into our hands.

I continued the pursuit till long after dark, and then discontinued it only on account of the fatigue of our troops, who had been engaged during twelve hours, and because I found myself on the same road with Marshal Blücher, who assured me of his intention to follow the enemy throughout the night. He has sent me word this morning that he had taken 60 pieces of cannon belonging to the Imperial Guard, and several carriages, baggage, etc., belonging to Bonaparte in Genappe.

I propose to move this morning upon Nivelles, and not to discontinue my operations.

Your lordship will observe that such a desperate action could not be fought, and such advantages could not be gained, without great loss; and I am sorry to add that ours has been immense. In Lieutenant-General Sir Thomas Picton His Majesty has sustained the loss of an officer who has frequently distinguished himself in his service, and he fell gloriously leading his division to a charge with bayonets, by which one of the most serious attacks made by the enemy on our position was repulsed. The Earl of Uxbridge, after having successfully got through this arduous day, received a wound by almost the last shot fired, which will, I am afraid, deprive His Majesty for some time of his services.

His Royal Highness the Prince of Orange distinguished himself by his gallantry and conduct, till he received a wound from a musket-ball through the shoulder, which obliged him to quit the field.

It gives me the greatest satisfaction to assure your lordship that the army never upon any occasion conducted itself better. The division of Guards, under Lieutenant-General Cooke, who is severely wounded, Major-General Maitland, and Major-General Byng, set an example which was followed by all, and there is no officer nor description of troops that did not behave well.

I must, however, particularly mention for His Royal Highness's approbation Lieutenant-General Sir H. Clinton, Major-General Adam, Lieutenant-General Charles Baron Alten (severely wounded), Major-General Sir Colin Halkett (severely wounded), Colonel Ompteda, Colonel Mitchell (commanding a brigade of the 4th Division), Major-Generals Sir James Kempt and Sir D. Pack, Major-General Lambert, Major-General Lord E. Somerset, Major-General Sir W. Ponsonby, Major-General Sir C. Grant, and Major-General Sir H. Vivian, Major-General Sir O. Vandeleur, and Major-General Count Dornberg.

I am also particularly indebted to General Lord Hill for his assistance and conduct upon this, as upon all former occasions.

THE WATERLOO DISPATCH

The artillery and engineer departments were conducted much to my satisfaction by Colonel Sir George Wood and Colonel Smyth; and I had every reason to be satisfied with the conduct of the Adjutant-General, Major-General Barnes, who was wounded, and of the Quartermaster-General, Colonel De Lancey, who was killed by a cannon-shot in the middle of the action. This officer is a serious loss to His Majesty's service, and to me at this moment.

I was likewise much indebted to the assistance of Lieutenant-Colonel Lord FitzRoy Somerset, who was severely wounded, and of the officers composing my personal staff, who have suffered severely in this action. Lieutenant-Colonel the Hon. Sir Alexander Gordon, who has died of his wounds, was a most promising officer, and is a serious loss to His Majesty's service.

General Kruse, of the Nassau service, likewise conducted himself much to my satisfaction, as did General Tripp, commanding the heavy brigade of cavalry, and General Vanhope, commanding a brigade of infantry, in the service of the King of the Netherlands.

General Pozzo di Borgo, General Baron Vincent, General Müffling, and General Alava, were in the field during the action, and rendered me every assistance in their power. Baron Vincent is wounded, but I hope not severely, and General Pozzo di Borgo received a contusion.

I should not do justice to my own feelings, or to Marshal Blücher and the Prussian Army, if I did not attribute the successful result of this arduous day to the cordial and timely assistance I received from them. The operation of General Bülow upon the enemy's flank was a most decisive one; and even if I had not found myself in a situation to make the attack which produced the final result, it would have forced the enemy to retire if his attacks should have failed, and would have prevented him from taking advantage of them if they should unfortunately have succeeded.

Since writing the above, I have received a report that Major-General Sir William Ponsonby is killed, and, in announcing this intelligence to your lordship, I have to add the expression of my grief for the fate of an officer who had already rendered very brilliant and important services, and was an ornament to his profession.

ON WATERLOO

I send with this dispatch three eagles, taken by the troops in this action, which Major Percy will have the honor of laying at the feet of His Royal Highness. I beg leave to recommend him to your lordship's protection.

> I have the honor to be, etc.,
>
> WELLINGTON

III.

LETTERS HOME[1]
Two letters by Clausewitz to His Wife Marie

Le Plessis-Piquet near Paris   3 July 1815

In sight of the great city, towards which the gaze of half the world has again turned, I sit down to write you a few words about the historic efforts of the last three weeks. It is an entirely delightful task to share news with a cherished friend after having completed one's labors, resting in a wonderful villa, surrounded by a beautiful park, at the foot of the shimmering battlements of the humiliated rulers of the world.

On 15 June, we quick-marched to Namur, arriving in the night. Two hours later, we broke camp and proceeded to Sombreffe, a few hours distant from the famous battlefield at Fleurus. The Prussian army was assembled here, but unfortunately faulty arrangements resulted in the absence of the 4th Corps, the strongest. We arrived at ten in the morning and took up our position on the left wing. The battle[2] began at three o'clock and continued until after ten in the evening. Our participation was limited, but in the evening, after Thiele brought the news that we had been ordered to retreat, and that the retreat was to be toward Wavre—not toward the Meuse but toward Brussels—we found ourselves in a dismal situation. We were cut off from the Field Marshal [i.e., Blücher] and had to make our own way. Our firefight ended with an unfortunate cavalry affair; I managed to escape the French cuirassiers only with great difficulty. Our troops were scattered in an extended position, out of which they could be extracted only with difficulty. Our strongest brigade was

---

1 From Karl Schwartz, *Leben des Generals Carl von Clausewitz und der Frau Marie von Clausewitz, geb. Gräfin von Brühl, mit Briefe, Aufsätzen, Tagebüchern und anderen Schriftstüden* [*The Life of General Carl von Clausewitz and Marie von Clausewitz, née Countess von Brühl, including Letters, Essays, Diaries, and Other Papers*], 2 vols. (Berlin: Dümmler Publishing and Books, 1878), 2:148-158. The initial translation of these two letters was provided to us by Dr. Stanley A. Riveles, U.S. Department of State, who was then a visiting professor at the National War College. We have included all of Schwartz's explanatory footnotes.
2 Of Ligny and St. Amand. (Schwartz, 149)

sent to help the 2nd Corps, and we had no more reserves available. The road to Namur, along which we were spread out, was filled and blocked by the countless wagons of the other army corps, who thought that this was the line of retreat because the army had come from there. The enemy cavalry was emboldened and made a charge during the night that was repulsed only by the strong stand of Pochhammer's battalion. The darkness was deep; the use of couriers impossible; and our retreat was conducted along a secondary road. I believe my hair turned gray that night, and, apart from the few moments it took to write my report to the Field Marshal, I did not dismount my horse. As always in such cases, the worst did not happen, and before daylight we were able to gather the small band of troops that remained and march to Gembloux. The enemy's pursuit was weak.

At noon on the 17th, the weary troops arrived at Gembloux in driving rain after having had to wade through a defile for half an hour in water above their ankles. The only food we had to eat for the next 24 hours was that which a small town of 2,000 inhabitants can give to a corps of 20,000 men. At two o'clock we again departed and marched toward Wavre via a detour, because we had to rejoin the Field Marshal's army. Once again a horrible downpour, once again a defile where the tired soldiers had to march along a slippery sunken road in an unceasing struggle. Half of the corps went through the small town of Wavre and arrived in their positions at 1 a.m. The other half remained on the road in front of the town because the column was constantly bogging down; heavy rain continued the whole night. It was only in the morning that the last of the infantry passed through; the cavalry did so only shortly before the beginning of the battle.

The 18th. The troops had no rations other than meat, yet hardly any time to butcher and cook it. Think what it is like to have to walk for a mile to get wood and water and then be your own cook. Our corps headquarters was in the very lovely Chateau La Bavette. Wellington's battle began at midday. The Prussian army had already set off in the morning and arrived at four in the afternoon on the left flank of Wellington's army, which had taken up a position in front of the *Bois de Soignie*. Our corps remained behind to observe the position at Wavre; in other words to defend the Dyle, thereby covering the road to Louvain, along which the Prussian army would retreat in the event of a defeat. Initially, there was

ON WATERLOO

little activity near Wavre, and we had begun our march toward the main body of the army to serve as a reserve force. However, the appearance of a strong enemy formation near Wavre forced us to turn back.

Our engagement got underway around four o'clock. The enemy attempted to force his way through the defile, but our position was strong and we turned them back. We had no knowledge that the great battle [at Belle Alliance/Waterloo] had ended by eight o'clock; our fight lasted long into the night. At ten in the evening, a battalion of the 2nd Corps defending one of the defiles left its position without informing us. Consequently, the enemy got into our position and threatened our right flank. Stülpnagel and his brigade[3] charged with a "hurrah" at this point (whereby Tiedemann was wounded), but this failed. The enemy held firm and we fell into disarray; we had great difficulty in restoring order. This continued until midnight. We still had not had any news of the victory. On the 19th at two in the morning, at first light, the newly arrived corps attacked Stülpnagel. I hurried over, collecting as many troops as could be spared. All at once the firefight became very intense, and it lasted until about eleven o'clock in the morning. At ten, we received news from General von Pirch [I] that a brilliant victory had been won. He also informed us that he intended to cut off the corps facing us. However, the locations where he intended to cut them off were so far removed from us that the action promised us no relief. Cut off as we were from the main body of our army as a result of the enemy's flanking maneuver, we were left to our own resources with Vandamme and Grouchy's superior force of 45,000 men against us.[4] We expected to be able to hold out for only another hour, and still no General Pirch. In addition, as a result of an error that I still find inexplicable, General Borcke marched off toward the main army with our strongest brigade[5]—thus with a quarter of our corps—and could not be recalled. At eleven o'clock we commenced our retreat toward Louvain having lost nothing else [i.e., no major pieces of equipment] than many dead and wounded. We proceeded for two hours along the road, then stopped in order to assemble our extremely weary troops. The enemy did not pursue.

---

3 The 12th Brigade of the 3rd Army Corps. (Schwartz, 151)
4 This force is overestimated; 32,000 French faced 15,000 Prussians. (Schwartz, 151)
5 Major General Borcke commanded the 9th Brigade. (Schwartz, 151)

The 20th. At daybreak, we broke camp and prepared to attack the enemy opposite us because we hoped that General von Pirch would now arrive. However, the enemy had already marched off during the night. Thanks to an amazingly rapid march of the cavalry, we reached his rear guard at Namur and captured 4 guns through a bold attack by the 8th Ulan Regiment. From Namur on the 21st we hurried after the main army, which had been in pursuit [of the French] ever since the 18th, and reached it between Avesnes and St. Quentin. From there we continued day and night in never-ending long marches via Ham, Compiègne, Dammartin, Argenteuil, St. Germain, and around Paris, until we reached here. Our exertions were so taxing that several men shot themselves out of despair; others dropped dead. Here on the southern edge of Paris, which is not fortified, the French Army has taken up positions, while Wellington has advanced on Montmartre. Over a two-day period, there were rather violent skirmishes contesting the village of Issy, which we then took and held. Yesterday, negotiations began. The French army will probably pull back over the Loire and we will occupy Paris.

At this point I will end my excessively military travelogue, which deals more with the corps than with me personally. I share this with you because you have sometimes reproached me for never sharing these matters with you. So if this has bored you, it is not my fault. Gneisenau is well and at the pinnacle of his fortunes: He has received the Order of the Black Eagle. The monarchs of Europe are expected in Paris any day; they have already assembled.

Farewell, dearest soul mate! Hopefully we shall be together again soon. Once peace has been concluded, I will write to you. I am already thinking about the arrangements for your journey. Fortunate, I feel inexpressibly fortunate, even after such epoch-making events, that I possess something more valuable to me than any triumph, and I eagerly anticipate a moment that will exceed any other. I never love you more than in moments of great fortune or great misfortune. You are worth more to me than any manifestation of the former, and this overshadows any impact that the latter could have on my fate.

Dohna is no longer with us; he has received command of a cavalry brigade in the 4th Corps and is well.

ON WATERLOO

Le Plessis-Piquet, near Paris   7 July 1815

We are still not in Paris yet. Today the 1st Corps will move in and begin a military occupation. We follow tomorrow but will remain only one day and then move to Fontainebleau, which is entirely pleasant to me. Since the tone of my last letter was perhaps too military, I will today add a few lines on more pleasant matters.[6]

Our first march from Namur was to Charleroi on the Sambre....

On the 22nd to Beaumont....

On the 23rd to Avesnes. This place has a rather strong fortress and the city itself is not without significance. General Zieten had shelled it for several days, and by chance one of the shells hit the powder magazine. The explosion was so enormous that two-thirds of the city lay in ruins. I have never seen a picture of such destruction in my entire life. We stayed in the house that had suffered the least damage; even so the door of my room had been lifted out of its hinges and the front door of the house had been wrecked to such an extent that it could not be opened. The number of inhabitants killed by the explosion was estimated at more than 100. Entire streets were full of rubble and impassable; in other streets all the roofs were gone. The scene was highly depressing, and I will never forget the impression made on me by a young child, who was looking out the window of such a shattered house and rejoiced at the sight of our troops marching by.

On the 24th to Nouvion....

On the 25th to Humbier via St. Quentin....

On the 26th to Guiscard via Ham. The latter place has a very strong citadel that contains the famous state prison to which most German prisoners were sent. The original intent had been to destroy this citadel completely once we had gained possession of it, but [its] commander did not want to surrender just because of the few shells we were prepared to throw at him. We finally had to settle for signing a convention with him, whereby the crossing over the Somme would remain open and the citadel would be guarded jointly by us and the French until a future government took it over....

---

6 Most of this letter is a travelogue commenting on art and architecture. We have left in only the military elements and those paragraphs most revealing of Clausewitz's personality and of his relationship with Marie.

On the 27th to Compiègne on the Oise. There is a royal hunting lodge here that was formerly the prince's headquarters. It was redecorated by Napoleon, who celebrated his marriage to Marie Louise here, and it is one of the most magnificent fantasy palaces [literally, "air castles"] I have ever seen. The bedrooms and baths, with walls entirely mirrored, show that Marie Louise lacked a noble and virtuous nature—everything breathes of sensuality and feminine vanity. Apart from the questionable furnishings, there are some works of art that make the chateau worth seeing. In particular there are two groups here, Amor and Psyche, one of which is by Canova, as well as several lovely landscapes. The exterior of the chateau is quite beautiful, and the town itself is one of the loveliest of cities.

On the 28th to Crépy on the road from Soissons to Paris....

On the 29th to Dammartin on the road from Soissons to Paris, nine hours distant from the latter city....

On the 30th to Gonesse, four hours from Paris....

On the 1st [of July] our exhausted troops remained at St. Germain. On this day Lieutenant Colonel Sohr marched with the Brandenburg and Pomeranian Hussar Regiments[7] from St. Germain through Versailles with the goal of reaching Longjumeau on the road between Paris and Bleau. His objective was to determine whether forces were rushing from there to help Paris. As fate would have it, the French had sent out a reconnaissance force from St. Cloud and Paris toward Marly and Versailles at the same time to observe our movements. Sohr seems to have committed some blunders. In any event, after he encountered the enemy between Versailles and Paris, he attacked and pursued them to within two hours of Paris. A superior cavalry force then counterattacked and drove him back; he then found the road behind him occupied by infantry. Both regiments were so badly mauled that of 800 horsemen, 300 were captured; 170 saved themselves, and the remaining 330 were lost. Sohr himself was wounded and taken prisoner. General Yorck's son, who had volunteered for the regiment, suffered a grave wound.[8] Gen-

---

7 Belonging to the 2nd Corps. (Schwartz, 156)
8 Of Sohr's 800-man strong regiment, 500, most wounded, were captured; 216 men died or were gravely wounded. Lieutenant-Colonel Sohr, who turned down an offer of surrender, was also wounded and fell into the enemy's hands. However, he recovered and became Major General and brigade commander in 1832; divisional commander in 1838. Heinrich von Yorck, the Field Marshal's son, succumbed to his wounds after several days. (Schwartz, 157)

eral Gneisenau's son had fortunately been detached; otherwise he could hardly have avoided a similar fate. The enemy succeeded in driving so close to St. Germain that we barely had time to send the 9th Brigade out to the nearby heights to oppose him and force him back.

On the 2nd of July the other two corps also passed through St. Germain, and we continued our march through Meudon and Chatillon. The royal chateau at Meudon is situated on the edge of the Seine valley, about two hours from the riverbank where Paris is located. From the terrace at Meudon, several hundred feet above the valley that spreads out below, the view of Paris, Passy, Sèvres, St. Cloud, and all the lovely villages and castles that fill the valley is surprisingly beautiful. It all looks like one enormous park. It is the most remarkable view of its kind that I have ever seen, and on the European continent can only be compared with Constantinople or Naples. St. Cloud, location of the Field Marshal's headquarters, is characterised by fine alleyways and groves of trees. The chateau is more elegant than grand. Grolmann is rolling around in Josephine's bed.

Dearest Marie, the time has come to close this diary. Once the peace agreement has been signed, then you will come to me, as I have imagined by way of Compiègne. This route is not much farther and a great deal more interesting than the direct road via Laon. I hope to be able to meet you in Compiègne, and together we will savor what I have seen only in haste. You and I will take the same route, through St. Germain, Versailles, and Meudon, that we have just traversed. In this manner, we shall arrive in Paris through the back way, having relished the beauty that Paris has to offer.

ON WATERLOO

IV.

CORRESPONDENCE WITHIN WELLINGTON'S CIRCLE

Liverpool[1] to Wellington,
10 September 1840
Wellington Papers[2] 2/71/28.

My dear Duke:

A German friend of mine in the course of the last Spring recommended to me the posthumous works of Gen. Clausewitz. My object was to learn something with respect to York's[3] going over to the allies in the campaign of 1812-13, but having dipped into this book I found it a work of exceeding interest. It is entitled a work "on war & the mode of conducting war." Several volumes are devoted to general principles & the others contain details of many of the campaigns of the revolutionary war in which the author's principles are exemplified by actions in many of which the author was an eye witness. One whole volume is devoted to the campaign of Waterloo. The greatest part of this I have translated & having submitted my translation to Col. Gurwood[4] I have begged him at a proper & convenient opportunity to lay it before you.

---

1 Charles Cecil Cope Jenkinson (1784-1851), Third Earl of Liverpool, inherited his title in 1828. During the Napoleonic Wars he had served as a British attaché in Vienna and as a volunteer in the Austrian Army during the Battle of Austerlitz in 1805, so he was quite familiar with the German language. See *Dictionary of National Biography* [hereafter cited as DNB], 63 vols. (London: Smith Elder & Co., 1885-1900), 29:310-311.
2 University of Southampton, Wellington Papers (hereafter cited as WP).
3 This refers to Prussian General Hans David Ludwig Yorck von Wartenburg (1759-1830), commander of the Prussian corps on the left wing of Napoleon's advance into Russia. On 30 December 1812, he signed the Convention of Tauroggen with the Russians, making his force neutral and paving the way for Prussia to change sides and enter the war on the side of the Allies. See Peter Paret, *Yorck and the Era of Prussian Reform, 1807-1815* (Princeton: Princeton University Press, 1966); John Keegan and Andrew Wheatcroft, *Who's Who in Military History from 1453* (Leicester, 1991), 337.
4 Col. John Gurwood (1790-1845) served as a captain in the 10th Hussars at Waterloo, where he was severely wounded. He subsequently became Deputy Lieutenant of the Tower of Lon-

CORRESPONDENCE WITHIN WELLINGTON'S CIRCLE

We both agree in thinking that if at your leisure you could read what I have translated your observations on this part of the work would be invaluable.

Pray believe that if I have any motive in this matter beyond the desire of acquiring accurate information it is that your great & admirable actions should be thoroughly known & duly appreciated.

This letter will be sent open to Col. Gurwood that he may use it or not with the translation which is in his possession as he may judge most proper.

Believe me dear Duke
with every feeling of
regard & attachment
sincerely yours,

Liverpool

Lt. Col. John Gurwood to Wellington,
The Tower,
12 September 1840
WP 2/71/37.

My Lord Duke:

I have the honor to inclose a letter from Lord Liverpool to your Grace, relating to a translation which he has forwarded to me, at different times during the last month, of that part of the posthumous work of General Clausewitz, giving a detail of the operations of the British, Prussian and French armies, previous to and at the battle of Waterloo. He's written on 50 sheets of foolscap paper, half margin, and with your Grace's permission I will forward it to you.

Gen. Clausewitz having died in 1830, and the work, 10 Volumes, having been published by his widow between 1836 & 1838,[5] it has not had

---

don and private secretary to the Duke of Wellington, during which time he edited the Duke's papers and published *Dispatches of the Duke of Wellington* (London, 1837-1844). See *DNB* 23:370.

5 Clausewitz actually died in 1831, and his works were published between 1832 and 1837.

the advantage of many corrections which would have presented themselves in your Grace's dispatches, since published.

General Clausewitz I understand to have been an officer of great reputation in the Prussian army; and Lord Liverpool's translation proves his anxiety to ascertain the truth, although his sources of information probably did not always enable him to obtain it.

It has not yet been translated into either French or English, and I have not been able to ascertain the opinions of any French officers, to whom I have written respecting the work, as they generally have a great contempt for anything military not exclusively French, but particularly when it is Prussian.

If I should be permitted by your Grace to forward it to you at Walmer castle, I shall send at the same time the few original letters of your Grace to the late Sir Robt. Barsley, which I have obtained from his niece, W. Gordon.

I have the honor to be
your Grace's faithful servant,

J. Gurwood

Wellington to Liverpool,
Walmer Castle
14 September 1840
The British Library [BL], Papers of the Third Earl of Liverpool, Additional Manuscripts [Add Mss] 38,196, fol. 143.

I am very much obliged to my dear Lord Liverpool for his letter which Col. Gurwood has sent me. I will receive with much interest your translation of Gen'l Clausewitz' Work. I should like most of all his account of Grouchy's operations at the period of the Battle of Waterloo.

Believe me yours most sincerely,

Wellington

CORRESPONDENCE WITHIN WELLINGTON'S CIRCLE

Gurwood to Wellington,
The Tower
22 September 1840
WP 2/71/72.

My Lord Duke:

I have the honor to forward to your Grace Lord Liverpool's translation of that part of Gen. Clausewitz's work relating to the operations of General Grouchy and Gen. Thielmann on the Dyle on the 18th & 19th of June, 1815.

Lord Liverpool writes to me "that there is a long military description upon the whole combined operation of Waterloo, but this I do not think worth troubling his Grace with, as it might be truly considered in the light of *Reveries*." I returned him for answer that there was no want of "Reveries" on this or any other military operation; the object was, if possible, to obtain a history of facts as they occurred, not as they might have occurred.

I have the honor to be
your Grace's faithful servant,

J. Gurwood

Charles Arbuthnot to Lord Francis Egerton,[6]
22 July 1842

Dear Lord F[rancis],

Last night the Duke read out to me your paper, which I had given him,[7] and said, "Oh, this will do exactly, but I will make some additional re-

---

6 Lord Francis Egerton (1800-1857) was born Lord Francis Leveson Gower and subsequently inherited the estates of Francis Egerton, Duke of Bridgewater. He became the First Earl of Ellesmere in 1846, so he did not yet have that title during the correspondence relating to Wellington's Memorandum. *DNB* 17:157-158.

7 Egerton's note: "The first rough draft of my Article." He is referring to a draft of his article reviewing Rauschnick's *Marschall Vorwärts* (a biography of Blücher), which was published in

marks." ... I had written this far when the Duke came into my room with his 12th volume[8] in his hand, and said, "I have it all here,"—said it with high delight. He stayed with me for some time, and read to me various pages from page 375 to 476. I took down the pages by his desire and send them to you. You never saw a man so delighted as the Duke is, and saying that he would go and write his Memorandum, and make out Alison[9] to be a damned rascally Frenchman. This between ourselves.

C.A.[10]

Arbuthnot to Egerton,
Apsley House,
25 July 1842
From Ellesmere, *Personal Reminiscences,* pp. 236-237.

I send you the paper which the Duke has drawn up,[11] and I return the one you gave to me for him to read. The Duke's paper contains a com-

---

the *Quarterly Review* in September 1842. Ellesmere (Egerton) recalled in his *Personal Reminiscences of the Duke of Wellington by Francis, the First Earl of Ellesmere* (New York, E. P. Dutton & Company, 1903), 90, that this "second article which I wrote for the *Quarterly* on Waterloo was partly a commentary on the work of the Prussian Clausewitz. A translation in MS. of this had been furnished to him by a friend—I believe the late Lord Liverpool. The Duke had some doubt of the competence of the translator, and would not look at it till I had gone over it and certified its accuracy, which I did. He then read it, and made on it comments, some of which appear verbatim in the article in question."
8 Egerton's note: "Gurwood's first edition of the Dispatches, I think."
9 Sir Archibald Alison (1792-1867) was the author of the 10-volume *History of Europe from the Commencement of the French Revolution in M.DCC.LXXXIX to the Restoration of the Bourbons in M.DCCC.XV* (Edinburgh and London: William Blackwood and Sons, 1833-1842). The final volume covered the events of 1815. *DNB* 1:287-290. The Duke strongly disagreed with Alison's allegation that he had been caught by surprise by Napoleon's attack.
10 From Egerton, *Personal Reminiscences,* 235-236. Charles Arbuthnot (1767-1850) was a civil servant who was best known for being the husband of Harriet Fane Arbuthnot, a close friend and confidant of the Duke of Wellington. After her death in 1834, he moved into the Duke's residences at Apsley House and Walmer Castle. For more information on the Arbuthnots, see The Seventh Duke of Wellington, ed., *Wellington and his Friends: Letters of the First Duke of Wellington to the Rt. Hon. Charles and Mrs. Arbuthnot, the Earl and Countess of Wilton, Princess Lieven, and Miss Burdett-Coutts* (London: Macmillan, 1965); *DNB* 2:61; Neville Thompson, *Wellington After Waterloo* (London: Routledge & Kegan Paul, 1986), 14, 23.
11 The paper mentioned was an early draft of Wellington's Memorandum on the Battle of Waterloo, dated 23 July 1842 (see WP 8/1/1), which served as the basis for Egerton's *Quarterly*

plete narrative of all that has happened from Napoleon's quitting Elba till the battle of Waterloo, and I think you will find it conclusive against a surprise. It details all that he had ordered, which proves that he had good reason for not collecting his troops until Napoleon had committed himself to the place of attack upon which he had determined. At the conclusion of the paper the Duke represents Alison as a Whig. Whether so or not I don't know, but you do probably. I think you will make a capital article from your own notions, and from the Duke's information. When written, you had better send it straight to the Duke, as I might not be returned to London.

C.A.

P.S.—Alison states his numbers from those which were to have been collected. The actual numbers were nothing like what had been intended, and the Duke had not more than 50,000 men on the field of battle.[12]

Gurwood to Liverpool,
70 Lowndes Square
1 August 1842
BL Add Mss 38,303 fols 191-192.

My dear Lord Liverpool,

I passed two hours with the Duke yesterday with more interest & satisfaction than on any previous occasion. He has written a Memorandum on the operations of the Waterloo campaign of considerable length, and great clearness in refutation of the charges made by Clausewitz & Alison. I shall be able to show you a copy of it some of these days, although I believe it will form the foundation of a paper that will be written and

---

Review article on Blücher. This version of the Memorandum did not mention Clausewitz's book, because Wellington had thus far seen only the portions of it dealing with Grouchy's movements and the Battle of Wavre (the chapters of Lord Liverpool's translation which he had received in September 1840). So at this time Wellington's main target was Alison's *History of Europe*.
12 Wellington's total troop strength on the morning of 18 June 1815 was around 70,000 men, so this figure may refer solely to his strength in infantry.

ON WATERLOO

published in the *Quarterly Review* (this "entre nous"). I know no one who will be more interested in this paper than yourself after what you have described to me in reading Clausewitz & Alison. The Duke does not confess it, but I think that the Memorandum was not wholly written the week before last, for he enters into the detail of the whole operations as I recollect stated in your translation of Clausewitz although his remarks are directly chiefly at the misrepresentations of Alison.[13]

I am at the Tower at night, but I pass the greater part of the day here.

Sincerely yours,

J. Gurwood

Luckily I have made no notes in your book that are not borne out in the Duke's memorandum.

Wellington to Gurwood,
Walmer Castle
28 August 1842
WP 8/3/1.

My dear Colonel

I return the inclosed paper which according to your desire I have shewn to Arbuthnot.

Lord Francis' design has been carried into execution very ably.

I do not exactly understand the corrections in Red Ink in the margins; that is whether they are made by you with knowledge of the facts from documents; or by Lord Francis himself.

I wish to add a Word about the Initiative, about which I think that I have not expressed myself clearly. All acquainted with Military Operations are aware that the Initiative of the operations between two Armies

---

13 As previously noted, Wellington had so far seen only the Grouchy and Wavre chapters of Liverpool's translation of Clausewitz's history of the Waterloo Campaign. There is no indication in the surviving correspondence that the Duke saw any more of the manuscript before September 1842.

en Presence is a great advantage, of which each Party would endeavour to avail Himself.

We the Allies in the Netherlands and on the Meuse in 1815 were necessarily on the Defensive! We were waiting for the juncture and cooperation of other Large Armies to attain our object.

But our defensive position did not necessarily preclude all idea or plan of attack upon the enemy.

The Enemy might have so placed Himself, as to have rendered the attack of His Army advisable and even necessary. In that case we must and we should have taken the Initiative!

But in the case actually existing in 1815 the enemy did not take such a position. On the contrary he took a position as is explained in my Mem^m in which His Numbers, His Movements, His Designs would be concealed, protected and supported up to the last moment previous to their execution by his formidable fortresses at the frontier.

We could not attack this position without being prepared to attack this superior Army so posted: and to lay on at least two sieges at the same period of time. We could not have the Initiative therefore in the way of Attack.

We could have it and we had it in the way of Defensive movement: But the object of my memorandum was to shew that such movement must have been founded upon Hypothesis: our original position having been calculated for the Defence and protection of certain objects confided to our care; any alteration previous to the first movement of the enemy; and the certainty that it was a real movement: which is much more than an Hypothesis, must have exposed to injury some Important Interest. Therefore no movement was made till the Initiative was taken by the enemy and the Design of his movement was obvious. If any movement had been previously made it would have been what is commonly called a <u>false movement!</u> And whatever people may think of Bonaparte; of all the Chiefs of Armies in the World, he was <u>the one</u> perhaps in whose presence it was least safe to make a false movement! This is what I endeavoured to explain in the Memorandum.

Therefore, I did not desire or order a movement till I knew on the 15th that a movement had been made: and its direction although I knew for days before that the whole Army with Bonaparte at its Head was at the frontier.

ON WATERLOO

When I was certain of the movement and its Direction I ordered the March and it is obvious that I was in time! And if foolish accidents had not occurred; upon which I ought not to have reckoned, the whole Army would have been at Quatre Bras on the 16th before the Battle commenced at the front of our position.

Wellington to Gurwood,
Walmer Castle
31 August 1842
WP 8/3/2.

My Dear Colonel

I return Lord Francis Egerton's letter and I send up in the Horse Guards' Bag[14] this day Lord Liverpool's Translation of Clausewitz, which I beg Lord Francis will cast his eye over. If it should be correct, I will read it: and afterwards my Mem^m upon the situation previous to the Battle of Waterloo, and the letter upon the Initiative which I wrote to you two days ago. I beg that Lord Francis will mark any passage in Clausewitz, which he may think requires explanation.

Having all these papers before me I shall be a better judge of the case. I beg you forward me the Mem^m and letter abovementioned, of which I don't know that I have copies.

Ever Yours most sincerely

W

---

14 The "Horse Guards" Barracks housed the administrative headquarters of the British Army.

CORRESPONDENCE WITHIN WELLINGTON'S CIRCLE

Gurwood to Wellington,
70 Lowndes Square
1 September 1842
WP 8/3/3.

My Lord Duke,

Agreeably to the orders contained in your Grace's letter, which I received this morning, I have forwarded to Lord Francis Egerton, Lord Liverpool's translation of Clausewitz, requesting that he would see that it is correct, and that he would make any remark which he thought might require explanation.

I received a letter this morning from Lord Francis in which he states that he has a severe attack of gout in his bridle hand wrist, but as his Yeomanry were yesterday dismissed, he hopes the gout will keep out of his right hand and not prevent him getting on with Clausewitz

I have seen Mr. Lockhart,[15] who has decided on including in the forthcoming number of the *Quarterly Review* only that part of Lord Francis's paper relating to Blücher, leaving out the battle of Waterloo, but noting the intention of dedicating a future article to it in answer to Clausewitz, Alison, etc.

This motive he will introduce in a note to the article "Blücher" by stating that Mr. Alison and others in presuming to attack your Grace and Marshal Blücher, were like the self sufficient Greek lecturer mentioned by Cicero, who requested Hannibal to attend his lectures on the art of war, in which he would point out the errors he had committed in the command of armies.

I have seen Colonel Freeth[16] this morning, who thinks he shall be able to find in the Archives of the QMG [Quartermaster General] Department the orders of movement of the 15th June 1815. Those which I inserted in the 12th volume of the Dispatches, I obtained from other quarters, as I had heard that Lady Delancy had destroyed the originals among her husbands papers. But there must be a copy of them in the QMGs department over which neither Sir William nor Lady Delancy could have

---

15 John Gibson Lockhart (1794-1854) served as editor of the journal *Quarterly Review* from 1825 until 1853. *DNB* 34:47-49.
16 Col. James Freeth is listed as Assistant Quartermaster General in the War Department's *The Army List for August 1842* (London, 1842), 6.

ON WATERLOO

had any control. I recollect however referring to Sir Willoughby Gordon for them when completing the 12th volume but without success. Colonel Freeth however thinks they are in the office. If so they will afford proof of the hours in which they were circulated to the different corps and divisions if they do not also state the exact hour they were received from your Grace for such circulation.

[Unrelated paragraph omitted.]

I have the Honor to be
Your Grace's faithful servant

J. Gurwood

Wellington to Gurwood,
Walmer Castle
4 September 1842
WP 8/3/4.

Many thanks for your note of the 3rd my dear Colonel. I will not lose a moment in perusing Clausewitz and in writing upon the subject if necessary after I shall have perused the same; when Lord Francis will return the manuscript.

The bag comes down from the Horse Guards every night.

Ever Yours most faithfully

Wellington

CORRESPONDENCE WITHIN WELLINGTON'S CIRCLE

Egerton to Arbuthnot,
Worsley,
5 September 1842
WP 2/91/148.

My dear Arbuthnot,

Ld Liverpool's translation of Clausewitz is not only correct but in my opinion remarkably good. The main error of the work is that he postpones <u>all</u> political & moral to the purely military considerations of the case, & even with respect to these makes nothing of the possibility of either Army losing its communications, or even its materiel. He seems to me free from national prejudices & nonsense. People will judge of things after the event, & it is difficult now to persuade them that the Duke could not know enough of the points on which Bonaparte was clustering his masses to be sure that he would not come on from Lille upon Mons. Clausewitz' main principle is that the Allied Generals might have forced B^e [Bonaparte] to fight them on their own field of battle by merely collecting & remaining together, & all that the Duke has to do is to shew the risk of such a proceeding.
[Unrelated material omitted.]
I think I shall translate & publish Clausewitz's Russian Campaign. It is full of curious particulars, & well worth being known to military readers here.[17]
[Unrelated material omitted.]

Ever Yours faithfully

F. Egerton

---

[17] Egerton published his translation—anonymously—as *The Campaign of 1812 in Russia* (London: John Murray, 1843).

ON WATERLOO

Gurwood to Wellington,
70 Lowndes Square
6 September 1842
WP 8/3/5.

My Lord Duke

The *Quarterly Review* will be published next Saturday week, the 17th inst., and will contain Lord F. Egerton's paper on Blücher, which, by being transposed according to chronological arrangement, with some additions which escaped Lord Francis, will, I think, very much interest its readers.

Lord Francis had quite overlooked your Grace's letter to Genl. Dumouriez,[18] 26 Sept 1815, where you disclaim ever having seen Fouché, or having had communication with him, previous to July. But I shall have the Honor to forward the corrected copy tomorrow, by which your Grace will see the changes made.

I was at the Horse Guards today, and I regret to say that Colonel Freeth has been unable to find any documents of movements between the 13 June & 3 July 1815. It appears that the QMGl's [Quarter Master General's] office, although in great pen and ink order when there is little to do, is always the contrary during very active operations, and there is no registries of memorandums of movement. Colonel Delancy, I hear, was particularly careless on these subjects, but after his death, these orders might have been collected from the corps, if not from the division, to which they were issued.

I have the Honor to be
Your Grace's
faithful Servant

J Gurwood

---

18 French General Charles-François Dumouriez (1739-1823) had won the battles of Valmy and Jemappes before falling out of favor with the Revolutionary government and going over to the Allies. From 1804 onward he lived in Britain, where he was active in many schemes against Napoleon and received a substantial pension from the British government. See J. Holland Rose and A. M. Broadley, *Domouriez and the Defence of England against Napoleon* (London and New York, 1909).

CORRESPONDENCE WITHIN WELLINGTON'S CIRCLE

Egerton to Gurwood,
Worsley
6 September 1842
WP 8/3/6.

My dear Gurwood,

I hope you will get Ld L's [Lord Liverpool's] Mss safe with this. It seems to me not only a correct but a remarkably good translation & leaves nothing to desire as the parts omitted have no interest for us.

 I do not quite understand why Clausewitz supposes that if the battle of Waterloo had begun earlier Blucher would have been earlier in the field. This would have been the case if the battle had begun earlier in consequence of <u>better weather</u>, but he is blaming Buonaparte for losing time by an ostentatious & needless deployment & parade of his forces. I dare say he is right & I hope he is.

 I have marked with pencil some passages which I think deserve the Duke's attention but I hope he will find an hour to read it through as it contains little verbiage, & he will nowhere find the argument on the other side more fully stated.

 It is founded after all on the notion that Brussels & our communication with England were of no value in comparison of a junction with the entire army with Blucher; & this is the real point at issue.

F. Egerton

ON WATERLOO

Gurwood to Liverpool,
70 Lowndes Square
12 September 1842
BL Add Ms 38,303 fols 195-196.

My dear Lord Liverpool,

[Unrelated paragraph omitted.]
    I have sent to the Duke the paper of Lord F Egerton on Marshal Forwards [Blücher] as arranged by Mr. Lockhart and myself. It will be out next Saturday. I have however requested the Duke, that as the *Quarterly Review* is but an ephemeral publication, and difficult of reference as a record of historical facts, to arrange his own memorandum as a document of authority, with the assistance of your translation of Clausewitz to particular parts of which Lord Francis has drawn his attention for elucidation. I shall know in a day or two whether he pays attention to my request, but it is very difficult to ascertain how to urge, when he is so overwhelmed with business of all departments of the State. I have been preparing a new edition of the Dispatches, and as there is much new matter, I have it set up in type for his consideration, before it is placed according to date in the sheets. He has had about 70 pages of this new matter ever since July last, and I have 15 sheets, or 240 pages, standing ever since in type, waiting his decision as to what letters of this new matter he approves of for insertion in them. He writes me long letters on the employment of his time, one half of which that he takes in writing to me would suffice for drawing his pen through what he does not wish to be published—and, after flaring up, he then apologises to me for the delay, as he knows that I have but one object in view—his honor. If I can get the Dukes memorandum before the 1st of next month, I shall run over to Bruxelles to make arrangements to have it printed in French, and in German at Berlin.

                                                  Sincerely yours

                                                  J. Gurwood

CORRESPONDENCE WITHIN WELLINGTON'S CIRCLE

Gurwood to Wellington,
70 Lowndes Square
16 September 1842
WP 8/3/9.

My Lord Duke,

[Three unrelated paragraphs omitted.]

The *Quarterly Review* is published, and I suppose it has been sent to your Grace. I see in the index under the head of "Wellington, the Duke of" "The Duke at Waterloo. 465. Fallacy of the theory that he was surprised 470 etc."

[Unrelated paragraph omitted.]

I have the Honor to be
Your Grace's faithful servant

J. Gurwood

[Unrelated postscript omitted.]

Wellington to Gurwood,
Walmer Castle
Sept 17 1842
WP 8/3/10.

My Dear Colonel

I return the papers inclosed in your letter of the 16th Inst with many thanks.
I am sorry to hear that Major Elrington is so unwell.

Ever yours most sincerely,

ON WATERLOO

I am trying to finish the Memo on Clausewitz for Lord Francis. I will send it to you as soon as it will be finished. But I am really too hard worked to become an Author and review these lying works called Histories.

Ever Yours most sincerely

W.

Egerton to Arbuthnot,
Worsley,
23 September 1842
WP 2/94/103.

My dear Arbuthnot,

Charge your glasses. I give you Nankin & Cabool with three times three!! I understand that Alison expresses himself much pleased with the Edinburgh review of his work which, being interpreted, means that he is much displeased with mine. I see also that Siborne,[19] the officer who made that curious model of the battle, is about to publish a detailed account. Under these circumstances I think it probably that a good opportunity may present itself of such further use of the Duke's mem^m. as may be required. When I first saw Siborne's model I suspected that he had been humbugged by the Prussians, & I remember mentioning my opinion to Fitzroy Somerset. I see he advertises something like a confes-

---

[19] Captain William Siborne (1797-1849) was a British Army officer who joined Wellington's army of occupation in France in August 1815. An expert surveyor, he was commissioned by the Army in 1830 to build an accurate scale model of the battlefield of Waterloo, and he lived at La Haye Sainte for eight months while carrying out his measurements. He also contacted a number of officers who participated in the battle in order to gather information about the positioning of their units on the battlefield. Siborne subsequently published a very detailed history of the campaign: *History of the War in France and Belgium in 1815* (London, 1844; 3rd Revised Edition of 1848 reprinted London, 1990, as *History of the Waterloo Campaign*.) Many of the letters he received in the course of his research were subsequently published by his son, Major General H. T. Siborne, as *Waterloo Letters* (London: Cassell, 1891; reprinted London, 1993), and additional ones have been published more recently in Gareth Glover, ed., *Letters from the Battle of Waterloo: the Unpublished Correspondence by Allied Officers from the Siborne Papers* (London and Mechanicsburg, 2004). For more information on Siborne see *DNB* 52:185-186.

sion of the fact, & says he has made corrections as to the position of their corps. I fully understand the Duke's objections, & knowing his position with regard to Prussia, I took care to state what I knew were his opinions with regard to Ligny in such a qualified form as might avoid offense to [2 words illegible], & might not commit him.

Wellington to Gurwood,
24 September 1842
WP 8/3/14.
London Sept. 24 1842

My Dear Col.

I send you the inclosed. A nice little Work for a Man who has so much to do as I have.
    You will see that it requires a good deal of revision and more illustration.

                          Ever Yours most faithfully

                                    Wellington

Gurwood to Liverpool,
24 September 1842
70 Lowndes Square24
BL Add MS 38,303 fols 197-198.

My dear Lord Liverpool,

The Duke left town for Windsor at ½ past 12—he is very well and in good spirits. He had been awake and left his bed at Walmer. He evidently feels a shock at Lord Wellesleys[20] illness, but I think it is as relates to himself for on remarking on it, he said, "but he is 8 years older than me". He sent

---

20 Richard Colley Marquis of Wellesley (1760-1842), Wellington's oldest brother. The illness proved fatal. Wellesley died on 26 September 1842.

ON WATERLOO

me last evening his revised memorandum, in which he has left out the remarks on Alison & taken up Clausewitz. I cannot send it to you, but I will send a copy of it to you when I have made it, which will take a little time as it covers 12 sheets of foolscap, half margin; & he has omitted to send me one of the sheets. The latter part is evidently written in a hurry & I shall bring it again before his revision when I shall have made a fair copy of it. There is now and then a bitterness, in allusion to Clausewitz, which I shall take the liberty to mark for correction, as I think it unworthy of him and that it does not strengthen his argument. The paper is much improved upon the one I sent to you. Let me know whether I shall send it to you to Buxted or keep it until you return to town.

Sincerely yours

J. Gurwood

Gurwood to Liverpool,
26 September 1842
BL Add MSS 38,303, fol. 199-200.

My dear Lord Liverpool

I have a note this morning from the Duke, who says that he shall be in town this morning and at Walmer Castle in the evening, where he shall possibly find the 7th sheet of his Memorandum on Waterloo, omitted in the copy he sent to me—I send you his notes to show you how good natured he is about it. Have the goodness to return them to me.

You are quite right about the truth. I have made it my object to endeavour to attain it—with discretion. I have, however, been occasionally indiscreet, it appears, and have always been shewn up—hitherto, without having lost the confidence of the Duke. I have had several lessons which, at time, have caused me much uneasiness, in the apprehension of misconstruction. Fortunately for me, the Duke has never attributed to me wilfulness, when what I have done has been misrepresented by others; and although not unassailed, I remain unblemished, as far as I can judge by his conduct to me. I am perhaps paying myself too high a compli-

CORRESPONDENCE WITHIN WELLINGTON'S CIRCLE

ment in saying that I am sometimes overconfident with those who are unworthy, when I have wished to elucidate and prove truth, and destroy common report by what I personally knew. All this causes wound to me, but, unfortunately, does not diminish any misplaced confidence. My great desire to save the Duke from controversy is a difficult task. I believe I have hitherto succeeded in so doing, in what I have hitherto done; but there are two persons about the Duke, Arbuthnot and Lord F. Somerset, who are always on the look out to catch me tripping. I am confident that if, unfortunately, I should stumble, that it will not be from deviating from rectitude of principle, but it may arise from too much zeal in a career, in which I am without a rival. This is not forgiven by them and others. I have never hinted at this to anyone but yourself. You may have guessed it, however, by what I have previously told you. It is painful to disguise one's feelings, particularly when it is possible that I may be mistaken, therefore for the object which I have always had in view, I am obliged to act with what I should otherwise call duplicity. In this I have however a great example in his Grace, when good is the object, but which however is difficult of attainment.

[Unrelated material omitted] I will send to you at Buxted the copy of the Memorandum on Waterloo, when I have made it and when I get, tomorrow or the next day, the 7th sheet of it, from the Duke on his arrival at Walmer.

Sincerely yours,

J. Gurwood

ON WATERLOO

Gurwood to Liverpool,
28 September 1842
70 Lowndes Square.

My dear Lord Liverpool,

My letter of yesterday, which you will have received this morning will account for my blunder.[21] I was about copying the Duke's memorandum to send to you but I received a note from the Duke this morning "I cannot find the 7th sheet any where. I must write another. But I must have the whole paper in order to be able to do so. If you will send it down to me by the bag I shall be able to write a 7th sheet which shall fit in. I am glad you like the paper."

When I get it back I will send you the copy of it. The Duke treats the complaint of Genl. Clausewitz of a want of a Return of the Duke's army, called 'A Line of Battle' and the assembly of the Army under the Duke as having taken place earlier than that under Blücher very satisfactorily. But he shows, on speaking of a position in which the Genl. Clausewitz recommends the position of the 2 Armies "It is obvious that the historian could not indicate such position. He was too wise to make the attempt." This shows a little humour, which may offend, but is very conclusive.

I am delighted at the paper and I am sure it will be agreeable to you to have the pleasing reflection that you are the cause of its having been written.

Sincerely yours,

J. Gurwood

---

21 This letter of 27 September 1842 has not been reproduced, as it concerns only the mix-up in letters to Siborne and Liverpool.

CORRESPONDENCE WITHIN WELLINGTON'S CIRCLE

Captain William Siborne to Gurwood
1 October 1842
WP 8/3/21.
Dublin, Oct. 1, 1842

My dear Colonel,

I beg to thank you for your very obliging letter of the 26th ult., by which I am glad to perceive that the Duke of Wellington has himself written a memorandum on the strategy of the campaign of 1815, as so valuable a document may hereafter be required to be made public in order to set aside the silly and groundless questions advanced by certain writers. I am well aware that my History will displease some people—I may not be able to tell the whole truth but I am quite satisfied that my account of Waterloo will be found to differ materially from all others hitherto published, and I feel very confident that it will prove far more satisfactory to military men.

> Believe me
> My dear Colonel
> Very faithfully yours
>
> W. Siborne

Philip Henry, 5th Earl Stanhope,
Notes of Conversations with the
Duke of Wellington, 1831-1851
(London, 1888; reprint edition New York:
Da Capo Press, 1973), p. 279.
4 October 1842

Walked with the Duke on the Castle ramparts. He then took me to his room and read to me a memorandum on the battle of Waterloo, which he has drawn up lately. It is of great length, filling thirteen folio sheets—or rather half-sheets, the other half being left blank as usual in drafts. It is a truly interesting and important document. Some erroneous statements

ON WATERLOO

of General Von Clausewitz in a German history of the campaign are refuted, and it is unanswerably shown that the Duke was not surprised, but was ready and prepared on all points. I was also much struck with the opinion incidentally expressed, that after the battle of the 16th it might have been a more judicious movement on the part of Napoleon to march against the right instead of the left of the English army—that is, along the chaussée from Mons to Hal and Brussels. But the Duke adds of Napoleon—that there never yet existed a general in whose presence it would have been more dangerous to make a false step.

This memorandum is written throughout in the third person. "The Duke of Wellington heard—the Duke of Wellington did." It is to be lent to Lord Francis Egerton, who wishes to write an article upon Clausewitz's work in the 'Quarterly Review.' Meanwhile it goes back by to-night's post to Gurwood. The Duke has had to replace and write over again one of the sheets which was lost.

Wellington to Gurwood,
Walmer Castle
4 October 1842
WP 2/93/17.

My dear Colonel,

I return this paper with another seventh sheet which I have had much difficulty to make out so you can put it in its place.

I could have written another paper more easily in a shorter space of time.

[Two unrelated or illegible paragraphs omitted.]

       Ever yours most faithfully

       W.

I don't mean that this paper should be published!
I have written it for Lord Francis Egerton's information to enable him to review Clausewitz's History.
I don't propose to give mine Enemy the gratification of writing a Book!

CORRESPONDENCE WITHIN WELLINGTON'S CIRCLE

Excerpt from a Wellington Memorandum
enclosed in a letter from Arbuthnot to Egerton,
10 October 1842, in Ellesmere, *Personal
Reminiscences*, p. 237.

I don't know that I can suggest any alteration of this. There is in some of my papers an argument upon the inconvenience and danger of taking up a false position, and of making a false movement, in front of such a Captain as Buonaparte, having an Army in such a position as that of the French frontier of the Department of the North covered (*hérisée*) with fortresses, in which he might cover and protect, and through which he might in safety and secrecy move hundreds and thousands of troops; while the allies, whether to correct or improve their position erroneously taken up, must have moved along the frontier, and confronted with this formidable position of the enemy, no part of which could be attacked by us, we should have been exposed to be attacked by each part in detail.

A common inspection of the map will show this. Place our right at Ostend, and the left at Namur on the Meuse, and take any central position you please. Then take the French position, with its right at Givet and Charleroi, by Le Quesnoi, Valenciennes, Courtrai, Lisle, Dunkirk, on the sea. And the folly and danger of a central position will be seen, we being, *par force* on the defensive, and moreover, we could not move without being attacked.

Even my position ... as it was in comparison, could not have been taken up if I had not fortified and rendered defensible against a *coup de main*, Mons, Ath, Tournay, Ypres, Ostend, and Nieuport.

Wellington

V.

THE CAMPAIGN OF 1815
Strategic Overview of the Campaign of 1815
by Carl von Clausewitz

Chapter 1.
French Forces. Creation of the Standing Army

When Louis XVIII left France, the army was by some accounts 115,000 men strong.[1] Bonaparte states that the number of men under arms was only 93,000.[2] On the 1st of June [1815], after ten weeks had passed, the army consisted of 217,000 men. Thus even if we accept the lowest estimate for the royal army as accurate, the actual increase in size amounted to only 124,000 men. While Bonaparte claims that there were also another 150,000 men in depots on the 1st of June, these were obviously not yet organized, because he certainly took all forces that were in any way useful directly to the battlefield.

There could not have been a shortage of manpower, that is to say trained soldiers, because if you add together what Bonaparte had available when the war ended in 1814—the army in Spain and opposing Wellington [in Southern France], the troops in Italy and the Netherlands, and all the fortress garrisons—the French army must still have contained at least 300,000 men. 100,000 prisoners of war definitely came back from captivity, so it seems that Bonaparte could have disposed of more than 400,000 veteran soldiers in 1815.

That there was also no shortage of weapons can be seen in the fact that 150,000 members of the National Guard received arms. Furthermore, the arrangements that Bonaparte made for increasing arms production provide little reason to believe that such a shortage existed. Equally implausible is the assumption that there was not enough cash available ini-

---

1 After the French army failed to offer any resistance to Napoleon's advance from southern France toward Paris, King Louis XVIII fled to Belgium on 19 March 1815.
2 Napoleon's *Mémoires*, 19, claims that the French army's "effective strength was 149,000 men, capable of putting into the field an army of 93,000 men of all arms."

tially. We must therefore conclude that, apart from the time required for training, there are definite limits to how fast armed forces can be raised, which are more constrained than they might appear at first glance.

For example, at the end of 1813, after Bonaparte saw his army destroyed at the Battle of Leipzig, replacements over the next three months amounted to only 150,000 men. Going back even farther, we find that at the beginning of 1813, when Bonaparte was almost the only one to return from the army that had been shattered in Russia, the increase in size of his forces from then until the armistice—a period of seven months— only came to about 200,000 men.[3] When considered in relation to the population and strength of France, these increases are quite modest. We must therefore be careful about crediting even the most energetic government—and Bonaparte's can certainly be counted as such—with the ability to mobilize huge numbers based solely on population and wealth. The situation is different with a *Landwehr* system,[4] or whatever other name one gives it, for which we can take the arming of the French nation in 1793 and 1794 as an example. It is well known how the French fielded such overwhelming masses of troops at that time.

Our own example is similar. At the beginning of 1813 our standing army was 30,000 men strong, and at the time of the start of the campaign in Saxony around 70,000. The increase in size was thus 40,000 in three months. In contrast, the increase by using the *Landwehr* from that time until the end of August—a period of around four months—was approximately 150,000. It is thus clear that a centralized administration like that of a standing army has much greater difficulty equipping exceptionally large forces within a limited period of time than do provincial administrations spread across the entire country, as long as these act simultane-

---

3 Napoleon signed an armistice with the Allies on 4 June 1813, which lasted until Austria declared war on 13 August 1813.

4 A *Landwehr* is an organized militia or reserve system, like the one that Clausewitz himself had helped organize in Prussia after the defeat by Napoleon. This system enabled Prussia to field armies in 1813-14 much larger than the small standing forces Napoleon had permitted that state to maintain. It was based on universal service but shorn of the revolutionary rhetoric and energy that had inspired the French *levée en masse* (the universal mobilization by which the French Revolutionary regime saved itself in 1793-94). The *levée en masse* is analyzed in Alan Forrest, "*La patrie en danger*: The French Revolution and the First *Levée en masse*," in Daniel Moran and Arthur Waldron, eds. *The People in Arms: Military Myth and National Mobilization Since the French Revolution* (Cambridge and New York: Cambridge University Press, 2003), 8-32.

ously and with the necessary zeal. Overall the main characteristic of a *Landwehr* system is that it is subject to far fewer inherent limitations in wartime than a simple expansion of the standing army, no matter how the latter is done.

Chapter 2
Depots and the *Armée Extraordinaire*

In addition to the 217,000 men that Bonaparte had under arms on 1 June, there were by his own account another 150,000 men in depots. He does not say how many of these were incorporated into the army or at what times, and it seems that up to the middle of June—thus at the decisive moment—no substantial numbers had entered.

In addition he lists an *armée extraordinaire* supposedly consisting of 196,000 men, mainly militia and naval troops, who were intended to garrison France's ninety fortresses. It is not certain if these 196,000 men were actually armed. He labels them "effectives," but because he also uses this term for the 150,000 men in the depots, it remains unclear how many of those 196,000 men were actually under arms.

The large number of fortresses could have swallowed up great masses of troops, but judging by the numbers of armed troops we actually encountered when we entered France, there is good reason to doubt the reality of those figures. According to them there should have been 217,000 men on the frontiers plus another 350,000 men inside France, including those in the depots. However, many of the 90 fortresses were either not garrisoned at all or only lightly manned, as can be concluded from the example of Strasbourg, since Rapp[5] had to throw his whole corps into it in order to be able to defend it. Furthermore, the entire French army in Paris and afterwards behind the Loire was not more than 80,000 men strong, of which at least 40,000 had come from Bonaparte's main army, so the reinforcements could not have amounted to more than 40,000 men.[6] All we want to point out with these figures is that when Bonaparte says that "on June first I had 560,000 men under arms," one should not regard this as a solid fact. If he had actually had such numbers, it would

---
5 General Jean Comte de Rapp commanded the corps-sized Army of the Rhine in 1815.
6 This refers to the period after the Battle of Waterloo.

certainly have been poor economy of force for him to bring only 126,000 men with him to the decisive battle on 16 June. The only certainty is that he had 217,000 troops opposing the enemy. The force that was behind the army and in the interior of the country in fortresses may not have been negligible, but as the results prove it was also not sufficient to provide a reliable source of support after a total defeat.

Chapter 3
Bonaparte's Boasting about His Resources

In the end, Bonaparte claims that he would have increased his forces to around 800,000 men by the 1st of October. But if we already have reason to doubt the previous numbers, this is even more the case with those 800,000 men. One cannot ignore the fact that the author of the *Memoirs* enjoys expounding upon his tremendous efforts and on this occasion—as on so many others in his works—does not stick very closely to the facts. Bonaparte and the authors who support him have always attempted to portray the great catastrophes that befell him as the result of chance. They seek to make their readers believe that through his great wisdom and extraordinary energy the whole project had already moved forward with the greatest confidence, that complete success was but a hair's breadth away, when treachery, accident, or even fate, as they sometimes call it, ruined everything. He and his supporters do not want to admit that huge mistakes, sheer recklessness, and, above all, overreaching ambition that exceeded all realistic possibilities, were the true causes.

If we confine ourselves to an overall impression of the situation, then Bonaparte seems like a land speculator who pretends to be richer than he actually is. He did not have much more than a couple of hundred thousand men available, and he tried his luck with them. Had he succeeded in overthrowing the coalition, or at least in securing France's borders, then afterward—while still far from having increased his strength—he would have revealed the miserable performance of his opponents by showing how his incomparable boldness had enabled him to accomplish so much with so little. But now that the attempt has failed, and actually seems to have been impossible all along, he does not want to look like a reckless adventurer. Instead he says his preparations were colossal and claims that the French people were making tremendous efforts for him out of enthusiasm and devotion. These are entirely natural expressions of his great vanity and low regard for the truth, but this side of his character reduces his significance as a writer of history far below that of other military leaders whose memoirs have become a primary authority for historians.

We are not wasting time here in some useless speculation, because our evaluation of the strategic relationships of this campaign would be completely different if we could truly believe that Bonaparte had been so confident in the French people, and so successful in all of his preparatory measures, that he might actually have achieved the results that he presents: to have 800,000 men under arms and abundantly provided with all necessary equipment within three months; also Paris and Lyon fortified, the former with 116,000 men and 800 guns, the latter with 25,000 men and 300 guns. Even if the Allies did not actually give him all three of the months he needed to complete this project, namely July, August and September, he still would have drawn closer to this great goal with every month that passed. It could therefore be predicted that if the Allies had advanced toward Paris in July, they would have encountered defensive forces that—in conjunction with the loss of strength that every strategic offensive suffers as a result of the need to secure its lines of communication—would have sufficed to bring the operation to a standstill, and thereby gradually led to the involvement of the entire populace. This would naturally have given the French a far greater chance of success than they had with the offensive that Bonaparte actually undertook. But if all of Bonaparte's numbers are more or less empty boasts, if he had to rest his hopes for a new start solely on an army of 217,000 men, then perhaps this offensive was so obviously the only possible means of resistance that nothing else could even be considered.

Chapter 4
Dispositions of the Army

The 217,000 men that Bonaparte had under arms at the beginning of June were divided into seven army corps, a Guards corps, four corps of observation,[7] and an army corps for the Vendée.[8] After deployment they consisted of the following forces:

1. The main army opposite the Netherlands		130,000
The Imperial Guard and five corps		
2. On the Upper Rhine		25,000
a) 5th Corps at Strasbourg under Rapp	20,000	
b) 1st Observation Corps at Hüningen under Lecourbe	5,000	
3. Opposite Italy		22,000
a. 7th Army Corps at Chamberi under Suchet	16,000	
b. 2nd Observation Corps in Provence under Brune	6,000	
4. Opposite Spain		8,000
a. 3rd Observation Corps at Toulouse under Decaen	4,000	
b. in Bordeaux under Clauzel	4,000	
5. In the Vendée under Lamarque		25,000
Total		210,000

which does not correspond exactly with the number of 217,000 men, but the difference is not significant.

The army aimed at the Netherlands was originally supposed to be 20,000 men stronger, but these were sent to the Vendée to deal with the immediate threat that had appeared there.

To be sure, Bonaparte had thereby concentrated his forces to a high degree against Blücher and Wellington, because he opposed the 220,000 Allied troops facing him on this front (which represented about one-third of the total enemy strength) with 130,000 men, that is to say more than two-thirds of the total forces he had available to place on the bor-

---

7 Observation corps (*corps d'observation*) were light formations deployed on the frontiers to observe enemy movements and provide initial resistance prior to the arrival of the main army.
8 The Vendée is a region in western France where royalist resistance to the Revolution had been especially strong. After Napoleon returned to power, it was again the scene of an armed uprising. He was forced to send a large force there to regain control.

ders. Nevertheless, we are tempted to say that he, the great master of the art of concentrating his strength at the decisive point, had fragmented his forces in this case. The troops on the Upper Rhine and those facing Italy and Spain were obviously insufficient even to make a show of defending the rivers and mountains that lay before them, yet they were not absolutely indispensable merely for garrisoning the fortresses. And considering that Bonaparte might have gained another 20-30,000 men for the main army out of the 55,000 stationed on the borders if he had immediately abandoned [his efforts to defend] the countryside, then it seems like a huge mistake not to have made the utmost efforts to assemble all of his strength at the decisive point. For in a position such as his, this appears to be the only thing that could have saved him. There is no doubt that another 20-30,000 men could have been very decisive in the battles of 16 and 18 June, even though it cannot be assumed that this would have guaranteed a French victory.

However, if we put ourselves in Bonaparte's position when he was forming and equipping his forces, we must step back from such a judgment. In analyzing strategy the main thing is always to put yourself precisely into the position of the individual who had to take action. This is often very difficult to do, of course. The vast majority of strategic criticisms would either disappear completely or be reduced to minor, theoretical differences if writers would want or be able to analyze all situations in such a manner.

Since Bonaparte was preparing to oppose all of Europe, he naturally had to consider the defense of all of his borders. He therefore placed small portions of his standing army on the borders of southern Germany, Italy, and Spain in order to form nuclei around which newly-raised forces could form. They were the cadres for the corps he intended to create there. When he gave these orders, there was no way he could predict in which particular week hostilities would be started by one side or the other. Nor could he know just how far his various rearmament measures would have proceeded. While he could generally foresee that his efforts would never enable him to assemble enough forces on the Upper Rhine to oppose the expected main enemy army there on anything like equal terms, he could still hope that a substantial force there would at least cause the usual initial delays, uncertainty, and caution found at the opening of any campaign, thus gaining time and slowing the enemy advance so that he would have time to rush there with his victorious main army from the Netherlands. We are not merely speculating that he saw the situation like this; rather, we have taken it from his memoirs. It makes a big difference whether or not a border is completely devoid of forces to defend it, especially when rivers and mountains pose an obstacle to the attacker, as is here the case with the Vosges, the Rhine, the Jura, the Alps, and the Pyrenees. If there is absolutely nothing in a province, then even the most indecisive, ponderous opponent, even the hundred-headed headquarters of a coalition army, is practically forced to advance, instead of being provoked by resistance into Daun-like caution.[9] Thus even the smallest force can cause substantial delays and indecision.

Another reason why Bonaparte could not consider completely stripping his eastern borders of troops was the impression this would have made on the French populace. He would thereby have been seen as giving up half of the Empire, thus exposing the complete weakness and uncertainty of his position. This would have had serious repercussions among the political parties in the country, as well as for the results of the rearmament effort. One could even go so far as to say that he would have been forced to keep troops in most of provinces in order to guard against the possibility of royalist uprisings. Finally, one should not overlook the fact that under the original plan the main army was supposed to have been 20,000 men stronger, and that the emerging danger in the Vendée forced Bonaparte to send some of the troops intended for the main army back to the Loire.

In mid-June the circumstances were such that he faced a force of 220,000 under Blücher and Wellington in the Netherlands, against which his 130,000 men had little likelihood of success, and on the Upper Rhine he could oppose the large [Austro-German] army of Schwarzenberg with just 30,000 men, even including the sixteen National Guard battalions he sent to Rapp. Bonaparte may well have wished he could completely eliminate the inadequate forces on the other borders in order to

---

9 Field Marshal Leopold Josef Count Daun, Prince of Thiano (1705-1766), commanded Austria's army during the Seven Years' War. He was known for his extremely cautious approach in the campaigns against Prussian King Frederick the Great. Clausewitz regularly used Daun, a commander of great reputation in his day, to exemplify what he regarded as the exaggerated caution of pre-Revolutionary warfare. See for instance *On War*, 172, where Clausewitz notes that "Daun's campaigns are, to some, models of wisdom and foresight; to others, of timidity and vacillation."

have a greater chance, or better yet complete certainty, of success in the Netherlands, but it was no longer possible to change all this at the last moment. He therefore had to try his luck with the 130,000 men that he had on the northern frontier.

Chapter 5
The National Guard

The actual arming of the people, that is to say the establishment of the National Guard, deserves a closer look.

In April Bonaparte had the idea of arming all male inhabitants between 20 and 60 years of age and organizing them into more than 3,000 national guard battalions, which would have given him over two million combatants.

This gigantic concept was unquestionably less than sound. It required three main elements: the unity of the people, enthusiastic energy on the part of his supporters, and the necessary equipment. It does not take much to see that of these three elements, the first was not present at all, the second only in insufficient quantity, and the third was even farther from being able to satisfy such an extravagant requirement.

It is not just this expanded mobilization that we must consider illusory, but also any sort of general arming of the population. This was not possible under the circumstances. Bonaparte most definitely felt this and expressly conceded as much when he spoke of the necessity of reducing the 44,000-man strong Parisian National Guard to 8,000 men while instead increasing the light infantry of the Parisian suburbs from 15,000 to 60,000. The situation in the Vendée and in the south also shows clearly that the cooperation of these departments could not be counted on. Bonaparte writes that even the mood in the northern departments was poor and unreliable.[10]

The result was that he limited his entire program of arming the people to just 248 elite [National Guard] battalions with a total strength of 150,000 men.

Of these, 16 battalions were sent to strengthen General Rapp, 16 battalions to General Suchet in the Dauphiné, and finally around 20,000

---

10 See Napoleon, *Mémoires*, 53, 55, 59.

men to Bordeaux and Toulouse. Thus approximately 40,000 men of the National Guard were deployed in the field. That leaves around 110,000 National Guardsmen who—along with naval troops, veterans, voluntarily reenlisted retirees (mostly officers and non-commissioned officers), and finally individuals still in the depots—made up the fortress garrisons and all the other forces located in the interior of the country.

Chapter 6
An Attack On the Allies in April

Bonaparte asks himself if on the 1st of April he could and should have taken all troops available at that time and attacked the Allied forces located in Belgium and on the Rhine. Three factors, he says, forced him to abandon this idea.[11]

1) In the north he had only 35,000 men available. In order to advance with this force into Belgium he would have had to strip bare all of the fortresses in the northern provinces. However, sentiment there was too unfavorable for them to be left to their own devices.

2) He did not want to appear to be the aggressor.

3) The Bourbons were still fomenting unrest in the south and west, so it seemed essential to him to force those princes to leave French territory and nip the internal war in the bud.

While the nature of Bonaparte's position makes the second reason seem like an illusion, a pretense at legal relationships, the other two reasons are quite compelling.

His failure to conduct such a precipitate attack is often seen as one of his great mistakes, but if we evaluate such an attack from the point of view of the Allies, there is even less reason to believe that it would have proven fruitful.

On the 1st of April the English-Hanoverian army under the Prince of Orange numbered 20,000 men and the Prussian army under General Kleist 50,000. Wellington arrived from Vienna early in April, and Bonaparte always had to reckon with this possibility. 70,000 men under Wellington and Kleist might well have been placed in some difficulty by 35,000 men under Bonaparte, but it is completely unreasonable to as-

---

11 Napoleon, *Mémoires*, 51-53, cited in Hahlweg, *Schriften* 2:954n.

sume that he could have dealt them a decisive defeat and smashed their armies. On the contrary, that would have been the most unlikely outcome of all. If Bonaparte's success against these two leaders had consisted simply in forcing them to give up part of the Netherlands, then such a result would not have been in any way decisive. Even gaining the Belgians—if that had been so certain as Bonaparte believed—would not have added much weight to counterbalance the overall situation.

Nothing is more important in strategy than ensuring that the forces that are to carry out an attack are not used in vain, that is to say, that they are not merely thrust into the air. But that is basically how an operation against Wellington and Kleist would have to be viewed, even if it had been successful.

Of course, if we only consider the force ratio of 35 to 70, then there was no reason for Bonaparte to expect better odds at a later time. Yet the issue is not just the likelihood of victory but also its impact. It is clear that a victory over one-tenth of the enemy's forces cannot be as decisive as one over a third of them. But if even a victory over this third (assuming that he won the Battle of Belle Alliance [Waterloo])[12] would still have left Bonaparte's ultimate success very much in doubt, then it is impossible to see how an unimportant victory such as one over Wellington and Kleist could have brought significant results.

Thus Bonaparte correctly abandoned the idea of falling on the Allies at the very first moment, and instead waited for a time when a force would be gathered against him whose defeat would be worth the effort.

---

12 The Prussians gave this name to the Battle of Waterloo in honor of the location where Wellington and Blücher supposedly met at the end of the battle. "La Belle Alliance" was a tavern, named in honor of an advantageous marriage in the previous century. For Prussians the name also signified a victory that had resulted from a "good alliance" of Prussian and Anglo-Allied forces. The Duke of Wellington, however, chose to name the battle "Waterloo" because that was where his headquarters was located and where he wrote his official report after the battle. The fact that it was not a French name may have also played a role in the selection. French writers frequently referred to the battle by its actual location, "Mont St. Jean." These three different names for the battle remained in use throughout the 19th century, but the Waterloo designation gradually attained preeminence thereafter.

Chapter 7
Defense

Bonaparte also raises the question of whether he should have remained on the defensive or instead attacked a portion of the Allied forces before they had all assembled, so as to place himself in a more favorable position from which to sustain himself afterward.

However confident he may have been about his rearmament efforts, he foresaw that before he could complete them, an enormously superior force would advance against him. He personally believed that 600,000 men would oppose him, but in fact between 600,000 and 700,000 appeared. If we compare these numbers with the 200,000 that he had in the field and add to them another 50,000 who were in the fortresses with which the enemy would come into contact, there still remains a superiority in numbers that even a Bonaparte had reason to fear.

Under these circumstances, the first thought had to be of defense. In particular, a defense in which he withdrew into the interior of the country, on the one side toward Paris, on the other side toward Lyon. This defense indeed would have been greatly strengthened because it would have brought into play a large portion of the French theater of operation and a number of fortified places, specifically Paris and Lyon, the former with 116,000 men and the latter with 25,000.

The immensely important advantages of such a form of resistance would have been:

1) Additional time. The main battles would have occurred four, six, or even eight weeks later, because one can never calculate how much time can be lost by indecisive commanders.

2) The weakening of the enemy force resulting from an extended theater of operations, in which a number of fortresses would have to be surrounded, and a number of roads secured by garrisons.

3) The increasing involvement of the French people, which could have become a true war of insurrection.

These three things, which constitute the essential advantages of a strategic defensive and whose effectiveness increases the farther the defense can be drawn back into the interior of the country, are offered by Bonaparte himself as the best arguments in favor of the defensive. And these arguments would have been so overwhelming that there could have been no question of any other form of resistance, provided the unspoken supposition on which they all depended had been true.

This supposition is of a loyal, devoted, undivided, and enthusiastic people. But this was inconceivable, because even though the Bonapartist party had grown stronger in 1815, it was still just one party, which was opposed by the royalists and the republicans. Even if we admit that the latter stood more for the Bonapartists than against them, they were still two separate elements.

As a result, the whole support of the people for providing regular and irregular assistance would have been weakened. In those parts of the country occupied by the Allies, a political party in opposition [to Napoleon] would have arisen and the defender, instead of feeling himself at home and in strength and comfort, would have been in an uncertain position, almost as if in a foreign land.

One subject that requires special consideration, moreover, is the capital. Every capital has great strategic importance, but some more than others. This is greater in those that embody the concept of a capital, and most of all where there is a knot of political parties. This was the case with Paris. Bonaparte had to hold Paris at all costs, and for this reason his entire strategy revolved around this strongpoint. Now Bonaparte had in fact already given thought to fortifying and defending Paris, but this gigantic project was completely illusory as long as he could not count on the undivided support of its inhabitants. That he could not is proved by his intention to disarm the Paris National Guard and replace it with another force based on the lower classes. Even if he did not have the courage to carry out this plan, it does show how much he feared the portion of the Parisian populace that was not completely loyal to him. The opposition Bonaparte encountered in the Legislative Assembly makes the political uncertainty of his position in France quite apparent. As long as he did not demand anything more than the relatively indirect efforts required by expanding the army, as long as he fought the war on foreign territory or on the borders, and did so more or less successfully, his uncertain situation would remain satisfactory and the preponderance of his intellect and his luck would continue. But as soon as direct, widespread, and prodigious efforts became necessary, as would be the case in a defense conducted in the interior of the country, then Bonaparte's precarious relationship with France would no longer have proven strong enough. The tool would have broken in use.

Bonaparte felt all of this clearly. If he does not state it explicitly in his memoirs, it is only because of his desire to appear as the idol of the French people. Nevertheless, he is forced to speak of the resistance in the western provinces and the uncertain spirit of the northern ones.

In such a situation Bonaparte must have considered the role of a defender like Alexander of Russia to be unsuitable, favoring instead one like Alexander of Macedonia.[13] He therefore preferred to place himself at the head of his excellent army and trust his fate to his lucky star and to his flashes of genius in bold ventures, rather than count on a more favorable development of the overall situation, which he could not contemplate with much confidence.

Such considerations are in this case much more important than a simple preference for attack. The latter can determine the actions of a commander in smaller, less decisive situations that do not place his entire existence at risk. But it cannot be considered in a case where a far greater destiny is at stake. There is probably no other commander who preferred the attack for himself and his army as much as Frederick the Great. Nevertheless, in 1761 he occupied the camp at Bunzelwitz when the situation forced him to pin all of his hopes on waiting.[14]

---

13 Alexander the Great, King of Macedonia from 356 B.C. to 323 B.C., was famous for his offensive campaigns. Czar Alexander of Russia, on the other hand, had presided over the famous retreat that had drawn Napoleon's forces all the way to Moscow, and to their eventual destruction, in 1812. In Clausewitz's history of that campaign, he does not portray this action as a positive decision by anyone, but merely as the natural reaction of an army confronting an overwhelmingly superior opponent. This is an illustration, perhaps, of how difficult it is for any political leader, much less one as self-willed as Napoleon, to deliberately allow an enemy army to enter his country. Carl von Clausewitz, "The Campaign of 1812 in Russia" (excerpted), in Clausewitz, *Historical and Political Writings*, eds./trans. Peter Paret and Daniel Moran (Princeton: Princeton University Press, 1992), 113-204.

14 With the Seven Years' War going badly for Prussia in 1761, King Frederick the Great of Prussia was forced to withdraw his army into a heavily fortified camp at Bunzelwitz, near the Prussian fortress of Schweidnitz in Silesia. He hoped that, with the passage of time, the already shaky coalition against him might fall apart. It did precisely that the following year, when Tsarina Elizabeth of Russia died. She was succeeded by her nephew, Peter III, whose pro-Prussian sympathies were well-known to Russia's generals and had made them reluctant to cooperate in Austrian plans to attack and destroy Frederick's army. The position at Bunzelwitz thus provided just enough of a tactical excuse to allow Russia's generals to act on their political premonitions. In contrast to Clausewitz's frequent criticism of what seemed to him the doctrinaire caution of warfare under the Old Regime, he often used Frederick's withdrawal to Bunzelwitz

ON WATERLOO

Chapter 8
Attack on Wellington and Blücher

Even before the Russians had arrived, and before the great Allied army on the Upper Rhine had assembled, there was already an Allied force in the Netherlands and on the lower Rhine for Bonaparte to contend with. This force was substantial enough that a decisive victory over it would greatly benefit his overall position, yet not so large that he could hold no hope of a successful outcome. Bonaparte was both willing and able to begin the war against this force before the others had crossed his frontiers. He chose the last possible moment, when Schwarzenberg had nearly assembled his forces and the Russians were only about fourteen days' march away. He probably delayed attacking until so late because most of his forces arrived only during the last few days. Otherwise it would have been decidedly more advantageous to have begun earlier, so as to have enough time to smash this force on the Lower Rhine before the others could begin to influence the situation.

The fundamental concept that Bonaparte adopted for the campaign was to burst forth with an attack on the Allied army in Belgium and on the Meuse, because it was the first one present and thus the first one capable of being brought to battle; because it was closest and thus the first one that could be reached; and because it was commanded by the most enterprising leaders and therefore the ones to be feared most. He therefore assembled a disproportionate part of his army against them, as we have already seen. There was certainly nothing better for him to do: This was indeed the only way—given his extremely difficult and precarious situation—for him to attain a more solid position. Only by a splendid victory over Blücher and Wellington, the two generals in whom the Allied sovereigns placed their greatest confidence, and by the total destruction of their armies, could he strike a blow that would cause admiration in France, dismay among the Allies, and astonishment in Europe. Only then could he hope to gain time and increase his power by a few more steps, thus becoming more of a match for his opponents. If he failed to

---

as a positive illustration of prudence based upon a sound understanding of the overall political and strategic situation. See *On War*, 389, 497.

gain this victory, or if it did not deter the Allies from immediately invading France, then it would be impossible for him to save himself from a second downfall.

Chapter 9
Allied Forces

In the first half of June, the forces that the Allies set into motion against Bonaparte had the following strengths and dispositions:

1. The army of the Netherlands	
Wellington in Belgium, consisting of English, Hanoverian, Dutch, Brunswick, and Nassau troops	100,000
Blücher on the Meuse	115,000
Germanic Confederation troops on the Moselle	20,000
Total	235,000
2. The Russian army, on the march towards the Middle Rhine	140,000
3. The Austrian army, together with Germanic Confederation troops from Southern Germany, on the Upper Rhine	230,000
4. The Austrians and Sardinians in Italy	60,000
[Grand] Total	665,000

Against these masses the French had approximately:

Standing Army	180,000
National Guard	15,000
Total in the field	195,000

If we add to these about 80,000 men from the fortress garrisons, who could have come into action during the course of the campaign, then the French with their 275,000 men are supposed to hold their own against 665,000 men or even defeat them. But the Prussians alone had another 100,000 troops moving up, namely the Guard, the 5th and 6th Corps, and several regiments belonging to the other four corps. Later on, the Neapolitan and Danish troops would have to be taken into account as well, along with the new corps being raised in Germany, such as the Prussian 7th Corps in Westphalia.

To get the better of such overwhelming forces would require almost a miracle, and Bonaparte's attempt in his memoirs to use the campaign of 1814 as proof that such a miracle was possible is mere sophistry. The successes that he had gained against the Allies in February 1814 were not tactical victories over an enemy two or three times his superior, for he defeated the forces one at a time, and in each engagement he had either superior or roughly equal numbers. Nor did these victories lead to overall strategic success against the whole alliance, for the campaign ended in his downfall. These victories were the result of well arranged operational combinations and tremendous energy. The fact that all their outstanding results could not bring about a favorable outcome for the campaign as a whole, however, shows the insurmountable difficulties that occur once a certain disproportion of forces is reached.

We do not mean to suggest that it was totally impossible for Bonaparte to bring the war to a successful conclusion. Rather, we are saying that in wars between civilized societies, where the forces and the mode of employing them are not very different, numbers generally decide more than has usually been admitted. Thus the numbers shown here—according to all theoretical and historical probability—had already determined the outcome of the war in advance.

Chapter 10
Opposing Forces and Order of Battle

The order of battle and disposition of the main French army at the beginning of June were as follows:

1st Corps (d'Erlon) at Lille	22,000
2nd Corps (Reille) at Valenciennes	24,000
3rd Corps (Vandamme) at Mezières	17,000
4th Corps (Gérard) at Thionville	16,000
6th Corps (Lobau) at Laon	14,000
The Guard (Mortier) at Paris	21,000
The four corps of reserve cavalry	15,000
Total	129,000

The Allied forces opposing this main French army were deployed as follows:

1. Wellington

   2nd Corps under General Hill, which however stood on the right wing, consisted of:

Clinton's English Division	6,800
Colville's English Division	6,700

   Prince Frederick of the Netherlands:

a) Anthing's Dutch Brigade	3,700
b) Stedman's Dutch Division	6,600
Total	23,800

   1st Corps, under the Prince of Orange, on the left wing from Ath to Nivelles:

Cooke's English Division	4,100
Alten's English Division	6,700
Perponcher's 2nd Dutch Division	8,000
Chassée's 1st Dutch Division	6,900
Collaert's Division of Dutch Cavalry	3,700
Total	29,400

   The Reserve under the direct command of the Duke of Wellington

Picton's English Division	7,000

Lambert's English Brigade and a Brigade of Hanoverian *Landwehr*	4,800
The Hanoverian *Landwehr* Division under General Decken[15]	9,300
The Duke of Brunswick's corps at Mechelen	6,800
Nassau troops at Brussels	2,900
The reserve cavalry under Lord Uxbridge, from Ghent via Ninove to Mons	9,800
Total	**40,600**
Total [of Wellington's army]	**93,800**

2. Prussian army under Blücher

1st Corps, General Ziethen, at Charleroi	27,000
2nd Corps, General Pirch, at Namur	29,000
3rd Corps, General Thielmann at Ciney	24,000
4th Corps, General Bülow at Liége	35,000
Total [of Blücher's army]	115,000

3. Germanic Confederation troops from Northern Germany under General Hacke at Trier — **20,000**

Total [Allied forces] — 228,800

Chapter 11.
Reflections on Wellington's Dispositions:
Assumptions That Must be Made

In order to draw any clear and instructive conclusions from the dispositions of the forces detailed above, we must have far more information than we presently possess. None of the previous historical writers who

---

15 The actual designation of this unit was the Hanoverian Reserve Corps, consisting of 13 battalions organized in four brigades. Clausewitz inserted a footnote here: "It must have been used to garrison Ostend, Ypres, Antwerp and Mechelen."

have written about this campaign have found it necessary to search for this data, and all that we have regarding the actual strategic relationships of the campaign, in terms of an exact representation of the situation prior to the two battles, is as fragmentary and scanty as for any old campaign of the 17th century.

The main points on which everything depends are:

1. An authentic and complete order of battle for Wellington's army, from which we can derive the disposition of the forces and the details of the chain of command. For example, in the order of battle above, the Hanoverian *Landwehr* Reserve under General Decken is counted as part of the main reserve. Yet it stood on the extreme right wing, took no part in the battle, and appears to have been used to garrison some fortresses, such as Antwerp, Ostend, and Ypres. Lyon's brigade, belonging to Colville's division, remained in Nieuport, did not come to the battle, and was probably also a garrison force. The 1st Corps under the Prince of Orange, which was supposed to have been the right wing, stood out of place on the left. Similarly, the divisions were out of order: for example, Perponcher and Chassée were reversed. As for Collaert's Dutch cavalry division, we do not know exactly what role was assigned to it prior to the 18th. In short, what we know about the order of battle of this army is so riddled with confusion that the numerous assumptions required for a strategic analysis of a campaign, which can normally be derived simply by examining the order of battle, are in this case either altogether absent, or confused and uncertain.[16]

2. The defensive preparations and intentions of the Duke of Wellington. Whatever plans Blücher and Wellington had made to invade France are immaterial to us, since Bonaparte forestalled them by attacking first. But every force assembled for an attack remains in a state of defense until it advances to attack, and there must be a plan for this situation. However, we know nothing of the defensive plan for the Allied army in the Netherlands.[17]

No such doubts exist with respect to the Prussian army. Two corps stood in the valley of the Meuse, where the cities of Liége, Huy, and Namur afforded quarters for large numbers of troops. A corps was on

---

16 Wellington's marginal note: "I do not know whether the examples required can now be afforded. It does not seem to me of much importance."
17 Wellington's marginal note: "This is an important chapter."

the Sambre around Charleroi, and another was on the right bank of the Meuse around Ciney, pushed forward like a pair of antennae. The headquarters was in the center at Namur, 13 to 18 miles[18] from the advanced corps and connected with Brussels by a major road. The position extended 35 miles in breadth and depth. The force could be collected at its center in two days and could well expect to have two days in which to do so. Once the forces were concentrated, they could either give battle—if they considered themselves strong enough for that purpose—or retire in any direction. Nothing tied them to a particular spot or prevented them from acting as freely as possible.

All this was clearly not the case with the army of the Duke of Wellington. The army stretched from Mons to the sea, a distance of more than 90 miles; its depth was from Tournai to Antwerp, or about 65 miles. The headquarters at Brussels lay 45 miles from the front line of the cantonments. Such an army cannot concentrate on its center in fewer than four or five days. Yet the line of the French fortresses was much too close for anyone to be able to count on having four to five days to collect the army. The great fortress of Lille, for example, was only one day's march from Tournai.[19]

But did the Duke of Wellington intend to concentrate his army at a single point? Was it sufficient simply to assemble the army, or did it have to concentrate at a particular point in order to protect something or enable him to act in concert with Blücher?

And if the intention of the Duke of Wellington was not to concentrate his forces at a single point but to defend with his forces more or

---

18 In Clausewitz's original text the distances were given in Prussian miles [*Meilen*], an obsolete measurement equivalent to 4.6 English miles or 7.4 kilometers. We have converted all distances from Prussian miles into English miles.

19 Clausewitz does not name the sources from which he obtained his order-of-battle information, and he is clearly aware of their inadequacy. In this instance, they caused him to exaggerate a contrast between Blücher and Wellington that was more imaginary than real. Wellington's deployment was actually slightly less extended than Blücher's. The forces in the most distant locations, such as Antwerp, Ostende, Nieuport and Ypres, were relatively small and generally consisted of lower-value Hanoverian militia units not intended for use in the front lines. Thus the width of the positions of his main combat units was less than 60 miles, and the depth less than 40. Conversely, Clausewitz's figures of 35 miles for the width and depth of the Prussian cantonments are too small. The frontage occupied by the Prussian 1st and 3rd Corps was over 55 miles, and the depth of the position was over 50 miles. See the excellent map of the Allied cantonments on 12 June 1815 in F. de Bas and J. de T'Serclaes de Wommersen, *La Campagne de 1815 aux Pays-Bas*, 2 vols. plus atlas (Bruxelles: Librairie Albert Dewit, 1908), Atlas map 1.

less divided, then we must ask: What was the purpose of the individual positions and how did it all fit together?

We find not a single word about any of this. It is easy to suppose that the duke considered Brussels to be of special importance, but even if we were to accept this and consider Brussels as the only object to be protected, much depends on the degree of importance accorded it.

3. The base for Wellington's army, in particular its ultimate point of retreat or, alternatively, the freedom it had regarding [the choice of] this point, is an extremely important factor in determining what it could do.

4. Finally, what was available in the way of real fortresses, meaning places that might be left for a time to fend for themselves? The information we have speaks of places where defensive works had been undertaken but does not say to what extent these works had been completed, and still less how well they were equipped.

The duke no doubt had a clear understanding of all these matters, but we know nothing about them, and therefore cannot judge how well his view of the situation corresponded to the actual circumstances. If we can make conjectures based simply upon appearances rather than definite information, then the duke's judgment must have been as follows: If Bonaparte attacks, he will advance against me and Blücher in several columns and on an extended front. It will therefore be necessary to take measures to ensure that Bonaparte encounters sufficient resistance everywhere while I keep a significant reserve that is ready to rush assistance to the point where the enemy's main force may be found, and that is then capable of fighting a successful battle before this main force reaches Brussels. If the French push forward with their main force on their left wing, that is, in the vicinity of Lille, the reserve in Brussels would, by joining with Hill, be able to give battle somewhere on the river Dendre near Ath, with half or even three-quarters of the army participating, provided time and circumstances allow the [Allied] left wing to close up. If the main enemy force advances in the center, that is, from the vicinity of Maubeuge or Valenciennes, the reserve would unite with the Prince of Orange's corps and, circumstances permitting, with a portion of Hill's corps in order to give battle on the road from Mons to Brussels. If the enemy advances with his main force on his right wing, that is, towards Charleroi or Namur, the reserve and perhaps a portion of the left wing could hasten to the assistance of the Prussians.

It is easy to see that a couple of days would be sufficient time for all of these plans, because all that was necessary was to combine the two corps of Hill and the Prince of Orange. Uniting with the Reserve at Brussels could then be accomplished simply by retreating one day's march toward Brussels. Given these assumptions, the duke's preparations appear adequate, for he could scarcely fail to have a few days' [warning] time.

It was along these lines that the duke and Prince Blücher must have reached agreement in their meeting at [Tirlemont][20] in the beginning of May. Thus when considering the duke's promise to concentrate his army at Quatre-Bras and come to the assistance of Blücher in his chosen position at Sombreffe, if the main enemy force turned that way, it must be understood that the term "army" meant only the greater part thereof, that which Wellington himself may have called his main force—his reserve together with his left wing. It was completely impossible for Wellington's whole army, stretched out over ninety miles, to concentrate in two days on its extreme left, at Nivelles or Quatre-Bras. At most, the 6000-man left-wing division of Hill's corps, namely Clinton's division, which was at Ath and Leuze, would be able to join in. The extended nature of Wellington's billeting area leads us to this assumption. Further confirmation seems to come from his decision to leave Prince Frederick of Orange near Hal, the fork in the road leading from Brussels to Lille and Valenciennes. These 19,000 men could certainly have reached the battle on the 18th. To this day there has been no explanation given for their being left behind, other than that they were to cover Brussels on that side.

Chapter 12.
Critique

If we now allow ourselves to consider these assumptions as historical facts and then submit them to critical analysis, it will be obvious that Bonaparte's way of operating and the circumstances of the moment have not been correctly understood. The whole expectation of a divided advance along a broad front is taken from other times, other commanders, and other situations. Bonaparte above all was one to gamble everything

---

20 In his original manuscript and the 1835 published edition, Clausewitz mistakenly had "St. Tron" [Saint-Trond].

on the result of a single great battle. We say "gamble," not because this may be more risky than when the forces and their efforts are divided. On the contrary, circumstances may arise in which the latter course of action is a thousand times more hazardous than the former.[21] We call it a gamble because, all rational calculation aside, the mind of man recoils from the idea of concentrating such an enormous decision into a single moment, as happens in a battle. It is as if our spirit feels confined in such a small space in time; we have the vague feeling that if we only had more time, we could find within ourselves a well of new resources. However, when these feelings are based not on objective circumstances but only on our emotions, this is merely the weakness of human nature. Strong-minded men will easily surmount such weakness, and in this respect Bonaparte must be reckoned among the strongest. Thus Bonaparte was first to venture everything in the tremendous act of a single battle. We must further state that he always preferred this kind of decision whenever circumstances permitted. However, seeking a decisive outcome through an all-encompassing battle can only come in circumstances where the overall goal is to reach a great victory. Furthermore, such a great victory can be the objective only:

1) if we know that our adversary seeks one and we cannot avoid it; [or]
2) if the impetus comes from us, and then only if we also have the means of carrying it through. One should only seek a great victory when one has the means of exploiting all its results, for a great victory and great danger stand side by side.

The latter was the case in all of Bonaparte's offensive wars; the former was the case now.

If Bonaparte never failed to seek an all-encompassing decision in the past, when he made war primarily to satisfy his thirst for fame and his lust for power, then surely nothing else could be expected of him now, when a modest success would be of no use and only an overwhelmingly

---

21 Images of Napoleon as a gambler recur throughout Clausewitz's work. He is often at pains to show that a willingness to make big bets may be a form of prudence, arising from a superior understanding of the situation and the adversary, rather than mere recklessness. See especially Clausewitz's defense of Napoleon's conduct in the Campaign of 1812, *Historical and Political Writings*, 201-4.

complete victory, surpassing all his earlier ones, offered him any hope of a better future.

The most compelling assumption was therefore that Bonaparte would burst forth with his whole force against a single point.

Lord Wellington had never personally commanded against Bonaparte. Perhaps this is the reason why such an assumption did not impress itself upon Wellington as strongly as it would have on anyone who had ever been struck by the lightning bolt of one of Bonaparte's great battles.

If Lord Wellington had made this assumption, he would have carried out quite different arrangements for billeting his forces. As things actually were, it would have been impossible for him to appear with his entire force and operate together with Blücher, no matter what part of Belgium was chosen as the battlefield. But regardless of the assumptions made by Wellington, he could not have intended to leave a considerable portion of his forces out of the action.

Chapter 13
Dispositions and Concentration of the Prussian Army

Let us now leave the intentions of Lord Wellington respecting his army in general, and his right wing in particular, in the obscurity from which they cannot be removed, because his original battle report makes not the slightest mention of this,[22] and because no other writer has properly considered the subject. Let us instead concentrate on the results arising from the actual situation, that in the event that the enemy attacked Blücher, Lord Wellington would come to his assistance with his reserve, with his left wing, and perhaps with part of his right wing. Our goal will therefore be to examine this further, and also the concentration of Blücher's army.

We have already said that the Prussian army was placed so that it stretched 35 miles in breadth and depth and could be concentrated on Namur within two days. However, an exception must be made for the corps belonging to the North German Federal troops that stood at Trier. While this force was under Field Marshal Blücher's command, it had been ordered to remain on the Moselle. This decision was no better than

---
22 This refers to Wellington's Waterloo Dispatch of 19 June 1815 (reproduced in Section II above).

that for Wellington's right wing,[23] but this was not the fault of Field Marshal Blücher, who did not count this corps as part of his army. As for his own force, we have already said that he had no plan other than to concentrate it once the enemy approached and then turn it in whichever direction the situation required. Against a commander like Bonaparte, and under the prevailing circumstances, this was absolutely the correct basis for all further decisions.

Chapter 14
Object of the French Attack

In order to be clear in our own mind about what the Prussian army's role would be after it had concentrated, we must ask ourselves what the objective of the enemy's strategic attack could be. Bonaparte's goal for this attack could only be a glorious victory over both Allied armies, as we have already said. If he inflicted a defeat on one or even both of them, such that Blücher was forced to retreat across the Rhine and Wellington into Zealand;[24] if he took hundreds of cannon and many thousands of prisoners as trophies of victory; if he shattered the morale of both armies; if he shook the courage of both commanders and weakened their initiative; then he could hasten to the upper Rhine with a portion of his victorious army—even if it was only 50,000 men—and unite with General Rapp to form there a main army of 80,000 men. In a few weeks, this force would grow to 100,000 through reinforcements from the interior of the country. The terrible blow on the Lower Rhine would inevitably have produced delay and indecision [among the Allied forces] on the Upper Rhine, and the arrival of Bonaparte would have changed hesitation into fear for their own safety. A hasty retreat of all Allied forces located on the left bank of the Rhine, or their unexpected defeat, would have followed next.

Although the remaining force ratios would have left no reasonable basis for delaying the Allied attack upon France beyond the point when

---

23 Clausewitz is referring to the force under Prince Frederick of Orange, which was left at Hal and did not participate in the fighting on 18 June.
24 Zealand is a watery province in the south-west corner of the Netherlands, consisting of islands and peninsulas deeply carved by the sea. The implication is that it would have been difficult to reconstitute a beaten army in such terrain.

Russian reinforcements had arrived and Blücher and Wellington had recovered somewhat, it is very probable—when one looks at the lessons of similar cases—that the moral effect of the French victory could not have been overcome so quickly. Shaken and weakened by the effects of such a defeat, the Allies would have imagined a mass arming of the French populace and new French armies seemingly rising out of the ground. The two most distinguished leaders, Wellington and Blücher, would not have been on the scene, with the latter more than 450 miles from Allied Headquarters. It is thus possible that an excessive amount of time would have elapsed before the Allies felt themselves strong enough to take a step forward.

On the other side, would not such a victory have electrified France! In the heady triumph of this victory the vain, self-satisfied French would have laid their monarchism and their republicanism aside for the most part. The weapons would have fallen from the Vendéeans' hands, and Bonaparte's position inside France would have been completely different.

We are, however, far from accepting the general opinion that after such a victory, Bonaparte's situation would have become as favorable, firm, and unassailable as it had once been precarious. Such complete reversals are generally contrary to the nature of things and a very unworthy means of historical analysis. On the contrary, we think that Bonaparte's prospects would still have remained immensely difficult after even the most splendid victory and that such a victory would have given him only the barest possibility of resistance against the collective power of his enemies. The fact that he personally thought the most important immediate result of such a victory would be the fall of the British government in England and peace with that power only strengthens our impression of just how weak and uncertain he considered his position to be, because he wished to conceal this fact with such illusions.

A brilliant victory over the united armies in the Netherlands was therefore Bonaparte's most urgent requirement. This being the case, there could be only one objective for his endeavors, and this was the combined Allied army, not any geographical position such as Brussels or the right bank of the Meuse or even the Rhine, etc.

When a great, all-encompassing decision is at stake, geographical points and the connections of the army to them cannot be operational objectives in themselves, because the immediate advantages that such points give are too insignificant, and the more remote, long-term influence they may exert on the course of the war takes too long to have an effect. The great event of a battle would be like a mighty river sweeping away such a weak dike. Bonaparte's efforts could have been directed toward a geographical object only insofar as it would have afforded him a more advantageous prelude to the battle, particularly if it had given him the means of rendering the battle greater and more decisive, for this was his real need. Outflanking the enemy's army in order to attack it from a different direction, thus forcing it away from its natural line of retreat, is in most cases an unfailing means of intensifying a military action. But not always, particularly in the present case.

On the Prussian side, much has been said about the necessity of maintaining possession of the right bank of the Meuse, and Blücher's position on both banks of the river resulted from this. Similarly, Lord Wellington is considered to have attached great importance to covering Brussels. But what would have happened if Bonaparte had gained possession of the right bank of the Meuse or even of Brussels before the battle? The armies would have lost some unimportant supply columns and elements of their baggage trains, and perhaps also some stores of rations. Furthermore, in the former case the Prussian army, and in the latter the English, would have been pushed away from their natural lines of retreat. Clearly this would not have been particularly disadvantageous for either commander, because Blücher could easily unite with Wellington for a short time and retreat toward Mechelen and Antwerp, just as Wellington could unite with Blücher and turn towards the Meuse. The losses that both commanders would experience in case of a lost battle would not have been noticeably increased thereby, for there was no reason to fear either a long retreat or the possibility of encirclement.

It could thus be foreseen that Bonaparte would not place any value on such an outflanking maneuver. It would have cost him the far more valuable advantage of a quick and successful thrust and—if unsuccessful—could have placed him in great danger. We therefore believe that the two commanders could have united their forces at a single point and been certain that, no matter where this point lay, Bonaparte would seek it out. This union could not take place in advance because of the difficulties with provisioning, but the choice of a point of union was entirely up to them and not in any way dependent on the direction that Bonaparte himself chose.

Chapter 15
The Point of Union of the Two Allied Armies

The most natural point for this union lay on the road from Brussels to Namur, where the two armies could join together most quickly. Blücher's headquarters had found that the area around Sombreffe—12 miles from Namur along this highway and barely 5 miles from the Brussels-Charleroi highway where Wellington intended to collect his left wing—was particularly well suited to serve as a battlefield against an enemy coming from the Sambre. The Ligny brook and one of its small tributaries, which run parallel to the highway between Sambre and Saint-Balâtre, carve out a strip of land that, while neither very deep nor very steep, is enough of both that the left side of the valley, which is higher, forms an excellent position for the employment of all arms. This position was of moderate extent (two or three miles), so that if occupied by one to two corps, it could be defended for a long time. In that case Blücher would still have two corps left for offensive operations, whereby he could win the battle either by himself or in conjunction with Wellington.

To be sure, the tactical characteristics of this position were only relevant against an enemy advancing from Charleroi. But since the strategic characteristics of this position completely met the requirements of all situations as well, the tactical advantages in this particular case played a role in the decision to select it.

If the two armies had united here in good time, either in a single position or in two sufficiently close that they could act in concert, they would have done everything their mission required, and could have left everything else to the decision of arms, which their great numerical superiority gave them no reason to fear. Whether Bonaparte's line of march took him toward Brussels or anywhere else, he was obliged to seek out his opponents. But we have already said that Lord Wellington seems to have been far from considering such a concentration of forces and such a simplification of the problem of combining them. If he remained in his extended position even after the French army began to show signs of movement, then concentration at a single point was completely impossible. Even if it had been possible, he did not desire it. The thought of exposing Brussels even for a short time seemed inconceivable to him, and because the city was quite open, it could not be protected against incursions by a garrison alone. It is therefore certain that if Bonaparte had advanced on Brussels from Lille or Valenciennes, Lord Wellington would have hastened to oppose him, in the former case on the road from Tournai, in the latter on that from Mons. Then Blücher, in order not to remain idle, would also have had to go there. This he could have accomplished in about 36 hours, moving from Sombreffe to the road to Tournai. His forces would have been able to oppose the enemy in the vicinity of Enghien or at the worst near Hal. As Sombreffe lay exactly on this route, it was a perfectly good choice as a point of concentration in this respect as well.

On the other hand, Sombreffe would have been quite unsuitable for a defense on the right bank of the Meuse if the enemy were to advance along it. But how could Blücher have imagined he could collect his army on the right bank of the Meuse in time? And there could be even less thought of [receiving] any assistance there from the English commander. Blücher therefore understood better than Wellington the need to put aside whatever was not urgently required by the situation. He was certain of Wellington's support on the left bank of the Meuse, and if Bonaparte wanted to attack there, then he would have to cross the Meuse himself.

Chapter 16
Calculation of the Time Required for Concentration: The Prussian Army

Thus we see the Duke of Wellington uncertain about where to expect the enemy and prepared to oppose him everywhere with the greater part of his troops. We see Blücher resolved—as soon as the enemy bursts forward—to concentrate his army at Sombreffe, where he is near enough to the duke's army to support it or be supported by it.

If we now look at the time both armies would require to concentrate, and compare it to the time that would have been available under the most unfavorable circumstances, based on the location of their forward corps, we find no satisfactory solution.

Charleroi is the closest place to the concentration point at Sombreffe and only about 12 miles away. If reports of the enemy's advance go from Charleroi to Namur, and then the order to assemble goes from there to Liége, the most distant billeting area, then we can calculate at least 16 hours for this process. If we then add the eight hours necessary for notifying and turning out the troops, 24 hours will have passed before the 4th Corps can begin its march. The route from the area around Liége to Sombreffe is 45 miles long, and for this distance even the fastest march requires two days. Consequently it would take a total of three days for this corps to arrive. The 3rd Corps in Ciney could be there in 36 hours; the 2nd Corps, from Namur itself, in 12 hours. General Ziethen's resistance on the Sambre and his retreat to the vicinity of Fleurus could not gain more than one day of time; that is, he might delay the enemy from morning until evening, after which the arrival of darkness would supply the remaining time.

Naturally, one would not expect the enemy's advance to be noticed only at the first cannon shot but at the very latest when he was in his final position prior to attacking our troops. Very probably this news would reach us a few days earlier by other channels. In that case there would be sufficient time to assemble the whole army. But if we were limited to what we could actually see,[25] then only the 2nd and 3rd Corps could have arrived in time to receive 1st Corps at Sombreffe, and the 3rd Corps only with difficulty. [Bülow's] 4th Corps could not have been there at all. This danger was fully appreciated at Blücher's headquarters, but there were all sorts of difficulties involved in moving Bülow's corps closer. Nevertheless, it received orders on the 14th—when the movements of the French army were noticed—to advance to the vicinity of Hannut, which is only 23 miles from the point of concentration. Consequently it might have reached there sooner than 3rd Corps, which was 30 miles away.[26] As we will see later on, this did not happen because a chance event prevented this approach march from taking place immediately.

---

25 This is the "most unfavorable" circumstance Clausewitz referred to earlier: in effect, the achievement of complete tactical surprise by the French.
26 The center of the 3rd Corps was in the town of Ciney, 28 miles from Sombreffe, but the most distant billets were in Fronville, over 40 miles away.

Blücher thus believed that he could collect his forces at Sombreffe in 36 hours. Although the chances were 100 to 1 that the enemy's advance would be known at least 36 hours before he reached the area of our battlefield, it was nonetheless very risky to remain in such an extended position when the enemy's advance guard was so close. The continual difficulties that the Dutch authorities made with respect to provisioning prevented Marshal Blücher from collecting his forces to a greater extent, so he intended to wait for more definite reports on the movements of the enemy's army. He cannot, however, be entirely absolved from blame.[27]

Chapter 17
Wellington's Army

We can form no judgment about the assembly of Wellington's army, because we do not know the intentions and dispositions for the right wing. But this much is clear: For the scenario in which the least time would be available, that is to say, if the enemy advanced via Charleroi, the consequences for Wellington's army had to turn out even more unfavorably [than for Blücher's]. In this case, even if no more than the left-wing division of the right-wing corps—namely, Clinton's—was to be brought over and the concentration was to take place at Quatre-Bras, this division had to march from Ath and Leuze, 37 and 47 miles respectively. This was the same distance that the news had to travel to reach Brussels, and the orders from Brussels to reach the corps. It is clear that this division would reach the battle even later than the Prussian 4th Corps. On the other hand, the left wing corps (whose furthest division was in Le Roeulx, 23 miles from Quatre-Bras), as well as the reserves around Brussels, could reasonably be expected to reach the battlefield within 36 hours. The fact that this did not occur resulted from circumstances we shall discuss later.

---

[27] This last sentence is not in Clausewitz's original manuscript but is found in all published editions of his work. See Hahlweg, *Schriften*, 2:976n.

ON WATERLOO

Chapter 18
Reflections

As long as it was known for sure that the French had one corps in the vicinity of Lille and another at Metz, there was no need to fear a sudden attack by concentrated forces. However, during the first days of June the French corps left Lille and Metz, and even though it was not known precisely what had occurred, the Allies received definite information around the middle of the month that the French 4th Corps had moved from the Moselle to the Meuse. From this moment onward, one could no longer count on having any additional warning before the outbreak of hostilities. It was now high time to draw closer together, and to do so in such a manner that all the corps could reach the field of battle within 24 hours. It is not necessary to describe all the changes in dispositions that would have been necessary, but it would have been very advantageous if the Duke of Wellington had placed his headquarters nearer to his corps and to that of Field Marshal Blücher, perhaps around Nivelles. This alone would have gained at least twelve hours and avoided much misfortune. But neither of these things took place. Only the Prussian 4th Corps received an order to concentrate in closer quarters near Hannut, and this order also came too late, as we shall see.

Part of the problem was the hope that more intelligence would be received before the outbreak of hostilities. Another part was Wellington's belief that when he assembled his forces he must direct them toward the enemy's main force, about which there was no definite information as yet. No declaration of war had been made, and it was not yet known that the [Imperial] Guard had left Paris (which occurred on 8 June). Thus the Allies remained in a lamentable state of indecision until the 14th, in a situation where they clearly felt endangered, and from which they had decided to extract themselves, but in which they were nonetheless caught by surprise.

THE CAMPAIGN OF 1815

Chapter 19
Bonaparte Assembles His Army

Bonaparte had decided to begin the campaign on 15 June. The 4th Corps departed Metz on the 6th. A few days later the 1st Corps left Lille. This movement was masked by strong pickets from the fortresses. On the 8th the Guard left Paris, the 6th Corps left Laon, and the 2nd Corps left Valenciennes. All these corps arrived between Philippeville and Avesnes on the 13th, the latter place being where Bonaparte himself also arrived that evening, having left Paris on the 12th.

From Metz to Philippeville is about 115 miles, which took the 4th Corps eight days. From Paris to Avesnes is 135 miles, for which the Guard needed only six days. The former distance, however, is over a lateral route without major roads. While it is impossible to judge a march without the fullest knowledge of all the details, we may safely assume that Bonaparte, whose main goal was to achieve surprise, had ordered his corps to proceed with the greatest possible speed. On the 14th the French corps drew even closer together, and took up the following positions in three columns:

The right wing, 16,000 men strong, consisting of the 4th Corps and some cavalry, around Philippeville.

The center, 64,000 men strong, consisting of the 5th and 6th Corps, the Guard and most of the cavalry, around Beaumont.

The left wing, 44,000 men strong, consisted of the 1st and 2nd Corps around Solre-sur-Sambre. This position was still 18 miles from Charleroi.

Since the move from Metz and Lille had not been merely a temporary concentration of the army's quarters but rather a genuine march of concentration, the Allies—if they had had a good intelligence system—should have found out about it before the 13th or especially the 14th—eight or nine days later; which would have dragged them out of their uncertainty earlier. But this did not happen. It was only on the 14th that they learned that the French were concentrating and that Bonaparte was with the army. It still remained uncertain just where this concentration would occur. It was not until the night of the 14th/15th that they learned through a report from General Ziethen that the enemy force facing him had been strengthened and that he expected an attack the next morning.

ON WATERLOO

Thus definite news was in fact received only 36 hours before the Battle of Ligny began.

Chapter 20
Blücher's Concentration at Sombreffe

In consequence of the news of the enemy movements and the arrival of Bonaparte, an order was sent from Namur to General von Bülow on the evening of the 14th to assemble his troops so that he could reach Hannut in a day's march. General Bülow received this order at 5 a.m. on the morning of the 15th and carried out the measures that had been ordered.

During the night of the 14th/15th, after General Ziethen reported the advance of the enemy, a second order was sent to General von Bülow to advance immediately to Hannut and establish his headquarters there. General Bülow received this order at 11 a.m. on the 15th. If he had then ordered to his troops to make the second march to Hannut after a short rest—which was certainly feasible, since Hannut is only 23 miles from Liége and most of his troops were stationed in-between—his corps could have been assembled at Hannut on the night of the 15th/16th. But General Bülow thought he could postpone obeying this order until the following day, first because he was convinced that the concentration of the Prussian army could take place only around Hannut and that there would therefore be plenty of time for him to reach this location; and secondly because he thought that as long as there was no declaration of war, there was no danger of hostilities.[28]

---

[28] The order to Bülow spoke merely of moving his corps "into close cantonments" near Hannut and concluded with the statement that "it would be most appropriate for Your Excellency's headquarters to be located in Hannut." The order thus contained no sense of urgency, although it did add that the French were expected to go on the offensive soon. Gneisenau also failed to mention that he had ordered the concentration of the Prussian army at Sombreffe, leaving Bülow still believing that the concentration would occur in Hannut, as had been stated in previous orders. Oskar von Lettow-Vorbeck, *Napoleons Untergang 1815*, 2 vols. (Berlin: Ernst Siegfried Mittler, 1904), 1:198, 279-281). But Bülow's dilatory action may also partly be explained by a somewhat delicate consideration that Clausewitz does not mention: Bülow, commanding a corps, was senior to Gneisenau, Blücher's chief of staff, from whom the order to move had come. On Gneisenau's side this meant that the order may have been phrased too much in the nature of a routine request, while Bülow may have felt the need to demonstrate that he was not at the immediate beck and call of someone who was nominally his junior. The operational subordination of field commanders to general staff officers remained an issue in

He reported this to headquarters and announced that he would be in Hannut at midday on the 16th. This report arrived after Marshal Blücher had left Namur. A third and then a fourth order dispatched in the course of the 15th from Namur to General Bülow ordered him to continue his march to Sombreffe on the 16th. As Sombreffe is 23 miles from Hannut, and Bülow's corps could only have reached Hannut during the night of the 15th, he might—by tremendous effort—have reached Sombreffe with his advanced guard by the afternoon of the 16th, but the rest of his corps could not arrive before the evening. It is obvious that there was not enough time for any of this.

Both of these orders were sent to Hannut, where General Bülow was supposed to go and was expected, hence they remained there. But General Bülow had remained at Liége on the 15th and first received these orders at 10 a.m. on the 16th. The loss of time was now so great that it was only at 3 a.m. on the 17th that he reached Haute et Basse Baudeset, an hour's march from Gembloux and three hours from the battlefield. Had he arrived twelve hours sooner, he might still have decided the outcome of the Battle of Ligny.

Unfortunate circumstances also prevented the Prussian 3rd Corps from receiving its marching orders until 10 a.m. on the 15th, although they had been written on the night of the 14th/15th. Nevertheless, this corps was on the field of battle at 10 a.m. on the 16th, having left behind only some troops who were in outposts. The 2nd Corps arrived shortly before.

Chapter 21
Wellington's Concentration

The news that Field Marshal Blücher received on the 14th, which led him to order the concentration of his army on the night of the 14th/15th, seems not to have induced Lord Wellington to take any decisive steps. Even on the evening of the 15th, when he received the report that General Ziethen had been attacked and driven back by the main French army

---

the Prussian army until the 1870s, when the extraordinary personal ascendancy of the elder Moltke, chief of the Prussian (later German) Great General Staff (*Großer Generalstab*), established it firmly.

ON WATERLOO

at Charleroi, Wellington still considered it unwise to march with his reserves towards his left wing, and even less advisable to weaken his right. Instead, he believed it was more likely that Bonaparte would advance on the road from Mons, and considered the clash near Charleroi to be a feint. Thus he was content simply to order his troops to be ready.

It was not until midnight, when news came from General Dörnberg (who commanded the outposts at Mons) that he had not been attacked and that the enemy appeared instead to be moving to the right, that Wellington gave orders for the reserve to begin its march, passing through the Soignies Forest. According to the account of General Müffling, this was carried out at 10 a.m.[29] From there it was only 14 miles to the battlefield at Sombreffe; the duke's reserve might therefore have arrived on time. But much time was lost while the duke first went to his left wing at Quatre-Bras, reconnoitered the enemy near Frasnes, and then hastened to Prince Blücher at Sombreffe, where he arrived at 1 p.m. The duke wished to see for himself whether the enemy was advancing here with his main army, and he also wanted to make the necessary arrangements with Prince Blücher. During this time the reserve appears to have waited for further orders at the edge of the Soignies Forest, where the road divides in the directions of Nivelles and Quatre-Bras. Even then there would still have been sufficient time, but the duke had completely splintered his forces in order to be able to meet any contingency and had previously not wanted to take the right wing of the Prince of Orange away [from Nivelles]. He was therefore too weak to be able to support Blücher, as we shall examine more closely.

---

29 Müffling was the Prussian liaison officer at Wellington's headquarters. See C[arl] von W[eis] [Carl Friedrich Freiherr von Müffling genannt Weis], *Geschichte des Feldzuges der engl.-hannover.-niederländ.-braunschweig. Armee unter Wellington und der preuß. Armee unter Blücher 1815* (Stuttgart: no publisher, 1817); in English as C. de M., *History of the Campaign of the British, Dutch, Hanoverian, and Brunswick Armies, Under the Command of the Duke of Wellington, and of the Prussians under that of Prince Blücher of Wahlstadt, in the Year 1815*, by C. de M, edited and translated by Sir John Sinclair (1816; reprinted London: Lionel Leventhal, Ltd., 1983).

THE CAMPAIGN OF 1815

Chapter 22
Bonaparte's Thrust is Directed at Blücher

Now that our reflections concerning the assembly of the armies have brought us to the moment when Bonaparte is about to attack General Ziethen, we must consider more closely Bonaparte's plan, how he chose this direction for his attack, and what the objective of this thrust was.

While still in Paris, Bonaparte must have had pretty good knowledge of the cantonments of both Allied armies. However, his plan of attack could have been based only on the general situation, not on the positions of individual corps like General Ziethen's at Charleroi, since those positions might easily have changed, given that his information must have been eight or ten days old. Therefore, we cannot assume that his thrust toward Charleroi was aimed specifically at the Prussian 1st Corps. He knew of Blücher's plan to concentrate and deploy his forces behind Fleurus, but he could not base his plan in Paris on anything as uncertain as a point of concentration, which might long since have been altered without his knowing it. Bonaparte could only be sure that Wellington and his army were in and around Brussels, and that Blücher was with his in and around Namur. He presumably had a reasonably precise estimate of their strength, but it is quite likely that he considered these accounts exaggerated. General Sarrazin relates in his book *De la seconde restauration*[30] that when Bonaparte was told that more than 200,000 men opposed him, he shrugged his shoulders and answered that he knew for certain that the English had 50,000 men and that just as many Prussians under Blücher were on the Meuse. Even supposing that Bonaparte made such remarks only to encourage his men, it is still very likely that he estimated Wellington's army at not over 60-70,000 men, and Blücher's at not above 80-90,000, thus altogether about 150,000 men, and of these he certainly expected that a substantial proportion would not come into action. We should not be misled if he gives relatively accurate strengths for both armies in the *Memoirs*.[31] It is easy to see that these details are drawn from

---

30 Jean Sarrazin, *Histoire de la guerre de la Restauration depuis le passade de la Bidassoa par les Alliés, 7 october 1813, jusqu'à le loi d'amnestie du 12 janvier 1816* (1816), 395; see Hahlweg, *Schriften*, 2:982n.
31 Napoleon, *Mémoires*, 77, gives the combined strength of Wellington's and Blücher's armies as 224,000.

later accounts, and Bonaparte was too much in the habit of underestimating his opponent not to have done so in this case, in all probability.

If Bonaparte concentrated in his center, thus between Maubeuge and Givet, which was the shortest distance and thus also the best route for achieving surprise, then he would find himself oriented more toward Blücher than toward Wellington. At the same time, most of Wellington's army was a day's march away from Blücher. If Bonaparte now went through Charleroi, he could hardly fail to encounter Blücher, for it could be taken for granted that the two Allied commanders would want to remain in contact and that Blücher would therefore assemble his army not on the right bank of the Meuse but on the left. The route via Charleroi thus would lead Bonaparte against either Blücher's main body or his right wing. To fall upon Blücher and attack him first was undoubtedly what Bonaparte preferred, in part because he clearly felt a much greater animus toward Blücher and the Prussians than toward Wellington and the English, in part because the Prussians were stronger than the others, and finally because they were more restless and combative. Our view concerning Bonaparte's plans has also been confirmed by his memoirs, for he says he knew that Blücher, an old Hussar and bold to the point of folly, would certainly hasten to assist Wellington more rapidly than the ever-cautious Wellington would move to assist Blücher.[32]

If Bonaparte encountered the main part of Blücher's army, he hoped to defeat it by a sudden attack before Wellington could come over. It would not be as good if Bonaparte fell on Blücher's right wing, but he could still expect that in pursuing it he would encounter Blücher himself and bring him to battle somewhat later, while also pushing him even farther away from Wellington. In both cases, Bonaparte expected that Blücher's force would not be properly concentrated while marching to join Wellington, as this march—being a strategic flank movement from scattered quarters—would not permit the forces to be completely united.

This, it seems, is how we must understand and explain Bonaparte's particular plan of operation. All the writers who have described this

---

[32] Napoleon, *Mémoires*, 78, states, "Blücher's Hussar qualities—his activity and bold character—formed a great contrast to the circumspection and slow marches of the Duke of Wellington. If the Prussian-Saxon army was not attacked first, it would be more active and eager in rushing to the aide of the Anglo-Dutch army than the latter would be in aiding Marshal Blücher. All of the actions of Napoleon therefore had the goal of attacking the Prussians first." See also Wagner, *Pläne der Schlachten und Treffen*, 4:12.

campaign begin by saying that he threw himself between the two armies in order to divide them. This expression has become part of technical military jargon, but there is actually no clear underlying concept behind it. The space between two armies cannot be the objective of an operation. For a commander like Bonaparte, who has to deal with an adversary twice his strength, it would be very unfortunate if, instead of striking one-half of his opponents' forces with all of his own, he would instead strike at the empty space between them, thus launching a blow into thin air. He would be wasting time, when only the strictest economy of time would enable him to get double duty out of his own strength.

Even if no time is lost, a blow against one army, delivered so as to push it away from the other, can still be very dangerous, since as a consequence you may be attacked in the rear by the other army. If, therefore, this other army is not far enough away to insure against such a threat, a commander is very unlikely to mount an attack merely to push an opponent away.

Bonaparte therefore chose the direction that led between the two armies, not in order to divide them by squeezing between them, but because he had reason to believe that in this direction he would fall upon Blücher, either concentrated or in separated corps.

Chapter 23
The Action at Charleroi

On the evening of the 14th, the French army was deployed in three columns at Philippeville, Beaumont, and Solre-sur-Sambre, 18 miles from Charleroi. There are no definite reports on whether or not General Ziethen observed their fires, or whether he had drawn his brigades together to the extent the defense of the approaches allowed. His outposts were driven in at four o'clock on the morning of the 15th. The three French columns pushed towards the three crossings of Marchiennes, Charleroi, and Chatelet. All three were defended by portions of the 2nd Brigade. General Ziethen's outposts withdrew, but the battalion that had defended Thuin for some time was lost to a cavalry attack while retreating toward Marchiennes.

ON WATERLOO

General Ziethen's outposts were drawn back from the vicinity of Binche, Thuin and Ham to the Sambre River at Charleroi, a march of two and a half hours.[33] This had been necessary for the security of the corps, but it is preferable in any case to pull back such extremely extended outposts once one has learned of the advance of the main enemy force and is therefore prepared, making it unnecessary to continue to place the outposts in jeopardy.

On the morning of the 15th, the positions of the centers of the brigades of General Ziethen's corps were:

1st, at Fontaine-l'Evêque
2nd, at Charleroi
3rd, at Fleurus
4th, at Moutier-sur-Sambre,
The Reserve Cavalry, divided between Gosselies, Charleroi, Fleurus, etc.

We can here consider the 3rd Brigade to be the reserve, the 2nd as the force that actually defended the Sambre, and the 1st and 4th Brigades as flank protection.

Accordingly, General Ziethen could not have intended to become decisively engaged on the Sambre, for he had personally chosen the 2nd Brigade's intended position near Gilly and wanted to defend the three crossings of Charleroi, Marchiennes, and Chatelet only as long as might be done without danger for the troops involved. A second stand was to take place near Gilly, in order to gain time for the flanking brigades to reach the area behind Fleurus. There the whole corps was to unite and, through its concentrated resistance, gain the time still needed to assemble the army.

On the whole, this plan was carried out successfully. It is true that the 1st Brigade, which had wanted to continue toward Heppignies, found the advanced guard of the enemy column that had advanced via Marchiennes already at Gosselies and therefore engaged it. But because the 1st Brigade was supported in this action by a regiment from the 3rd Brigade

---

33 Clausewitz's original sentence reads: "General Ziethen's outposts were drawn back from the vicinity of Binche via Thuin and Ham to the Sambre, two and one-half hours from Charleroi." This confuses the relationship between the Sambre River and the town of Charleroi, which is on the river, not two-and-a-half hours away. That would have Ziethen's men marching in the wrong direction.

at Fleurus, which had been sent to meet it, the 1st was able to continue its retreat without great difficulty to the vicinity of Saint-Amand.

The left wing brigade was not attacked by the enemy. This is probably the reason it pulled back its outposts so much later and reached Fleurus only that evening. It had therefore not suffered any losses at all.

The situation of the 2nd Brigade was as follows:

The outposts were attacked at 4 a.m.; the attack on Charleroi did not begin until 8 a.m. and lasted until 11 a.m. During this period the French also took Marchiennes, but the French right-wing column did not reach Chatelet. The 2nd Brigade now withdrew toward Gilly. The French awaited the arrival of their 3rd Corps under Vandamme, which had lost its way and therefore arrived only at 3 p.m. The time from 3 to 5 p.m. was lost in reconnoitering and in passing through Charleroi. Finally, between 5 and 6 p.m., just as General Pirch II[34] was about to begin his withdrawal toward Fleurus, the attack began. General Pirch therefore had to conduct a fighting withdrawal, during which he lost many men. In addition, one of his battalions was overrun by the enemy's cavalry before he could reach the woods at Lambusart. At nightfall Ziethen's brigades reached the area around Fleurus, and the enemy took up a position in the Lambusart woods.

Since the enemy had already begun attacking at four o'clock in the morning and had therefore spent the night and the whole previous day on the move and in combat, it was pretty clear that he would neither undertake anything further during the night, nor even resume his attack very early the next day. It could thus be foreseen that if a battle was going to take place at Sombreffe on the 16th, it could begin only in the afternoon, so the armies would have until mid-day to assemble.

General Ziethen's losses on the 15th are given as 1,200 men, but they may have been as high as 2,000. With this sacrifice, the 1st Corps had delayed the enemy's army for 36 hours, which is no unfavorable result.

Only the center and the right wing of the French pursued General Ziethen. Bonaparte gave command of the left wing to Marshal Ney, who had arrived at Charleroi at 4 p.m., along with instructions to advance

---

34 Two Prussian generals named Pirch fought in the Waterloo Campaign. Prussian accounts typically designated the senior one, Major General Georg Dubislaw Ludwig von Pirch, commander of the 2nd Corps, as Pirch I. His younger brother, Major General Otto Karl Lorenz von Pirch, commander of the Second Brigade in General Ziethen's 1st Corps, was referred to as Pirch II.

against the English army on the highway through Frasnes to Quatre-Bras, smash whatever he encountered, and take up a position at that crossroads.

Ney had found Reille's 2nd Corps near Gosselies with one of its divisions (that of Girard) detached against Fleurus and d'Erlon's 1st Corps still between Marchiennes and Gosselies. At Frasnes he encountered a brigade of Perponcher's Dutch Division. Because he had received a report from Girard's division that large masses of troops had been seen at Fleurus, he did not have the nerve to press on to Quatre-Bras, partly because his troops were not all together and partly because he may have been concerned about getting too far away from the decisive battle. He was therefore content merely to drive the Dutch brigade under Prince Bernhard of Saxe-Weimar out of Frasnes and occupy that place with his advance guard.

That evening the position of the French army was as follows:

Left Wing
The advanced guard of the left wing in Frasnes
The 2nd Corps between Mellet and Gosselies
The 1st Corps between Marchiennes and Gosselies
Center
The 3rd Corps and the cavalry in the woods in front of Fleurus
The Guard between Charleroi and Gilly
The 6th Corps behind Charleroi
Right Wing
The 4th Corps near Chatelet
Bonaparte's headquarters was in Charleroi, that of Ney in Gosselies.

Chapter 24
Situation the Morning of 16 June

As we have said, Blücher had already issued his orders for concentrating his army on the night of the 14th/15th. Wellington did not issue his until the night of the 15th/16th, thus 24 hours later.

Blücher's 2nd and 3rd Corps began marching on the 15th. By midday on the 16th, 36 hours later, they were on the battlefield ready to receive the 1st Corps. As we have already shown, the 4th Corps could have reached the field of battle by midday with no more than its advance guard, the other brigades [arriving] in the evening. But it did not arrive at all, because by a series of unfortunate circumstances the orders that General Bülow might have received on the 15th at 2 p.m., reached him only on the 16th at 10 a.m., twenty hours later. As a result, instead of being at Sombreffe at six o'clock on the evening of the 15th, the 4th Corps was still three hours away at six o'clock the next morning, a difference of about fifteen hours.

What was happening on Lord Wellington's side?

It was not until midnight on the 15th that Lord Wellington issued his orders for a march to the left. To what extent his troops—particularly his right wing—had already assembled earlier is not recorded anywhere. This must of necessity have happened already if the right wing really was concentrated at noon on the 17th near Hal, as has been asserted. For it stands to reason that orders could not have gone to Nieuport, and the troops then have marched from there to Hal, between the night of the 15th and midday on the 17th.

We must leave this unresolved and merely state what we know, namely that the English army was in the following positions on the morning of the 16th:

1. Perponcher's division and one brigade of Dutch cavalry, consisting of eight squadrons, at Quatre-Bras.

2. Chassée's Dutch division, probably with the other two brigades of Dutch cavalry consisting of twenty squadrons, at Nivelles.

3. Picton's division, the brigades of Lambert and Pack, and the Nassau and Brunswick troops on the march from Brussels to Quatre-Bras.

4. Cooke's and Alten's divisions, belonging to the left wing, on the march from the vicinity of Enghien to Quatre-Bras.

5. The cavalry under Lord Uxbridge on the march from their quarters to Quatre-Bras.

6. Clinton's division, belonging to the right wing, on the march from the vicinity of Ath and Leuze to Quatre-Bras.

7. Mitchell's brigade of Colville's division, likewise belonging to the right wing, on the march from the vicinity of Renaix to Quatre-Bras.

8. Stedtman's and Anthing's divisions, two brigades of Colville's division (Johnston and Lyon), and Estorff's Hanoverian Cavalry brigade on

the march from their quarters to Hal, where they did not arrive until the 17th.

Thus at noon, when the battle of Ligny began and that at Quatre-Bras could have begun, Lord Wellington had about 8,000 men at Quatre-Bras. By and by—throughout the whole engagement and continuing until nightfall—reserves arrived from Brussels and Cook's and Alten's divisions, perhaps also some cavalry, and the duke's strength may have risen thereby to about 40,000 men. The duke could not bring himself to abandon the road from Nivelles, which to be sure would have been dangerous because the columns of the right wing were rushing over and crossing this road. Even toward evening, 40,000 out of the duke's 90,000 troops were still on the march. Of the 50,000 already in position, 10,000 men (namely Chassée's division and twenty squadrons of cavalry) were at Nivelles, a place that was not attacked.

Chapter 25
The Battle of Ligny

On the morning of the 16th Bonaparte's forces were not yet fully concentrated for an attack.

The left wing under Ney was "in echelon," as the French say, from Frasnes to Marchiennes, a distance of about nine miles. The center and right wing were similar, because the 6th Corps stood behind Charleroi. Furthermore, the French troops had attacked the Prussian outposts at 4 a.m. on the 15th, so they had probably marched the better part of the night and then spent the whole of the 15th, well into the evening, either in combat or in readiness and on the march. On the morning of the 16th it was therefore impossible to mount an attack on Blücher at Sombreffe or on the Dutch troops at Quatre-Bras. Bonaparte had become convinced of this by the situation at Sombreffe, and he gave no thought to beginning the action there during the morning. However, the very same situation existed at Quatre-Bras. Thus his reproach of Ney for not having seized Quatre-Bras with his whole force, either on the evening of the 15th or early in the morning of the 16th, is accordingly frivolous and unjustified.

If it had actually been possible for the tactical engagement of the main forces to have occurred on the morning of the 16th, it would have been a tremendous mistake to have delayed it, for Blücher was still assembling his troops, as Bonaparte knew. Furthermore, since the overall strength of the Prussian force was so superior to the 75,000 men that Bonaparte could deploy against them, nothing could be more important than to begin the action before that whole force was assembled. The Prussian 3rd Corps, for example, arrived on the battlefield only at 10 a.m. But the French troops needed time to rest, get rations, prepare a meal, and then draw closer together. All this could not be done during a short summer night, and it is not surprising that these activities continued into the morning of the 16th. Between 11 a.m. and noon the French troops once again advanced against General Ziethen, who had already sent his brigades back into the positions allotted to them, though he himself had remained with his cavalry on the plain of Fleurus. The maneuvers by which this cavalry was pushed back to the main position lasted until 1 p.m. Bonaparte then reconnoitered the Prussian position. The real attack could begin only around 3 p.m.

Chapter 26
Blücher's Dispositions

Blücher's original idea, as we have already said, was to occupy the Sombreffe position along the Brussels highway and then, while Bonaparte was developing his attack there, to fall upon his flank with the largest part of the Prussian force. When the army assembled at Sombreffe on the morning of the 16th, concern arose about the need to immediately post strong forces to secure the area from which the Duke of Wellington was supposed to arrive with part of his army. A position was therefore chosen for the 1st and 2nd Corps between Saint-Amand and Sombreffe. But it was also thought that the area between Sombreffe and Balâtre could not be left unoccupied, because General Bülow was approaching there through Gembloux. The 3rd Corps was therefore ordered to occupy this position. As a result, there were two front lines. These formed an inward-pointing right angle. It was probably assumed that the enemy would not make the exposed right flank the principal object of his attack,

ON WATERLOO

because the Duke of Wellington was expected to arrive on that side with a considerable force. Against a secondary attack, however, this flank was considered fairly strong because of the string of villages extending from Saint-Amand to Wagnelée.

The principal Prussian mistake was to believe that the whole enemy force was opposed to them and that they could therefore count on Wellington's assistance with a substantial force (40,000 to 50,000 men). And it is true that a flank can be willingly exposed if 40,000 or 50,000 men are in echelon behind it. They must have thought that Bonaparte would attack both Prussian front lines, thus placing himself in a very disadvantageous position. This expectation proved false, and there would have been time during the battle to correct this mistake.

Chapter 27
Dispositions on the Front at Ligny

The front from Amand to Sombreffe was occupied as follows: 1st Corps formed the actual front line; 2nd Corps remained in reserve behind the heights. 1st Corps had, through various mischances, gotten its troops rather oddly intermingled. While the 1st Brigade had three battalions in Bry, the other six stood behind Saint-Amand. On the other hand, the 3rd Brigade had three battalions in Saint-Amand, while the other six formed the rearmost reserve. [See Map 1, on p.103 below.]

The essentials of the deployment were: Bry was occupied by three battalions of the 1st Brigade; Saint-Amand by three of the 3rd Brigade; and Ligny by four battalions of the 4th Brigade. The remaining six battalions of the 1st Brigade were at the front in two lines just behind Saint-Amand (B).[35] The eight battalions of the 2nd Brigade (one battalion having been lost), along with the remaining two battalions of the 4th, were in a second line between Bry and Ligny (C and D). Finally, the six remaining battalions of the 3rd Brigade were in a third line just behind the 2nd and 4th (E).

---

35 Clausewitz's note: "These letters are all references to August Wagner's maps of the battle." This refers to the excellent maps contained in Wagner, *Pläne der Schlachten und Treffen*, which have not been included in any prior published edition of this work. See Map 1, below, which is a detail of Wagner's map of the Battle of Ligny.

The 1st Corps' reserve cavalry stood initially in front of the villages to observe the enemy, and afterwards placed itself as a reserve just in front of the 3rd Brigade (W).

The 2nd Corps stood along the Brussels road as the main reserve, the brigades next to each other (H, J, K, L,) in their prescribed order of battle of three lines in column. The reserve cavalry was behind (M). The artillery was for the most part still with the brigades. Just the three heavy batteries of the 1st Corps had been advanced between Ligny and Saint-Amand.

The intention was to fight only a preliminary action in the villages of Saint-Amand and Ligny, in order to disrupt the enemy's force, and then to fall upon it as soon as it advanced from the villages.

Chapter 28
Dispositions on the Front at Sombreffe

The 3rd Corps placed its 9th Brigade to defend the extended villages of Sombreffe and Mont-Potriaux, as well as the ridge on which they are located; the 11th Brigade to defend the highway from Point-du-Jour; the 10th to defend the ridge of Tongrines and Tongrinelle; with the 12th Brigade and the reserve cavalry behind them as a reserve. The 9th Brigade initially occupied the village of Mont-Potriaux with only one battalion, while the other eight battalions remained in reserve behind the village (P). The 11th Brigade occupied the valley [of Ligny Brook] with one battalion (R) and kept the other four in the rear (Q), one battalion having remained at the outposts on the Meuse.

The 10th Brigade occupied the valley with two battalions and placed the other four on the ridge.

The intention was to use the skirmish line to hold the enemy in the valley at all points for as long as possible and then, when this line could no longer be held, to engage the enemy on the ridge with full battalions.

The artillery was distributed mainly on the heights in front of Mont-Potriaux, on the main road in front of Point-du-Jour, and on the heights at Tongrinelle.

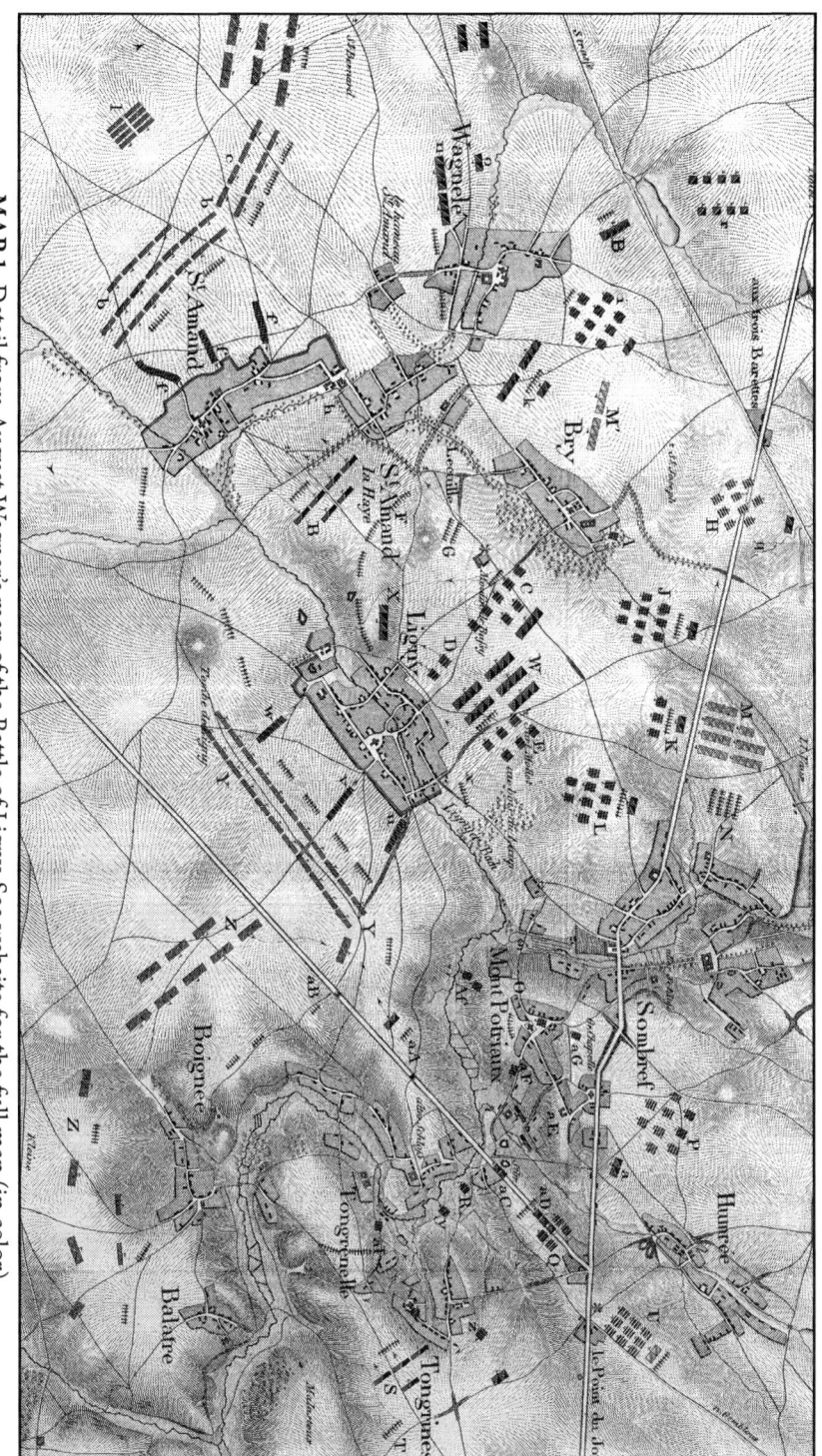

MAP 1. Detail from August Wagner's map of the Battle of Ligny. See website for the full map (in color).

Chapter 29
Arrival of the Duke of Wellington

These arrangements were carried out very calmly by noon, because—as had been foreseen—the enemy could not begin his attack before then and did not in any way impede General Ziethen's withdrawal from Fleurus into this position.

At 1 p.m. the Duke of Wellington came to Marshal Blücher at the windmill of Bry. The duke told the field marshal that his army was at that moment assembling at Quatre-Bras, and that in a few hours he would hasten with it to assist Blücher. "At four o'clock I will be here," are supposed to have been the duke's words as he spurred his horse away.

It would have been unreasonable to suppose that the duke could arrive in a few hours with his whole army. Wellington must have meant nothing more than his left wing united with his reserve, which nonetheless amounted to 40,000 to 50,000 men. Both commanders thought that the whole French force (estimated at 130,000 men) was facing the Prussians. Blücher had assembled around 80,000 men, so if the duke came with another 40-50,000 there would have been a rough equality of forces. They were also counting on Bülow's arrival, although not without some uneasiness on that score. If his 35,000 men arrived, victory seemed pretty certain. Even though these ratios were not as advantageous as they might have been, given the Allies' great superiority of numbers, they still seemed satisfactory. A withdrawal in order to delay giving battle for a day seemed fraught with difficulties because of the two armies' diverging lines of retreat. Each army might have abandoned its natural line of communication for a short time and turned toward the base of the other, if they had been together. But they were not together, and a simultaneous march to the rear would actually have impeded their union. Furthermore, it would have made a bad impression on the troops and the public. All these reasons—which were indeed sufficient—confirmed Field Marshal Blücher's resolution to stand and give battle. The battle was therefore undertaken in the belief that the Prussians would have to face a great superiority of numbers at first, but that by the end of the day the superiority would be on their side. It was only a matter of putting up sufficient resistance until then.

ON WATERLOO

Chapter 30
Bonaparte's Plan of Attack

As we know, on the 15th Bonaparte had sent Ney forward on the road to Quatre-Bras with the 1st and 2nd Corps, the light cavalry of the Guard, and a division of cuirassiers, altogether 48,000 men. While this mass of troops was advancing from Marchiennes, where they had crossed the Sambre, Girard's division of the 2nd Corps was employed against General Steinmetz at Gosselies. Since it moved closer to the French center while pursuing [Steinmetz] toward Heppignies, Bonaparte kept it with him. The main army advancing against Blücher now consisted of about 75,000 men. Bonaparte gave it the following dispositions and objectives:

The 3rd Corps (Vandamme), together with Girard's division and supported by a brigade of light cavalry of the Guard, 24,000 men in all, would advance via Wagnelée to attack Saint-Amand.

The 4th Corps (Gérard), 15,000 men strong, would turn to the left and advance to attack Ligny.

Grouchy would advance against Point-du-Jour and Tongrinelle with two corps of cavalry and some infantry (no one says from which corps, but probably from the 4th).

The Guard was placed in reserve to the left of Fleurus. The 6th Corps (which arrived somewhat later) and Milhaut's cavalry corps were placed in reserve to the right.

These reserves and Grouchy's cavalry, which merely scouted, amounted to a force of about 36,000 men.

Bonaparte did not know the position of the Prussian 3rd Corps. He believed that all three Prussian corps were deployed between Saint-Amand and Sombreffe. He was all the more certain that what he saw in this position was the whole Prussian army because he saw numerous masses of reserves in locations H, I, K, L, and P. Assuming the villages were strongly held, these could easily have comprised the total of 80,000 men he had in front of him. Whether he knew for certain that the 4th Corps had not yet arrived cannot be determined. Later on he claimed as much, in order to put his attack plan in a more favorable light. But it is scarcely possible that he could have been completely sure of this, since even the prisoners he had taken at the start of the battle could not have known for certain. We will therefore leave this question open and turn to his own description.[36] There he saw the Prussian army as being deployed along a line with the Brussels road behind it, which meant that the Prussians had completely abandoned their original line of retreat and had exposed their right flank to him.

In reality, the principal orientation of the Prussian position, even without considering Thielmann's [3rd] corps, was not as Bonaparte conceived it. On the contrary, the Brussels road was more parallel than perpendicular to it. But Bonaparte did not see things this way, and this mistake is quite understandable, because it was very difficult to form an idea of the orientation of the whole shape based on the many individual masses of the Prussian brigades. It was very natural to imagine that the line from Saint-Amand to Ligny, plus the line of the latter village itself, which were the most forward occupied posts, was the dominant line of the whole force. The Prussian deployment amazed Bonaparte and led him to conclude that Blücher was not expecting a battle on that day. Thus Blücher had chosen this position—astonishing under the circumstances—in the hope of gaining time until the next day and of then seeing the English army take up its position in line with the Prussians. Bonaparte attributed the fact that Blücher continued to maintain this deployment while face-to-face with the French army partly to the old man's audacity and desire to maintain an imposing countenance, and partly to the apparently unthreatening nature of Bonaparte's own position near Fleurus, where a portion of his troops was completely concealed.

Bonaparte was now almost certain that Wellington could not arrive. On this point he was much more likely to have had definite news than about Bülow. Furthermore, he thought that he had dealt with that threat by the orders he had given Ney. Everything thus depended on Ney, who, having missed his chance on the 15th, was supposed to press forward to Quatre-Bras as quickly as possible on the 16th, thereby holding off whatever aid might have come from Wellington. Ney was then to send 10,000 men back on the Quatre-Bras-Namur road into the rear of the Prussian army. In his enthusiasm for this plan, Bonaparte said to General Gérard, who had come to him for instructions: "It may be that in three hours the fate of the war will be decided. If Ney executes his orders properly, not a

---

36 Napoleon, *Mémoires*, 90.

single cannon of the Prussian army will escape. They have been caught *en flagrant délit*."[37]

Chapter 31
Critical Analysis

There is strong reason to doubt that Bonaparte's intentions at the time he gave his orders for the battle were truly as he has stated. In his narratives and dictations he has demonstrated all too often that he is not truthful and forthright. It may well be that in this case he also wished to appear to be less of a gambler, not just in his attack on Blücher but in his whole second appearance on the political stage. He was destroyed by the combined strength of Blücher and Wellington, but his vanity requires that this appear not to have resulted from the force of circumstances, but from mistakes by individuals. This brief for the defense, as the lawyers call it, therefore requires him to argue that the Prussian army would already have been lost on the 16th if Bonaparte's plans had been carried out.

No study to date has been able to show to what extent Marshal Ney actually acted contrary to Bonaparte's orders on the 16th, because Gamot's defense of the Marshal also does not clear this up completely.[38] However, it will definitely contribute to a better understanding of the matter if we present word-for-word the four orders that Marshal Ney received in the course of the 16th, according to Gamot's book.

First Order

Charleroi, 16 June 1815

Marshal! The Emperor has just ordered Count Valmy, commanding the 3rd Cavalry Corps, to concentrate and head for Gosselies, where he will be at your disposition.

---

37 Napoleon, *Mémoires*, 94.
38 M. Gamot, *Réfutation, en ce qui concerne le Maréchal Ney, de l'ouvrage ayant pour titres: campagne de 1815, ou relation des operations militaires qui ont lieu pendant les cents jours, par le general Gourgaud, écrite à Sainte-Hélène* (Paris, 1818), 12ff; cited in Hahlweg, *Schriften*, 2:997n.

THE CAMPAIGN OF 1815

His Majesty's intention is that the Guard Cavalry, which had been on the road to Brussels, remain behind and rejoin the remainder of the Imperial Guard; but in order that it should not have to make a retrograde movement, you can replace it in the line and leave it a little to the rear and he will send its orders for the day there. Lieutenant General Lefebre-Desnouettes will send an officer to pick up the necessary orders.

You will inform me whether the corps has carried out its movement and of the exact position this morning of the 1st and 2nd Corps and of the two cavalry divisions which are attached, informing me what enemy forces are in front of you and what has been learned.

Signed: Chief of Staff,
the Duke of Dalmatia

Second Order
Charleroi, 16 June 1815

Marshal! An officer of lancers has just told the Emperor that the enemy has appeared in force near Quatre-Bras. Unite the corps of Counts Reille and d'Erlon and that of Count Valmy, who is just marching off to join you. With these forces you must engage and destroy all enemy forces that present themselves. Blücher was at Namur yesterday and it is unlikely that he has sent any troops toward Quatre-Bras. Thus you will only have to deal with the forces coming from Brussels.

Marshal Grouchy is going to move on Sombreffe as I informed you, and the Emperor is going to Fleurus. You should address future reports to His Majesty there.

Signed: Marshal of the Empire,
Chief of Staff, the Duke of Dalmatia

ON WATERLOO

Third Order
In front of Fleurus, 16 June, at two o'clock.

Marshal! The Emperor has directed me to warn you that the enemy has gathered a body[39] of troops between Sombreffe and Bry, and that at two-thirty Marshal Grouchy will attack it with the 3rd and 4th Corps. His Majesty's intent is that you should attack all that is in front of you, and that, after having vigorously pushed it back, you should advance toward us to assist in enveloping the force I just mentioned. If this force has already been smashed, then His Majesty will maneuver toward you to speed up your operation in turn. Immediately inform the Emperor of your dispositions and of what is happening on your front.

Signed: Chief of Staff,
Marshal of the Empire,
Duke of Dalmatia

Fourth Order

In front of Fleurus, 16 June 1815,
at three-fifteen

Marshal! I wrote to you an hour ago that the Emperor would attack the enemy at two-thirty in the position he has taken between Saint-Amand and Bry. At this moment the engagement is very fierce. His Majesty has directed me to tell you that you must maneuver onto the field in such a manner as to envelop the enemy right and to fall with full force on his rear. The enemy army will be lost if you act vigorously. The fate of France is in your hands. Therefore do not hesitate an instant to move as the Emperor has ordered, and head toward the heights of Bry and of Saint-Amand to cooperate in a victory that may be decisive.

---

39 The original French, "*corps,*" has sometimes been misinterpreted as referring to an army corps ("*corps d'armée*"), which would suggest that Napoleon had grossly underestimated the size of the Prussian force facing him. By itself, however, "*corps*" may refer to any substantial body of troops. Here it clearly refers to a force far larger than a single corps.

The enemy has been caught *en flagrant délit* while trying to unite with the English.

> Signed: Chief of staff,
> the Duke of Dalmatia.

In contrast, Bonaparte wrote in his previously mentioned memoirs:

An officer from the staff of the left wing reported that, at the moment when Marshal Ney was marching into position in front of Quatre-Bras, he was stopped by the sound of cannon on his right flank and by reports that the Anglo-Dutch and Prusso-Saxon armies had already linked up in the vicinity of Fleurus; that had he continued his movement under these circumstances he would have been outflanked; and that he was ready to execute any commands the Emperor should send him, once His Majesty became aware of this new development. The emperor blamed him for having lost eight hours already. What Ney claimed was a new development had in fact existed since the day before. The emperor reiterated to Ney the order to carry all before Quatre-Bras, and that as soon as he had taken the position he was to detach a column of eight thousand infantry, together with Lefebre-Desnouettes's cavalry division and twenty-eight guns, via the road through Marbais, in order to attack the rear of the enemy army on the heights of Bry. With this detachment gone, there would still remain to him thirty-two thousand men and 80 guns at Quatre-Bras, which will be sufficient to hold in check the detachments of the British army that might arrive on the 16th. Marshal Ney received this order at 11:30 a.m. He was near Frasne with his advance guard; he ought to have taken up his position in front on Quatre-Bras at mid-day. Now, from Quatre-Bras to the heights of Bry is eight thousand yards; the column that he detached against Marshal Blücher's rear should therefore have reached Marchais by two o'clock. The line that the French army occupied near Fleurus was not aggressive. Part of it was masked; the Prussian army should have had no cause for concern.[40]

---

40 Napoleon, *Mémoires*, 90-93.

ON WATERLOO

Although it cannot be said that this narrative contradicts the four orders, the following must be noted:

1. A specific mission such as the one described [in the *Memoirs*] cannot be found among the orders to the Marshal. Perhaps it was verbal, perhaps it has been lost.

2. The third order does not make reference to any previous order along similar lines, but instead presents the situation differently; Soult would probably have been the one who wrote the order mentioned by Bonaparte, or at least would have had precise knowledge of it.

3. Anyone who has a little experience in these matters will find that the four orders reproduced by Gamot have a greater ring of truth than the account given by Bonaparte in his memoirs.

4. Finally, Bonaparte's account lists the Guards Cavalry Division among the forces allocated to Marshal Ney, while the first of the three orders clearly calls for it to remain behind. On St. Helena Napoleon may have forgotten this situation, but not a few hours after he gave the order.

And now for the internal consistency of this deployment.

1. Ney is to advance nine miles toward Brussels with around 40,000 men, where he is likely to encounter 50-60,000 English and Dutch troops. He is supposed to defeat them, and no doubts are raised about the certainty of his success, even though English troops led by Wellington had on many occasions defeated French marshals quite decisively.

2. Around midday the main body of Marshal Ney's force was still at Gosselies, three hours' march from Quatre-Bras. This force must first cover that distance, for even though Ney himself is with the advanced guard at Frasnes, that is not sufficient. Then he must begin and end a battle, and afterward march 10,000 men three hours toward Saint-Amand to help end another battle, which has been going on at the same time. If all this was not completely impossible, it was certainly not very realistic.

3. Why should the appearance of 10,000 men in the rear of the 80,000-man Prussian army, in open countryside with complete visibility all around, have necessarily caused it to collapse completely? By simply appearing on the field they might tip the scales in an undecided battle and force Blücher to retreat earlier; but that is still a long way from collapse, i.e., complete destruction such as at Jena.[41]

---

41 Clausewitz regarded the destruction of the Prussian army in the twin battles of Jena and Auerstädt (7-13 October 1806), as exemplifying what the total defeat of an army entailed—not

We must therefore conclude that this Bonapartist narrative, written in solitude on St. Helena, is a kind of bombast, and that at the moment of action Bonaparte's entire concept was simpler and more natural.

He saw the greater portion of Blücher's army in front of him, estimated it as smaller than it really was (because he thought the 3rd Corps arrived only during the course of the battle), and hoped in any case to defeat Blücher quickly. In the meantime Ney, with around 40,000 men, would be able to hold off the assistance being rushed over by Wellington and to send any extra troops against Blücher's rear. This was more or less his plan. Just how big his victory over Blücher would be was something Bonaparte could not determine in advance, given his situation. He would have to be satisfied with whatever results a very forceful blow could bring. Time, forces, and circumstances were insufficient for an overwhelmingly destructive plan to be realized. If a moderate victory would not help him, if it did not pull him back from the abyss toward which he was tottering like a great daredevil, then it only shows how insecure his position was, how dangerous his game—and it is precisely about this that he wants no word to be said.

Chapter 32
Principal Moments of the Battle

There are three distinct but simultaneous acts to distinguish among in relating the course of the battle itself: the fighting around the village of Saint-Amand; the fighting around the village of Ligny; and the demonstration against the 3rd Corps.

The first of the three acts was the bloodiest, the second the most decisive. The third was unimportant in itself but must be considered an effective feint by the French.

[1. The Fighting at Saint-Amand]
Events regarding the fight for the village of Saint-Amand can be grouped roughly as follows.

---

just death and destruction on the battlefield, but its ultimate dismemberment as a fighting force. See his "Observations on Prussia in Her Great Catastrophe," in *Historical and Political Writings*, 30-84, and chapters 44 and 52 of the present work.

1. The southernmost village, that is Saint-Amand proper, was attacked at 3 p.m. by Lefol's division of the French 3rd Corps. The Prussian 1st Brigade, which had six battalions posted behind the village, supported the three battalions of the 3rd Brigade inside it. 1st Brigade maintained the action for an hour, during which the village changed hands several times, and the three battalions that had stood in Bry were brought forward and used up. At 4 p.m. the village was lost and the 1st Brigade was no longer able to continue fighting; it was withdrawn and reformed behind Bry. (See item G on Map 1.) The advance of Girard's division into Saint-Amand-la-Haye presumably contributed to this success.

2. Field Marshal Blücher decided on a strong attack in two columns in order to retake the villages of [Saint-Amand and] Saint-Amand-la-Haye.

One column, consisting of the 2nd Brigade, which had stood in reserve near Bry with its eight battalions, was to attack the broad side of the latter village. Meanwhile, General Jürgass with the 5th Brigade and seventeen squadrons of cavalry—namely ten from his own brigade and seven from Marwitz's brigade brought over from the 3rd Corps—was to advance through and alongside of the village of Wagnelée so that he could attack the left flank of Girard's division defending Saint-Amand-la-Haye. In this manner the Prussians hoped to regain possession of this village and subsequently also Saint-Amand itself.

General Pirch [II] made two attacks. The first miscarried completely; the second, under Blücher's personal leadership, went right into the village and resulted in the capture of the churchyard.

General Jürgass also made two attacks, but these do not appear to have been well coordinated with those of General Pirch [II]. In the first attack, the 25th Regiment, which was leading the advance out of Wagnelée, fell quickly into disorder, and the attack must be considered a total failure. General Jürgass then renewed it with the same troops after reforming them in the rear, and this time he was more successful; that is, he pressed forward into the area around the village of Saint-Amand-le-Hameau, and here the fighting ground to a halt for some time.

In response, Bonaparte reinforced his left wing with a division of the Young Guard and the French renewed their attacks. Because the 2nd Brigade was exhausted and had expended all of its ammunition, four battalions of the 6th Brigade were brought forward from its position behind Bry and General Pirch moved the 2nd Brigade back behind that village.

The 7th Brigade likewise advanced to reinforce the 5th. There is no precise account as to what took place on either side at this point. The fighting was probably confined to a rather small space, fluctuating back and forth. Both sides may have been in nearly the same situation, since each occupied a portion of the village of Saint-Amand-la-Haye. From what we can garner from the various accounts, it would appear that the battle always remained on the far side of the small brook where the villages of Saint-Amand are located.

Nothing clear and definite can be said about the effect and the employment of cavalry and artillery because the accounts of the use of these arms are too disjointed, perhaps because their employment was, too. Many units from these arms do not even appear in the accounts of this action. If we add together the reserve artillery of the 1st Corps as well as the batteries of the 1st, 2nd, 5th, and 7th Brigades, which were undoubtedly there, this makes ten batteries or 80 guns. There were probably several reserve batteries of the 2nd Corps also in action here as well, and taken all together this makes a total of 100 guns that were fighting in a space of around 3,000 paces.

The artillery of the French 3rd Corps consisted of 38 guns, that of Girard's division 8 guns. If we add to this around 30 guns belonging to the Guard and the reserve cavalry, the total number of French guns must have amounted to only 76. At any rate, the number was considerably smaller than that of the Prussians. If we are nevertheless obliged to agree that the Prussians lost more in killed and wounded, this is surely due to the fact that we hold too much artillery in reserve and relieve a battery as soon as it has expended its ammunition. For this reason some gunners try to expend their ammunition as quickly as possible.

Cavalry seems to have been employed very little on either side and merely observed each other. Three French regiments attempted to turn the Prussian right wing but were checked by the eight squadrons sent against them by Colonel Marwitz.

3. Finally, we must consider as the third principal act in the fighting around Saint-Amand the time when Field Marshal Blücher, believing on account of the movement of the French Guard that the French army was retreating, led the last available battalions—three from the 8th Brigade—to Saint-Amand in order to break through the French there and then pursue them. This decision reveals that the fighting at Saint-Amand

must have hung in the balance, for otherwise the thought of attempting a breakthrough and pursuit with fresh troops could never have arisen.

A summary of the results of this entire struggle shows that our side had gradually committed around 40 battalions, thus perhaps 28,000 infantrymen, while on the French side, the 3rd Corps, Girard's division of the 2nd Corps, and Duhesme's division of the Guard, altogether about 24,000 infantrymen, had been committed and had maintained the fight for six hours, for the Prussians retained possession of the villages until 9 o'clock. But on the whole we were somewhat at a disadvantage, since we had lost all of Saint-Amand and half of Saint-Amand-la-Haye, we had suffered more casualties in killed and wounded, and overall we had been weakened more, with more of our units burnt out and fewer that could still be employed compared to the French, for it is not likely that all of the French battalions had been involved in the actual fighting. It was therefore a setback for us that we had already suffered noticeably more in this fight than the enemy. However, this success was clearly not decisive, but rather an almost imperceptible tipping of the scales.

[2. The Fighting at Ligny]

We now turn to Ligny. Here the action was even simpler than at Saint-Amand. It consisted of a five-hour-long firefight, principally in the village itself, during which the French were generally in possession of the half of the village lying on the right bank of the brook, while the Prussians had the other half.

The attack on Ligny was carried out by the French 4th Corps under Gérard, and the decisive stroke was made by the Guard itself under Bonaparte. It began somewhat later than the attack on Saint-Amand. The following events can be considered the most important ones:

1. Ligny was occupied by four battalions of the [Prussian] 4th Brigade. The attack advanced in three columns, consisting of the three divisions that made up the [French 4th] corps, though we must assume that the greater part of these divisions was held back in reserve. The two remaining battalions of the 4th Brigade also moved into the village, and the first attack was repulsed.

2. The French renewed the attack, the 4th Brigade gradually became too weak to resist, and the 3rd Brigade, after leaving two battalions to protect the artillery batteries, moved four battalions into the village for

support. General von Jagow wanted to advance with them out of the village and go over to the attack, but the fire of the enemy batteries made it impossible to break out. This led to disorder among the troops in the village itself, which is probably why half of it was lost.

3. So as not to lose the other half, the remaining four battalions of the 6th Brigade were ordered to Ligny. (One battalion had already been used up in Ligny, and four others had been employed by General Pirch in the attack on Saint-Amand.) These were later followed by five battalions of the 8th Brigade, which had previously moved from the area around Sombreffe to the mill of Bussy. Of the remaining four battalions of this brigade, one stayed at the mill and the other three were those that Field Marshal Blücher led into Saint-Amand. With respect to the use of cavalry and artillery, we know even less than we do concerning Saint-Amand. Assuming that the Prussian artillery at Saint-Amand consisted of 100 guns, then there could not have been more than 60 at Ligny, for the whole complement of artillery for both corps was only 160 guns.

The French 4th Corps had forty cannon, but it is likely that part of the Guard's artillery, as well as that of the cavalry reserve, was employed here, so at this place it is unlikely that our side had any superiority in artillery.

The Prussian cavalry had for the most part been drawn away to the right wing, for when the French cavalry broke through later on only three [of our] regiments were found here.

The contest in Ligny now continued in a very confined space and with the most bloody exertions. The mass of Prussian infantry employed there amounted to 20 battalions, thus about 14,000 men. The French 3rd Corps may have been equally strong in infantry.

At about 3 p.m. Field Marshal Blücher ordered General Thielmann to send a brigade of his reserve cavalry. This was done, and Colonel Marwitz was placed under the command of General Jürgass, as we mentioned in describing the action near Saint-Amand. Around four o'clock, General Thielmann received orders to send a brigade of infantry, too, whereupon the 12th Brigade marched off to Ligny. It was placed in reserve between Sombreffe and Ligny in place of the 8th. The 12th Brigade pushed its skirmishers forward as far as Ligny Brook and covered the left flank of the troops in Ligny in an engagement that was not without importance.

The brigade did not suffer very heavy losses, however, and thus could still be considered a reserve.

Bonaparte resolved to break through the position at Ligny with the main body of his Guard and thereby force a decision in the battle. This thrust occurred at about 8 p.m. and was the final phase of the action at Ligny.

4. Eight battalions of the French Guard and 3-4,000 cavalry advanced for the decisive blow against Ligny, and drove the Prussian troops out of the whole place. The French cavalry pushed through the center of the Prussian position, which was nearly devoid of infantry. The reserve cavalry of the 1st Corps rushed over by brigades to counterattack the enemy's cavalry and infantry, but was repulsed at all points. Field Marshal Blücher's horse was wounded while he was leading one of these counterattacks, and he escaped capture only by chance.

[3. The Action of the Prussian 3rd Corps]

Two corps of cavalry and some infantry, probably from the 4th Corps under Grouchy's command, were employed to demonstrate against the Prussian troops between Sombreffe and Saint-Balâtre and thus keep them occupied. This goal was accomplished, because the 10th and 11th Brigades (with eleven battalions) and the 2nd Brigade of the reserve cavalry (with six squadrons) were thereby fixed in place. On the other hand, the 12th Brigade and one brigade of the reserve cavalry moved over to the other two corps, and the 9th Brigade, posted behind Sombreffe, can be considered as a reserve. The infantry action was unimportant in itself and took place almost entirely on the terrain occupied by the 10th Brigade between Tongrinelle and Boignée.

Between 7 and 8 p.m. General Thielmann saw the skirmishers of his 12th Brigade, which was between Sombreffe and Ligny, crossing the stream. He saw also that the cavalry opposing him was dwindling down to few troops. He therefore believed that the enemy was retiring, and decided to advance across the defile with his remaining brigade of cavalry. Two squadrons were sent forward, and a battery of horse artillery imprudently followed close behind. Scarcely had these units approached the nearby heights when some enemy regiments threw themselves on the two squadrons and took five guns from the horse artillery battery, which had attempted to unlimber its guns instead of turning back. The remaining three guns had time to save themselves.

To summarize our impression of the battle as a whole, it is—like all recent battles—a slow consumption of the forces opposed to each other in the front line, where they engage in a firefight of many hours' duration with very little fluctuation, until at last one side acquires a noticeable superiority in reserves, that is, in fresh masses of troops, with which it then gives the decisive blow to the already shaky enemy force.

Bonaparte advanced with about 75,000 men against Blücher, whose three assembled corps together made a force of 78,000 men, thus a force of comparable strength.

Bonaparte used about 30,000 men to engage the two principal points of Blücher's position, Saint-Amand and Ligny, from 3 p.m. to 8 p.m. He employed around 6,000 men to occupy the Prussian 3rd Corps, and kept 33,000 waiting calmly in reserve, far behind the battle line. Of these he used about 6,000 to maintain the struggle at Saint-Amand.

He decided as early as 6 p.m. to deliver the decisive blow on Ligny with his Guard, but then he suddenly received reports that a sizeable force had appeared an hour's march from his left flank. Bonaparte halted his movement, as this could be an enemy force coming from Brussels. In fact it was d'Erlon who, acting on orders the source of which is still not known, was marching from Frasnes towards Saint-Amand. Scouts were hastily sent to reconnoiter this force, but nearly two hours elapsed before the news was brought back that this was the French 1st Corps. It is for this reason that the thrust against Ligny did not begin until 8 p.m.

Bonaparte did not even deliver this blow with the whole mass of his reserves, but with only about half of it (that is, with the remainder of the Guard), while the 6th Corps remained behind, still in reserve.

At the beginning of the battle, Blücher had the 1st Corps (27,000 men) in Ligny and Saint-Amand, and the 3rd Corps (22,000 men) deployed from Sombreffe to Saint-Balâtre. Only the 2nd Corps (29,000 men) was kept behind in reserve. While it is true that the 3rd Corps had not been seriously attacked, and thus could have been concentrated and used as a reserve, and also that Blücher was counting on the arrival of Bülow, neither of these things occurred, so the ratio of Prussian reserves to those of the French always remained unfavorable. As we have seen, 2nd Corps, the actual reserve, was gradually used up in maintaining the action. Therefore nothing remained with which to deliver a decisive blow if the battle had remained wholly in the balance or had even taken a turn in our favor.

As the end of the day approached, the situation of the opposing forces was approximately as follows.

Blücher had committed 38,000 infantry to the two villages. They had suffered substantial losses and in some cases had used up their ammunition and now had to be considered mere cinders, in which little living energy remained. There were still 6,000 infantry standing behind the villages, scattered in solitary battalions that had not yet been engaged. The remaining 56,000 men in the 1st and 2nd Corps were cavalry and artillery, of whom only a small portion were still fresh.

If the 3rd Corps had been concentrated, or if appropriate steps to do so had been taken in time, it could have constituted a reserve of 18,000 men. One could therefore say that at the decisive moment Blücher still had a reserve of around 24,000 men.

Although originally a few thousand men weaker than Blücher, Bonaparte now had several thousand more fresh troops than his opponent. The reason for this was his greater restraint, his greater economy of force during the firefight.

This small superiority of numbers in the French reserve naturally would not in itself have been very decisive, but it still must be considered as the first reason for the victory.

The second was the unequal results obtained in the firefight thus far. To be sure, when Bonaparte made his advance against Ligny we still held part of that village, but we had nonetheless lost the rest. Likewise we still held on between Wagnelée and Saint-Amand, but here too we had lost villages and terrain. Thus the battle had already turned a little to our disadvantage everywhere, and in such cases the stage is prepared in advance for the decisive blow.

But the third and most important reason for the outcome was indisputably that Blücher did not have close at hand the troops who had not yet been engaged, namely the 3rd Corps. To be sure, the 12th Brigade was near by, but this was too little. The 9th was also not far away, but insufficient attention had been paid to it and to the whole of Thielmann's corps. For this reason the 3rd Corps might as well not have been there at all as far as the decisive moment was concerned. It could only be useful in the retreat. Nevertheless, we may possibly (even probably) consider the scattered disposition of Thielmann's corps to be an advantage overall. If the 3rd Corps had been at hand, it would have been used up in the same manner as the rest, without increasing the prospects for success. Given the turn of events that had already occurred, a successful outcome [for the Prussians] could only have been obtained by a decisive superiority in numbers, as would have occurred with the arrival of Bülow's corps. Had the 3rd Corps been consumed along with the others, our losses in the battle might well have been 10,000 more.

Chapter 33
Critical Observations on the Whole Battle: Blücher

1. Blücher's main mistake appears to have been a certain lack of clarity in his plans, which resulted in the occupation of two fronts and the neutralization of 20,000 men. The position from Sombreffe to Saint-Balâtre was good if the intention was to preserve the line of retreat towards the Meuse. In that case, however, it would have been necessary to remain along that front and to view the connection with Wellington as solely a matter of fighting a common enemy, not one requiring direct union. In such open countryside it would be easy to see if Wellington was advancing on the road from Quatre-Bras, so direct union was so unnecessary as to be a disadvantage. [As it was,] Wellington's natural line was like that of a corps sent against the enemy's flank, a form of attack that is always sought with the greatest care, and which is warranted as the most decisive form whenever one is stronger and has the broader base.

If, however, it was intended in the worst case to give up the line of retreat to the Meuse, then the position at Sombreffe was quite unnecessary. It should have been held by a single brigade at most, in order to keep the enemy hemmed in. It was not necessary to occupy this position in preparation for Bülow's arrival. Just as with the preceding example of Wellington, 35,000 men operating as a flanking force would have been able to cross Ligny Brook even if the enemy had held [Sombreffe], which was not all that likely.

In preparing so great an action as a battle, nothing seems more essential than to have a clear idea of the general relationships involved. Of these, none is as important or influential as the roads to be used for a retreat, for these determine the position of the front and all the key lines of possible movement during the battle. In this case Blücher remained stuck in half measures, that is to say, caught between two contradictory ones.

2. Even during the course of the battle, i.e., between about 4 and 5 p.m., orders might have been given to General Thielmann to assemble his corps and to advance from Mont-Potriaux and Point-du-Jour against the enemy right flank. In that case, Gérard's corps would either have had to give way or would have required earlier support from the Guard. Even if General Thielmann had then been attacked by Grouchy and the Guard, and forced to retire back over the brook, the French reserve would still have been absorbed earlier, and the blow against the center at Ligny would probably not have taken place at all. In that case, the battle would probably not have been decided on the evening of the 16th. In any event, it would have weakened the French army much more.

3. With respect to defending the villages, the defense of Saint-Amand proper appears to have been a damaging diversion from the main effort. If Saint-Amand was supposed to be an advanced post, then it must be said that such posts can be justified only on two accounts:

a. If they are inherently very strong, so that they force the attacker to commit disproportionate forces against them because he cannot bypass them; to which must be added that apart from their inherent strength, such posts must also be more or less supported by the front line of the army. If these advantages are not present, such a post will fall to an enemy attack from all sides. It is soon lost, and if you attempt to regain it, you often get involved in unplanned and disadvantageous engagements.

b. Occasionally one is forced to occupy a point that is in front of the line because it would give too much protection to the attacker in his approach. In that case it is a necessary evil.

Saint-Amand proper had no great inherent strength, it could receive almost no support from the front line of the army, and it did not even command this front sufficiently to prevent an attack on Ligny, for instance. Thus there was clearly no reason to occupy the village in accordance with the first consideration. Under the second consideration, it could be linked to the village of Saint-Amand-la-Haye, whose defense became tougher. But Saint-Amand's connection with this village was only at its narrowest end, in the vicinity of the castle, where this castle offered the means to cut the line of defense. With respect to the front between Ligny and la Haye, Saint-Amand did not represent a threat. On the contrary, its location strengthened this front, because if the French had attacked us from there they would have had to deploy at a distance of 800 paces under the fire of our canister rounds. As a matter of fact, the French never advanced from it against the heights. The defense of this village consumed a whole brigade and probably caused no corresponding losses for the French. Its loss produced the adverse impression that we had lost a portion of our terrain.

4. The premature attack against Saint-Amand-le-Hameau and the attempt to mount another one from Ligny were likewise out of harmony with the whole scheme of battle. The defender must naturally incorporate into his defense a certain offensive principle; he must combine resistance with counterattacks. But such a counterattack must take place only when and where it can be done advantageously, e.g., if the enemy's advance has placed him in the midst of our forces or if he has become severely weakened and can barely maintain himself. As a rule, therefore, [such counterattacks are wise] only after his forces have exhausted themselves against our resistance. General Jürgass' attack at Wagnelée against Saint-Amand-le-Hameau obviously came much too early to produce any decisive result at that point. If this general advanced up to the heights of la Haye, as he in fact did, he still had to stop there, and then found himself in a very unfavorable defensive position. But one does not choose the defensive in order to fight under unfavorable conditions. If Wagnelée had been occupied from the very beginning, and strongly provisioned with artillery, the enemy certainly could never have occupied la Haye. Wagnelée would have been a very decisive point, and because of its quite rearward position would have been very troubling to the French commander. But even after la Haye was occupied by the French, it seems that we would have done better to be content with occupying Wagnelée and thus holding the occupiers of la Haye in check. As long as Wagnelée, Bry, and Ligny were in our hands, the enemy could not possibly break out of either of the two villages of Saint-Amand. The whole position seemed instead to be well suited to gain time and inflict terrible losses on the enemy. The moment to break out of Wagnelée would have come only if we could have contemplated achieving a decisive success for the en-

tire battle, in which case the advance should have taken place in greater strength. If, however, the situation was such that a counterattack could not be expected to result in a transformation of the whole battle, then it should have been omitted altogether, for the forces would have been far better employed simply by remaining on the defensive.

General Jagow's attempt to advance out of Ligny is even less justifiable. Even the most favorable outcome of this attack would still have left General Jagow out in the open in the midst of the French divisions, thus in a position that he could not have maintained and where he would have suffered heavy losses.

Our generals are too taken with the idea that it is better to advance than to stand and fire. Each of these actions has its proper place.

5. We consume our troops too quickly in a standing fight. Our officers call for assistance too soon, and it is given them too easily. As a consequence we commit more men than the French without gaining any ground—thus we have more killed and wounded—and we thereby transform fresh masses of troops into burnt-out cinders sooner.

We need not point out here that, with battle plans and all sorts of retrospective accounts in front of us, and with the events behind us, it is very easy to discover the actual causes of failure and, after thoroughly considering all the complexities of events, to highlight those things that can be deemed mistakes. But all of this cannot be done so easily at the time of action. The conduct of war is like movement in a resistant medium, in which uncommon qualities are required to achieve even mediocre results.[42] It is for this reason that in war, more than in any other area, critical analysis exists only to discover the truth, not to sit in judgment.

In considering the above-mentioned mistakes, we must also take into account that the Prussian troops consisted mostly of *Landwehr* who were only in their second campaign; that among them were many new formations from provinces that had never before belonged to the Prussian state, or at least not recently; that the French army, although also newly formed, still consisted of elements that had belonged to the best army in the world; and that Bonaparte was the greatest commander of his time. Under the circumstances, the overall results of Ligny cannot appear out of the ordinary. It is a battle which 78,000 men lost to 75,000 by a very

---

[42] This passage recurs almost verbatim in *On War*, 120, illustrating Clausewitz's concept of "friction."

slight tipping of the scales, after a long struggle, and without any truly glorious results for the victor, since his trophies consisted of only 21 guns and perhaps a few thousand prisoners.

Chapter 34
Bonaparte

1. The simplest way for us to describe Bonaparte's original plan of attack is that, as we have already said, he advanced against Blücher with two thirds of his army (75,000 men) and that he sent one third (some 40,000 men) against Wellington to stop whatever aid might be rushed from there to the Prussian commander. Bonaparte must have calculated that Wellington's force was not a whole army, and that 40,000 men led by a man like Ney would buy him enough time to complete his victory over Blücher. The thought that Ney could participate in [the battle with Blücher] could not yet have occurred to Bonaparte on the 15th or early on the morning of the 16th in Charleroi, because it was based on Blücher's position, which surprised Bonaparte and seems to have given him the idea that if Ney sent a detachment back along the road from Quatre-Bras to Namur, this would make the battle at Ligny much more decisive. This idea is first expressed in the third of the orders we have presented earlier.[43] But the order seems to make cooperation only a secondary consideration—and in the nature of things it could not be anything else, because Bonaparte could not know whether Ney would have a single man to spare. And since the order was written at 2:15, which made it very uncertain whether there would even be time for Ney to do his part, given the three hours' march separating the battlefields, it is impossible to believe that such cooperation was in any way an essential element of Bonaparte's plan. Nor can we believe—as Bonaparte wishes us to—that it was merely an unfortunate accident, a mutilation of his original plan, that the Prussian army was not attacked simultaneously from the front and the rear, which according to Bonaparte would have brought about its complete and unavoidable destruction.

2. Furthermore, the fact that Bonaparte did not try to turn the exposed Prussian right flank and send a column via Wagnelée, but instead

---

43 See chapter 31.

preferred to advance on Ligny with the second column—in fact even made his main thrust in this direction—means that we cannot consider his plan to have been based upon the idea of an attack by Ney into the rear of the Prussians, and then cooperating to cause the destruction of the Prussian army. Rather, the direction of Bonaparte's main thrust was determined by the following factors:

a. As Bonaparte saw the Prussian position, the Prussian army's right flank was at Saint-Amand proper, its center at Ligny, and its left wing at Sombreffe. Saint-Amand-la-Haye appeared to lie to the rear of the right wing. He therefore believed that if he attacked Saint-Amand and had a division march on Saint-Amand-la-Haye, this would already constitute an envelopment of the right wing. He wished to combine this with the attack on the center so that the battle would not be fought in too confined a space, which would have strengthened and prolonged the Prussian resistance. This therefore seems like a very simple and commonplace plan.[44]

b. The attack on Ligny would certainly threaten the Prussian right wing, so one could expect that resistance there would be shaken by it. It was also very possible that part of the right wing would be completely lost as a result.

c. The attack on Ligny threatened the natural line of retreat of the Prussian army, and if they were determined to retain this at all costs, they would suffer heavy losses.

d. Finally, Saint-Amand and Ligny were the nearest possible points of attack for the front line of the French army at Fleurus. A wider envelopment via Wagnelée would have delayed the attack by as much as an hour, but it was already past noon when Bonaparte reconnoitered the Prussian position, so there was not much time to lose.

Thus the reasons for this form of attack seem to be sufficiently motivated by the immediate circumstances, and in war such immediate circumstances have the greatest weight in decision-making.

3. However, if we look at the matter from a more comprehensive point of view, we must first ask ourselves whether it was better for Bonaparte to attack Blücher in such a way as to drive him towards Wellington, or away from him. And we must of course reply that the latter approach would have had a much more decisive impact on the whole campaign.

---

44 This last sentence comes from Clausewitz's original manuscript. For some reason it was not included in the published editions of the work. Halhlweg, *Schriften*, 2:1015.

If Bonaparte had attacked Saint-Amand with his right wing, Wagnelée with his left, and advanced with a third column toward the Brussels highway, then in the event of a defeat the Prussian army would have been obliged to retreat along the Roman road, that is, towards the Meuse. Union with Wellington during the next few days would then have been very uncertain, perhaps impossible.

4. If Bülow had arrived that afternoon, which was possible, and then been employed with Thielmann in an attack from Point-du-Jour, Bonaparte would have been obliged to fight a superior enemy force under the worst possible circumstances, namely with both flanks turned, on the left from Wagnelée, on the right from Point-du-Jour. Since Bülow was expected to come from Liége through Point-du-Jour, this could have been yet another reason for Bonaparte to turn the right flank of the Prussian army.

We do not know whether Bonaparte considered these matters or not, or whether his thinking may also have been influenced by concern that he was not safe from the direction of Brussels despite having detached Ney. If the latter supposition is true, then the form of his attack is sufficiently justified. But if he had no such concerns and organized his attack solely on the basis of the immediate circumstances, one could certainly say that this plan was not entirely worthy of him and also not adequate to his precarious situation.

5. We are completely in the dark about the reasons for the movements of the French 1st Corps. Gamot, Ney's defender, is convinced that Bonaparte himself pulled it over from Frasnes but is unable to produce any proof of this.[45] Bonaparte believes that Ney left the corps behind out of indecisiveness in order to cover his line of communications.[46] It seems almost impossible that Bonaparte could have called for it himself, for in that case how could its appearance have created his fear that the force was English; how could d'Erlon have turned around again; and how would it have been possible that the dispositions and orders given to Vandamme make no mention of this? One could well ask, however, why did Bonaparte, after finding this corps in his vicinity, not use it to envelop Blücher? In all probability because it was too late. He seems to have received the news of the appearance of this corps only at half past five.

---

45 Gamot, *Réfutation*, 19, cited in Hahlweg, *Schriften* 2:1017n.
46 Napoleon, *Mémoires*, 181, cited in ibid.

It was seven p.m. before news was brought him that it was d'Erlon, and an hour would have been required for d'Erlon to receive the order and perhaps another hour before he could show up in the area around Bry.

But all this is only an attempt to explain the matter, and there is no denying that the meager information that exists concerning the movements of this corps gives rise to suspicions against Bonaparte. Gamot names Colonel Laurent as the man who brought the order.[47] Why does this individual not come forward with an explanation? It cannot be out of regard for Ney's memory, for even if Colonel Laurent were to declare that he had carried no order from Bonaparte changing the employment of the 1st Corps, this would not result in much blame being placed on Ney. There is simply no other way to explain this obscurity than to suppose that loyalty and respect for the former emperor have closed the mouth that could speak.

In any event, this useless movement to and fro of 20,000 men, at a time when forces were needed so desperately, is a cardinal error that must always be blamed at least in part upon Bonaparte, even if he had not himself recalled the corps, because in that case the orders given to Marshal Ney must not have been sufficiently clear and precise.

Given all this, it can already be said that even on the 16th Bonaparte was no longer equal to the task that fate had imposed upon him.

Chapter 35
The Action at Quatre Bras

We have already seen how Ney's troops were situated on the morning of the 16th. Ney left his 2nd Corps near Gosselies and instructed General Reille to wait for Bonaparte's orders. He himself hurried to his advanced guard at Frasnes and reconnoitered the enemy, which during the entire morning consisted solely of the greater part of Perponcher's division and two regiments of cavalry, thus around 6-8,000 men.

At eleven o'clock, General Flahaut, Bonaparte's adjutant, came to Gosselies with the order that Ney should advance and attack with his corps. This is probably the order to which Bonaparte refers and which he says

---

[47] Gamot, *Réfutation*, excerpted in Hahlweg, *Schriften* 2:1017n.

was in Ney's hands at 11:30 a.m. By the time the 3rd Division of the 2nd Corps reached Frasnes it was 1 p.m.

At this time, then, Ney was at Frasnes with 3 infantry divisions (of the 2nd Corps) and 3 cavalry divisions (Kellerman and the cavalry of the 2nd Corps), a total of about 23,000 men and 48 guns. He had left the light cavalry of the Guard behind Frasnes, as Bonaparte had specifically ordered this, and the 1st Corps was still on the march.

On the Allied side, Perponcher's division still found itself opposing him alone. At this time the Duke of Wellington was meeting with Blücher. It was only then that he became convinced that the main enemy force stood opposed to Blücher, and it seems that only then did he send the order to the divisions of his reserve, which had been standing at the exit of the Soignies Forest since 10 a.m., to start their movement toward Quatre-Bras. This explains why the first of these divisions—namely Picton's—did not arrive before 5 p.m. It is over 13 miles from Bry to Waterloo, and from there to Quatre-Bras more than nine miles.

The battle itself began at 3 p.m. and can be divided into three main phases.

In the first, Perponcher's division was driven from the terrain it had occupied halfway between Quatre-Bras and Frasnes. It lost four guns in the process and retreated in part into the woods of Bossu.

In the second, Picton's division—which arrived around 5 p.m.—restored the situation, took up a position along the Namur highway, and recaptured the village of Pierremont on its left flank. The Brunswickers arrived a little later and advanced on the road toward Charleroi, where they occupied the sheep farm. Now both sides were nearly balanced, for Wellington was also around 20,000 men strong, but Wellington only had about 1,800 cavalry while Ney had around 4,000.

The fight remained evenly balanced for a few hours. The French retook the village of Pierremont and maintained their hold on the Gemioncourt farm, next to the highway. Ney received Bonaparte's subsequent urgent order to advance, overwhelm his opponent, and then participate in the Battle of Ligny. Indeed, Ney brought his reserve—Jerome's division—into action and made the utmost efforts with his superior cavalry forces to push through to Quatre-Bras along the highway. It was probably around this time that he sent the order to d'Erlon to rush over to him. Upon receiving it around 8 p.m., d'Erlon turned back in the vicinity of Villers-Perwin. The French cavalry's efforts resulted in their taking 6 or 8 guns, overrunning a few battalions, and penetrating partly into Picton's second line, but this did not lead to overall success. Both Piré and Kellerman were repeatedly forced to retreat when fire poured upon them from all sides. Nevertheless, in general the French seemed to gain the advantage in this fight, and they continued to advance farther into the Bossu woods.

Third Phase. Cook's and Alten's divisions, which constituted the right wing of the Prince of Orange's corps, arrived between 7 and 8 p.m. Cook's division was employed on the right wing in the Bossu Wood, Alten's division on the left wing against the village of Pierremont. Both overpowered the enemy and thereby caused a general turn of fortune in the battle. The resistance of the French remained very obstinate, however, and it was not until 10 p.m. that the Allies became masters of the farm of Gemioncourt. Ney retreated to the area in front of Frasnes, where he took up a position. The losses were pretty nearly equal and were estimated at 4-5,000 men on each side.

Chapter 36
Reflections

Bonaparte and all the critics after him have raised a great clamor that Ney was negligent in failing to seize the position at Quatre-Bras before a substantial English force arrived, just as if Quatre-Bras were a fortress whose capture would have completely accomplished the objective of the operation. The expression "position" here is like one of those terms which, if used blindly like an algebraic formula, leads to hollow phrases and empty assertions.

Ney had been ordered to stop everything that Wellington could send to aid the Prussians. He could accomplish this either by defeating the force sent with this purpose or by simply blocking its advance. The former required superiority in numbers, the latter a good position

As for the force that Ney could expect to encounter, it was difficult for him to estimate its size because it consisted not only of what could be assembled against him in the course of the 16th, but also what might be there by noon on the 17th. We have seen that this could have been nearly the whole Anglo-Dutch army, or at least 80,000 men of it. Initially, as Ney could have foreseen, he encountered very few enemy troops at Frasnes and Quatre-Bras, or at least far fewer troops than he had himself. If he had defeated this handful, it would have been a small advantage, but would it also have been such an effective opening that he could view it as a virtual guarantee of complete victory? Impossible! Granted, he could have defeated the part of Perponcher's division that stood before him on the evening of the 15th or early on the morning of the 16th, and then taken up the pursuit. But in that case a commander like Wellington would have adjusted his actions accordingly and chosen a position for the first reserves farther back, so that they could receive the defeated division, and then stand fast to gain time for the other divisions and corps to assemble. The farther Ney advanced, the more he hastened the moment when Wellington would be concentrated. Thus no matter how bold and fortunate Ney might be, the result would always be a great inequality of forces and a very dangerous situation. To reach any other conclusion, we would have to assume that the Duke of Wellington's army would have been literally shattered by Ney, thrown into complete confusion, with individual divisions wiped out and so on. Such a supposition would be completely illusory.

Now one could well say that even if Ney had encountered a far superior enemy on the evening of the 16th or the morning of the 17th, he would still have fully accomplished his objective by preventing this enemy from taking part at Ligny, and that the marshal could then have pulled back. But could Ney know for sure that no such overwhelming force was already facing him at midday on the 16th? Could he be certain—having been ordered to advance with his head down along a single road—that when he finally looked up he would not find himself surrounded and trapped by enemy columns on the right and especially the left? Would he not recall the fate of Vandamme in 1813?[48] What military commander has ever been required to advance 40,000 men up a single road between two enemy forces?

---

48 Clausewitz is referring to French General Dominique Vandamme's crushing defeat at the battle of Kulm on 30 August 1813, when his 32,000-man force, attempting to cut off an apparently beaten Austrian army after the Battle of Dresden, advanced into Bohemia without support and was surrounded by overwhelmingly superior Allied forces. For one version of this incident, see David G. Chandler, *The Campaigns of Napoleon* (New York: Macmillan, 1966), 912.

ON WATERLOO

Based on these reflections, we see that Ney could never have thought that his offensive would rout the enemy forces coming toward him, but rather that his objective could be nothing more than to gain possession of Quatre-Bras and drive back whatever might already be there. This was all that Bonaparte had asked of him. One therefore comes to regard Quatre-Bras as a very good position, by means of which the marshal was able to hold off a superior enemy force throughout the 16th.

But is Quatre-Bras such a position? When the expression "position" is used, this seems to be assumed. But such a supposition is quite arbitrary, for no one has proved it, no one has ever suggested it, indeed no one has even spoken of it. Such an unfounded supposition can have no place in critical analysis.

In order to judge the value of Quatre-Bras as a position for Ney, one must have been there, for positions cannot be judged by maps alone and we do not even have a good map of this place. In general, however, we must say that such crossroads are disadvantageous as a position, because it is not possible to have a line of retreat perpendicular to the front. But even supposing that Quatre-Bras was a very good position, it certainly was never a strong one, and as Ney had no time to establish himself in it, he could not expect to gain much advantage from it in attempting to hold off a far superior enemy force.

Bonaparte had ordered Marshal Ney to Quatre-Bras because the two main roads met there, and therefore the road from Brussels to Namur—that is, from Wellington to the Prussians—would be cut. Nothing was more natural than these orders, and if Marshal Ney could have carried them out without danger, he would have been wrong to have failed to do so. But since Ney's appearance near Frasnes prevented Wellington from going to the assistance of the Prussians via the Namur highway in any case, Ney's failure to capture the crossroads was of no consequence. Indeed, in view of the reflections we have made here, one could go so far as to say that, no matter what Ney had done on the evening of the 15th or the morning of the 16th, the events brought about by or because of him either could not have occurred much differently than they did, or would have turned out much worse for the French.

Ney completely accomplished his objective of preventing Wellington from providing assistance [to Blücher]. The idea that Ney could contribute to the battle of Ligny occurred to Bonaparte only much later, namely after he had reconnoitered Blücher's position, and when he had not yet heard from Ney about a considerable enemy force. But by then it was too late to do anything. If Bonaparte had had this idea on the evening of the 15th, it would have been foolish to have made Ney's force so strong. Instead Bonaparte should have sent a corps down the Roman road to attack Blücher in the rear. Making Ney strong at first and then weakening him later was the opposite of what was required, for at the beginning he could just as well have been weak, but with every hour that passed the number of enemy troops opposing him increased.

The whole outcry against Ney is merely an attempt by Bonaparte to make his plans appear more brilliant and splendid than they really were at the time of execution. His intentions were far simpler and more commonplace, and it was impossible for the marshal to have acted on a concept that was developed only after the events.

Admittedly, Ney could easily have driven Perponcher back early in the morning and stood at Quatre-Bras; admittedly he could even have sent an entire corps against the Prussian right flank via the Namur highway, without having the events at Quatre-Bras turn out much worse for him. But it is only now that we can all see that he could have done this, after considering all of the random circumstances that could not have been foreseen back then.

Chapter 37
Movements on 17 June: Blücher

The retreat of the Prussian 1st and 2nd Corps through Tilly toward Wavre took place partly on the night of the 16th and partly on the morning of the 17th. That of the 3rd Corps, which did not begin until around four or five in the morning, was directed toward Gembloux and from there to Wavre.

The 1st and 2nd Corps reached Wavre at midday on the 17th and then took their positions on both sides of the Dyle, having left part of their cavalry as a rear guard a few hours' march behind them. The 3rd Corps remained at Gembloux until 2 p.m. and then proceeded towards Wavre, where it did not arrive until evening. The 4th Corps spent the night of the 16th in Haute- and Bas-Bodecé, two hours' march behind

Gembloux, and then during the 17th went to Dion-le-Mont, where it deployed to receive the other corps.

While the Prussian corps were carrying out the better part of these movements (that is to say, until noon of the 17th), the French were doing very little in the way of a pursuit.

During the night of the 16th, Bonaparte ordered General Pajol to conduct the initial pursuit of Blücher, using his cavalry corps and Teste's division from the 6th Corps. This general set out on the morning of the 17th and sought the Prussians first on the road to Namur. It is impossible to understand how the French failed to see that the Prussian 3rd Corps had [in fact] taken the road to Gembloux, since it did not move off until broad daylight. Even more incomprehensible is the French belief that Blücher would move his entire army toward Namur. This impression may have been prompted to some extent by the actions of a Prussian battery from the 2nd Corps, which was just arriving from Namur when it learned that the battle was lost, attempted to turn back, but was captured on the road. But the main source of this absurd idea was Grouchy, from whom Pajol had received his detailed instructions. Grouchy himself was also supposed to pursue the Prussians, but because his troops definitely needed a few hours of rest, Bonaparte did not rush to send him out. Instead, he took him to the battlefield on the morning of the 17th and did not release him until noon. Grouchy was given Gérard's and Vandamme's corps, Teste's division from the 6th Corps, Exelmans' cavalry corps, and half of Pajol's, which together made a force of 35,000 men.

As we have said, Pajol was put in motion early. Exelmans was sent on the road to Gembloux somewhat later, but Gérard's and Vandamme's two corps were still in their old bivouacs near Ligny and Saint-Amand at 3 p.m. It would be evening before Grouchy was able to combine them at Point-du-Jour.

Bonaparte's intention was to have Grouchy get Marshal Blücher moving so fast that he would not be able to think of supporting Wellington right away. Bonaparte himself intended to turn toward Ney with the remaining 30,000 men, thus uniting a force of around 70,000 men against Wellington, and then achieve a second victory over him.

Since Bonaparte needed to let his troops rest until noon on the 17th, he could not confront Wellington before the evening of the 17th, and thus could not commence this second battle before the 18th.

THE CAMPAIGN OF 1815

Bonaparte supposedly instructed Marshal Grouchy to stay between Blücher and the road from Namur to Brussels, for the second battle had to take place on this road and the possibility of Grouchy participating in the battle was thereby greatest. But there is no trace of any such order except in the scarcely credible account by Bonaparte himself[49] and by those who have based their accounts on his. The account that Grouchy gives concerning the movements on the 17th has too much the character of simple truth not to be believed.[50] According to this account, Bonaparte's instructions dealt only in general terms with the pursuit of Blücher, and were expressed very vaguely. At 10 a.m. on the morning of the 18th Bonaparte finally did give Grouchy such an order, but how could it have any effect? It reached Grouchy only when he was already at Wavre.

Bonaparte never thought that Blücher would move towards Wavre in order to unite with Wellington, as his memoirs would have us believe. Instead he assumed that Blücher would above all seek to unite with his 4th Corps and then head toward the Meuse. He thought that 35,000 men under a resolute commander would give the Prussians no rest for several days, and that he would therefore be able to fight his battle with Wellington without having to fear anything from them.

It is truly strange that on the morning of the 17th the Prussian army was not pursued or sought at all in the direction of Tilly and Gentinnes, where two corps had gone, but only in the direction of Gembloux, where just one corps had gone, and in the direction of Namur, where none had gone. Virtually the only explanation for this astonishing fact is that when Bonaparte tasked Marshal Grouchy with the pursuit, his two cavalry corps were [already] facing toward Gembloux, because they had been fighting Thielmann all day. If Bonaparte had ordered the Guard cavalry and the 3rd Corps to conduct the pursuit, they would have picked up the trail more easily. The casual way in which Bonaparte did everything prevented him from giving Grouchy more detailed instructions. Furthermore, Bonaparte himself seems to have held so firmly to the idea

---

49 Napoleon, *Mémoires*, 115-117, cited in Hahlweg, *Schriften*, 2:1025n.
50 *Observations sur la relation de la campagne de 1815, publiée par le général Gourgaud: et réfutation de quelques-unes des assertions d'autres écrits rélatifs à la bataille de Waterloo, par le Comte de Grouchy* (Paris, 1819), 5ff, cited in Hahlweg, *Schriften*, 2:1025n. Grouchy's account was published in English as *Doubts of the Authenticity of the Historical Memoirs Attributed to Napoleon and First Refutation of Some of the Assertions They Contain* (Philadelphia: J. F. Hurtel, 1820).

ON WATERLOO

that Blücher had to go to the Meuse that no thought was given to any other direction than Gembloux and the Roman road. At any rate we can see that a pursuit along the two roads to Gembloux and Namur must have been Bonaparte's intention, because they are mentioned in a message written by Marshal Soult to Ney from Fleurus on the 17th and published by Gamot.[51] These were obviously instructions to harass the Prussian army on its way to the Meuse, rather than to block its way toward Wellington. If Bonaparte had thought that Blücher was going to Wavre, it would have been more natural for him to send a strong force there via the left bank of the Dyle.

There is still too little explanation for Pajol's movements—first in the direction of Namur, then towards Saint-Denis between Namur and Gembloux, and then back toward Mazy. Whether Grouchy or Bonaparte ordered this strange movement remains uncertain, but the result was that after wandering around aimlessly on the 17th,[52] Pajol and his corps, plus Teste's division, found themselves still near Mazy in the evening, thus more or less back on the battlefield of Ligny.

Even Grouchy with the 3rd and 4th Corps was only able to reach the area around Gembloux by 10 p.m.,[53] where they had to spend the night, while Exelmans was sent forward to Sart-à-Walhain. But even this corps then sought quarters for the night and had only two regiments in front as an advance guard.

The overall result of this day on the French side was that for all practical purposes they failed to pursue the Prussian army. Blücher was able to reach Wavre unimpeded and unite his corps there on the evening of the 17th.

While this seems to contrast strongly with previous French practices, we must also carefully consider the differing situations. The extraordinarily energetic pursuits that brought Bonaparte such spectacular results in his earlier campaigns were simply a matter of pushing far superior forces forward in pursuit of a totally defeated enemy. But now he had to turn his main force—in particular his freshest corps—against a new op-

---

51 Gamot, *Réfutation*, 20; excerpted in Hahlweg, *Schriften* 2:1017n.
52 Clausewitz's manuscript and the 1835 edition of his works both have the 16th, which must be wrong. The error was corrected in the 1862 edition but was resurrected in Hahlweg, *Schriften*, 2:1027.
53 The 1862 edition contains the following footnote: "Because both corps had to use a single road."

ponent who had not yet been defeated. The troops who were supposed to conduct the pursuit were the 3rd and 4th Corps, precisely the ones who had been engaged in a very bloody struggle until ten o'clock in the evening, and now needed some time to get themselves back into order, eat their rations, and replenish their ammunition. To be sure, the cavalry corps had not suffered and would therefore have been able to press the Prussian rear guard quickly. That they did not do so may well have been a mistake, but cavalry alone could not have produced results like those achieved in earlier victories by a general advance of the French army, because the terrain is too broken for cavalry alone to achieve much.[54]

Blücher had abandoned his natural line of retreat in order to maintain contact with the Duke of Wellington, because he felt that the first battle had to some extent been bungled and was therefore determined to fight a second. So he informed the Duke of Wellington that he would come to the duke's assistance with his entire army.

Blücher, who did not know what had become of the French, had naturally assumed, because his rear guard had not been pressed at all, that Bonaparte must have turned his entire force against Wellington. He therefore believed that he had to leave only a few troops at the defile of Wavre and could advance with virtually his whole force to join with the duke.

This decision by Blücher is unquestionably worthy of the highest praise. Ignoring all the false courses of action that traditional practices and misplaced prudence might have suggested in such a case, he followed his common sense and decided to turn toward Wellington on the 18th, preferring to abandon his own line of communications rather than adopt half-measures. The battle he had lost had not been a rout. It had reduced the size of his force by only about one-sixth, and with nearly 100,000 men he could undoubtedly turn the battle that the Duke of Wellington was confronting into a victory. In addition, he felt the need to wash out the stain that his military reputation had received on the 16th. He also wished to achieve the renown that comes from standing by an ally, even supporting him beyond all expectations, even though on the day before, and contrary to expectations, that ally had not been able to

---

54 Given the detail with which Clausewitz analyses this phase of the campaign, it is surprising that he fails to note that, had the cavalry alone pursued the Prussians immediately, it would at least have been able to identify the direction of its retreat correctly.

provide support [to him]. There can be no greater motivation than this, resulting as it did from both reason and emotion.

We will describe Blücher's movements on the 18th when we consider his role in the battle of Belle Alliance.

Chapter 38
Wellington on 17 and 18 June

On the evening of the 16th, Wellington had assembled the Prince of Orange's corps and the reserve at Quatre-Bras, with the exception of Chassée's division and two Dutch cavalry brigades, which remained at Nivelles. During the night and on the morning of the 17th, Clinton's division and a brigade of Colville's division arrived from Lord Hill's corps, which had constituted the right wing. The remainder of Hill's corps assembled at Hal under Prince Frederick of the Netherlands.

Wellington therefore had an army of about 70,000 men near Quatre-Bras and Nivelles on the morning of the 17th. He learned of Blücher's retreat around 7 a.m., let his troops cook a meal, and at 10 a.m. began his retreat toward the position of Mont-Saint-Jean in front of the Soignies Forest, where he had found a good battlefield and had resolved to give battle if Blücher could come to his assistance with two corps, thus with about 50,000 men.

Ney was supposed to advance in the early part of the morning of the 17th against Wellington's rear guard, but because the duke did not leave his position before 10 a.m., Ney was not able to advance. The French did not immediately notice his retreat because the duke left his numerous cavalry (7-8,000 horsemen) behind, and Ney therefore remained quietly in his bivouac near Frasnes until 1 p.m.

By midday Bonaparte had put the following forces into motion on the road from Namur to Quatre-Bras: the 6th Corps, the Guard, Milhaud's cavalry corps, a division of Pajol's corps, and Domon's cavalry division belonging to the 3rd Corps. This was his whole force, except for Girard's division, which according to Bonaparte was deliberately left behind at Saint-Amand because it had suffered too heavily, but which must actually have been forgotten, which is all the more understandable because this division belonged to the 2nd Corps.[55] None of the other corps commanders concerned themselves with it, and General Girard, who had commanded it, had been severely wounded. To have left it behind intentionally would certainly have been an even greater mistake than to have forgotten it.

Around two o'clock this mass of troops advanced from the area around the village of Marbais on the road to Quatre-Bras, and Marshal Ney was brusquely ordered to advance at the same time. The English cavalry began their withdrawal, the two French columns came together on the Brussels road and continued the pursuit until they encountered strong resistance towards evening at Mont-Saint-Jean, and Bonaparte convinced himself that he had the English army in front of him. Torrents of rain and extraordinarily bad road conditions, both on and off the highway, had delayed the march and exhausted the troops, so there could be no thought of giving battle on that day. Bonaparte placed his army in front of Plancenoit and established his headquarters in Caillou.

Chapter 39
The Battle of Belle Alliance
Wellington's Deployment

By the morning of the 18th Wellington had assembled his army—except for the 19,000 men posted at Hal—at Mont-Saint-Jean, giving him a strength of 68,000 men.

When the battle began, his deployment was such that the right wing lay on the road to Nivelles, his center behind La-Haye-Sainte, and his left behind the farms of Smohain, Papelotte, and La-Haye.

The ground between the two roads sloped gently downward, and to the left of the Namur road a sunken way also hindered any approach to the front. The two wings basically had no real anchors, but the right was somewhat protected by the villages of Merbes, Braine, and Braine-l'Alleud, and the left by the low ground near Frischermont. About an hour's march behind the front was the Soignies Forest, which Bonaparte and many armchair critics considered to be a deathtrap for Wellington's army in the event he lost the battle, but which in reality must not have

---

55 The 2nd Corps was part of Ney's force, and thus far away from the Ligny battlefield.

been as bad as they imagined, since otherwise such a careful commander as Wellington would not have accepted having it so close to his rear. A forest traversed by many paths actually seems to offer a lot of protection for a defeated army.

In general the duke's deployment was such that the front was about 5,000 paces long, with 30 battalions of infantry in the first line, some 13 battalions in the second line, sixty squadrons of cavalry in the third and fourth lines. In addition another 38 battalions and 33 squadrons were placed at other points, either farther to the rear or on the flanks, and could be considered as reserves. Thus one could say that the deployment was exceptionally deep.

In front of the lines lay three strong points: the farmhouse of Hougoumont 1,000 paces in front of the right wing, La-Haye-Sainte 500 paces in front of the center on the main road, and La Haye 1,000 paces in front of the left wing. All three were occupied by infantry and more or less prepared for defense.

Wellington expected to be attacked by the whole French army, because it was possible that Bonaparte had left only some cavalry opposed to Blücher. He then would have had to face around 100,000 men with just 68,000, and thus had to count on Blücher's support, which had already been promised on the 17th. For Wellington everything came down to holding out on the defensive until Blücher arrived. Blücher's assistance would then develop independently, in part by supporting the Allied left wing and in part by falling on the right flank of the French. Blücher's support was definitely offensive in nature, which made it all the more appropriate that Wellington should limit himself to the defensive and thereby seek to take full advantage of the terrain. Wavre is roughly nine miles from Wellington's battlefield. From the moment that the Duke of Wellington saw the enemy appear in his front until Blücher could arrive, perhaps six to eight hours might pass, unless Blücher had not already begun his march earlier. A battle against 70,000 men cannot be initiated, fought out, and decided in such a period of time, however, so there was no reason to fear that Wellington could be beaten before Blücher arrived.

Chapter 40
Bonaparte's Plan of Attack

Bonaparte, as he give us to understand, allowed his corps to leave their bivouacs rather late only in order to give the rain-soaked ground some time to dry out a bit. He then lost several hours forming them up in front of Belle Alliance, about 2,500 paces from the English position and parallel to it, in two lines of infantry and a third and fourth of cavalry. It was not until 11 a.m. that all this was accomplished.

There was something strange about this parade formation, the image of which seems to be one of Bonaparte's most pleasing memories. It was extremely uncharacteristic, and nothing like it happens in any of Bonaparte's other battles. It was also completely unnecessary, for afterwards the corps had to form into columns again in order to attack. Instead of concealing his forces from the enemy as much as possible, as is usually done in order to approach undetected, he had them deploy as broadly and systematically as possible, as if all that was required was a show of force. We can only think of three reasons for this: either he wished to bolster the courage of his own soldiers, or he wanted to awe his opponents, or it was an extravagant piece of folly by a mind that was no longer completely balanced.

Whether Bonaparte was intending to attack all along the line, break through in the center, or push in one of the wings, is something that cannot be clearly discerned, either from the measures that were actually taken or from the direction that the fighting took, and even less from what Bonaparte himself says regarding his plan.

Judging by the distribution of forces and the initial advance, it was purely an attack all along the line; judging by the main efforts made during the course of the action, the intent was to break through the center. But the latter seems to have been inspired more by the needs of the moment than by a clear plan, so as far as the preparations for the attack go we have only the following atypical aspects to offer:

The 2nd Corps (Reille), supported by Kellerman's cavalry corps and Guyot's Guard cavalry division—in all, three infantry divisions and four of cavalry—attacked the enemy's right wing. Two divisions of the 1st Corps (d'Erlon), supported by the 6th (Lobau), which had only two divisions present, plus two divisions of cavalry, Milhaud's cavalry corps, and a division of the Guard cavalry—in all, four divisions of infantry and five divisions of cavalry—were directed against the center. Two infantry divisions of the 1st Corps and a cavalry division were intended for the attack on the enemy's left wing. The infantry of the Guard remained in reserve in the rear of the center.

No other systematic concept for this attack can be found, at least none that makes any sense, for what Bonaparte says himself about his intention to attack Wellington's left wing is self-contradictory, and does not correspond to the actual course of events in the battle, as we shall see later.[56]

The dispositions that Bonaparte made demonstrate that the thought that Blücher would arrive and participate in the battle had never crossed his mind. Instead, as at Ligny, he was counting to some degree on assistance from his own detached wing. He had given Grouchy orders along those lines, as he had done with Ney, but in both cases the orders were too imprecise, too late, and too little in accord with the actual space, time, and circumstances. We will discuss this later, and note it here only because it is somewhat related to the battle plan. But truly only somewhat, because Bonaparte does not appear to have counted very much on such assistance.

Chapter 41
Key Events of the Battle: Wellington's Defense

The battle appears to have been divided into two separate acts: Wellington's resistance and the attack of the Prussians on the French right flank. The battle—that is to say Wellington's resistance—began at noon; the participation of the Prussians began at half past four; and the battle ended with nightfall, thus between 8 and 9 p.m.

It seems to us that the French attack on Wellington's position can only be presented in the following manner.

---

56 Napoleon wrote in his Memoirs, page 135, that he "had preferred to turn the enemy's left first, rather than his right, in order to cut them off from the Prussians, who were at Wavre." He added that he also did not want to push the English toward the Prussians—which would have been the case had he attacked the right wing—but away from them, toward the sea. He also considered the English left to be their weakest side and noted that he was expecting some of Grouchy's forces to arrive on this side of the battlefield.

1. At noon, Reille's corps attacks the farm of Hougoumont with its left flank division (Jerome's), while the other two remain in reserve. The French gain control of the small woods but not the buildings. This strong point is supported by the English guards from Cook's division of Wellington's right wing. Foy's division (the center one of the French 2nd Corps), is employed in supporting the attack, but the French never gain control of this place, and a steady firefight continues throughout the day. It almost seems as if this was only supposed to be a feint, as if Reille was conserving his forces. At any rate, the corps' right wing division remained in reserve and was later utilized in the center.

This attack accomplished nothing except to absorb the right wing of both lines of the English army, as well as the Brunswickers, who were brought up in support.

2. It was not until two hours later, after Bonaparte had already become aware of Bülow's approach and had sent the 6th Corps and the two cavalry divisions of Subervie and Domon to advance against the Prussians, that d'Erlon's corps began its attack at around 2 p.m. The main thrust was made by three divisions against La-Haye-Sainte and that part of the Allied center that was to the right of the main road (from the French perspective) and had the sunken road in front of it. The 4th Division advanced to attack La-Haye, Papelotte, and Smohain. This last attack was of quite a different nature from that on the center; we will therefore separate it from the other and consider it first.

The villages [just mentioned] were occupied only by light infantry from Perponcher's 2nd [Netherlands] Brigade, which formed the extreme left wing of Wellington's army. They lost this position at some point during the battle—there is no agreement precisely when—but it is certain that the French never advanced from there against the main Allied line and were content with a continuous firefight. They retained possession of these villages (which, however, they appear to have occupied only lightly) until Bülow advanced past Frischermont, detached troops from his right wing against them, and drove them out. However, since d'Erlon's right-wing division still had most of its strength intact, it regained possession of this point and held it for a couple of hours, that is, until between 6 and 7 p.m., when General Ziethen arrived at the left wing of the English army and advanced against that area.

Thus more or less the same situation occurred at this advanced post on the English left wing as on the right. What happened was more like a demonstration, or at most a supporting attack to cover the center's flank, rather than a serious attack.

3. As we have already said, in the center the attack was made by d'Erlon's three remaining divisions. Because the 6th Corps and Subervie's and Domon's cavalry divisions had already been deployed against Bülow, the infantry in the French center consisted solely of those three divisions, and there was nothing left in reserve but the cavalry corps and the Guard.

By all accounts, d'Erlon's first attack was very violent and precipitous. Thus the second column, which fell upon the 1st Brigade of Perponcher's division, actually penetrated it but naturally had to fall back when confronted by the fire of the reserves and the charges of the English cavalry. Pursued by two English cavalry brigades under Lord Ponsonby and Vandeleur, this column suffered a rather severe defeat, which also extended to the third column. The French cavalry under Milhaut then forced the English cavalry back in turn and with some loss, as one may well imagine.

This first attack thus appears to have been almost a kind of skirmish, which on the whole degraded the French situation more than it advanced it. As the stage had not been set for this action, that is to say the forces opposed to each other were not yet exhausted, any success could not be decisive. D'Erlon's left-wing column, which advanced against La-Haye-Sainte, appears to have been fought to a standstill. This advanced post was reinforced by the English army and the action continued, with both the fortunes of war and possession of the post itself going back and forth.[57]

D'Erlon assembled his forces again, and the engagement continued until between 5 and 6 p.m. without any overall success and without any noteworthy events. One must imagine it as a violent struggle of artil-

---

[57] In reality La-Haye-Sainte fell to the French only once, after a series of heavy assaults. The timing of its fall remains one of the mysteries of the battle. Many English accounts place the fall of La-Haye-Sainte at around 5:30 p.m., but Dutch engineer W. B. Craan, who prepared a highly detailed map of the battle based on interviews with participants in 1815-1816, wrote that the farm fell much earlier, at 3 p.m. See Arthur Gore, *An Historical Account of the Battle of Waterloo Fought on the 18th June, 1815 ... Intended to Explain and Elucidate the Topographical Plan Executed by W. B Craan* (Brussels: T. Parkin, 1817), 41. The differing accounts may have caused Clausewitz's impression that the place changed hands repeatedly.

lery and skirmishers, interspersed with individual attacks of battalion columns or battalions in line. From time to time the cavalry stepped in, cutting down individual battalions that sought to regain possession of La-Haye-Sainte. In this manner three Allied battalions were lost, and the French cavalry advanced up to the English positions but was always obliged to retire again with losses.

After the forces had worn each other down in this manner, during a struggle lasting three or four hours, the Prussians appeared on the field of battle and deployed out of the Paris woods. Ney now sought to gain victory against Wellington through the use of cavalry. Since a sunken way to the right of the Namur road prevented the employment of cavalry there, he tried to force his way through on the left of the road using Milhaud's cuirassiers and the Guard cavalry division commanded by Lefebvre-Desnouettes. More than once they reached the ridge that formed the position of the first English line but were obliged each time to retire to regroup in the valley. As these forces had not achieved their objectives, the cuirassier corps of Kellerman and the other cavalry division of the Guard, commanded by Guyot, were employed in the same way, that is, to support the others. Around this time Bachelu's division from the 2nd Corps must have also been drawn into the engagement. The more the action expanded into the French rear through Bülow's advance, the more Ney threw in everything he had in a last-ditch effort to break through the front. Now the whole mass of the French army was involved in the battle, except for the Guard infantry, and fighting continued another two hours without any real result, until around 7 p.m. In this action the opposing forces grew increasingly exhausted, and the consensus seems to be that Wellington could hardly have defended himself from further French efforts, and that he was about to lose control of the battlefield.

This opinion requires closer analysis, however. Around 5 or 6 p.m. Wellington probably felt so weakened that, when he thought of the Guard standing in reserve and making a decisive thrust against him, without being turned away by the Prussians, he may have considered himself too weak, and the whole situation in danger. But if you set aside the Guard and consider only the troops engaged with each other at six p.m., it would appear that the scales of victory were tipping more toward Lord Wellington than toward the French. Even if we concede that the Allied army was noticeably more weakened because it was not composed of such good troops as the French, we still must not forget that Wellington had 68,000 men, while the portion of the French army which was engaged with him numbered only about 45,000.[58] Furthermore, it seems that the French had already employed all of their cavalry and that their infantry reserves were completely exhausted. If we recall the boundless confusion into which they [would all be] thrown a few hours later, there can be no doubt of this. On the other hand, Lord Wellington still appears to have had many troops that had either not been engaged at all, or only slightly, as for example Chassée's division, the 10th British Brigade (marked M on Map 2, p.146 below), Collaert's cavalry division, etc.

We may therefore consider this violent struggle in the center to be a final, weary grappling of combatants who had been driven to such a state of exhaustion that a decisive blow would be all the more decisive, such that the defeated side would not be able to rally again. This decisive blow resulted from the attack of the Prussians.

But before we proceed to this subject, one last act of desperation in the center must be mentioned. Bülow was victorious, Plancenoit was lost, and the mass of Prussian troops on that side was constantly growing. Half of the Guard had already been employed against them and still there was no prospect of defeating them. At that moment, Bonaparte in desperation decided to play his last card in order to break through Wellington's center. He led the remainder of the Guard forward onto the main road towards La-Haye-Sainte and the enemy's position. Four battalions of the Guard made a bloody assault, but all in vain. Ziethen's advance had completely driven in the French right wing, the four Guard battalions were forced to retreat, and the other eight could not stem the tide of flight and confusion. Thus it happened that the whole army disintegrated to its very core, that it was destroyed as a fighting force, and that Bonaparte left the battlefield more or less alone.

---

58 Here Clausewitz is referring to the fact that Napoleon had already been forced to divert a substantial portion of his original force of around 70,000 men to face the growing Prussian threat to his right flank, an issue that his account has not yet addressed.

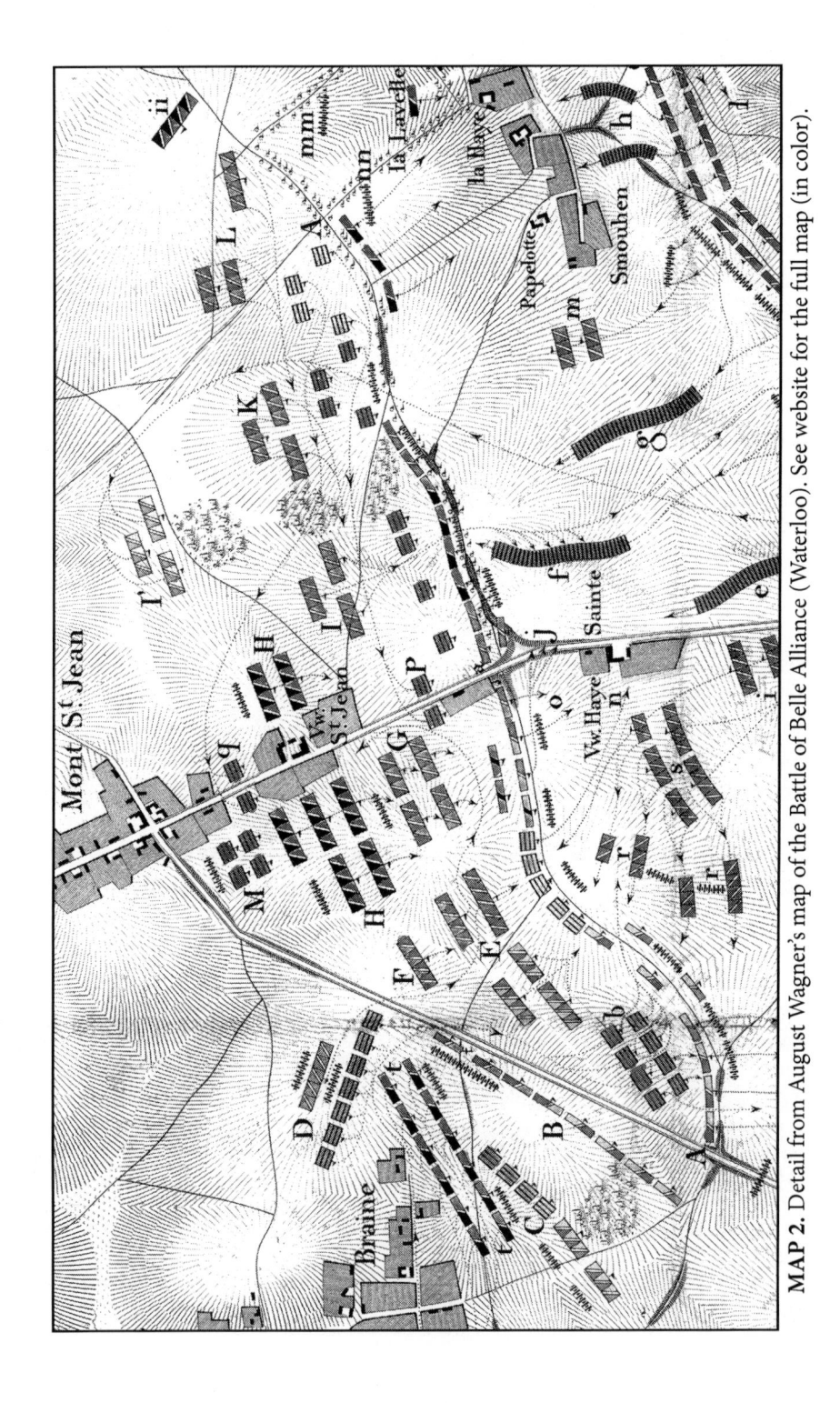

MAP 2. Detail from August Wagner's map of the Battle of Belle Alliance (Waterloo). See website for the full map (in color).

ON WATERLOO

Chapter 42
The Attack of the Prussians

When Blücher saw that his corps were in no way being harassed or pursued during their retreat on the night of the 16th and on the 17th, he naturally assumed that Bonaparte had turned his whole force against Wellington. Blücher therefore decided to leave only a few battalions behind in Wavre and to hasten to help Wellington, who wanted to fight a battle [south] of the Soignies Forest. These arrangements between the two commanders were made on the 17th, and on the morning of the 18th Blücher was able to put his force in motion. The 4th Corps was to begin the march.[59] It left its bivouac at seven o'clock in the morning, went through Wavre to Saint Lambert, which it reached at noon, and concentrated there. Apparently it was already noticed in this position by the French.

The 2nd Corps was to follow the 4th Corps, and both were ordered to advance against the French right flank, that is towards Plancenoit, which would greatly endanger the French line of retreat. The 1st Corps was to march via Ohain towards the Duke of Wellington's left wing, because the duke was concerned that this flank could be turned and had expressly requested this.

The 3rd Corps was to form the rear guard, occupy Wavre with several battalions and, if no substantial enemy force appeared, make its way towards Couture, thus also towards Plancenoit. Should the enemy appear in strength at Wavre, however, the 3rd Corps was to take up a position there to stop him.

In this manner about 20,000 men provided direct support to the English left wing and 70,000 appeared on the enemy's right flank and rear. The whole affair could not have been arranged more simply, naturally, and practically. The only possible criticism is that the 1st Corps, which had bivouacked near Bierge, was sent towards Saint-Lambert, while on the other hand the 2nd Corps, which first had to cross the Dyle, was sent to Ohain. This caused the columns to cross and led to delay.

---

59 Although the Prussian 4th Corps, commanded by General von Bülow, was bivouacked farthest away from the Waterloo battlefield on the night of 17 June 1815, placing it at the head of the Prussian advance made considerable military sense. The 4th Corps had not participated in the Battle of Ligny and was therefore the strongest Prussian corps in terms of manpower and ammunition supplies.

Various unforeseen circumstances meant that the overall march was so slow that the 4th Corps arrived at Frischermont only at 3 p.m., even though it had to go only about 9 miles. Several defiles, a fire at Wavre, repeated concentrations, and very poor roads fully explain this loss of time.

Because it followed the 4th Corps, the 2nd Corps naturally arrived on the field of battle several hours later. Due to other unforeseen circumstances, however, the 1st Corps arrived on the duke's left wing later still, in fact only around 6 p.m.

One could say that Blücher arrived too late, not because of the way things actually turned out, but rather in view of the mission. If Bonaparte had attacked in the morning, the battle would probably have been decided by the time the Prussians arrived. In that case an attack by Blücher—while not impossible or useless—would certainly have been much less certain of success. But we must not forget that if Bonaparte had attacked earlier, everything on Blücher's side would have been speeded up. Most of the missed opportunities that may have occurred took place before noon, before a single cannon shot had been fired at Wellington. If Wellington had already been under heavy fire at 8 or 9 a.m., Blücher's first troops would possibly have reached the field by noon or 1 p.m.

The 3rd Corps was likewise in the process of starting its march when its rear guard, which was still on the other side of the Dyle, came under pressure from a formidable enemy force, and considerable masses of cavalry showed themselves. For the time being, therefore, this corps occupied a position behind the Dyle to await further events.

The French claim that they had already observed Bülow's approach and his first position around Saint-Lambert at midday. At this time—which was before d'Erlon's attack—Bonaparte ordered the 6th Corps and Subervie's and Domon's cavalry divisions, which had stood in reserve behind the center, to march in the direction of Saint-Lambert and take up a hook-shaped position approximately in line with his right wing. There is no explanation of whether or not this position had any tactical advantages, and map study alone cannot be conclusive. But if we do rely on this, then it would have been more advantageous if these troops had been placed farther forward, between Frischermont and Pajeau, anchoring their flanks in these villages.[60]

Bülow had reached the woods of Frischermont with his first two brigades, the 15th and 16th, around 3 p.m. and had taken up a covered position which, however, could not and in fact did not conceal his presence from the French. He waited there for the arrival of his remaining brigades. But when Field Marshal Blücher saw that the French were pressing very strongly against the English center, and feared that they might penetrate it, he ordered General Bülow to attack the enemy's 6th Corps with his two brigades and the reserve cavalry. This happened at half past four; the two other brigades followed soon after as reserves for the 15th and 16th. The enemy's initial resistance was not great, on account of Bülow's numerical superiority and the minimal advantages offered by the terrain, and the 12,000 men under Lobau were obliged to make a fighting withdrawal in the direction of Belle Alliance. General Bülow then received the order to incline his attack further to the left, in order to reach the village of Plancenoit and make it the objective of his attack. But Bülow's right wing had already become engaged with the enemy near the village of Smohain, so the 4th Corps' position became rather overextended, robbing the attack on Plancenoit of the strength which it otherwise could have had.

For his part, Bonaparte sent the division of the Young Guard to reinforce General Lobau as soon as he saw that Lobau was being forced to retreat towards the main road. The action now became a standoff because General Bülow could not advance further until he gained possession of Plancenoit. A long contest for the possession of this village ensued, with success going back and forth. Since the other two divisions of the French

---

60 Belgian historian Bernard Coppens believes that Napoleon did not react this early to news of the Prussians—or possibly did not even receive it this early—and thus took no measures to protect his right flank. Contrary to Napoleon's claims that he sent the 6th Corps out to guard this flank, Coppens argues that the 6th Corps was already on the right side of the French line, behind the 1st Corps, and simply turned to face the Prussians when their attack began late in the afternoon. He provides French and Prussian eyewitness accounts in support of this allegation. He also shows that Napoleon's initial account of the battle in 1815 did have the 6th Corps in such a location. By 1821, however, he had placed their starting position much farther to the west to account for the fact that they were only on the right edge of the French line when the Prussians began their attack. Bernard Coppens and Patrice Courcelle, *La Papelotte*, series Waterloo 1815, Les Carnets de la Campagne, no. 4 (Brussels: Tondeur Diffusion, 2000), 11-12, 67-71.

Guard stood close behind the village and gradually supported it with four battalions, it is easy to understand the protracted uncertainty about the results at this place, with the tide not turning in our favor until the 2nd Corps moved up and directed part of its strength against the village, whereby it fell into our hands for good. This must have been between 7 and 8 p.m.

During this struggle for Plancenoit, the French cavalry masses made their efforts against the English center, and from the other side General Ziethen arrived and advanced against the French right wing. Finally, towards 8 p.m. came the desperate gamble by the last twelve battalions of the Guard, attempting to decide the battle against Wellington. It would be very interesting to know if the Prussians were already firmly in possession of Plancenoit when Bonaparte marched off with these last reserves, throwing them into the very jaws of destruction. If that was the case, his conduct would appear even more to be that of a desperate gambler indifferent to all rational calculation.

Chapter 44[61]
Combat at Wavre on the 18th and 19th: Grouchy's March

We have already seen that Grouchy did not arrive in Gembloux with his two corps until late in the evening, and Pajol's cavalry corps and Teste's division even spent the night at Mazy. A heavy rainstorm had soaked the roads traversing the rich farm land and thus greatly impeded the march. It also hindered an early start. Although Marshal Grouchy says in his defense that he started the march at sunrise, Maréchal de Camp Berton, who was with the corps, states quite definitely that Exelmans' [cavalry] corps did not set off before 8 a.m. and the infantry corps began to march only between 9 and 10 a.m.[62] The truth must lie somewhere in between. The 3rd Corps, which led the way, arrived in front of the Prussian rear guard at Wavre around 2 p.m.; since it had marched fourteen miles from Gembloux to Wavre, it must have left around 6 or 7 a.m. The 4th Corps' [13th] division, under Vichery, arrived a few hours later, but

---

61 There is no chapter 43 in Clausewitz's manuscript, nor in any published version of his text.
62 Jean-Baptiste Berton, *Précis histoirique, militaire et critique des batailles de Fleurus et de Waterloo dans la campagne de Flandres en juin 1815* (Paris: 1818), 54f; cited in Hahlweg, *Schriften*, 2:1041n.

the remaining two did not arrive until close to evening. All used a single road, which easily explains the late arrival, especially if one recalls all that these two corps had done during the past four days.

General Pajol was sent with his column from Mazy to Saint-Denis, Grand-Leez, and then Tourinnes, thus to the right of the main column, where he was to await further orders. From there he had to be pulled back to Wavre and did not arrive at Limale until 8 p.m., having been ordered there by Grouchy after he saw that he would not be able to break through at Wavre.

There can be no doubt that in the morning Grouchy had no clear idea of the direction that Blücher had taken with his army. Grouchy himself says this, and when he departed Gembloux, his march was directed only toward Sart-à-Walhain, not yet toward Wavre. This explains the sideward move of Pajol and the way the French were tapping blindly around, which slowed the march. It was only the encounter with the rear guard of the Prussian 2nd and 3rd Corps in front of Wavre that drew Grouchy toward that place.

This failure to recognize the true line of retreat of the Prussian army borders on the incomprehensible, because it requires an assumption of the highest degree of clumsiness and negligence on the part of the French generals, which is not at all easy to make.

On the other hand, we do not find the slowness of Grouchy's movement toward Wavre as astonishing as most others do. In recent wars we have become accustomed to rapid movements and marches of 20, 25, or 30 miles in a single day and therefore feel justified in demanding them, since great speed may be very valuable. But such speed results more from favorable march conditions than from the urgency of the requirement. This is all too clear to anyone who has had to deal with such matters and has had to struggle with all of the difficulties that can arise. Weather and the state of the roads, lack of rations and quarters, fatigue of the troops, lack of information, and so forth, may—despite the best intentions—reduce a march to one-half or even one-third of what was thought possible on paper. Let us take the example of the French after the battles of Jena and Auerstädt, when they were completely victorious and had the greatest reason to hasten their movements. Although they were at that time at the peak of their military efficiency, they did not exceed an average of 10 miles per day during their pursuit.

If we assume that Grouchy's corps did not leave the field of battle at Ligny before 2 or 3 p.m. [on 17 June], then it is not surprising that these corps did not reach the neighborhood of Wavre before 2 or 3 p.m. [on 18 June], that is to say, 24 hours later, since Wavre is 25 miles from the Ligny battlefield on the road that Grouchy took, [which passed] through a range of hills; plus the conditions were very unfavorable, as we have already seen. The cavalry might certainly have begun the pursuit much sooner, but while this would not have been completely useless, it still would not have achieved the results that some commentators argue could have achieved by Grouchy with respect to the battle of Belle Alliance. The only reproach that can clearly be made against General Grouchy is that he sent his whole force down a single road, which naturally resulted in the last divisions of the 4th Corps arriving only around evening.

Chapter 45
General Thielmann's Dispositions

The Prussian 3rd Corps arrived at Wavre on the evening of the 17th, where it was rejoined by the previously detached 1st Brigade of the Reserve Cavalry. Three brigades, the 10th, 11th, and 12th, as well as the Reserve Cavalry, went through Wavre and then encamped at La Bavette. The 9th Brigade remained on the far side of the river because it had arrived too late. Together with the 8th Brigade of the 2nd Corps it now formed the advanced guard against Grouchy. On the morning of the 18th, as the 4th Corps marched towards Saint-Lambert, General Thielmann received orders to form the rear guard for the other three corps. If no significant enemy force showed itself, he was to follow the others by taking the road via Couture, while leaving several battalions behind in Wavre to prevent any French patrols from causing problems on the road to Brussels while the armies fought at Waterloo. But if a considerable enemy force showed up in front of Wavre, General Thielmann was to occupy the strong position on the Dyle there and cover the rear of the army.

The departure of the 2nd and 1st Corps from the position at Wavre took until around 2 p.m. Since nothing at all had been seen of the enemy up to that time, the Prussians were even more convinced that Bonaparte had turned his whole force against Wellington. General Thielmann therefore formed his corps into columns and was about to lead it down the Brussels road when a lively engagement began against the 9th and 8th Brigades, which were still on the left bank of the Dyle. General Thielmann therefore halted his troops until the situation became clearer. In the meantime, the 8th Brigade of the 2nd Corps left altogether. The 1st [Corps], which had stopped for a while, recommenced its march but left behind a detachment of three battalions and three squadrons under the command of Major Stengel at the village of Limale.

General Thielmann now occupied the Wavre position as follows: the 12th Brigade was placed behind the crossing at Bierge, the 10th to the right behind Wavre, the 11th to the left behind Wavre on the main road. Wavre itself was occupied by three battalions of the 9th Brigade, and the remainder of this brigade as well as the Reserve Cavalry were designated as the reserve and placed in the vicinity of Bavette.

The three forward brigades kept as well concealed as possible in brigade assembly areas, with the greater proportion of their force in columns, and employed only individual battalions or half companies of skirmishers for the defense of the bridges and the river itself. Meanwhile, all of the artillery—with the exception of one battery (totaling 27 guns) kept in reserve—was spread along one side of the valley and immediately went into action against the enemy coming down the other side.

The position of the 3rd Corps extended 2,000 paces from Bierge to Lower Wavre, so it was not too extensive for a corps of 20,000 men. There were four bridges across the river—one near Lower Wavre, two at Wavre, and one at the mill of Bièrge. The Dyle itself was fordable if necessary. On the other hand, the left bank of the river valley was rather high, perhaps 50 to 60 feet, and so steep that it could be considered a significant obstacle to any approach, while still offering full fields of fire. Since the countryside in the vicinity of the right and left wings was open, and some strong points presented themselves farther to the rear, the position could certainly be considered among the strongest that could be occupied immediately without much preparation.

General Thielmann's directions were designed to expose as few troops as possible, to maintain the firefight with the smallest possible numbers of infantry, and to rely mainly on artillery, so that if the enemy troops attempted to break out of the valley by storm, he would be able to send a mass of fresh men against them. The actual reserve was to be used to attack the flank of any enemy that attempted to envelope one of our flanks.

Misfortune caused one of these arrangements to fail.

The 9th Brigade, which had withdrawn via Lower Wavre after the enemy had deployed in strength, had occupied Wavre with two battalions and placed a third behind it. Owing to some unexplainable misunderstanding, the brigade then failed to keep its remaining six battalions, two cavalry squadrons, and eight guns in reserve near La Bavette, and instead followed the other corps going via Neuf Cabaret to Couture, which had been the original destination for the whole corps. No one noticed this mistake because at the moment when General Borcke withdrew through the lines at Lower Wavre, everyone's attention was focused on the deployment of the enemy's force in front of the lines. It was not until about 7 p.m., when it was realized that the reserve might be needed, and a preparatory order was sent, that it was discovered that General Borcke had marched away instead of remaining with the Reserve Cavalry. Officers were sent out to see whether he had taken up some other position in the area, but when they returned without having found out anything, General Thielmann let the matter rest, because, as he said, the place where the heavy cannonade of a great battle could be heard was the place where the whole affair would be decided, and whatever might happen at Wavre would have no effect on that; so perhaps it was even better that another [brigade] would be there.

Thus it was that on June 18th and 19th General Thielmann had only 24 battalions of infantry, 21 squadrons of cavalry, and 35 guns, for a total of about 15,000 men, to oppose Marshal Grouchy, whose total strength could not be seen because of the woods, although about 10-12,000 men were visible by around 3 p.m.

Chapter 46
Grouchy's Attack on 18 and 19 June

The Battle of Wavre can be divided quite naturally into two different acts, namely the engagement along the Dyle from 3 p.m. until nightfall on the 18th, and then the engagement on the left bank of the Dyle, between that river and the Rixansart Woods, from daybreak until about 9 a.m. on the 19th.

On the 18th Grouchy had wanted to take Wavre with the 3rd Corps and force a passage over the Dyle there. The 3rd Corps, which was leading the way, attacked Wavre with most of its forces between 2 and 3 p.m., while somewhat later a detachment attacked the mill of Bierge. But two Prussian battalions commanded by Colonel Zepelin, which were subsequently supported by two more, maintained possession of the town and both bridges. Equally unsuccessful was the attack on the bridge at the mill of Bierge, where the 12th Brigade was defending the river crossing with only light infantry and artillery posted on the left bank. When the French 4th Corps (Gérard) arrived, a part of the [14th] Division (Hulot) was also sent to Bierge. After having been repulsed at Wavre, the French generals placed great hopes on the attack at the Bierge mill and were therefore present in person, but they were not able to gain control of this crossing. Hulot's division later—that is to say between 8 and 9 p.m.—moved to Limale, where it was joined by the other two divisions, which arrived considerably later after having been directed there from La Baraque.[63] Pajol also proceeded in that direction with his cavalry corps and Teste's division of the 6th Corps.

All these troops reached Limale just as darkness fell. They found the town and the river crossing undefended, probably because Colonel Stengel was already withdrawing to follow the 1st Corps. The French therefore crossed over the Dyle in the dark and pushed forward in thick masses up to Delburg on the rim of the Dyle valley, facing the right flank of General Thielmann.

It was not until around 10 p.m. that the 12th Brigade reported that the enemy had crossed the river at Limale. General Thielmann thought that it was a detached column, consisting perhaps of just one division, and ordered Colonel Stülpnagel to go there with all the forces he could collect and drive the enemy back over the river. A brigade of the Reserve

---

63 This is the wording in the 1835 and subsequent published versions of the book. The original manuscript contains a somewhat shorter and slightly different account for the three sentences beginning with "Equally unsuccessful": "The 4th Corps (Gérard) was supposed to attack the position at Bièrge. The [13th] Division (Vichery) was used to attack the mill but could not gain control of the crossing, and later—that is to say between 8 and 9 p.m.—moved to Limale, where it was joined by the other two divisions, which arrived considerably later after having been directed there from La Baraque." In Hahlweg, *Schriften*, 2:1046n.

Cavalry was sent at the same time. General Thielmann hurried over to the threatened point himself. The attack took place in the dark, but it was not successful, in part because the attacking battalions were thrown into disorder by a sunken road, and in part because the enemy was already too strong.

Colonel Stülpnagel was therefore forced to take up a position very close to the enemy in order to tie them down and prevent them from spreading out. The first cannon shots began at dawn, at a distance of 500 paces. A violent struggle now commenced, during which the French methodically pushed their four divisions forward under the protection of a large line of skirmishers. The 3rd Corps resisted in three different positions. The first was in the low ground near the small wood, with the 12th Brigade and Colonel Stengel, who was still nearby. The next position was between Bierge and the Rixansart Woods, with fourteen battalions of the 12th, 10th, and 11th Brigades and the Reserve Cavalry, while six battalions remained behind Bierge and Wavre, and four remained in Wavre.

The resistance in this second position lasted the longest, and it was here that General Thielmann learned that the battle [Waterloo] had been won and that the Prussian 2nd Corps had been ordered to take his opponent in the rear by advancing via Glabaix and La Hutte.

These places were so far from the field of battle that General Thielmann could expect no assistance, so he could only hope that his opponent had also heard of the outcome of the great battle and would quickly begin to retreat out of fear of being cut off. General Thielmann therefore had his troops shout loud hurrahs and show signs of rejoicing. But this hope was in vain. The enemy continued to press forward, and General Thielmann was forced to retire further, and finally to begin a general retreat in which he also ordered Colonel Zepelin to withdraw from Wavre.

General Thielmann withdrew in the direction of Louvain as far as Saint-Achtenrode, three hours' march from the battlefield, and lost only a few thousand killed and wounded. The 3rd Corps' 9th Brigade had continued its march towards Saint-Lambert, spent the night of the 18th in the woods there, marched back towards the cannon fire of Wavre early on the 19th, and finally reunited with the rest of the 3rd Corps at Gembloux on the 20th after passing through Limale.

ON WATERLOO

Chapter 47
Combat at Namur

Grouchy actually seems to have received the news of the loss of the Battle of Belle Alliance on the morning of the 19th, just about the time that Thielmann began his retreat. This made his opponent's withdrawal easier, since Grouchy lost any desire to continue seeking small advantages at a time when he had to be greatly concerned about his own retreat. He realized that he could no longer head for Charleroi and thus resolved to go to Namur. At midday he sent Exelmans' cavalry corps ahead, which is supposed to have arrived at 4 p.m., though this seems doubtful since the battlefield of Wavre is almost thirty miles from Namur. The infantry followed at nightfall in two columns, one via Gembloux, the other by the most direct route. The cavalry divisions of Maurin and Soult formed the rear guard.

The French infantry reached Namur between 8 and 9 a.m. [on the 20th].

General Thielmann reached the area of Achtenrode around noon [on the 19th]. He had decided that under no circumstances would he send his utterly exhausted troops to pursue the enemy that day, as they were greatly in need of rest and it could be foreseen that the enemy's rear guard would not withdraw before nightfall, making it impossible for an advance to be decisive. He therefore preferred to have his troops rendezvous at daybreak near Ottenbourg, where his advance guard was placed, in order to advance in good time in pursuit of the enemy. Assembling the force was delayed for about an hour, and at around 5 a.m. the cavalry set forth via Gembloux on the road to Namur, with the infantry following.

The cavalry first encountered enemy cavalry at Gembloux, but these immediately withdrew. The pursuit proceeded as quickly as possible on the most direct route to Namur, but the Prussians did not find the enemy again until they were about 45 minutes from town.

General Thielmann's cavalry thus covered the distance to Namur in five or six hours, while the infantry remained at Gembloux.

Several enemy battalions along with some cavalry and artillery were encountered in front of Namur. They were attacked, lost three guns, and withdrew closer to the town.

THE CAMPAIGN OF 1815

Some masses of enemy troops stood on the Brussels-Namur highway, apparently to cover a retreat. While they were being observed, an enemy division, marching in column, was discovered on the road itself. As soon as they spotted General Thielmann's cavalry, they formed squares, placed artillery and skirmishers out on the left, and under this cover continued their march into the city. It was the last division of the 4th Corps, which arrived at Namur a little later than the 3rd. Almost immediately afterward came General Pirch with the Prussian 2nd Corps.

After the battle [of Waterloo] this general had received orders to proceed toward Gembloux and fall on Grouchy's rear. He had marched all night, passing through Maransart and Bousval, and reached Mellery on the morning of the 19th. Here he bivouacked and sent out patrols. However, as these brought no news of either General Thielmann or the enemy, he remained there through the night and set out for Gembloux only after receiving a report, at five in the morning on the 20th, that the enemy was retreating through that place. Thus it was that he ended up hanging on to the tail of the column of the French left wing. When this column withdrew into the town, General Pirch tried to gain possession of the Brussels gate. But because the gate and the remaining pieces of the ramparts connected to it were strongly held by enemy infantry, a very sharp infantry action took place, which lasted several hours and is supposed to have cost the 2nd Corps 1100 men killed and wounded, without achieving anything. The effort had to be abandoned, and the enemy did not leave the town until 6 p.m., heading towards Dinant, where it was followed, on Blücher's orders, only by Colonel Sohr's brigade of cavalry.

If General Pirch had continued his march toward Namur and gotten there before Grouchy's infantry, as he well might have, Grouchy would have had no way to cross the Meuse, and would have had to turn towards Charleroi. This would have happened on the 20th. On that day the Prussian 1st Corps, having followed the defeated main French army through Charleroi, had already passed through there and was near Beaumont. On hearing the news of Grouchy's move, it would probably have given up its advance towards Avesnes and turned towards Philippeville. But it is very unlikely that it could have cut off the retreat of Grouchy's corps, since Grouchy would have reached Philippeville first, and in the worst case could have gone to Givet. Nevertheless, Grouchy might have suffered greater losses, as individual units would have been cut off, etc. Things would have turned out quite differently if the Prussian 1st Corps had been ordered to remain on the Sambre on the 19th and 20th in order to block Grouchy. In that case 50,000 men would have been united against this marshal on the morning of the 21st, and it is hard to believe that he could have avoided capitulating, penned in as he would have been by this superior force and two rivers. Bonaparte himself said in a letter written at Philippeville to his brother Joseph, "I have heard nothing from Grouchy at all. If he has not been taken, as I fear, I can have 50,000 men in three days."[64] But of course early on the 19th—when these dispositions would have had to have been made—Blücher's headquarters knew far too little about Grouchy's situation to make cutting him off a major objective of immediate operations.

In any case the attack on Namur is hard to justify, since little would have been gained by forcing a way into the town and just beyond the town was the bridge over the Sambre, [whose destruction by the French] could have put an end to all further pursuit. On the other hand, another passage over the Sambre could probably have been found; and because the Namur-Dinant road runs on the left bank of the Meuse, that is to say in a deep and steep valley between the two rivers (in effect a continuous defile), then if the Prussians had gained control of the heights they could have greatly impeded the French retreat, inflicting heavy losses upon Marshal Grouchy, and above all delaying his retreat, thus preventing him from reaching Laon before the Allies. But in war it is seldom the case that everything is done that can be done. The mission that was here assigned to General Pirch was in no sense routine; rather it required an exceptional degree of energy.

Chapter 48
Reflections on the Battle: Bonaparte

If we take a probing look at the outcome of the great drama which took place on the 17th and 18th of June, we must focus our attention on the following subjects:

---

[64] Pierre Alexandre Édouard Fleury du Chaboulon, *Mémoires pour servir à l'histoire de la vie privée, du retour et de règne de l'empereur Napoléon en 1815*, 2 vols. (London: Longman, 1820), 2:196; Hahlweg cites a later edition in *Schriften*, 2:1050n.

THE CAMPAIGN OF 1815

1. First we must ask: Could and should Bonaparte have attacked in the morning instead of at midday on the 18th? His entire offensive against the Allied field armies had to be conducted with the greatest speed if it was to succeed, since he wanted to defeat them one at a time, if possible even before they had completely assembled. We might even criticize him for having already lost a few too many hours on the 16th. However, his troops' need for rest, coupled with various measures and preparations required for strategic and practical reasons, are sufficient to explain why the attack on the 16th did not take place earlier, and on the whole critics far away in place and time are rarely in a position to argue over a couple of hours. But on the 18th there really does not seem to be sufficient justification for delaying half a day. Bonaparte arrived in front of Wellington's position on the evening of the 17th and even regrets in his memoirs that he did not have a few more hours of daylight so that he could have started the battle on the 17th.[65] There was thus no reason why he could not have set his columns in motion at daybreak on the 18th, which would have allowed the battle to start at around 6 or 7 a.m. Under such pressing circumstances, 4 or 5 hours of rest would have to suffice for the troops. Bonaparte had two things to fear: first, the complete concentration of Wellington's army, and second, Blücher's participation in the battle. A rapid attack was the only means of dealing with either. But Bonaparte did not believe

1. that Wellington would accept battle if he was waiting for more troops to arrive, or, which he thought even less likely,
2. that Blücher would be able to come quickly to Wellington's aid.

Bonaparte therefore thought that a few hours more or less were not significant. We personally do not believe that an attack early that morning would have guaranteed victory, because we know that Wellington did not receive any more reinforcements in the course of the day. Furthermore, if the battle had begun at 6 or 7 a.m., Blücher would probably have arrived 3 to 4 hours earlier, thus still in good time. But what we know now was hidden from the French commander at that time, and neither of his assumptions concerning Wellington and Blücher proved to be well founded.

In looking at the unnecessary assembling and parading of his army, through which Bonaparte lost several hours of time, one might almost

---

65 Napoleon, *Mémoires*, 182; excerpted in Hahlweg, *Schriften*, 2:1052n.

ON WATERLOO

suspect that his aim was not a battle but an English retreat, which he hoped to achieve with this bombastic display. But such a wish would have been so contrary to his interests under the circumstances, and also so far removed from his previous methods, that it could only be seen as the result of an inner crippling and dimming of his spark of genius. All of this would only be a fleeting thought, an unproved suspicion, a mere premonition of the truth, and it would scarcely be permissible to include it in the list of observations were it not for the fact that another consideration, of which we shall speak in a moment, also leads to the same conclusion.

2. The second issue to consider is the role that Bonaparte wanted his right wing to play in the battle. We regard his entire account of this as completely dishonest, a scheme conceived only after the fact. Grouchy's situation—and the way Bonaparte uses it in self-justification—is very similar to Ney's situation on the 16th. On that occasion the left wing originally was supposed only to stop the British, or perhaps force their leading divisions to move back somewhat. Only later, when it was obviously too late, did it receive the completely unrealistic order to take part in the main battle itself. Similarly, on the 17th the right wing under Grouchy was only supposed to pursue the defeated Blücher, to prevent his forces from assembling, recovering, or even turning back. It was only later—and once again too late and contrary to the true nature of the situation—that Grouchy received the order to participate in the main battle. According to Grouchy's account in his own defense,[66] there is no order listed in the order book of the chief of staff, Marshal Soult, as having been sent to Grouchy on the 17th. The instructions that he received concerning the pursuit of the Prussians consisted solely of those given to him verbally by Bonaparte on the battlefield of Ligny, in the presence of General Girard.

On the other hand, we find two letters from Marshal Soult to Grouchy on the 18th, which read as follows:

---

66 Grouchy, *Observations*, 55f.

THE CAMPAIGN OF 1815

1.

To Marshal Grouchy
(carried by the aide, Major Lenovich)

In front of the farm of Caillou,
18 June, 10 a.m.

Marshal, the Emperor has received your last report dated from Gembloux. You speak to his Majesty of only two Prussian columns that have passed at Sauvenières and Sart-à-Walhain. However, other reports say that a third column has passed at Gery and Gentinnes, heading toward Wavre.

The Emperor directs me to tell you that at this moment his Majesty is going to attack the English army, which has taken position at Waterloo near the Soignies Forest. Thus his Majesty desires that you direct your movements on Wavre in order to draw near to us, place yourself in touch with our operations, and link up your communications with us, driving before you those portions of the Prussian army that have taken this direction and may have stopped at Wavre, where you should arrive as soon as possible. You will follow the enemy's columns on your right, using some light troops to observe their movements and gather up their stragglers.

Inform me immediately about your dispositions and your march, also about any news of the enemy, and do not neglect to link up your communications with us. The Emperor desires to have news from you very often.

Signed: Major-General,
Duke of Dalmatia

ON WATERLOO

2.

From the battlefield of Waterloo
the 18th at 1 p.m.

Marshal, you wrote to the emperor at 2 o'clock this morning that you will march on Sart-à-Walhain, thus your plan is to proceed to Corbaix or to Wavre. This movement conforms to his Majesty's arrangements which have been communicated to you.

Nevertheless, the Emperor directs me to tell you that you should always maneuver in our direction. It is up to you to see where we are located in order to regulate your movements accordingly, and to link up your communications with us so as to be always ready to fall upon and wipe out any enemy troops that may attempt to annoy our right flank. At this moment the battle is in progress on the line of Waterloo. The enemy's center is at Mont-Saint-Jean, so you should maneuver to join our right.

Signed: Duke of Dalmatia

P.S. A letter that has just been intercepted says that General Bülow is about to attack our flank. We believe we can see this corps on the heights of Saint-Lambert, so do not lose an instant in drawing near and joining with us in order to crush Bülow, whom you will catch *en flagrant délit*.

In contrast, Bonaparte maintains that at 10 p.m. on the evening of the 17th he sent an officer to Grouchy

> to inform him that he had the intention of fighting a great battle on the morrow, and that the Anglo-Belgian army was in position in front of the Soignies Forest, anchored on its left in the village of La Haye, and that Marshal Blücher would certainly operate in one of the following three directions:
> 1. retreat toward Liége;
> 2. advance toward Brussels; [or]
> 3. remain in position at Wavre.

THE CAMPAIGN OF 1815

In all three cases he would have to maneuver via Saint-Lambert in order to overrun the left wing of the English army and join with the right of the French army. In the first two cases, however, he would have to execute his movement with the bulk of his forces combined, and in the third it would only be necessary to leave a detachment, whose strength would depend upon the nature of the position, in order to occupy the front of the Prussian army.[67]

Furthermore, Bonaparte asserts that he repeated this order in a duplicate sent early on the morning of the 18th. Bonaparte immediately adds, however, that Marshal Grouchy never received these two orders. The marshal, on the other hand, declares his conviction that they were never even sent,[68] and in reality a closer examination of the issue seems to support this view because:

1. The orders are not contained in the chief of staff's order book.

2. The two letters by Soult on the 18th do not mention them and are not even consistent with them.

3. It is unlikely that two separate letters carried by officers would both be lost. One must ask if the officers also were lost.

4. Bonaparte should have named the officers who were supposed to have carried these orders.

5. It is revealing that the statement that Grouchy did not receive these orders comes from Bonaparte.

6. It is curious, and most suspicious, that on the 16th a similar order failed to reach Marshal Ney.[69]

---

67 Napoleon, *Mémoires*, 115-117.
68 Grouchy, *Observations*, 72f., states his doubts that such letters were even written.
69 Clausewitz's arguments are accepted by most modern historians, who share his belief that the alleged messages described in Napoleon's memoirs have no basis in fact and were simply designed to shift the blame for defeat at Waterloo to Grouchy. For the most recent examination of this issue, see Bernard Coppens, *Plancenoit*, 40-41. However, Grouchy's assertion that he received no written orders at all on 17 June is also incorrect. A message sent by Napoleon shortly after midday ordered Grouchy to search in the direction of Namur and Maastricht and pursue the enemy. "It is important to discover what Blücher and Wellington are intending to do and if they propose to reunite their armies to cover Brussels and Liege and attempt to give battle. In that case keep your two infantry corps united in terrain having several avenues of retreat and place detachments of cavalry in-between to maintain communications with the headquarters." The existence of this message did not become known until the 1840s, which is why Clausewitz was unaware of it. Had he been, however, it seems unlikely that it would

ON WATERLOO

At any rate, Marshal Grouchy is correct when he states that he cannot have been expected to carry out orders that even Bonaparte says did not reach him, and that he could therefore act only on the basis of the verbal instructions that Bonaparte gave him around midday on the 17th. Bonaparte had told Grouchy on the evening of the 16th, when the latter asked for more instructions, that they would come on the following morning. Grouchy then states:

> I was at his headquarters the next morning before sunrise, waiting for orders. Around 7:30 he sent word through the chief of staff that he was going to visit the battlefield and I should accompany him.
>
> Meanwhile, General Pajol, who had been ordered to pursue the Prussians with his light cavalry and a division of infantry, was just then sending back several cannon captured on the road to Namur. This circumstance may have led to the belief that Blücher was retiring toward that town.
>
> Between 8 and 9 a.m., Napoleon left Fleurus in his carriage to go to the battlefield. The difficult condition of the roads, across fields cut by ditches and deep furrows, delayed him so much that he decided to mount his horse. Arriving at Saint-Amand, he had himself guided around the diverse avenues by which this village had been attacked the evening before. Then he walked on the battlefield, stopping to care for and question several wounded officers who were still there, and passing in front of the regiments who formed up without arms on the fields or who were bivouacked there, saluted them and received their acclamations. He spoke to almost all of the corps with interest, expressing satisfaction at their conduct the evening before. He then dismounted and spoke for a long time with General Gérard and myself about the state of opinion in the Parisian assembly, the Jacobins, and diverse other subjects; all of which were extraneous to that

---

have altered his general view that Napoleon's intentions with respect to Grouchy's force were marked by hesitancy and cross-purposes, which he subsequently sought to represent as a daring but poorly executed plan. See Charras, *Histoire de la Campagne de 1815*, 5th ed. (Geneva, 1907), 240-241, and the detailed discussion of this message in John Codman Ropes, *The Campaign of Waterloo: A Military History* (1893; reprinted Tyne & Wear: Worley Publications, 1995), 355-361, which strongly criticizes Grouchy's truthfulness.

which seemingly should have occupied his thoughts exclusively at such a moment.

I am entering into such minute details because they serve to reveal how that morning was spent, the loss of which was to have such disastrous results. It was not until midday, after having received the report from a patrol that had been sent to Quatre-Bras, that Napoleon began to issue orders relating to the dispositions he intended to adopt. He then put into movement the corps of infantry and cavalry that he wanted to take with him and directed them toward the route to Quatre-Bras, and afterward gave me the verbal order to take command of the corps of generals Vandamme and Gérard and the cavalry of generals Pajol and Exelmans and to pursue Marshal Blücher.

I then commented to him that the Prussians had commenced their retreat at 10 p.m. on the night before, and that considerable time would be needed before the troops could be put into motion, for they were scattered across the plain and had disassembled their arms for cleaning and were making their soup and were not expecting to march that day; also that the enemy were 17 to 18 hours ahead of the corps that were being sent after them; that although the reports of the cavalry did not give any more precise details on the direction taken by the mass of the Prussian army, it seemed that Marshal Blücher's retreat was in the direction of Namur, and that in pursuing him, I would therefore find myself isolated, separated from [the emperor], and outside the radius of his operations.

These remarks were not well received. He repeated the order that he had given, adding that it was up to me to discover the route taken by Marshal Blücher, that he was going to battle the English, that I was to complete the defeat of the Prussians by attacking them as soon as I had reached them, and that I was to communicate with him via the paved road which led from a point not far away from that on which we found ourselves at Quatre-Bras. The brief conversation that I then had with the chief of staff [Marshal Soult] concerned only the extraction, from the corps under my command, of the troops to be sent

ON WATERLOO

toward Quatre-Bras. These are word for word the only directions that were given to me, and the only orders I received.[70]

On the basis of Marshal Grouchy's recounting of what occurred with Napoleon on the morning of the 17th, we see:
1. that in all probability this marshal truly received no instructions for his actions on the 17th other than a very general one to pursue the Prussians;
2. that Bonaparte had no idea that the Prussians were withdrawing toward the Dyle and even saw some merit in the view that they were heading toward Namur; therefore he did not direct the marshal toward Wavre;
3. that at 10 a.m. on the 18th Bonaparte did have a report that one Prussian column had gone to Wavre, but that he still believed the main portion had gone toward Liège and therefore that General Grouchy would undoubtedly be able to drive the Prussians from Wavre and place himself between Bonaparte and the Prussians;
4. that Bonaparte truly demonstrated a kind of lethargy and carelessness that corresponded neither with the position he was in nor with his previous methods. This is the second sign that causes us to think that something had changed within him.

If he had wanted his cavalry to take up the pursuit that evening, why not have them mount up at daylight on the 17th to look for the missing Blücher, so as to at least be clear about the direction he had taken and thus about the best direction to send the force directed against him? Why does he drag the general who is supposed to lead the pursuit around with him for 3 or 4 hours without sending him off on his mission, and how could his thoughts be so occupied with things occurring in Paris that he lost sight of the most essential elements of the conduct of war?

In any case, the whole story leaves the impression that Bonaparte had undoubtedly written off the Prussians and no longer thought that any further fighting against them would matter in relation to the battle that he was now about to fight with Wellington. Thus there was no thought that either Blücher or Grouchy would participate in the battle that was about to take place on the road to Brussels. Bonaparte's assertion that he viewed the separation of the opposing forces on the 17th as two col-

---

[70] For the original, see Grouchy, *Observations*, 10-13; cited in Hahlweg, *Schriften*, 2:1057.

umns heading toward Brussels, one consisting of Blücher and Grouchy via Wavre, the other of Wellington and himself via Mont St. Jean, is just a view he patched together afterwards, and would not be worth mentioning if it had not been taken up by other writers.[71]

Now that we have shown that, in all probability, the participation of the right wing in whatever was going to happen on the left did not occur to the French commander at all on the 17th, which is to say, in time to matter, we must look more closely at the nature of the assistance that was ordered on the 18th, much too late.

If on the 17th Bonaparte had ordered Marshal Grouchy not to pursue and press Prince Blücher on all of his avenues of retreat, but merely to observe him while always staying between the main [French] army and Blücher, then Grouchy could have played a role on the 18th, either by placing himself in front of the advancing Blücher or, if Blücher did not advance, by detaching forces toward Mont-Saint-Jean. This role is clearly completely different from one of pursuing and pressing. Such an order would naturally have led Grouchy to the Dyle, because this river was a key terrain feature separating the two Allied armies; but the route would not have been by way of Gembloux, but rather by way of Tilly in order to reach the left bank as quickly as possible. If the Prussians remained on the right bank of the Dyle, then Limale and Wavre would have been the natural assembly points for Grouchy. If, however, he heard that the Prussians had headed for Wavre, then the area around Neuf-Cabaret, or anywhere else [that kept] his right wing on the Dyle and his front parallel to the road from Wavre to Brussels, would have been a good position from which to hold Blücher in check, get in front of him, or remain on his flank.

In this position Grouchy would have been only around 4 or 5 miles from Bonaparte and could have kept in direct contact through the usual flank patrols. It would thus not have been impossible for Grouchy to have been under Bonaparte's direct orders, even on the day of the battle.

In contrast, following Blücher via Gembloux, without any intervening forces [between himself and Bonaparte], was a huge divergence that not only placed Grouchy's force even farther away from the main army but also made communications with it very difficult, even uncertain, because of the circuitous path that was required. Thus we see that an order

---

71 Napoleon, *Mémoires*, 185-186.

written at 1 p.m. on the 18th did not reach Grouchy's hands until 7 p.m. This is not surprising, because the chief of staff had found it necessary to send the officer carrying this order via Quatre-Bras and Gembloux; he therefore had to travel about 30 miles. How can a corps that cannot receive orders in less than 6 hours be considered part of one and the same battle? How can a commander claim to be able to lead such a corps from the battlefield, based on constantly changing information on that very day? But that is how it looks when we read the end of the second letter:

> At present the battle is in progress on the line of Waterloo. The enemy's center is at Mont-Saint-Jean, so you should maneuver to join our right.

and even the postscript:

> A letter that has just been intercepted says that General Bülow is about to attack our flank. We believe we can see this corps on the heights of Saint-Lambert, so do not lose an instant in drawing near and joining with us in order to crush Bülow, whom you will catch *en flagrant délit*.

If Grouchy had received this order at 4 in the afternoon, which in this case would have been quite unlikely, and if the marshal had been able to start his march right away, he still would not have made it from the Wavre area to the vicinity of the [Waterloo] battlefield before 9 p.m., for one does not march with 40,000 men through rough terrain in the presence of the enemy at the same speed as one man alone, and the distance that Grouchy had to cover was more than 9 miles. If we consider the many instances of lost time that are a constant occurrence in warfare and must always be taken into account, then the order to Grouchy cannot be taken seriously. And what does that order presuppose? That Grouchy was not occupied with the enemy and was ready to march at a moment's notice. But Grouchy had in fact been ordered to pursue Blücher, and Bonaparte therefore had to expect that Grouchy's forces would either be engaged in close combat, or spread out over a number of roads in the course of the pursuit. Either way it would be quite unreasonable to expect that he would be ready to march off at once to the battle of Waterloo.

THE CAMPAIGN OF 1815

The truth is that when Bonaparte heard on the [morning of the] 18th that part of the Prussians had gone to Wavre, he began to be concerned that they could support Wellington, but he considered this column to be only a small fraction of the Prussian army, which Grouchy could easily drive away. Only [later in the day] did Bonaparte begin to realize the importance of having Grouchy between himself and the Prussians, and only then did his directives begin to have the tone that they would have had from the very beginning if, on the 17th, he had given Grouchy an order like that we have shown above, which is to say, if his arrogance had not led him to count Blücher out. As his position worsened in the battle, he transformed the idea of having Grouchy between himself and the Prussians into a different one: that Grouchy was nothing more than the right wing of his own line of battle and could be called over to fall upon the rear of the Prussian corps that had arrived alongside the English. But armies do not move like thoughts, and if one starts off with false assumptions, one must generally bear the consequences.

Bonaparte has always spoken only of Bülow, as if the rest of the Prussians were incapable of further action after the battle of Ligny. But this was a foolish assumption that was in no way justified by the outcome of that battle and the small number of trophies taken. In assuming that what was visible at Saint-Lambert could only be Bülow, not Blücher, Bonaparte had even less reason to believe that Grouchy would thereby be drawn toward him as well, because Grouchy had been sent out against Blücher, not Bülow, and had to be considered as engaged with the former, not the latter.

From our perspective the result of these considerations is:

1. that on the 17th Bonaparte did not expect Blücher and Grouchy to participate in the battle on the 18th, that he had not even considered it, and that—when the overall arrangements are considered—he was completely surprised by Blücher's appearance on the 18th.

2. that the orders on the 18th calling for Grouchy to participate [in the battle of Waterloo] seem to have been last-minute expedients issued in desperation and could not possibly have been carried out.

So much for Bonaparte's characterization of his right wing's relationship to the battle [of Waterloo]. We will look at Grouchy's actions later.

Now let us look at the battle itself, which leads us to the following observations.

3. We can discern nothing about an actual plan of attack. The deployment and advance of the French army take place parallel to the enemy front and the distribution of forces is practically uniform along the entire line. At the same time it seems that the attacks on the advanced post of Hougoumont and the village of La Haye had so little energy, and the attack on the center was so large, that Bonaparte's intention must have been to break through the Allied army in the center, while merely keeping it occupied on the flanks. Since the main avenue of retreat was directly behind the center and it is generally assumed that the other entrances into the Soignies Forest were not suitable for all arms, such a breakthrough in the center would indeed have had decisive results, and there was certainly no other way to bring about a total defeat of the Allied army so quickly. Considering that Bonaparte had the 6th Corps following in the center, and also that the Guard was behind the center, one can well imagine such a plan being successful. Namely, if the 3 divisions of the 1st Corps, which formed the attack on the center, could substantially weaken and drain the strength of the Allies through several hours of fighting, then the 6th Corps could move forward for the moment of decision and make the actual breakthrough, with the Guard in reserve in case Wellington's flank forces attempted to improvise an attack on the French flanks. Such a spur-of-the-moment reaction is seldom very sustained or strong, so the French Guard would probably have been able to withstand this thrust, and victory in the center would have continued to develop and become more dangerous for Wellington.

Thus one can imagine Bonaparte's attack being crowned with a spectacular triumph; but the essential factors should not be mixed up or placed in false relationships to each other.

Against forces in extended positions in hilly country, where everything seems to be nailed in place and a counteroffensive is not realistic for several reasons, a breakthrough in the center is the simplest, most decisive and least dangerous form of attack.

But this is not the case for a position with great depth, owing to concentrated forces or the presence of large reserves. In that case breaking through in the center—if successful—may still be the most decisive course of action, but it is also the most unnatural and dangerous one, because:

1. The attacker does not have the extended space in which to mass far superior forces at the decisive point.

2. It is much harder for him to hide his intentions and dispositions.

3. If the opponent goes over to an attack on the flanks, this leads to the most disadvantageous form of battle.

If battles still consisted solely of an instantaneous blow,[72] and if armies were like brittle objects whose crystalline structure could be smashed by such a blow, then there would be little reason to consider the third of these disadvantages. But our battles last for half or even a whole day; for the most part they are a slow grinding and consumption of the two armies, whose fronts touch each other like two hostile elements that destroy each other wherever they meet. Thus the battle burns slowly and with limited intensity, like wet powder, and only when most of the opposing forces have already been burned out into useless cinders is a decision achieved by what is left. In this kind of warfare, a thrust by a reinforced center, like a battering ram against the enemy front, is actually a very unrealistic form of attack.

We often hear it said that breaking through in the center was Bonaparte's favorite maneuver. Bold, ruthless, overpowering and arrogant as he was, and always thirsting for the greatest triumphs, one could well believe that he must have preferred this form of attack. However, if we look at all the important battles in which he was the attacker, we see that such an assertion is completely unfounded.[73]

Perhaps more than anything else, this proves just how unnatural a thrust at the enemy center is, and how strongly the attacker is always drawn to the flanks.

If we nevertheless regard a French victory at Mont-Saint-Jean as possible, it is only because we believe that 70,000 Frenchmen led by

---

72 Compare to *On War*, 79, in which Clausewitz considers at length his own proposition that "war does not consist of a single short blow." In this passage, that insight is still presented as historically contingent, and is applied to battles and armies rather than to war as such. Yet the generality of Napoleon's problem is apparent throughout Clausewitz's discussion: Napoleon needs, somehow, to strike a single blow that will transform the politics of Europe. The problem of how to break Wellington's center is no more than a tactical manifestation of this overarching, and ultimately insoluble, dilemma.

73 Clausewitz's original manuscript contained a footnote citing some of Napoleon's great victories: "The battles which lead to this opinion are those of Marengo, Austerlitz, Eylau, and Wagram. Marengo, Austerlitz and Wagram were actually defensive battles in which Bonaparte acted offensively." In Hahlweg, *Schriften*, 2:1064n.

Bonaparte and Ney were more than a match for 70,000 Allies, of whom a third consisted of Hanoverian militia and new units, and a third of Belgian units that had just been formed and whose officers and men could not be trusted. These units melted away in the battle much faster than the French, as is confirmed by all eyewitness accounts. The fact that Wellington's position was so precarious at around 5 p.m., despite the fact that not a single man from the 6th Corps or Guard had fought against him, clearly shows the superiority of the French troops.

If we therefore believe that the thrust against Wellington's center could have succeeded, it is only because:

1. we think the quality of the troops was so disparate, and
2. Wellington does not seem to have considered or prepared for a counterattack.

Under these circumstances, it is difficult to consider the wedge-shaped thrust against Mont-Saint-Jean as a mistake for a commander like Bonaparte, who must always have his eye on the boldest strokes in order to achieve spectacular results.

But this is only correct if the 6th Corps and the Imperial Guard are included. Once Blücher appears, and the entire 6th Corps as well as half of the Guard must be used against him, then this thrust at the center truly becomes no more than a melée, a wild attempt at overrunning the enemy. This is also a fair characterization of the premature and wasteful employment of the cavalry. From this point onward nothing is in its proper relationship: the forces on the flanks are just as strong as those in the center, so there is no superiority in numbers, and therefore no basis for success. The fact is, no matter how much Wellington's army had melted away, or how threatening the position of the French cavalry confronting Wellington's line may have been, Wellington's reserves were not yet exhausted, and if no large masses of fresh troops followed the French attack, then these tremendous endeavors were just wasted effort. Thus because Bonaparte lacked the forces to prepare the attack on the enemy center properly, as one must nowadays prepare every attack, and because he lacked time and therefore had to do everything too hastily, he was no longer carrying out a carefully planned and properly executed plan, but basically acting in sheer desperation.

We can therefore see that Blücher's arrival did not just snatch victory out of Bonaparte's hands, which would have also been the case had Turenne, Frederick the Great, or any other great commander been placed in the same situation. It also provoked the emperor into hurling his forces in helpless rage against Wellington's rocklike stand, shattering them, and thereby placing them in a state of complete disintegration as this remarkable day ended.

4. Most critics have claimed that Bonaparte should have attacked Wellington's left wing and enveloped it.

Wellington's left wing was weak in and of itself, and if one completely ignores the possibility of Blücher's assistance, then such an attack would seem to be much easier—although less decisive—than one against the center. If Bonaparte considered Blücher's appearance to be more or less impossible, then there would have been much to say for this course of action. However, if one does consider the possibility that the Prussians could advance via Lasne and Saint-Lambert, then it is clear that an attack on the left flank would have been just about impossible.

The right wing of Wellington's army was stronger than the left due to the terrain, because near Braine-l'Alleud and Merbe-Braine there are a considerable number of depressions that greatly hinder an attack. Also, an attack on this side, that is to say against the right wing and on the right flank, would have taken several hours longer, which in Bonaparte's position was a particularly weighty consideration. Furthermore, he would have completely given up his natural line of retreat, and if defeated he would have had to fall back through Mons toward Maubeuge or Valenciennes. Finally, such an attack would obviously have been the least decisive of all, because even if successful it would have neither split Wellington's army nor separated him from Blücher. These considerations are so numerous and important that in most cases the idea of attacking from this direction would have to be set aside completely. However, if we accept that Blücher's arrival with a significant force (c. 50,000 men) was sufficiently possible that it had to be taken into consideration for planning purposes, and that [if he were to appear] neither an attack on the center nor on the left wing offered any possibility of victory, then we must return to the attack on the right wing, because having at least some chance of success must be the highest priority.

If Bonaparte had marched his army to the left and had advanced against Wellington's right flank via Braine-l'Alleud, Wellington would have been forced to form a new front toward the west. In that case Wellington would have had a front that was perhaps even stronger, but there would have two important advantages for the French. First of all, in this position Blücher would most likely not have been able to fall upon the French right flank, but would have supported his ally from the rear; the battle would thus not have taken on such a disadvantageous form for the French. Second, the Soignies Forest would have been on Wellington's right flank, and as he had always shown great sensitivity and concern about the road to Brussels, Bonaparte could have exploited the woods to cause Wellington to occupy it strongly, thus splintering his strength. Then the French would not have faced such a deep and dense position, and would have encountered less resistance.

A complete defeat of Wellington was unlikely in this case, but there could still have been a blow comparable to the one against Blücher at Ligny, which might have led to disunity and indecision between the two Allied leaders. Grouchy's appearance in Blücher's rear on the 19th could then have achieved all that for which there was not enough time left on the 18th. Both Allied commanders had already abandoned their natural lines of retreat, and this had to cause uneasiness with their situation and weaken their resolve. In short, it is quite possible that if [the two Allied commanders] were not able to wrench a victory out of their opponent's hands on the 18th, there could have been a parting of the ways that would have been the overture to much greater results.

Therefore we believe that an attack on Wellington's left wing and in the left flank was the least feasible. One against the center was the shortest and most decisive, and it was feasible as long as there was reasonable assurance that it could be completed before Blücher arrived. But if an early and powerful appearance on the part of Blücher had to be taken into account, then an attack on the right wing and the right flank offered the only hope of victory.

5. Napoleon's failure to garrison the valley of Lasne and Saint Lambert immediately with some light troops may have been a mistake, but it would not have made much difference to the overall outcome of the battle. Deploying an entire corps like the 6th in that area would have required a completely different plan, a completely different point of view than that of Bonaparte. Admittedly Lobau['s Corps] could have offered stronger and longer resistance at Lasne and Saint-Lambert than at Frischermont, but he would have been attacked much earlier, and if Blücher had advanced forces by way of Couture, then Lobau would have been in danger of being cut off completely. In that case, Bonaparte would have been forced to send more troops to this area and, in short, would have found himself fighting on a battlefield twice as large, which would not have been to his liking and which he would have had great difficulty controlling. On the other hand, it does seem that Lobau's corps would have been better positioned between Frischermont and Pajeau, making that its main line of resistance.

6.[74] Finally, our last observation about the battle from Bonaparte's perspective concerns the previously mentioned use of the last reserves. A cautious commander like Turenne, Prince Eugene [of Savoy], Frederick the Great, who would not have found himself in such an extraordinary position, and who would have had either a greater sense of responsibility or more to lose, would not have fought the Battle of Belle Alliance. That is to say, at noon, when Bülow appeared, he would have broken off the engagement and withdrawn. If it were possible to confine the rules for the conduct of war merely to objective relationships, we would say in this case that it was against all the rules to try to carry on with the battle. Earlier critics would not have failed to point this out but would also have added that a genius cannot be bound by the rules. But we do not share this opinion. If the conduct of war should for the most part be based on fundamental principles, then these must encompass every situation in which a warring party can find itself, and in particular the greatest and most far-reaching situations.

---

74 In the original manuscript (see Hahlweg, *Schriften*, 2:1068n), this paragraph is numbered 7 and is preceded by a draft paragraph 6, which Clausewitz deleted. Perhaps he did so because he did not like to "second-guess" decisions taken in battle too explicitly: "6. If, knowing all that occurred, we were to propose an improved plan for Bonaparte, which is no real achievement but more to be considered as a useful employment of the experience gained, we would make the following points. 1. The attacks on the right and left wings, thus on Hougoumont and La Haye, which were only diversionary attacks, should be made with fewer troops. A cavalry division and an infantry brigade would have sufficed to fix the troops on these wings in place. 2. Organize the attack on the center with the remaining 6 divisions so that 3 would constitute the reserve and be able to deliver the decisive blow after the first 3 had taken the time to prepare this decision, which is always the *conditio sine qua non*. 3. As soon as Blücher's troops at Saint-Lambert are discovered, place Lobau's corps between Frischermont and Pajeau in order to make their main resistance there. It is not very likely that the battle would have been won with this disposition, but at least there would have been some possibility of victory, and the form of the entire struggle would have been less disadvantageous."

ON WATERLOO

Bonaparte was balancing on the tip of his sword not only the crown of France but a number of other crowns as well, and by relying solely on daring and bold defiance he had made his way through a world of fixed relationships and rules that constantly opposed him. How can he be measured on the same scale as a Turenne, who belonged to a comprehensive political order that defined him far less than he defined it, and who can merely be seen as one of its more prominent members? How can one criticize Bonaparte for not avoiding a battle, even though he saw on his flank the flash of the sword that Blücher had drawn—thirsty for revenge—and realized how little hope of victory remained? After all, this was the only path to his goal, the last hope remaining at a time when his fate was hanging from a slender thread. As he advanced toward Wellington, with victory almost certain, something like 10,000 men appeared on his right flank. The odds were 100-to-1 that another five to six times as many would follow them, and then the battle could not be won. But it was also possible that those troops were only a small detachment and that uncertainty and caution would prevent them from intervening effectively. Otherwise, all that lay ahead for him was inevitable ruin. Should he allow what was simply a dangerous situation to scare him into certain defeat? No, there are situations when the greatest prudence can only be sought in the greatest boldness, and Bonaparte's situation was one of them.

Thus we judge his perseverance in his decision to give battle, and it therefore remains for us to show, from [Bonaparte's] point of view, that our disapproval of his sacrifice of the last reserves is not based on mere normal caution. As Blücher's forces grew to between 50 and 60 thousand men, as Lobau was overwhelmed and forced back to the main line of retreat, as new, dark-coated masses under Ziethen moved into the empty spaces in Wellington's line as night began to fall, ending any hope that Grouchy might come to his aid, there could no longer be any thought of victory. His duty as commander—as well as the wisest course of action—was to throw part of his reserve against Bülow to relieve the situation and gain room for a retreat, and then to begin withdrawing immediately, covered by the rest of the reserve. The battle was lost, perhaps a complete downfall no longer avoidable, but for Bonaparte's subsequent dealings there was still a huge difference between being overwhelmed by far superior numbers and making a brave, fighting withdrawal from the battlefield at the head of his indomitable band, or returning [as he did] as a virtual fugitive, burdened with the reproach of having ruined his entire army and then abandoned it.

Bonaparte may have never made a greater mistake. Clearly a commander will not win very many battles if he gingerly pulls out of the struggle whenever the scales tip slightly against him, and such a view of battle is incompatible with Bonaparte's art of war. Quite a few [of his] victories were achieved only through perseverance and the efforts of the last reserves of strength. But a critic can demand that a commander not seek to attain the impossible, and in so doing sacrifice forces that would better be employed otherwise. In this case Bonaparte does not seem to be acting in the manner of a great man but rather in vulgar exasperation, like someone who has broken an instrument and in his anger smashes the parts to pieces on the ground.

Chapter 49
The Allies

We have little to say about the conduct of the Allied commanders in the Battle of Belle Alliance.

Wellington's position was by all accounts very favorable. As for the alleged danger posed by the forest of Soignies Forest lying close to his rear, we must first look at the condition of the secondary roads before making any judgment. It has always seemed unlikely to us that in this cultivated area such a small forest would be difficult to pass through. If this was not the case, then having the forest nearby was advantageous.

One of the chief virtues in the duke's dispositions is his numerous reserves, or in other words, the limited extent of his position in relationship to the size of his army, which allowed many troops to be left in reserve. However, more could have been done to prepare and fortify the three forward posts.

In deploying his divisions the duke sometimes split them apart completely. Very likely he did this in order to mix them up so as not to leave too many unreliable troops—namely the Belgians—next to each other. In actuality this measure showed itself to be effective when the battalions under General Perponcher fell back under the French attack. If the whole division had been together here, the gap would possibly have become too large.

Certainly the principle of mixing good and bad troops with each other is better than that of leaving the bad troops together and placing them at less important points.

That the duke gave no thought to a counterattack is quite natural, since he had to leave this to the Prussians.

As for Blücher's contribution to this victory, there is not much that needs to be said. It lies primarily in his decision to march. We have already spoken of this, as well as of the simplicity and expediency of the execution.

But one special and very great service lies in his tireless pursuit throughout the night. It cannot be calculated how much this contributed to an even greater dissolution of the enemy army, and to the number and splendor of the trophies that glorify this battle.

Chapter 50
The Battle of Wavre

If we start from the situation at midday on the 17th—namely that nothing significant had been done by way of pursuing the Prussians and that the direction of their retreat was not known but was assumed to be toward Gembloux and Namur, thus towards the Meuse, and also that it was only at midday that Grouchy was finally allowed to depart, with very general instructions from Bonaparte to stay on the heels of the Prussians—then we cannot actually find it surprising that this marshal did not think of heading for the Dyle and going down this river, either on its right bank or, as would have been even better, the left. The most one could have expected was that he would send a considerable detachment, around one division of infantry and cavalry, toward Mont-Saint-Guibert in order to maintain some sort of contact with Bonaparte. But the French were never wasteful in dividing their forces. Their system was to concentrate everything at one spot and to make only the most necessary detachments. Furthermore, their attention was focused on the Meuse, and that made the Dyle uninteresting. We thus do not find it remarkable that Grouchy pursued Blücher by way of Gembloux—or at least thought he was pursuing him—and turned to the Dyle only when the Prussian trail led him there.

But as soon as he learned that Blücher had turned to the Dyle, which happened during the night of the 17th in Gembloux, then his innermost thoughts should have been that this could only be happening in order to regain contact with Wellington, for one does not leave one's natural line of retreat without reason. From that moment onward, Grouchy should have taken for granted that his mission was not to follow on the heels of Blücher's rear guard but to place his force between Blücher and Bonaparte in order to get ahead of Blücher, in case the latter marched to his right. Accordingly, Grouchy should have taken the shortest route possible from Gembloux toward the Dyle, thus via Mont-Saint-Guibert, in order either to drive away the Prussian corps that might be in this area or to take up a position himself along the left bank if it was still unoccupied, and thus hold the corps at Wavre in check. This seems to us to be the conclusion that Grouchy could have drawn through a simple and natural consideration of his position, and this consideration—not the cannon fire of Belle Alliance—should have turned him away from the direction he was taking and brought him to the upper Dyle.

Bonaparte and many others have criticized Marshal Grouchy for not listening to the advice of Exelmans and Gérard, who drew his attention to the fearsome cannonade of the main army and urged him to set forth immediately in that direction. In this respect reference is often made to the principle hastily fabricated by Rogniat,[75] that the commander of a detached column should always head in the direction where heavy firing signifies the crisis of a decisive battle. But this principle can only apply in cases in which circumstances have placed the commander of a detached column in an uncertain position, in which the clarity and precision of his original task becomes lost amidst uncertainty and overtaken by events, as so often happens in war. Instead of remaining inactive or marching around without a definite aim, it is clearly better for such a commander to hurry to the aid of his neighbor when heavy firing suggests that he is in need. But to demand of Marshal Grouchy that he should have taken no further notice of Blücher, but instead should have marched to where

---

75 Joseph Vicomte de Rogniat (1767-1840) was a French engineer general and military writer. Chapter 10 of his *Considérations sur l'art de la guerre* (Paris: Magimel, Anselin, et Pochard, 1816) refers to this issue. Cited by Hahlweg, *Schriften*, 2:1073.

another part of the army was fighting a battle against a different enemy, would have been contrary to all theory and experience. That General Gérard actually gave this advice at noon on the 18th at Sart à Walhain proves only that he who does not bear the responsibility for a decision should not be too emphatic in formulating it.[76]

Grouchy for his part never seems to have realized that Blücher's move toward Wavre actually altered his own mission. Instead, without giving it much thought, he headed his whole corps along a single road toward Wavre with the intention of attacking his opponent and pinning him down. If he had been as strong as Blücher, then we could accept this plan, but trying to pin down an enemy who is three times stronger by means of a simple frontal attack is an impossible task.

Even if Marshal Grouchy intended to carry out such a frontal attack, he should have divided his forces coming out of Gembloux and sent the greater portion to look for a crossing over the Dyle upriver from Wavre, which would have led him to Limale. How could he expect to force his way through Blücher by heading right up the main road? Even if he did not know that the Dyle was an excellent defensive position in the Wavre area, he could still have seen from the map that a numerically superior enemy could cause him a lot of difficulty there, and that an envelopment would therefore be necessary. Such an envelopment could naturally take place only on the left, because that way he would move closer to the main [French] army.

That the attacks on Wavre and Bierge were not more successful is sometimes attributed to a lack of energy, but it should be remarked that Vandamme and Gérard were not the ones who were lacking in that respect; that in addition to Gérard several other generals were wounded; and that Grouchy even placed himself at the head of a battalion at Bierge. If mistakes were made in these attacks, they were due more to clumsiness than to lack of effort. In order to make a decisive attack on Thielmann the French had to cross the Dyle in 5 or 6 places, partly over bridges and partly by wading, and then storm the heights. This was certainly not easy, as one can scarcely imagine a stronger position than Thielmann's.

---

76 This last sentence was not in Clausewitz's original manuscript, which instead contained the following sentence: "Generals Exelmans and Gérard could never have suggested such a thing, and Grouchy also denies this fact." Hahlweg, *Schriften*, 2:1074.

Admittedly Grouchy could have done more damage to General Thielmann on the 19th if he had made use of his superiority in cavalry (5,000 men versus 2,000). But he already sensed the uncertain nature of his situation in his bones, and this was hampering his actions. Finally we come to the question of whether Grouchy could have prevented Bonaparte's defeat by appearing at Saint-Lambert. We do not think so, but believe instead that he too would have been drawn into the maelstrom, that the success of the Allies would thus have been noticeably greater, since Grouchy's force would not have made it back to Paris in such strength and good order. No matter where Grouchy was located on the left bank of the Dyle at midday on the 18th, and no matter how he employed his forces against Blücher, he would have tied down two Prussian corps at best, and the other two would have been able to march to the battle of Belle Alliance. These would have sufficed to decide that battle, for when we look at what Prussian forces actually fought there, it was scarcely two entire corps.

It is not even likely that Bonaparte himself would have been able to reach Grouchy's troops on the evening of the 18th, so that in all probability his personal fate would have been the same as it actually was.

Chapter 51
A Second Battle against Blücher

One key strategic question remains, and that is whether on the 17th it might have been better for Bonaparte to pursue Blücher with his main army, either to force him into flight and confusion by means of an energetic pursuit, thus driving him back across the Meuse; or—if Blücher dared to risk a second battle on the 17th or 18th—to inflict a total defeat upon him?

To be sure, it is one of the most important and most effective principles of strategy to exploit success in battle as quickly and thoroughly as circumstances permit, since all efforts made while an opponent is in a crisis will have much greater impact than otherwise. It is thus a misuse of forces to pass up such a favorable opportunity. Furthermore, employing the remaining superiority in numbers at another location leads to a loss of time and effort on the march, which, if the situation does not absolutely require this different deployment, truly appears to be an unnecessary expense.

Moreover, it is a great strategic maxim that, when a major decision is at stake, the greatest priority must be the destruction of the enemy force. The more decisive the battle, the more important this goal is, and the more this is the case, the less important is the location where the destruction takes place. Wherever the destruction can be the greatest is thus the most effective location. Naturally, certain factors can still have a noticeable impact, such as the reputation of the commander and the army, the closeness of the capital city, relations with Allies and so on. All these and similar matters must be considered as secondary factors, but military theory must rightfully consider the destruction of the armed forces as the main goal.[77]

From this standpoint it seems to us that Bonaparte's main objective had to be to render ineffective as many of the 215,000 men facing him as possible, and it made almost no difference if this took place against Blücher or Wellington or both. While we freely admit that the psychological impact of the overall victory would have been greater if Wellington's unblemished fame and the reputation of the English troops had been destroyed at the same time, this is just a minor nuance that cannot be considered significant when compared to the possibility of a much greater destruction of the Allied forces.

We therefore believe that if Bonaparte was in a position to make a second victory more likely and more consequential by means of a second battle with Blücher rather than Wellington, he must unquestionably choose the former. By seeking a second victory, he would not have lost some of the fruits due to him from the first victory. Pursuing Blücher and seeking out a second battle would have been one and the same action.

---

[77] See *On War*, Book One, "On the Nature of War," Chapter Two, "Purpose and Means in War," 90-99. Given Clausewitz's quite false reputation as a proponent of "Total War" (a term he neither invented nor used) and other extreme measures, we must note the way (90) he defined "destruction of the enemy force": "They must be *put in such a condition that they can no longer carry on the fight*. Whenever we use the phrase "destruction of the enemy's forces" this alone is what we mean." Note also that in this paragraph of his *Campaign of 1815*, he is referring to particular circumstances, i.e., "when a major decision is at stake." (This was certainly the case in 1815, especially from Napoleon's point of view.) In the cited chapter of *On War* (96), he comments that "there are many reasons why the purpose of an engagement may not be the destruction of the enemy's forces" and that "objectives can often be attained without any fighting at all."

The first and second victories would have united into a greater whole and given a much greater result than two separate battles against different opponents, just like two flames give a much greater glow when they are united.

But was it certain that Blücher could have been forced into a second battle? At least as certain, if not more so than forcing battle against Wellington, since an army that has not yet been thrown off balance can withdraw without suffering serious consequences and thus gain time, but a defeated army cannot do that. If the pursuer presses it too heavily, it must decide to resist, or it will be caught up in a rout with heavy casualties and the loss of its honor. This moral aspect of victory should not be underestimated.

In this connection we want to suggest that if Blücher had wanted to avoid a second battle and had withdrawn back to the Meuse, a vigorous pursuit by Bonaparte would have resulted in full—or certainly partial—compensation for having missed the chance for a second victory. If this had happened—if Bonaparte had driven Blücher back 50 or 75 miles—he still would have had the opportunity to do what he did on the 17th: turn with his main force against Wellington.

What would Wellington have been able to do in the meantime? We think he would more likely have moved backwards than forwards, but we want to consider the most favorable case, namely that he inflicted a complete defeat on Marshal Ney and drove him across the Sambre. Even so, it must be admitted that one cannot gain the same advantages against 40,000 opponents as against 115,000. Every trophy that Wellington won would have been paid for three times over by Blücher. To be sure, there would have been no doubt of a victory by Wellington over Ney, while one by Bonaparte over Blücher was not so certain; but Bonaparte's position was such that when he had to choose between a greater probability of success or more decisive results in the event of success, he always had to choose the latter. Commanders who conduct campaigns against evenly matched forces, and who neither fear the worst nor seek the greatest result, can choose the lesser but more certain success. Such caution would have led Bonaparte into the abyss.

Thus if the second of the basic principles we spelled out at the beginning is correct—that in cases where interests clash violently and great decisions are at stake, the destruction of the enemy's forces is the main objective, so that the effects of all geographic and geometric considerations are overwhelmed and swept aside—then whatever apparent advantages the Allied armies may have derived from their relationship to their bases and to [other] geographic points in the area cannot be taken into consideration.

If, for example, Wellington throws Ney back past Charleroi, he stands in Bonaparte's rear and cuts his lines of communication. This would have an impact if Bonaparte wanted or needed to stay in that position, or if Charleroi were Paris; but why should a commander in the full flush of victory be concerned if he loses his line of communications for a week? What prevents Bonaparte from establishing a new one via Huy and Dinant, so as to have a line of retreat in an emergency? And if Bonaparte now turns and heads toward Wellington or Brussels, then that general must undoubtedly return there post-haste. Wellington's greater dependency on his lines of communications lay not in the [geometric] relationship of the opposing lines of communication, nor in the more substantial base of operations enjoyed by Bonaparte, but in the most general features of their positions and in the specific details of their personal situations. That which Bonaparte could risk—because he was his own master—and that which he had to risk—because only by taking great risks could he retain power—could never have been considered by a responsible subordinate commander like Wellington. The result is that if Bonaparte had maintained an unrelenting pursuit of Blücher, he would have been sure of a ripe harvest of victory that outweighed whatever he might lose in his rear, and that a single thrust toward Brussels would have brought the Duke of Wellington recoiling back there like a spring, which would have opened the way for another victory by Bonaparte.

We have assumed here a retreat by Blücher toward the Meuse, because this is what Bonaparte assumed, and he therefore based his decisions on this view. Furthermore, this situation always had to be taken into consideration. Now we come to the case that actually occurred, namely that Blücher went to the Dyle with the intention of uniting with Wellington.

Once such a union after the first battle is included in the list of possible combinations, it obviously makes no difference, either to the likelihood or the extent of success by Bonaparte, whether this union took place at Wavre or Belle Alliance. Everything depended on the single question whether such a union was more to be feared if Bonaparte sought his second battle against Blücher, or against Wellington. We are fully convinced that the latter was the case.

Blücher's ability to reassemble his forces on the 17th, and establish a sufficiently firm footing that he could accept battle at Wavre on the 18th, resulted from the mistakes, failures, omissions, caution, and inadequate forces of his pursuer, Grouchy. If Bonaparte had followed with the main army, he would have been ready to fight at Wavre early on the 18th, and it is doubtful whether Blücher would have been in a position to accept a battle at that time and place, and even more doubtful that Wellington could have rushed over in time.

We do not want to get ourselves lost in examining every possibility that could have thereby occurred, but simply want to emphasize that a second battle could have occurred much earlier against Blücher than against Wellington, because no change of direction would have been necessary and because Wellington—out of uncertainty about what had happened and what was going to happen to Blücher—would have been much less able to make a decision to aid Blücher than could Blücher to aid Wellington. Blücher knew his own situation precisely and knew that Wellington's forces were intact, but Wellington knew only his own situation and nothing about Blücher's. Bonaparte let go of Blücher too soon, which was consistent with his frequent tendency to underestimate his opponents and overrate himself. Furthermore, the thought of gaining Brussels quickly attracted him. He made the same mistake in 1813 at the Battle of Dresden and in 1814 after the battles on the Marne. In the former case he should have pursued the Allied army past Prague, and in the latter he should have ruthlessly pushed Blücher back to the Rhine. There is almost no doubt that in both instances his momentum would have pulled the whole force of events with him, and caused a complete reversal of the overall situation.

In all three cases Bonaparte—who was used to seeing defeated opponents flee far away or waver indecisively like Beaulieu after the battle of Montenotte[78]—did not believe that his beaten foe was capable of turning and standing firm so soon. This resulted from his characteristic underestimation of his opponents.

---

78 The battle of Montenotte (12 April 1796) was Napoleon's first victory in the Italian campaign. He defeated an Austro-Piedmontese force while an Austrian force under General Jean Pierre Baron von Beaulieu (1725-1819) stood nearby.

This seems more like a mistake than a fundamental error. But we maintain that in all three cases changing direction undermined the whole result, and that the reasons for these changes were not strong enough to justify deviating from the general principle of our theory. For this reason we must consider it to be a true error.

But even if after reviewing the whole series of events we now believe that this was clearly an error by Bonaparte, a deviation from the law that had heretofore directed his meteoric path, we do not think it would have been easy to avoid. The decision to ignore Blücher on the Elbe [in 1813], Schwarzenberg on the Seine [in 1814], or Wellington on the Sambre [in 1815] would have been enormous for a general in ordinary circumstances or possessing a normal amount of willpower. But the enormousness comes not from theory but from the mission, from Bonaparte's situation and his goal. Strategy is like the art of perspective, in that the standpoint of the viewer determines the position of every line. If an object appears enormous, it is either because the draftsman's eye is not yet accustomed to it, or because the natural proportions have been transgressed, and a task bordering on the impossible has been selected.

Chapter 52
Consequences of the Battle

The French calculate their losses in the Battle of Belle Alliance at 25,000 men including 6,000 prisoners, and their total losses for all five days at 41,000 men. If you include just dead, wounded, and prisoners taken on the field of battle, these figures are not too low, but it would be a great mistake to assume that of the 115,000 men who, according to the French, marched off to this campaign, 74,000 remained. The extent of a victory, that is to say, the destructive effects which it inflicts on the enemy army, can naturally have countless gradations, but among these there is one major dividing line: when the defeated army is no longer capable of forming a rear guard in order to slow down and control the victorious pursuer. Then the retreat is truly flight, everything is in dissolution, and the army for the moment must be considered destroyed. Prince Hohenlohe at Jena and Bonaparte at Belle Alliance are examples of this. Such success must always result when the individual who has seen the tide of victory turning against him tries to force a turnaround with a final sacrifice, thus using up the reserve that could have formed the rear guard. This is what Bonaparte did with the last eight battalions of the Imperial Guard. The extent to which an army can regroup following such a total dissolution naturally varies greatly according to the circumstances. The time of day when the battle ends, the area and terrain where it is fought, the morale of the army, the political situation of the people and the government—these things all play a role. In his *Mémoires de St. Hélène* Bonaparte claims that 25,000 men of the defeated army were reassembled at Laon.[79] This was not impossible, but there is a big difference between possibility and realistic probability.

The battle ended at nightfall. The result was that on the one side the confusion and dissolution became even greater. It might have been possible for Bonaparte to form a rear guard of 10 or 15,000 men and thus stage some sort of a retreat instead of flight, if darkness had not made his personal intervention impossible. On the other hand, it is also certain that the night made the flight of individuals easier and that a few more hours of daylight on the 18th would have greatly increased the numbers of prisoners taken. Under the cover of darkness, everyone who could move could save himself. It is well known from the *Memoires de Chaboulon* that Bonaparte passed through Charleroi between 4 and 5 a.m. on the 19th and tried in vain to halt the fleeing troops there and restore order. He then continued his flight toward Philippeville. Charleroi is around 15 miles from the battlefield, so whoever was already in Charleroi at this time must have been running all the way.[80]

Fugitives had already reached Philippeville on the 19th, and they were equally incapable of resistance, so Bonaparte hurried that same day toward Laon. What is truly revealing is that in Laon, most likely on the morning of the 21st, thus around 60 hours after the end of the battle and ninety miles from the battlefield, Bonaparte received a report that a considerable body of troops was approaching. He sent his adjutant to see who it was, and it was his brother Jerome with the generals Soult, Morand, Colbert, Petit, and Poret de Morvan, who were arriving with around 3,000 infantrymen and cavalrymen they had gathered together.

---

79 Napoleon, *Mémoires*, 170.
80 Fleury du Chaboulon's account of the events in Charleroi after the battle is found in his *Mémoires* 2:194. No mention of the time is found here, however, so Clausewitz must have taken that from Napoleon, *Mémoires*, 169.

ON WATERLOO

Regardless of how much respect one may have for the French army, this can only be called complete dissolution, a flight without equal.

It was Jerome, however, who had been designated by Bonaparte to collect the army at Avesnes, and of whom Bonaparte said in his *Memoirs* that he had already assembled 25,000 men there on the 21st. Bonaparte also has Jerome bringing 50 cannon back with him, but it is well known that all of the 240 guns comprising the French artillery had been captured either on the battlefield or during the retreat.

As the pursuing Prussian corps advanced beyond the Oise down the road from Soissons to Paris, they encountered Grouchy on the 28th. For several days a few weak remnants of the defeated army had flitted past them like shadows, so it is certain that there was no organized body of 25,000 men assembled in either Laon or Soissons, and that those troops who were there did not unite with Grouchy but fled to Paris before he arrived. Grouchy himself speaks in his reports to the government commission about the low morale and disaffection of the army.[81]

The strength of the army at Paris also proves this. Not counting the National Guard, this army had 60,000 men, of whom 19,000 had come from the depots, so only 40,000 could have been from the main army and of these, around 25,000 had come with Grouchy, so the remaining 15,000 must have been the residue of the army that had been defeated at Belle Alliance. It is thus clear that between the battlefield and Paris this army had disappeared as a factor in the course of events.

Strategically, a victory of this scale has to be regarded as in a class by itself, deriving from exceptional circumstances and leading to results of a most exceptional kind. As for the causes that led to it, they are mainly as follows:

1. The extreme effort that the French army had already made by the time the victory was decided. The more exhausted the forces are before the decisive blow in a battle occurs, the more effective and consequential this blow will be. In this case, as we have already said, the exhaustion of French forces had been taken to the limit, if not beyond it, because Bonaparte had recklessly thrown his last reserves, which should have been his rear guard, into the destruction of the firefight, as he had already done with the entire cavalry. The use of the last reserves can be forgiven, or can even be quite natural, in a battle whose outcome remains in

---

81 Fleury du Chaboulon, *Mémoires*, 2:325.

the balance until the last moment; but not when the scales have already tipped so heavily in favor of the opponent. In that case [such a move] can only be regarded as contemptible foolhardiness, lacking the wisdom of the true commander.

2. Nightfall, which made it impossible to control the increasing chaos.
3. The outflanking form of the Prussian attack.
4. The great numerical superiority of the Allies.
5. The very energetic pursuit.
6. Finally, the influence of all the political elements, which more or less permeate every war, but which naturally imposed themselves even more strongly in this one and proved to be liabilities of the worst kind.

The less the preparations for a decisive event are firmly grounded in the natural conditions and interests of the people, and the more they are artificially inflated, based on luck, and undertaken in the spirit of bold risk-taking, the more destructive will be the impact of an unfavorable outcome that releases all these tensions.

All of these circumstances have contributed to the magnitude of the victory in the present case, and we are only justified in setting our sights so high when several of them are in our favor.

As to the consequences that follow from the destruction of an entire army, they generally depend primarily on political factors, the condition of the people and the government, the relationships with other peoples, and so forth, just as the strengths and actions, means and ends of strategy move ever deeper into the realm of politics in accordance with their size and scope; for war can never be seen as an independent matter, but only as a modification of political relationships, as the implementation of political plans and interests via the domain of battle.[82]

There was never any doubt that such a victory in the present case would lead directly to Paris, and to peace. Prior to Paris, resistance was out of the question, because no enemy force of any importance could be fielded. Even in Paris itself, resistance was quite unlikely, because the defense of such a large city is always very difficult, although not impossible, and it requires more favorable conditions than were at hand in this case. Even if the forces available in Paris had sufficed for the moment to secure the city against Blücher and Wellington, the rest of the inadequately defended country stood open to the other Allied armies. These armies

---

[82] See *On War*, Book 1, chapter 1, and Book 8, chapter 6.

would appear in front of the capital after a few weeks, having conquered half of France on the way. How could a population riven by political factions have offered resistance under such circumstances, and would not this impossibility have given the first impetus to internal reaction in Paris itself?

All that Bonaparte and his supporters have said about the great forces that were still available, about the possibility—yes, even the ease—of continued resistance, is mere blather. In placing the loss of 40,000 men into a simple mathematical relationship to the initial forces, they want to give the impression that this was an insignificant portion of the whole, but even they do not have the courage to state this laughable argument openly. It is not 40,000 men that France lost on the fields of Ligny and Belle Alliance; it was an army of 80,000 that was destroyed. This army was the cornerstone of the entire defense structure, on which everything depended, in which all security lay and where every hope was rooted. The army was destroyed, and the commander who led it, in whose miraculous abilities half of France believed with an enthusiasm bordering on superstition, the great magician, was—as he himself said of Blücher at Ligny—caught *en flagrant délit*. Thus all trust in the mind that was directing everything collapsed along with the military structure that was supposed to protect France's borders.

For these reasons no victory has ever had greater psychological power than this one, and what was accomplished by this power—the sudden overthrow of the huge faction that had formed against the Bourbons, plus the exile of Bonaparte, who was still worshipped by half of France—is therefore not remarkable and cannot be attributed to the actions of individuals. Indeed, it would have been almost a miracle if things had turned out otherwise.

The full extent of this victory was already clear to the two Allied commanders on the day after the battle, because trophies of victory comprising 240 guns (their entire artillery park), plus all the field equipment of the enemy commander-in-chief, leave nothing to be desired. They are the unmistakable sign of an army that has been totally destroyed and driven from the field.

Chapter 53
The March on Paris: Initial Pursuit

The Allied commanders thus clearly understood that they would encounter no opposition before Paris, and that if the enemy could actually meet them again on anything like equal terms there, the rapid approach of the other Allied armies would make a real setback difficult in any case. The march on Paris was thus legitimate, and in strategy whatever is legitimate must be done. Only *this* march made proper use of the brilliant victory, and was worthy of it and of the two commanders and the fame of their arms. Any lesser venture would have left the circle of victory incomplete and been a true waste of energy, because the fruits for which the price had been paid at Ligny and Belle Alliance would not have been harvested.

Since the Allies advanced on Paris as quickly as possible, they continued to pursue the beaten enemy up to the walls of the city, took new prisoners, and were hopeful of driving isolated units away from this central point of enemy power, shattering all organized resistance up to there, and bringing about terror, confusion, and disunity in Paris itself. If they brought in no appreciable number of new prisoners, if no enemy forces were driven off, if the catastrophe of Bonaparte's fall took place before the Allied advance on Paris was known in the capital, these intentions remain no less valid from the point of view of Blücher and Wellington, for in war we can never know in advance exactly how events will unfold. But the rapid march on Paris nevertheless hastened the end of the whole drama by depriving the republican party, which was again starting to stir, of the time and energy necessary even to attempt to reconstitute itself.

If we here give such precise reasons for the march on Paris, it is not because it requires justification. There can be no question of that, since it involved no danger, and that being so the honor of arms alone would already be sufficient reason. Rather, we dwell on it to draw attention to how, in the conduct of war, all the likely consequences of an event have to be thought through and brought into consideration, and that in this respect the ceaseless advance on Paris appears to the critic as an absolutely essential component of this campaign.

The two Allied commanders agreed on the battlefield itself that the Prussian army would undertake the subsequent pursuit, because it was less strained and weakened by the battle, and because it was further forward owing to the nature of its attack. It was also agreed that the Prussian army should strike out along the road through Charleroi to Avesnes, thus toward Laon, the other Allies on the road through Nivelles and Binche toward Péronne.

The English army thus remained on the battlefield, while most of the Prussians were on the march. The 4th Corps was in the lead. Lieutenant General von Gneisenau placed himself at the head of its most forward troops and urged on the pursuit throughout the night. He had the drums beat incessantly, so that this sign of approach would alarm the fleeing enemy from all sides, frighten them out of their bivouacs, and keep them constantly on the run.

Bonaparte had left the battlefield with a small entourage, and initially thought of remaining at Quatre-Bras and of drawing Girard's division to him. This was supposed to be the first way-station on the retreat, the first concentration point. But Girard's division was nowhere to be found, and the terrifying drumbeat of the Prussians drove everything onward without rest to the Sambre.

At daybreak the mass of fugitives reached this river at Charleroi, Marchiennes, and Châtelet, but there too no pause was possible. The Prussian advance guard, which had pressed forward to Gosselies, sent its cavalry to the Sambre, and the fleeing army continued on toward Beaumont and Philippeville.

In all probability this energetic initial pursuit is responsible for a large part of the overall success. The flight, the disorder, the demoralization, and thus the dispersal of the army were all heightened by it. It is well known that the majority of the captured artillery was found on the roads used in the retreat, because in the haste and confusion of flight they were all jammed and jumbled together in the defiles, for instance at the bridge over the Dyle in Genappe, so that the artillerymen, convinced of the impossibility of saving their weapons, simply set the horses free in order to escape on them. The rich and brilliant trophies of the imperial carriage, for which Bonaparte was so reluctant to answer, were also due only to this fortunate idea of pursuit. If we call it that, it is not because pursuit following a victorious battle is not basically natural in itself, and necessary in all circumstances, but rather because ordinarily [even] the best of wills gets stuck in a thousand problems and points of friction in the machinery. In the present case the enormous exertions of the Prussian troops prior to the victory made the execution of the [pursuit] so difficult that in the end the force with which General Gneisenau pressed on so relentlessly was really nothing more than a fusilier battalion and its tireless drummer, whom the general had put on one of Bonaparte's coach horses.

This is striking proof, not to mention a most vivid image, of the enormously different effects that identical expenditures of energy can have in war.

An army like the French, glorified by a string of victories over more than twenty years, which originally displayed the compact structure, the indestructibility, and, one could even say, the brilliance of a gem, whose courage and order were not dissolved or dissipated by mere danger in the blazing fire of battle, such an army, if the ennobling forces that gave it its crystalline structure are broken—its faith in its commander, in itself, and the sacred discipline of service—such an army flies in breathless terror before the sound of a drum, before a threat from its opponent that bordered on a joke.

In the conduct of war it is a great thing to correctly evaluate the innumerable gradations that lie between these two extremes; it is a matter of individual, intuitive judgment, which can be inborn, but which, more than any other quality of a commander, can also be cultivated through experience, that is, through practice. Only to the extent that we allow ourselves to be led by this intuition will we always find the right degree of effort to make in war—and indeed in great things no less than small, in the conduct of a campaign as of a patrol—so that no opportunities are missed on the one hand, nor effort wasted on the other.

Let us return now to the battlefield, to examine the relationship of the opposing forces more clearly. Prince Blücher's dispositions on the evening of the 18th were as follows:

a) the 4th Corps was in pursuit of the enemy so that he could not pause and regroup;
b) the 2nd Corps was cutting off Marshal Grouchy;
c) the 1st Corps was following the 4th in support.

ON WATERLOO

Had Prince Blücher known Grouchy's strength on the evening of the 18th, he could rightly be criticized for not giving the 1st Corps the same orders as the 2nd. For since Grouchy had some 30,000 men, and since it really was a question of cutting him off, it can well be argued that 20,000 men (the 2nd Corps would still have been about this strong if it was all together) were not enough. To be sure, Thielmann also had about 20,000 men, only it was very uncertain whether these would be on hand at the moment when Grouchy, hastening to his rear, fell upon the 2nd Corps. But at that point Blücher thought Grouchy was only 12-15,000 men strong, because the last reports of General Thielmann suggested no more. For such a force the Prussian 2nd Corps would have been enough. Moreover, the prince did not actually think Grouchy's whole force would be captured; instead he probably thought General Pirch should simply attack from the rear and perhaps cut off one part or another, for it was naturally assumed that Grouchy had begun his retreat that night, and would have advanced too far for anyone to be able to get directly in front of him while still on the way to Namur.

Nevertheless, if we consider that at the end of the Battle of Belle Alliance Grouchy still had to retreat; that the only way he had across the Meuse was at Namur, and that there were certainly no pontoons around with which to build a bridge elsewhere; that if we took this spot away from him he had to force his way across the Sambre, where we could easily have had sufficient light troops to hold him back; that taking even 12-15,000 prisoners was a very important thing—then we cannot refrain from counting it as an error on the prince's part that he did not send the 2nd Corps down the same road to Namur. If Marshal Grouchy could be blocked anywhere, it naturally had to be easiest at the most distant point. There was nothing to fear except reaching too far, and that the enemy—having been informed of the loss of Namur—could turn toward the Sambre, but in that case we could have been ready to oppose him there. In the tumult at the close of a battle, with its hundred demands of the moment, all these things were not so clearly and carefully weighed and considered as they are so easily by us now, and the result was a half measure.

As a consequence of the dispositions described above, Prussian forces on the night of the 18th-19th were located as follows:

THE CAMPAIGN OF 1815

a) the 1st Corps north of Genappes;
b) the 2nd on the march from Planchenoit via Glabbaix la Hutte to Meilleraux;
c) the 3rd at Wavre;
d) the 4th between Genappe and Gosselies, with the advance guard at the latter place;
e) Wellington's army remained on the battlefield.
f) Blücher's headquarters was in Genappe.
g) Wellington's headquarters was in Mont-Saint-Jean.
h) The French army was in flight, crossing the Sambre at Charleroi, Châtelet and Marchienne, partly on the road to Beaumont, partly to Philippeville.
i) Bonaparte in flight via Charleroi toward Philippeville; Grouchy at Wavre.

On the 19th Prince Blücher's orders for the day were as follows:

a) The 1st Corps was to advance to Charleroi and push its advance guard out to Marchiennes-au-pont.
b) The 2nd Corps was to march to Avesnes and push its advance guard out to the Sambre to cross it on the two bridges at Thuin and Lobbes. If the enemy wished to make a stand on the Sambre, the sluices [would] have to be opened so the water subsided, making the river fordable at several places. If the bridges at Lobbes and Thuin were destroyed, they would have to be rebuilt at once.
c) The 4th Corps was to advance this day toward Fontaine l'Evèque and immediately establish communications with Mons, etc.

We see from these orders that the only report the prince had from the 2nd Corps was that it was at Meillereaux but had heard nothing about the enemy, and that as a consequence he completely gave up the idea of that corps cutting off Grouchy, since he deployed it in a completely different direction. He could not have received a report from the 3rd Corps, since the enemy still stood in between.

ON WATERLOO

Thus on the 19th, the day when the actual arrangements to cut off Grouchy would have had to have been made, Blücher believed [Grouchy had] already escaped, and he was all the more set on continuing his advance via Avesnes.

On the evening of the 19th the positions of the opposing armies were:

>a) the 1st Corps at Charleroi, having completed a march of sixteen miles;
>b) the 2nd Corps at Meillereaux, which it reached only toward midday;
>c) the 3rd Corps at Saint-Achtenrode;
>d) the 4th at Fontaine l'Evèque, having likewise marched sixteen miles.
>e) the 5th brigade of the Second Corps, which was not with the Corps, at Anderlues, not far from Fontaine l'Evèque;
>f) the English army in the vicinity of Nivelles;
>g) Blücher's headquarters in Gosselies; Wellington's headquarters in Nivelles;
>h) the French main army around Beaumont and Philippeville, some already moving toward Avesnes;
>i) Bonaparte reached Philippeville at 10 a.m. and left there around 2 p.m. for Laon;
>j) Grouchy was on the march from Wavre to Namur.

On the evening of the 20th:

>a) the 1st Corps at Beaumont, after a march of eighteen miles;
>b) the 4th Corps at Colleret, not far from Maubeuge, after a march of sixteen miles;
>c) the 5th Brigade surrounding Maubeuge;
>d) the 2nd Corps at Namur;
>e) the 3rd at Gembloux and Namur;
>f) the Allied army in the vicinity of Binche;
>g) Prince Blücher's headquarters at Merbe le Chateau
>h) Wellington's headquarters at Binche;
>i) the main French army partly at Avesnes, partly further to the rear;

j) Bonaparte in Laon;
k) Grouchy in Dinant.

On the evening of the 21st:

a) the 1st Corps surrounded and bombarded Avesnes;
b) the 4th Corps between Avesnes and Landrecy, surrounding the latter place;
c) the 2nd Corps at Thuin;
d) the 3rd at Charleroi.
e) The Allied army between Mons and Valenciennes.
f) Blücher's headquarters at Nogelle sur Sambre.
g) Wellington's headquarters at Malplaquet.
h) The defeated [French] army begins to assemble at Laon and Marle.
i) Bonaparte arrives in Paris, where he will be forced to abdicate the following day.
j) Grouchy at Philippeville.

On the 21st General Ziethen had a battery of six ten-pounders, four seven-pound howitzers, and eight twelve-pounders drawn up within six hundred paces of Avesnes, and began the bombardment with it.

The force occupying the fortress consisted of 1,700 national guardsmen and 200 veterans. The initial fire achieved little, but when it began again that night, a ten-pound shell from the fourteenth volley fell in the fort's main powder magazine, blew it into the air, and laid waste to a large part of the town; whereupon its occupation followed on the 22nd.

Chapter 54
The March on Paris: Critical Comment

We have followed the movements on the first three days following the battle rather closely in order to make the actual results of that catastrophe clear. After these three days the direct consequences of the victory had come to an end, the defeated army had gained the necessary head start, Grouchy had successfully avoided being cut off and had directed the rest of his retreat down the highway to Rheims. Now we simply want to have the general situation in view, so we will content ourselves with describing only the main lines of the marches.

The Allied commanders knew the enemy had made Laon the main focus of his retreat and his assembly area. Now, what the enemy could deploy there was scarcely capable of mounting significant resistance or even of making a second decisive battle necessary, but it could still hamper the march of the Allies through rear guard actions and force them into circuitous marches. The Allied commanders therefore decided to proceed not toward Laon but along the right bank of the Oise, so as to cross this river between Soissons and Paris, roughly at Compiègne and Pont-Saint-Maxence. They hoped in this way to gain the following advantages:

1. To induce the enemy force, since it would not be pressed, to stay in place for a while and so perhaps get a head start on it toward Paris.

2. To be able to march unhindered, without expending a lot of effort on tactical precautions, and therefore faster.

3. To march in an area not already traversed by the retreating army, which was thus generally fresher and also somewhat better in itself, and so make the march easier for their own troops; a very important consideration because their earlier exertions had been so exceptional, and one certainly ought not to arrive at Paris unduly weak.

Since the diversion that the closest Allied column had to make involved only about a day's march, namely the piece of road it had to cover to reach the Soissons-Paris road again, and since there was no doubt that this diversion would easily be made up by the undisturbed advance later on, this plan, which presented itself so naturally, cannot be rejected out of hand. But if we consider the matter closely, the following questions arise:

1. Is it perhaps a mistake to think that a totally unpursued enemy would retreat more slowly? At first he might be tempted to ease up some, but a lateral march occurring so near to him would become known soon, and then he would make it the yardstick for his own movement.

Now it is obvious that a march without rear guard actions can be much faster, for the rear guard's movements in the face of the enemy have to be made while expending a lot of incidental tactical effort, by which its retreat must be greatly delayed; but you cannot leave your rear guard in the lurch all the time, so its delays are inevitably shared by the whole army.

Prince Blücher had actually decided to have twelve squadrons under Lieutenant-Colonel Sohr, which were supposed to be his advance guard, follow the enemy down the road to Laon; but these few cavalrymen were not sufficient for tying down the enemy columns very often or for long. It would thus have been better, for the purpose of outflanking the enemy and pushing him away from Paris, if the most forward corps, that is, the 1st, had remained on the Laon highway and kept steady pressure on the enemy rear guard, while the 3rd and 4th Corps proceeded along the right bank of the Oise.

There is no denying that in this way the 1st Corps would have been confronted with the possibility of fighting at a disadvantage, but this fighting would have been richly repaid by the lost time it would have cost the enemy. It was perhaps the only way to imagine him really being driven away from Paris.

2. Considering that on the morning of the 22nd Grouchy was still holding on at Namur, while Blücher had already reached the vicinity of Beaumont, we certainly think a direct advance along the road to Laon must have deflected Marshal Grouchy from there, as well as from Soissons, and consequently prevented him from uniting with the defeated army this side of Paris.

Now that in itself was not so important, but the main point would have been to cut Grouchy off from Paris, and this was still possible in the first instance only if he was already cut off from Soissons.

To tell the truth, it is never easy with a small head-start to cut someone off from a large city, least of all if the city lies on one or more rivers. This is the case with Paris. A glance at a map shows how the considerable extent of the city, the convergence of several excellent highways, and the way the countryside is cut up by the Marne and Seine, still provide means for a retreating force to reach the city, even if its opponent has gotten to the outskirts a day earlier, or even two, by the most direct route. To totally surround a city like Paris, and thereby keep your opponent away from it completely, requires several days and a very substantial force, which meant awaiting the arrival of all the other columns, since they cannot all arrive at the same moment by the same direct route.

The campaign of 1814 offers two examples of this kind. Marshals Mortier and Marmont, who were cut off by Yorck and Kleist on March 26 while on the road from La Ferté Gauche, reached Paris by way of the road from Provins; and Bonaparte himself could not have been cut off when he returned from his move toward Saint-Dizier, if the city had not already gone over to the Allies in the meantime.

It is thus very doubtful whether the Allies, had they been able to get in front of Grouchy at Soissons, would have been in a position to drive this general completely away from Paris; indeed we actually consider this most unlikely. It then came down to further maneuvering, i.e., a march to Meaux, then to Melun, and so forth.

But this much is certain: that if Grouchy could not be cut off from Paris before Soissons, it was even less possible to do so if he was allowed to reach that city. Consequently, the hope of driving the enemy force completely away from Paris by means of the flank march does not seem to rest on a really clear understanding of the situation.

But the less possible it seems to cut Grouchy's force off from Paris, the more important it becomes to take good care of one's own troops. So we can well say that on the whole the routes chosen for the march to Paris, even at present when all the circumstances are known, do not seem inappropriate.

Chapter 55
Table of Marches

The following table provides a survey of the main stages of the whole march:

	1st Corps	4th Corps	3rd Corps	Wellington	Grouchy
19th	Charleroi	Fontaine L'evèque	St. Achtenrode	Nivelle	Wavre
20th	Beaumont	Coleret, near Maubeuge	Gembloux	Binche	Dinant
21st	Avesnes	Landrecy	Charleroi	Malplacquet	Phillippeville

THE CAMPAIGN OF 1815

22nd	Etrouenge	Fesmey, by Nouvion	Beaumont	Chateau-Cambrésis	Rocroy
23rd	—	—	Avesnes	—	Morfontaine
24th	Guise	Bernonville	Nouvion	—	Rethel
25th	Cerisi, between St. Quentin and La Fère	St. Quentin	Homblieres	Cambrai	—
26th	Chaunay, between La Fère and Noyon	Lassigny, between Noyon and the road from Péronne to Pont St. Maxence	Compiègne	Péronne	Soissons
27th	Gelicourt. Engagement at Compiègne	Pont St. Maxence. Engagements at Creil and Senlis	—	Nesle	Villers-Cotterêt
28th	Nanteuil. Engagement at Villers-Cotterêt	Marlis-la-Ville	Crépy	Orville	Meaux
29th	Aunay	Bourguet	Dammartin	St. Martin Longueau	Paris
30th	Aunay	Engagement at Aubervillers and St. Denis	En route to St. Germain	Louvres	
1st	Le Menil, below St. Germain	en route to St. Germain	St. Germain. Engagements at Versailles and Marli	Gonesse	
2nd	Meudon. Engagements at Sèvres and Issi	Versailles	Plessi-Piquet		
3rd	Engagement at Issi				
4th	Convention for the evacuation of Paris				

ON WATERLOO

This survey reveals:

1. That the Prussian army marched in two columns, the left wing consisting of the 1st Corps, the right wing of the 4th, both only a few miles apart, and that the 3rd Corps followed the other two as a reserve, sometimes on the one road, sometimes on the other.

2. That the column on the left crossed the Oise at Compiègne, the one on the right at Pont-Saint-Maxence and Creil.

3. That the left column advanced to Avesnes, Guise, and La Fère, whereby the first, with its garrison of 1,900 men, was taken after a bombardment of a few hours on the 22nd. Guise, with its garrison of 3,500 men, was taken on the 24th without a bombardment and occupied by 3,500 men; and La Fère was shelled without success for several hours and then observed by an infantry battalion and a squadron of cavalry.

4. That the Duke of Wellington proceeded via Cambrai in a third column and fell in behind the 4th Corps a day later at Pont-Saint-Maxence.

5. That he encountered the fortresses at Cambrai and Péronne, both of which, not being particularly defensible, were taken by him through an easy storming of the outer works.

6. That the Prussian army's march from the battlefield to Paris lasted eleven days and covered 165 miles up to Gonesse, so the speed of the march was certainly very considerable, which is also evident from the fact that only one day of rest was allowed.

7. As far as Grouchy's march is concerned, it is uncertain what route he took from Rethel to Soissons. He joined up there with the remnants of the defeated army and then began his further retreat to Paris, during which, as we will see later, he would be driven from the direct road and forced to go over Meaux. He was still at Wavre on the 19th, and reached Paris on the 29th. During these ten days he covered about 230 miles and fought several engagements.

While the two Allied armies thus hastened to Paris in three columns, they left a portion of their forces behind to besiege the nearest fortresses.

By agreement between them the Prussians undertook the siege of all the fortresses on the Sambre and to the east of this river, the Anglo-Dutch army those that lay to the west.

Prince Blücher assigned this task to the Prussian 2nd Corps and the federal troops from North Germany, under the overall command of His Royal Highness, Prince August [of Prussia].

The Duke of Wellington likewise assigned 15,000 men under His Royal Highness, Prince Frederick of the Netherlands.

After thus detaching around 60,000 men, the remaining strength of the Allies marching to Paris was about 70,000 men under Blücher, about 60,000 under Wellington. But of course we still have to subtract some 10,000 men that each of these armies left behind in garrisons and for other purposes, so that they arrived in front of Paris with no more than 100,000 men [between them].

If it had still been possible for a second decisive battle to occur there before the arrival of the other Allied armies, it would have been a mistake for the two commanders to leave so many troops behind, since nothing compelled them to besiege or surround so many fortresses at the same time, and 30 or 40,000 men would have been sufficient to surround those directly on the [Allied] lines of communications, and to observe the others. But one could foresee with certainty that even at Paris there was no question of resistance in the countryside, or even less of a counterattack, and if Paris turned out to be occupied too strongly, one could await the arrival of the other armies. It thus gained time to leave significant numbers of troops behind in order to be able to besiege several fortresses at once, and so gain actual possession of the country sooner. Moreover, it might be expected that some of these places would give way more quickly, thanks to the effects of the initial panic.

The army engaged in marching to Paris first encountered the enemy again when it crossed the Oise on the 27th.

The advance guard of the 1st Corps did so at Compiègne at 3 a.m. It had just entered the town, which lies on the left bank of the river, when it was attacked by General d'Erlon. An insignificant fight ensued. Since the French marshal had presumably arrived in too little strength, and too late in any event, he soon withdrew on his own, and the 1st Corps advanced along the Soissons-Paris road as far as Gelicourt, while sending forward its 2nd Brigade, reinforced by a regiment of dragoons, to seize control of the highway at Villers-Cotterêt and cut off any French troops that might still be in Soissons.

The 4th Corps had found Pont-Saint-Maxence unoccupied, and likewise the bridge at Creil, but nevertheless, its vanguard encountered a weak enemy detachment at Creil, which immediately gave way.

ON WATERLOO

When the advance guard of the 4th Corps reached Senlis, it found the town occupied by the enemy. It was then engaged for a time, and gained possession of the town at ten in the evening.

All of these detachments seem to have come from the defeated main army, and in fact their weakness, their limited resistance, and their failure to occupy the Oise bridges suggest that these remnants were certainly not going to be found in appreciable strength and a decent state of readiness.

Toward evening on the 27th the utterly exhausted troops of Marshal Grouchy's 4th Corps arrived at Villers-Cotterêt, and those of the 3rd at Soissons. He quartered his troops in the nearby villages, in order to provide them with essential food and rest as quickly as possible, and decided at two o'clock the following morning to continue the march to Nanteuil. Since he must have gotten news at Villers-Cotterêt of the battle that had taken place that morning at Compiègne, it was very risky for him to continue the march on the Soissons road. It would have been more sensible to turn immediately toward Meaux, via Ferté Milon, for at Nanteuil he could have run into three Prussian corps and been destroyed within sight of Paris. Most probably the thought of taking his weary troops on a new detour over terrible roads repelled him, and the hope of still getting though on a good quality and straight major road attracted him. He did not in fact achieve his goal, for he still had to abandon the road, but he also did not suffer the catastrophe that had threatened him. This is because the Prussian forces were not sufficiently concentrated to mount a concerted attack on him.

As we have already said, General Pirch and his 2nd Brigade were detached toward Villers-Cotterêt and on the night of the 27th-28th reached Longpré, about an hour away, at one a.m. He allowed his troops some rest and broke camp again at 2 o'clock. He initially ran into a train of horse artillery, 14 guns and 20 munitions wagons, which were trying to reach the highway from their camps at Viviers, Montgobert, and Puiseux, and were moving with virtually no escort; they were thus captured immediately. After this General Pirch advanced to attack Villers-Cotterêt itself.

Grouchy assembled his troops, 9,000 strong (presumably Gérard's corps), and offered resistance. On the other side Vandamme came up from Soissons with the French 3rd Corps. Although the sound of cannon fire on the Paris highway immediately caused a kind of panic-stricken terror to set in, as cries that they might be cut off led most of the troops there to strike out at once by way of Ferté Milon for Meaux, Vandamme nevertheless succeeded in advancing up the road with about 2000 men and came to Marshal Grouchy's assistance. General Pirch had only 5 under-strength battalions, 5 squadrons of cavalry, and 13 cannon; General Ziethen and most of the Prussian 1st Corps were on the march from Gilicourt to Crépy , around 3 hours away, and were not near enough to provide support. Vandamme advanced against Pirch's left flank, Grouchy maneuvered against his right, and under these circumstances General Pirch correctly decided a bold assault was ill-advised and so began to retreat toward Compiègne, from which he later turned toward Crépy by way of Fresnoy. General Ziethen had not yet assembled his troops at Crépy, so when the French corps passed by he could move against the highway only with the 3rd Brigade and half the reserve cavalry. The village of Levignen, through which the French passed, was shelled and the rear guard pursued to Nanteuil, where two cannon were taken.

The French corps now presumably learned that another Prussian corps had already crossed the river the day before at Creil and Pont-Saint-Maxence and did not consider it advisable to continue along the Soissons-Paris highway, but instead turned left via Assi to Meaux, and from there via Claye to Paris, where it arrived on the 29th, presumably in a rather weakened state. In addition to the 2 guns, the Prussians took about a thousand prisoners during these two days.

Thus on the 29th the Prussian army found itself in front of Paris, with its right wing behind Saint-Denis and its left by the Bondi woods. The Duke of Wellington's army was supposed to arrive on the evening of the 30th, and then Prince Blücher wanted to march off to the right with his own, crossing the Seine somewhere below Saint-Denis, in order to surround the south side of the city, or rather to establish a position there from which to attack.

Meanwhile, in order to get the most use from the initial panic, an attack against the enemy lines and outposts behind the Ourq canal was to be attempted on the night of the 29th-30th by a brigade from the 1st and 4th Corps, with the rest of the corps advancing in support. The attack took place and resulted in a sharp fight with the advance guard of the French 4th Corps at Aubervillers, but generally the enemy was found to be in good order.

Because Prince Blücher had learned that Bonaparte was in seclusion at Malmaison following his forced abdication on the 22nd, Major von Colomb of the 8th Hussars was ordered to find out whether the bridge at Chatou, on the Paris-Saint-Germain road, might still be intact, and perhaps proceed to nearby Malmaison and take Bonaparte into custody. If he found the bridge already demolished, he was to seize the one at Saint-Germain. The bridge at Chatou was in fact destroyed, so it was through this detachment that the Prussian army gained control of the bridge at Saint-Germain, which was supposed to have been demolished as well and which was very important in crossing the Seine, because this could now be accomplished a day or two sooner.

The 3rd Corps, which departed from Dammartin at 5 a.m. on the 30th, reached Gonesse at midday and had to continue its march around Paris that evening, while the 1st and 4th Corps remained opposite the enemy pending the arrival of Wellington's army. The 3rd Corps proceeded behind St. Denis via Argenteuil to Saint-Germain, where it arrived at 3 a.m., having covered thirty-two miles in less than twenty-four hours. It remained at Saint-Germain.

Lieutenant-Colonel von Sohr, with six squadrons of Brandenburg and Pomeranian Hussars, thus about 600 horse, had been ordered to push forward past Saint-Germain and Versailles toward the Orleans road. He crossed the Seine before the 3rd Corps and was in Versailles when this corps reached Saint-Germain.

The 1st Corps followed the 3rd at 11 p.m., crossing the Seine below Saint-Germain at Le Menil, which it reached at seven the [following] evening, and where it remained.

The 4th Corps proceeded toward Saint-Germain at noon on the first, arriving there that night.

Lieutenant-Colonel Sohr had fed his horses at Versailles and remained there for several hours with his detachment. The French, having learned of this, laid a trap for him in the woods between Versailles and Marli with two regiments of cavalry and some infantry. As Lieutenant-Colonel Sohr left Versailles around midday on the road to Plessis-Piquet, he encountered enemy dragoons, who fled from him. The Prussians followed too impetuously, as far as the vicinity of Plessis-Piquet, where they were fallen upon by four regiments under General Exelmans and driven back through Versailles. They had thus already suffered heavy losses when they fell into the trap on the other side and were completely dispersed. Under these circumstances it is amazing that a couple of hundred horse from the detachment were nevertheless assembled again the next day. As a result of this engagement the French advanced toward evening as far as Marly, where they ran into the 9th Brigade, comprising the advance guard of Thielmann's corps, and fought an insignificant engagement with it.

Since Lieutenant-Colonel Sohr's unit was not the advance guard of a corps, and consequently would not be supported, but was instead sent out several miles ahead as a raiding party, he should have conducted himself with all the caution of a guerrilla, and least of all fed his horses in a place like Versailles, thereby revealing his location and sparking the plan for his encirclement.

The three Prussian corps thus assembled at Saint-Germain on the 1st and on the 2nd set out on the march.

The 3rd Corps advanced through Versailles as far as Plessis-Piquet without encountering a significant enemy force.

The 1st Corps' route led to Sèvres, which was strongly occupied. It was attacked by the 1st brigade and courageously defended for several hours. The enemy finally had to abandon Sèvres when General Ziethen reached the heights of Meudon with his right wing. They retreated to Issi. The 1st brigade followed over Moullineau, where it fought a second brisk engagement up to Issi. This village was attacked at 7 in the evening by the 1st brigade. The enemy held it strongly, the 2nd brigade had to support the 1st's attack, and even so the fighting lasted until around midnight, when the French pulled back.

But already at three in the morning the French had turned back to attack Issi in two columns coming from Vaugirard and Montrouge, under Vandamme's command. The result was a fight for possession of the village that lasted more than an hour, albeit in vain for the French. The 1st and 2nd brigades held, and the French retreated to their positions behind Vaugirard and Montrouge.

As the Convention of St. Cloud was concluded that same day, this was the final act of the war.

ON WATERLOO

Chapter 56
The Condition of Paris

Paris was in a strange situation. On the 21st Bonaparte arrived and set himself up in the Elysée Palace. He had his ministers called in to advise on the situation. In this meeting he received a declaration from the Chamber of Deputies, in which, having been informed of recent events by Bonaparte's Bulletin, they declared themselves in permanent session and ordered the ministers to appear before them without delay. Bonaparte understood immediately that an abyss was opening under his feet, and all at once his spirit seemed to be crippled, his courage broken. He was no longer the reckless soldier of *Vendémiaire* and *Brumaire*,[83] who could win everything while losing nothing, who boldly cut through political factions with the sword, dispelling a popular rising or overwhelming a Chamber of Deputies like an outpost. Already, among the thousand counterweights that always act in so many ways to restrain and moderate the actions of princes and commanders who operate within, and depend upon, a fixed order of things—already one of those thousand counterweights had acquired great significance for him. It was the question of his son and his dynasty.

France was not entirely pro-Bourbon, and neither was Paris. The party that ruled in the Chamber was the party of republicans and revolutionaries. Lafayette was the ringleader, and many other well-known names from that period were to be found within it. Bonaparte had high hopes of satisfying the party that now rose against him by abdicating in favor of his son. He imagined that the manifold revolutionary interests of this group would energize it and direct it specifically against the Bourbons, and that whoever became the leader in this situation would also necessarily become the center of the whole nation's political opposition to the will of the Allies.

---

83 Clausewitz here refers to two episodes in Bonaparte's early rise to power, signified by the respective months of the Revolutionary calendar in which they occurred. On 13 Vendémiaire [5 October] 1795, Bonaparte assembled a scratch force of cavalry and artillery that crushed a Royalist uprising threatening to overthrow the Revolutionary Convention—a deed accomplished, in Thomas Carlyle's famous phrase, by "a whiff of grapeshot." 18 *Brumaire* [9 November] 1799 was the day of the *coup d'état* by which Napoleon, having already established himself as the French government's military protector, overthrew it and made himself First Consul of the Republic. In Clausewitz's day these events were so famous that no explanation of them would have been required.

It is obvious that this has to be regarded as half fantasy, and Bonaparte himself was anything but inwardly reconciled to this idea. On the contrary, he foresaw in the meantime that the rising factions would wipe out France's last resistance and hasten the reversal of fortune he so hated. But still, the possibility [of his son's succession] kept him from gathering a few hundred of his loyalists and using force against the Chamber, and led him, following some futile resistance, to consent to abdicate.

After sending first his minister Regnauld and then his brother Lucien to the Chamber of Deputies, and trying in vain to pacify it; after the Chamber became more and more vocal; after they finally gave him only an hour to decide between abdicating or being deposed; after first Regnauld, then Bassano and Caulaincourt, and finally Joseph [Bonaparte] and Lucien advised him to give in—after about twelve hours of this struggle he signed his abdication in favor of his son, on the morning of the 22nd.

A Government Commission of five members was now named by both Chambers, to which Quinette and Caulaincourt were elected from the Lower House, and Carnot, Fouché, and Grenier from the Upper. Fouché became the Commission's president.

The internal factional struggle was in no way resolved by Bonaparte's abdication in favor of his son.

The true Bourbon loyalists were totally against recognizing the son, and the republicans and revolutionaries were not entirely for it either. A third party, whose leader was Fouché, and which in fact wanted the Bourbons but with some conditions, likewise saw this form of abdication as a great obstacle to compromise. By this time the proponents of these three points of view distrusted each other so much that no consensus could emerge; and, what was most important, they all feared the remnants of the Bonapartist party, which was still not entirely insignificant in Paris itself, and which could find powerful support among the troops [in the city] and the armed forces in the surrounding towns. The result was that the opposition that immediately arose against Napoleon II was suppressed, and people preferred to leave matters uncertain. Fouché and his party, who were the real leaders, still found sufficient means in the midst of this unresolved crisis to guide things toward their goal.

Fouché was President of the Government [Commission], and he was in secret contact with Wellington and the Bourbons, besides which his personality and his earlier connections suited him to play the leading role. He should thus be regarded as the head of the government, although he was of course watched with apprehension by the other members of the Commission and by the Chambers, and his actions were very constrained, being limited to the ways of intrigue and dissimulation. Next to him Davout has to be considered the most important person at this moment. He was minister of war and was named chief of the army after Soult and Grouchy declined. Moreover he entirely shared Fouché's point of view, which was the one that had the greatest chance of prevailing. It was mainly these two together who brought about the Convention of 3 July.

Considering the political situation in Paris and the nature of the authority wielded by the government, at a time when the fleeing army was hastening to return there and the Allied commanders, hot on their heels, were appearing at the gates, we can understand how difficult it must have been to think of organized resistance, of exhausting all the means still available, and so we have found it necessary to dwell on the point for a moment.

Bonaparte remained secluded at the Elysée from the 22nd to the 25th, in drab, empty rooms, accompanied by only a few friends and protected by only a single sentry from a detail of old grenadiers. Naturally his proximity must have aroused fear of unrest, which might break out either for or against him, and could lead to a catastrophe. The Government Commission therefore compelled him to move to Malmaison on the 25th, and to wait there for the passports for a journey to America that he had requested from Lord Wellington.

The Government Commission now sent the well-known delegation of Lafayette, Sebastiani, Benjamin Constant, Pontécoulant, d'Argenson, and La Forest to the Allied headquarters to announce Bonaparte's removal and to appeal for a cease-fire. All these gentlemen and all the parties in Paris wanted to prevent an occupation of the city, partly in order to avert various sacrifices and dangers, partly to be able to use this kernel of resistance later as a bargaining chip in negotiations, through which better terms might be obtained and a final agreement reached.

Even Fouché and Davout were initially of this view; but as they saw the growing danger of an explosion by those who thought differently, as the [French] army reached the city, and as they were confronted by its continuing Bonapartist spirit and hatred of the Bourbons (which also expressed itself unmistakably against them, as the Bourbons' secret tools), they also tried to promote the possibility of surrendering Paris and of placing the army beyond the Loire.

Bonaparte's removal likewise lay close to their hearts. On the 28th, when he heard the cannon fire from the fight at Villers-Cotterêt, he was naturally overcome by a state of exaltation. All the passions of war and battle were awakened again, and drove him to offer his services to the Government Commission as a general. He succeeded in getting General Becker, who was charged with watching him, to hurry personally to Paris with this offer, and had the few horses remaining to him saddled up. But his offer was received with derision by Fouché and Davout. They both saw that it was high time to get rid of him, if they did not want to run the risk of suddenly seeing him take center stage once more. To which add that Blücher's plan to have him seized at Malmaison became known, which made Bonaparte himself somewhat more eager to begin his journey. Thus, at five o'clock on the afternoon of the 29th, he proceeded to Rochefort in the company of General Becker, where the first opportunity was to be taken to sail for America.

On the 26th the delegation sent to the headquarters of the Allied commanders was directed to go to the headquarters of the monarchs [instead], the cease-fire was turned down, and the path of negotiation was rejected out of hand.

Now, during the eight days between Bonaparte's arrival and that of the beaten army, from the 22nd to the 29th, nothing much happened as far as organizing resistance was concerned, nothing that could have led to a basic transformation of the situation. The available guns were moved into place and the nearest depot troops called in; but nothing was done in the way of arming significant new forces or carrying out serious work on the city's fortifications.

On the 28th the corps of the main army arrived under the overall command of Reille; those of Grouchy [arrived] on the 29th. The Prussians not only followed right on their heels but, as we have seen, were already at Saint-Germain on the left bank of the Seine the next day, in order to threaten Paris from its unfortified side. The French army therefore had to divide itself immediately and occupy the southern side of the city with half its strength.

We do not have any clear and definite information on the fortifications that were supposed to protect the capital. For the most part they existed only on the north side. The main works were at Montmartre, just as in 1814, only this time completely finished. From there the lines extended toward Vincennes. Saint-Denis was considered to be an outpost. Some reports describe these fortifications as having fortress-like strength, others, namely those of the delegation sent from Paris, represent them as insufficient. The following data, which are not subject to doubt, will suffice for our purposes:

1. The frontage that had to be covered on the north side of the city extended from the Seine past Charenton back to the Seine again at Chaillot, nine miles without taking Saint-Denis into account. If a defensive line was to be held between La Villette and Saint-Denis, this distance would not be any less.

2. At a council of war that the government held on the 30th, Soult declared that, since the Prussians had taken Aubervillers, it was dangerous to think of mounting a defense even on the right bank of the Seine, because if the line of the canal joining Saint-Denis and La Villette were breached the enemy could advance pell-mell among the French troops manning the fortifications at Saint-Denis. This in no way suggests fortress-like strength overall.

3. All accounts are agreed, and we ourselves are convinced, that the works on the left bank have to be regarded as very insignificant. The village of Montrouge was hastily prepared for defense, and since it had stone houses and walls exceptional resistance was certainly possible. It lay directly in front of the center on the south side, so it could well have become an objective of the main attack, and would then have cost an enormous amount of blood to take. But such a strongpoint cannot secure the area a mile or two to its left or right, and in the end people realized that Paris could be taken without taking Montrouge, no less than without taking Montmartre; and in that case the French would have been limited merely to a defense by force of arms, without appreciable cover.

4. The frontage on the south side, from the Seine back to the Seine again, which was also almost completely without defenses and so would have had to be manned by sufficient troops, extended 11,000 yards, thus almost seven miles.

The French army thus had to hold a line 16 miles, or 39,000 paces (26,000 yards) long, whose defenses were partly non-existent, partly incomplete. We must say that this state of fortification provided no special refuge and support for a shattered army.

With the 20,000 men brought in from the depots, the French army was 60,000 strong, to which were added 20,000 armed men from the suburbs who, however, were normally counted on to defend Paris itself. The fortifications were equipped for the most part with iron cannon and other dismounted guns that were available in Paris; thus sufficient numbers of these weapons were probably available for the fortifications; as for field artillery, however, the Loire army took no more than 70 guns with it. This is surely very few and, especially for the southern side, where the fighting would be more or less in the open field, far too few to think of mounting effective resistance. What can 70 guns do, spread out over 7 miles?

The Allied armies, as we have already said, reached Paris with about 50,000 men under Wellington, 60,000 under Blücher, thus almost double what the French could put opposite them in front of Paris. But the worst was that the latter could never know in what ratio the Allies would divide their forces on the two banks of the Seine, so it was still necessary for them to man their fortifications on the right bank with appreciable numbers of troops. Wellington held a bridge at Argenteuil and an outpost at Courbevoye, and so was in uninterrupted contact with Blücher. Since the countryside was very cut up due to heavy cultivation, the French could never know how many of his troops would have been moved directly onto the left bank of the Seine. It was thus easily possible that while the French had to leave 20,000 men in their fortifications, so as to be able to accept a battle around Montrouge with 40,000 men and 70 cannon, they could be attacked there by 80,000 men with 300 cannon. This did not promise a favorable result. Moreover it is noteworthy that on July 1st Davout's headquarters was still in La Villette, for the last council of war would be held there on the night of the 1st-2nd; thus at that time the better part of the French army must still have been on the north side of the city.

Having set down these relationships side by side, we want to present the decision of the final French council of war word for word; it will now make more sense and also bring the results of our reflections together in a single point.

It was held under the chairmanship of Davout, and included all those officers of exceptional reputation who found themselves in Paris, namely Marshals Masséna, Lefebvre, Soult, and Grouchy, Generals Carnot, Grenier, and many others.

Questions posed by the Government Commission to the Council of War Assembled at La Villette, 1 July 1815

1. What is the state of the fortifications erected for the defense of Paris?
Answer: The state of the fortifications and their armaments on the right bank of the Seine, although incomplete, is generally satisfactory. On the left bank the fortifications can be regarded as non-existent.
2. Is the army capable of covering and defending Paris?
Answer: It can do so, but not indefinitely. It must not expose itself to a loss of provisions or its line of retreat.
3. If the army were attacked at all points, could it prevent the enemy from penetrating into Paris on one side or the other?
Answer: It is difficult for the army to be attacked at all points simultaneously; but if that were to happen there would be little hope of resistance.
4. In case of a reversal, could the general-in-chief reserve or recover sufficient means to oppose an entry into the city by brute force?
Answer: No general can answer for the outcome of a battle.
5. Does sufficient ammunition exist for several engagements?
Answer: Yes.
6. Finally, what can be said about the fate of the capital and how long it can hold out?
Answer: There can be no guarantees in this regard.

Signed Marshal Davout,
Minister of War, Prince of Eckmühl,
July 2, 3 a.m.

Taking all of this into account, our conclusions are as follows:

1. Accepting a defensive battle under the walls of Paris was not completely impossible for the French, but the battle would in all probability have been lost, in which case they had to fear that they would be forced to submit to much worse terms.

2. Even if the battle were won, that is, if the attack were repelled, the result would be nothing more than a few weeks reprieve, until the arrival of the other [Allied] armies; but this reprieve would not lead to a different outcome, nor to any change in the situation, because no major efforts of any kind were made to organize other resistance. Nor could they be, given the condition of the government. The French would thus have been fighting solely for the honor of their arms.

3. An attack on the Prussian army in its position between Meudon and Plessis-Piquet, if it arrived unexpectedly, would perhaps have promised more advantages, but the position in and of itself was very strong, so it would have been difficult to overwhelm an enemy there that was still substantially superior in numbers.

If a kind of siege were to have ensued, however, this would again have led to nothing, for the French either had to retreat toward Paris or turn toward the Loire; in the latter case the march would itself have become a kind of flight.

It is thus obvious, given the facts of the situation, that, if it were not allowed to withdraw, the army bottled up in Paris could be defeated and compelled to lay down its arms.

But this too would have served only the interests of martial glory, for under existing circumstances such an action could have no further influence on the terms of the peace.

On the other hand, speeding up the take-over of the capital could also speed up the take-over of some of the other fortresses, and the possession of the fortresses was of great importance from the point of view of guaranteeing the treaty.

Thus the interests of the two sides came together in the conclusion of the Convention, which was adopted on 3 July at St. Cloud between representatives of the two Allied commanders and the city of Paris. By its terms a cease-fire was declared and the French army surrendered the city and withdrew to the Loire. They carried out their march on the 4th, 5th, and 6th, the Prussian 1st Corps moved in on the 7th, and Louis XVIII himself arrived on the 8th.

Chapter 57
Advance of the Remaining Armies into France

In the middle of June Schwarzenberg's Army of the Upper Rhine stood as follows: Wrede was located between Mannheim and Kaiserslautern; the Crown Prince of Württemberg was as far as Bruchsal; the Austrians under Colloredo, the Prince of Hohenzollern and Archduke Ferdinand stood between Basel and Lake Constance.

On June 23, upon hearing the news of the events in the Netherlands, the Army of the Upper Rhine began to move; on this day Wrede crossed the Saar at Saarbrücken and Saargemünd following an easy fight, and the Crown Prince of Württemberg crossed the Rhine at Germersheim. On the 25th the Austrian corps crossed at Basel.

Wrede proceeded toward Nancy, the Crown Prince of Württemberg turned upstream along the Rhine toward Strasbourg. One Austrian corps under Colloredo drove Lecourbe before it and went to Belfort, the other under the Prince of Hohenzollern crossed the Rhine farther down and likewise advanced toward Strasbourg, and the reserves under Archduke Ferdinand moved toward Nancy.

On June 28 the Crown Prince of Württemberg fought a kind of engagement with General Rapp at Strasbourg, in which the latter withdrew into the fortress and the crown prince surrounded it.

At the end of July the Russian army under General Barclay reached the Rhine.

The French under Marshal Suchet also began hostilities in Upper Italy on June 15, and sought to reach the alpine passes before the Austrians. The latter arrived first, however, and, together with the Sardinians, advanced into Savoy in two columns, 50-60,000 strong, under Frimont's overall command. Meanwhile, a third column, composed of Sardinian troops, moved against Marshal Brune in the county of Nizza.

The right-wing column, under Frimont's personal command, crossed the Simplon Pass and moved through Meillerie, Geneva, Fort l'écluse, and Bourge en Bresse to Maçon. That under Bubna went over Mont Cenis, Mont Melian, les Echelles, and Lyon.

Grenoble had already fallen on 3 July, and both columns reached the Saone on 10 July, following several tough fights with Marshal Suchet's troops.

Chapter 58
The Conquest of the Fortresses

Prince Frederick of the Netherlands took the fortresses at Valencienne, le Quesnoi, and Condé.

The 2nd Prussian Corps, under the supreme command of His Royal Highness Prince August, took Maubeuge, Landrecy, Marienburg, Philippeville, Rocroy, and Givet, but not, however, Charlemont.

The North German troops under the command of General Hake took Charleville, Mezières, Montmédi, and Sedan.

Luxembourg was occupied under the command of His Excellency Prince Louis of Hesse-Homburg.[84]

Most of these conquests took place more as a result of envelopment than of actual siege, and when the latter occurred it lasted only a few days. Right down the line, these places lacked appropriate garrisons and armaments.

On the 20th of September the order was given to desist from these operations, so that the remaining fortified places in France could change hands by virtue of political submission to Louis XVIII. Those that were captured, however, would be regarded as bastions for the army of occupation.

---

84 In Clausewitz's original manuscript this sentence was followed by one reading "Longwy was taken by the Russians under General Langeron," but all the words except Longwy were struck out by Clausewitz, perhaps because he was not sure of their accuracy. The published editions placed Longwy after Hesse-Homburg without the period separating them, thus incorrectly giving the impression that Longwy was part of the Prince's name.

ON WATERLOO

VI.

MEMORANDUM ON THE BATTLE OF WATERLOO
by the Duke of Wellington

24th Sept., 1842.[1]

In discussing the Battle of Waterloo, and the military movements previous thereto, it is necessary to advert to the state of Europe at the moment, and the military position of the Allies on the one hand, and of Buonaparte and France on the other.

The Powers of Europe had, in 1814, made peace with France, governed by Louis XVIII. A Congress was assembled at Vienna, composed of ministers from the principal Powers engaged in the previous war, and from His Most Christian Majesty, to regulate and settle various points left unsettled by the treaties of peace, not only as between France and the Powers engaged in the war, but questions affecting the relative interests of all, arising out of the long and extensive warfare, the consequence of the French Revolution.

Buonaparte having abdicated his power, and having retired to the island of Elba under the sanction of a treaty, returned to France early in March, 1815, with a detachment of his Guard which had attended him to the island of Elba, arrived at Paris on the 20th of March, and overturned the government of King Louis XVIII., who fled to Lille, and subsequently to Ghent, in the Netherlands; when Buonaparte usurped the government of France.

Whatever we may think of the settlement of the government of France, of the state of possession of the different parts of Europe and of the world, as fixed by the treaties of peace, and by the subsequent diplomatic transactions at Vienna, at that moment completed, they constituted at the time the public law of Europe, and the state of possession of the several Powers, under authority thereof. This must never be lost sight of in the consideration of this subject.

---

1 *Supplementary Despatches*, 10:513-531. Note from original: "Written by the Duke of Wellington after reading the statements of General Clausewitz."

MEMORANDUM ON THE BATTLE OF WATERLOO

From the moment at which Buonaparte drove Louis XVIII from Paris and usurped his throne, it was obvious that the war would be renewed; and the first thing that was done by the ministers of the Allies at Vienna, upon learning the invasion of France by Buonaparte, his march upon Paris, and his usurpation of the Government, was to renew, and to render applicable to the circumstances of the moment, their former treaty of alliance, concluded at Chaumont in the month of March, 1814.

Field Marshal the Duke of Wellington being the plenipotentiary of His Britannic Majesty at the Congress at Vienna at that period, having concluded and signed the treaty of alliance on the 25th of March, and all the arrangements connected with that instrument, and having been appointed to command the Allied army assembled in the Netherlands, set out from Vienna and reached Bruxelles in the first days of April.

The treaty of peace of 1814 had rendered necessary the occupation of the provinces, commonly called the Belgian provinces, by an army composed of British, Hanoverian, and Dutch troops, under the command of His Royal Highness the Hereditary Prince of Orange; the German provinces on the left bank of the Rhine, extending from the province of Loraine to the Junction of the Rhine with the Meuse, by Prussian troops; the Italian provinces, forming what had been called the Kingdom of Italy, by the Austrian army (indeed this Austrian army was at about this time engaged in the active operations of war with Murat, King of Naples); the provinces in Poland, forming the kingdom of Saxon Poland, by the Russian army.

Thus then the armies of the Allies were distributed over Europe, while the greater part of that of England had been detached to North America; and notwithstanding that the treaty of peace had been concluded at Ghent, on the 24th of December, 1814, between His Britannic Majesty and the United States, sufficient time had not elapsed to enable His Britannic Majesty's ministers to bring back the troops to Europe.

On the other hand, Buonaparte found an army in France completely organized, consisting of not less than 250,000 men, with cannon, and all that was required to render them efficient for the field. There were besides many old soldiers available for the service, who had been prisoners of war in England, in Russia, and elsewhere, besides the men discharged from the corps of the Imperial Guard.

ON WATERLOO

It is obvious that the first measures of the Generals commanding the armies of the Allies must have been defensive. Those in the Belgian provinces, and those on the left bank of the Rhine, must have been strictly and cautiously formed upon these principles. Their forces were weak in comparison with the French force opposed to, or which might be brought against them. The latter enjoyed other advantages in the nature and strength of their frontier.

These Allied troops were at the outpost. They were destined to protect the march of the other armies of the Allies to the countries which were intended to be the basis of the operations to be carried on against the enemy, for which the treaty of the 25th March had made provision.

The army in the Belgian provinces, under the command of the Duke of Wellington, from the first days of April, had particular interests to attend to, as each of the other armies had, each in the districts under its charge, besides the general operations of the war. That army, composed of British, Dutch, and Hanoverian troops, had to preserve the communications with England, Holland, and Germany. It was connected with the Prussian army by its left, the communication of which with Germany was absolutely necessary.

The Prince Sovereign, afterwards King of the Netherlands, to whose government the Belgian provinces had been ceded by the Congress of Vienna, had fixed its seat at Bruxelles; and the King Louis XVIII., having found himself under the necessity of withdrawing from France altogether, had determined to reside at Ghent.

Buonaparte had great advantages, whether for an offensive operation on the positions of the Allies, or for the defence of his own, in the number, the position, and the strength of the fortresses on the north-east frontier of France. He might fix and organize his armies within these, out of sight, and almost without the knowledge, of the Allied Generals, even to the last moment previous to an attack; and it was impossible for the Allies to attempt to carry on an offensive operation against the French position which should not include the means of carrying on one or more sieges, possibly at the same moment.

The inconveniences, difficulties, and disadvantages of this defensive system were aggravated by the uncertainty of the length of time which it might last: that is to say, till the Austrian armies, having terminated their operations in Italy against Murat, should have reached the Upper

MEMORANDUM ON THE BATTLE OF WATERLOO

Rhine, and there formed a junction with the armies of Bavaria and Wurtemberg, and the Russian armies should have retrograded from Poland, should have crossed Germany, and have formed upon the Rhine, the Maine, and the Moselle.

It is complained of by the Prussian historian Clausewitz that he had never been able to obtain the sight of a return of the army under the command of the Duke of Wellington made up in the form of what is called "a line of battle." This at best is the complaint of a want of a return made up in a particular form; and it would not have been noticed here if it were not desirable to draw the attention of the reader to the general temper and tone of this History.

The reputation of its army, and above all of the Generals commanding the same, is an object of the greatest importance to any nation; and we find the historians of all nations, not excepting, as we see, those of the British, too ready to criticize the acts and operations not only of their own Generals and armies, but likewise of those of the best friends and allies of their nation, and even of those acting in co-operation with its armies. This observation must be borne in mind throughout the perusal of Clausewitz's History.

In respect to the return mentioned, it is forgotten by General Clausewitz that the army under the command of the Duke of Wellington was not, like that under the command of Marshal Prince Blücher, composed of the troops of all arms, and establishments of and belonging to one nation, but they belonged to several, the infantry, cavalry, and artillery in some cases belonging each to different nations; that the several corps of troops composing the Allied army in question were not of uniform strength of numbers, whether considered by nations, by battalions, by brigades, or by divisions; that the discipline and military qualities of the several corps of troops, and, above all, their efficiency and military experience in the field, were very various. The greatest part of some of the corps composing the army was composed of men lately recruited. The whole of the Hanoverian army was a militia, excepting some battalions of the Hanoverian Legion, which properly belonged to the *British* army, and had served under the command of Field Marshall the Duke of Wellington in Spain.

It was necessary to organize these troops in brigades, divisions, and corps d'armée with those better disciplined and more accustomed to war, in order to derive from their numbers as much advantage as possible. But these arrangements in allied armies, formed as this one was, are not matters of course. The same national feeling respecting its armies, even in the least powerful nation, which has been already adverted to as having an influence over the critical morality of the historian, is not without its influence in the formation of such arrangements of organization. No troops can be employed in an allied army excepting each corps and detachment is under the immediate command of its own national officer.

The organization and formation of corps to serve together, and under the command and superior direction of what officer, become therefore, and became in this case, a matter which required great attention and labour, and of great difficulty. To these considerations was to be added, that some of the troops were fit only for garrison duties; while, on the other hand, the importance of the fortresses was so urgent as to require for their garrisons a proportion at least of the very best troops.

This statement will serve to show that the formation of a return of the army under the command of Field Marshal the Duke of Wellington, as "a line of battle," was not very easy.

The two Allied armies, the one in the Netherlands, the other in the provinces on the left bank of the Rhine, were, as has been already shown, necessarily on the defensive. They were waiting for the junction of other large armies to attain by their co-operation a common object. But their defensive position and immediate objects did not necessarily preclude all idea or plan of attack upon the enemy. The enemy might have so placed his army as to render the attack thereof advisable, or even necessary.

In that case the Allied Generals ought, and in all probability would, have taken the initiative. But in the case existing in 1815 the enemy did not take such a position as is thus supposed. On the contrary, he took a position in which his numbers could be concealed, his movements protected, and his designs supported by his formidable fortresses on the frontier, up to the last moment.

The Allies could not attack this position without being prepared to attack a superior army so posted: they could not therefore have the initiative of the operations in the way of attack.

They had the option of taking the initiative in the way of defensive movement. But such defensive movement, or alteration of the well-considered original position taken up by each of the Allied armies, must have been founded on a conviction that such positions were faulty, and might be improved, or upon an hypothesis of the intended movements of attack by the enemy. There was no reason to believe that the first was the case; and it must never be lost sight of, that to found upon an hypothesis which might, and probably would, prove erroneous, considering what the advantages were of the position of the enemy on the frontier, the alteration of the position of the Allied armies might have occasioned what is commonly called a false movement; and it must be observed, that whatever may be thought of Buonaparte as a leader of troops in other respects, there certainly never existed a man in that situation, in any times, in whose presence it was so little safe to make what is called a false movement.

The initiative then rested with the enemy; and the course to be pursued by the Allied Generals respectively was to be prepared to move in all directions, to wait till it should be seen in what direction the attack should be made, and then to assemble the armies as quickly as possible to resist the attack, or to attack the enemy with the largest force that could be collected.

There is a good deal of discussion in the History of General Clausewitz upon the expediency of the maintenance of the defensive position taken up by the Allied armies, particularly by that under the command of Field Marshal the Duke of Wellington; and that even for the attainment of the objects in view for the position of the last mentioned, it would have been best to occupy a position in the country having for its sole object the early junction of the two Allied armies, with a view to fight a great battle with the enemy under the command of Buonaparte.

It is not difficult to criticize the particular positions occupied by any army, which positions were never, as in this case, the object of actual attack. It is not so easy a task, first to define precisely a particular object for the operations of a defensive nature for any army, taking into consideration not only political objects and views, but likewise those of a merely technical and military nature: such as, in this case, the preservation of the communications of the army with England, with Holland, and with Germany; and next to define the positions to be occupied by two armies in order to carry on such operations.

Bruxelles, Ghent, the communications with Holland and Germany, according to the view of the historian, ought to have been given up, and

ON WATERLOO

the armies united, or prepared to unite, in order to fight a general battle with the enemy, as the best mode of securing all the objects of their respective defensive positions. But it is not stated, or even hinted, where each was to be posted, where they were to unite, nor where was to be the great battle on which the contest was to be decided. It is obvious that the historian could not indicate such positions: he was too wise to make the attempt.

He could not but be aware that when the Allies should have abandoned their defensive positions in the Netherlands, and should have left in the power of the enemy to occupy, with his hussars and light troops, Bruxelles and Ghent, the communications with England and Holland through Antwerp, and with England through the towns on the Lys and Ostend, they would not have been nearer the attainment of the object of fighting a general battle than while in the positions having for their objects to maintain and secure these advantages.

The initiative for such general battle must still have been in the hands of Buonaparte. He might have avoided it by merely remaining with his main body within the French frontier; while with his hussars and light troops he would have possessed Bruxelles and Ghent and the communications with England and Holland, and with Germany through Holland.

The historian shows in more than one passage of his History that he is not insensible of the military and political value of good moral impressions resulting from military operations. He is sensible of the advantage derived by the enemy from such impressions.[2] He is aware of the object of Buonaparte to create throughout Europe, and even in England, a moral impression against the war, and to shake the power of the then existing administration in England. He is sensible of and can contemplate the effect of the moral impression upon the other armies of Europe, and upon the governments in whose service they were, resulting from the defeat or even want of success of the Allied armies under the command of the Duke of Wellington and Prince Blücher. But he is not sensible of, and cannot calculate upon, or even consider the effect of, the moral impression resulting from the loss of Bruxelles and Ghent, the flight of the King of the Netherlands, and of the King Louis XVIII., the creatures

---

2 The published memorandum omits here a line from the manuscript version: "But he cannot calculate the advantage on the one hand or the disadvantage on the other resulting from such impressions in cases in which it is the object to blame the course of Operations directed by a General, supposed to be a Rival in Reputation to one of the Prussians taken."

MEMORANDUM ON THE BATTLE OF WATERLOO

of the treaties of peace, and of the acts of the Congress of Vienna; and this with the loss of the communications of the army under the Duke of Wellington with England, Holland, and Germany, without making the smallest effort to save any of these objects.

If this historian had, however, inquired, in England or elsewhere, he would have found that the feeling upon such events would have been as strong as he admits it would have been in case of the want of success of the operations of the Allied armies whose operations are under discussion. In England in particular these supposed events would have been severely felt. But let us consider whether the abandonment of all the objects which the Allies had in view in maintaining any position in the Netherlands would have enabled the Generals of the Allied armies the better to fight a great battle with the enemy.

The enemy would have had the option whether to fight the battle or not, and the initiative of the movements preparatory to it, after having had all the advantages placed in his hands, and the Allied Generals having thus given up those objects the possession[3] of which alone, in a political or even a military point of view, could justify their fighting a battle at all, at least till they should be in a state of co-operation with the other armies of Europe.

The enemy having the initiative would have moved across the communications of the army under the command of the Duke of Wellington. In the possession of the great towns, of all the roads, and of the resources of the Belgian provinces, he would have had to decide whether he would, or not, force the two Allied armies to retire from the Meuse. But in the hypothesis that the enemy would fight a battle for such an object, why should the Allies? The Duke of Wellington would have lost all for which as the commander of an army he ought to desire to contend; and neither his position, nor that of the army under Prince Blücher, could have been improved by a great battle, even under the hypothesis that the result would have been a great victory.

Such a one would not have restored to the Duke of Wellington the advantages which he enjoyed in the state of preparation of the army under his command for the advance into France, in co-operation with the other Allied armies when they should have taken their stations, and should have been prepared to advance.

---

3 The manuscript reads "protection."

The restoration of the communications with England, Holland, and Germany, which would have been the result of such successful battle, would not have immediately restored and replaced his magazines not located in fortresses, and which would have fallen into the enemy's hands by the supposed change of position with a view to fight this great battle. After all, the initiative of this battle must have rested with the enemy; and there could be no military reason for fighting it, or political reason, excepting the moral impression throughout the world of its successful result.

It is useless to speculate upon supposed military movements which were never made, and operations which never took place, or the objects of the several chiefs of Generals opposed to each other.

But although it was not desirable that the Duke of Wellington should break up his defensive positions in the Belgian provinces with a view to take one with the army under his command having solely in view the object of fighting a great battle in cooperation or in conjunction with the Prussian army, it was still desirable that he should occupy this defensive position in such manner, and take such precautionary measures, as would enable him to assemble at the latest period of time the largest disposable force at his disposition, after providing for the defence and security of his military communications with England, Holland, and Germany, and of the objects entrusted to his care and protection under the treaty of peace and acts of the Congress, and by the Allied ministers in conference at Vienna. He accordingly from the moment at which he arrived in the Netherlands in the beginning of April turned his attention to the strengthening the posts on the frontier; and works were constructed at Ostend, Nieuport, Ypres, Menin, Courtray, Oudenarde, Tournay, Ath, Mons, Charleroi, and Namur. It is true there were field works, generally on the site of the ancient works by which these towns were defended; the defence of which was aided by the ancient ditches and means of inundation. His orders at that time to the Quartermaster-General and the General officers show what his instructions were in the various hypothetical cases therein stated.

There are several great roads leading from the northern department of France, and the great fortresses therein situated, by each of which

MEMORANDUM ON THE BATTLE OF WATERLOO

these provinces might have been invaded, and which it was necessary at least to observe:

One from Lille:[4] upon Menin, Courtray, and Ghent.
One from Lille: upon Tournay and Ghent, or upon Ath and Bruxelles.
One from Condé: upon Tournay, Ath, Enghien, and Bruxelles.
One from Condé and Valenciennes: upon Mons and Bruxelles.

Each of these was a great paved road, upon which there was no obstacle of a defensive nature, excepting the field works of which it appears the Duke of Wellington ordered the construction.

The historian Clausewitz has detailed the positions of the Prussian army, the distances of each part from the other, and the length of time which would elapse for the completion of the assembly of the whole. It cannot be stated that the Allied army under the Duke of Wellington could have been assembled in any equally short period of time; but if it is considered that the objects for the protection of the army under the command of the Duke of Wellington were extended over a tract of country of greater length than were those protected by the Allied army under the command of Prince Blücher, it will be found that this part of the country, continuous in its whole extent to the French frontier, and traversed in all parts by excellent paved roads leading from some one or other of the French fortresses, required for its protection a system of occupation quite different from that adopted by the Prussian army under Prince Blücher.

But what follows will show that not withstanding the extension of the Allied army under the command of the Duke of Wellington, such was the celerity of communication with all parts of it, that in point of fact his orders reached all parts of the army in six hours after he had issued them; and that he was in line in person with a sufficient force to resist and keep in check the enemy's corps which first attacked the Prussian corps under General Zieten at daylight on the 15th of June; having received the intelligence of that attack only at three o'clock in the afternoon of the 15th, he was at Quatre Bras before the same hour on the morning of the 16th, with a sufficient force to engage the left of the French army.

It was certainly true that he had known for some days of the augmentation of the enemy's force on the frontier, and even of the arrival of Buonaparte at the army; but he did not deem it expedient to make

---

4 These two references to Lille were misprinted as "Lisle" in the published version.

any movement, excepting for the assembly of the troops at their several alarm posts, till he should hear of the decided movement of the enemy.

The first account received by the Duke of Wellington was from the Prince of Orange, who had come in from the out-posts of the army of the Netherlands to dine with the Duke at three o'clock in the afternoon. He reported that the enemy had attacked the Prussians at Thuin; that they had taken possession of, but had afterwards abandoned, Binch; that they had not yet touched the positions of the army of the Netherlands. While the Prince was with the Duke, the staff officer employed by Prince Blücher at the Duke's head quarters, General Müffling, came to the Duke to inform him that he had just received intelligence of the movement of the French army and their attack upon the Prussian troops at Thuin.

It appears by the statement of the historian that the posts of the Prussian corps of General Zieten were attacked at Thuin at four o'clock on the morning of the 15th; and that General Zieten himself, with a part of his corps, retreated and was at Charleroi at about ten o'clock on that day; yet the report thereof was not received at Bruxelles till three o'clock in the afternoon. The Prussian cavalry of the corps of Zieten was at Gosselies and Fleurus on the evening and night of the 15th.

Orders were forthwith sent for the march of the whole army to its left.

The whole moved on that evening and in the night, each division and portion separately, but unmolested; the whole protected on the march by the defensive works constructed at the different points referred to, and by their garrisons.

The reserve, which had been encamped in the neighborhood, and cantoned in the town and in the neighborhood, of Bruxelles, were ordered to assemble in and in the neighborhood of the park at Bruxelles, which they did on that evening; and they marched in the morning of the 16th upon Quatre Bras, towards which post the march of all the troops consisting of the left and centre of the army, and of the cavalry in particular, was directed.

The Duke went in person at daylight in the morning of the 16th to Quatre Bras, where he found some Netherland troops, cavalry, infantry, and artillery, which had been engaged with the enemy, but lightly; and he went on from thence to the Prussian army,[5] which was in sight, formed

---

5 Note by J.G. [John Gurwood]: "About 1 o'clock, at the Windmill of Bussy, between Ligny and Brie: so Hardinge told me."

on the heights behind Ligny and St. Amand. He there communicated personally with Marshall Prince Blücher and the head quarters of the Prussian army.

In the mean time the reserve of the Allied army under the command of the Duke of Wellington arrived at Quatre Bras. The historian asserts that the Duke of Wellington had ordered these troops to halt at the point at which they quitted the Forêt de Soignies. He can have no proof of this fact, of which there is no evidence; and in point of fact the two armies were united about mid-day of the 16th of June, on the left of the position of the Allied army under the command of the Duke of Wellington. These troops, forming the reserve, and having arrived from Bruxelles, were not joined by those of the 1st division of infantry, and the cavalry:[6] and notwithstanding the criticism of the Prussian historian on the positions occupied by the army under the command of the Duke of Wellington, and on the march of the troops to join with the Prussian army, it is a fact, appearing upon the face of the History, that the Allied British and Netherland army was in line at Quatre Bras, not only twenty-four hours sooner than one whole corps of the Prussian army under General Bülow the absence of which is attributed by the historian to an accidental mistake, but likewise before the whole of the corps under General Zieten which had been the first attacked on the 15th, had taken its position in the line of the army assembled on the heights behind Ligny, and having their left at Sombref.

It was perfectly true that the Duke of Wellington did not at first give credit to the reports of the intention of the enemy to attack by the valleys of the Sambre and the Meuse.

The enemy had destroyed the roads leading through those valleys, and he considered that Buonaparte might have made his attack upon the Allied armies in the Netherlands and in the provinces on the left of the Rhine by other lines with more advantage. But it is obvious that, when the attack was made, he was not unprepared to assist in resisting it; and, in point of fact, did, on the afternoon and in the evening of the 16th June, repulse the attack of Marshal Ney upon his position at Quatre Bras, which had been commenced by the aid of another corps d'armée under General Reille. These were the troops which had attacked on the

---

[6] Note in original: "The Duke of Wellington was at Quatre Bras about 3 o'clock, on his return from Ligny."

15th, at daylight, the Prussian corps under General Zieten, which corps the Allied troops, under the Duke of Wellington, relieved in resistance to the enemy.

The Prussian army, after a contest of some hours' duration upon the heights behind Ligny, having been under the necessity of retiring, that part of the Allied army under the command of the Duke of Wellington which was engaged at Quatre Bras maintained its ground at Quatre Bras, and even gained ground upon the enemy.

The fields of battle were in sight of each other, and a report was received. But although the exact result of the battle was not known, it was judged that it had not been successful to the Prussian army. Field Marshal the Duke of Wellington was informed of some of the details at night; but still he considered that, his own positions being untouched, and the continued march of the troops under his command giving him an increase of strength at every moment, he felt the utmost confidence in the final result of the operations in progress.

The Prussian army retreated towards Wavre.

It must be observed in the historian's account of these battles that the corps of Reille,[7] at the commencement of the battle of Quatre Bras, joined with the corps of Ney. In point of fact, it was seen in the field. That corps was, during the battle, ordered, and did march, to its right, towards the main body of the French army. It was then halted, and countermarched towards its original destination. The reasons for these eccentric movements are not known. Certain it is that the corps of Reille did not fire a shot after the commencement of the battle of Quatre Bras. That which it is reasonable to suppose is that Marshal Ney had required that the corps of Reille should be sent back to him upon finding that he could make no impression upon the position of the Duke of Wellington at Quatre Bras, whose army was at every moment receiving reinforcements of cavalry, infantry, and artillery from Nivelles and other places on its right.

Field Marshal the Duke of Wellington's aide-de-camp Colonel the Hon. Alexander Gordon, with two squadrons of hussars, shortly after daylight on the morning of the 17th, drove in the enemy's videttes upon the ground of the Prussian contest on the afternoon of the 16th June. These retired into the villages of Ligny and St. Amand, &c., on the stream.

---

[7] Egerton, in his *Reminiscences*, 229, noted that "This is perhaps a slip of the pen. Here and elsewhere in this paragraph it is probably d'Erlon's corps that is meant."

MEMORANDUM ON THE BATTLE OF WATERLOO

Colonel Gordon communicated with General Zieten at Sombref, and ascertained exactly the line of retreat of the army under Marshal Prince Blücher upon Wavre. As soon as the exact position of the Prussian army was ascertained, and the intentions of its General were known to the Duke of Wellington, he broke up from the position of Quatre Bras shortly before midday, in presence of the whole army of the enemy, without interruption or molestation, and ordered the march of the infantry of the army under his command to the ground in front of Waterloo, with the exception of the light troops at the outposts, with which and the cavalry the Duke remained on the ground at Quatre Bras.

The Duke saw throughout the day of the 17th the movements of the Prussian army upon the field of battle of the preceding day. No pursuit was made of the Prussian army or movement of any kind made by the French army till a late hour on the afternoon of the 17th; and indeed the account given by Marshall Grouchy, in a pamphlet in his own defence, published in the United States, shows that the account given in the History is, as nearly as possible, an accurate representation of what passed on the 17th according to the reports in the Allied army under the Duke of Wellington. Would it not have been a fair conclusion for the historian to draw, that the position occupied by the Allied army under the Duke of Wellington at Quatre Bras, and the successful resistance of that army in the battle of the preceding day, might have had some effect in producing the unusual tranquility of the French army throughout the day of the 17th, the morrow of a successful attack upon the position of any enemy's army which had retired?

The enemy did not move till between 3 and 4 o'clock in the afternoon, at which hour large masses of troops appeared on the Prussian field of battle. One body marched in the direction of Namur, another in the direction of Wavre, which last is supposed to have been the corps under the command of Marshall Grouchy. The largest body and the great mass of the cavalry moved down the high road leading from Sombref to Quatre Bras, towards the left of the British troops of the army of the Duke of Wellington, which still remained on that ground. These were put in motion as soon as their outposts were touched by those of the enemy, and joined the main body of the army posted in front of Waterloo. Here were all the troops composing the army under the Duke of Wellington, excepting a small corps de reserve still remaining at Hal, on the high road

ON WATERLOO

from Bruxelles to Mons. All the remainder, whether engaged at Quatre Bras on the 16th, or who had joined on the evening of the 16th, or who had been turned off from Nivelles to Waterloo, and the troops falling back from the position at Quatre Bras, were on the position at Waterloo on the 17th, in the evening.

The whole of the Prussian army was, at the same time, in the position at Wavre.

The two Allied armies communicated with each other throughout the night of the 17th June, and the cavalry of General Bülow's Prussian corps of Marshal Prince Blücher's army was on the ground, in front of Ohain, through the defile between the positions of the two armies, at daylight on the morning of the 18th.

Thus, then, it appears, by the report of this historian, that, after the affairs at Ligny and Quatre Bras, the two Allied armies were collected, each on its own ground, in presence of the enemy, having a short and not difficult communication between them; each of them in presence of the enemy, and between the enemy and Bruxelles; all their communications with England, Holland, and Germany, and all the important political interests committed to their charge, being secure.

It has been stated and believed that the cavalry of Bülow's corps was seen on the heights in front of Ohain, between the Allied army under the command of the Duke of Wellington and the defile leading to Wavre, at an early hour on the morning of the 18th.

It is a curious fact in elucidation of the movements of the Allied army under Marshal Prince Blücher, that Marshal Grouchy has published in his Defence, printed in the United States of America, a letter from Marshal Soult, addressed to him, dated the 18th June, at 1 o'clock P.M., in which Marshal Soult states *"Nous apercevons la cavalerie Prussienne,"* which was the very cavalry seen by the Duke of Wellington, as stated, shortly after daylight in the morning of that day.

It is a curious circumstance that this cavalry should not have been observed in the French army at an earlier hour than one o'clock in the afternoon. It must be concluded that at that hour no knowledge existed in the French head-quarters that other troops had passed the defile, or had been engaged on the left of the army under the command of the Duke of Wellington.

MEMORANDUM ON THE BATTLE OF WATERLOO

The first heard of the operations of Marshal Prince Blücher's army was a report, brought from the right of the army under the command of the Duke of Wellington, at about 6 o'clock in the evening, that at that moment the smoke of the fire of artillery could be perceived at a great distance beyond the right of the enemy's army, which firing was supposed at the time to be at Planchenoit.

The report of the battle made at the time by the Duke of Wellington to the British and the Allied governments of Europe has long been before the public. In that report he does full justice to the exertions made by his colleague the Prussian Commander-in-Chief and by the General officers and troops to aid and support him, and to the effectual aid which they gave him. He states no detail, excepting that the battle was terminated by an attack which he does not report that any Prussian troops joined, because, in fact, none were on that part of the field of battle. He states, however, that the enemy's troops retired from the last attack upon his position "in great confusion, and that the march of General Bülow's corps by Frischermont upon Planchenoit and La Belle Alliance had begun to take effect; and as he could perceive the fire of his cannon, and as Marshal Prince Blücher had joined in person with a corps of his army to the left of our line by Ohain, he determined upon the attack, which succeeded in every point." He added that he "continued the pursuit until long after dark, and then discontinued it only on account of the fatigue of the troops, who had been engaged during twelve hours, and because he found himself on the same road with Marshal Blücher who assured him of his intention to follow the enemy throughout the night." He then adds, "I should not do justice to my own feelings, or to Marshal Blücher and the Prussian army, if I did not attribute the successful result of this arduous day to the cordial and timely assistance I received from them. The operation of General Bülow upon the enemy's flank was a most decisive one; and even if I had not found myself in a situation to make the attack which produced the final result, it would have forced the enemy to retire if his attacks should have failed, and would have prevented him from taking advantage of them if they should unfortunately have succeeded."

When the two Field Marshals met on the same road, it is well known that they embraced in the presence of their troops, and were cordial friends up to the day of the death of Prince Blücher. Surely the details of the battle might have been left in the original official reports.

Historians and commentators were not necessary.

The battle, possibly the most important single military event in modern times, was attended by advantages sufficient for the glory of many such armies as the two great Allied armies engaged.

The enemy never rallied; Buonaparte lost his empire for ever; not a shot was fired afterwards; and the peace of Europe and of the world was settled on the basis on which it rests at this moment.

It is impossible to close this paper without observing that Field Marshal the Duke of Wellington's letters, published by Colonel Gurwood, afford proofs that he was convinced that the enemy ought to have attacked by other lines rather than by the valleys of the Sambre and the Meuse; and that even up to the last moment previous to the attack of his position at Waterloo, he conceived that they would endeavour to turn it by a march upon Hal. He states this in letters to the Duc de Feltre on the 15th, and to the Duc de Berri and King Louis XVIII, dates at 3 ½ A.M. 18th June; and there are orders to his patrols of cavalry, on the nights of the 16th and 17th June, to observe particularly the enemy's movements towards Nivelles.

It might be a nice question for military discussion whether Buonaparte was right in endeavoring to force the position at Waterloo, or the Duke of Wellington right in thinking that, from the evening of the 16th, Buonaparte would have taken a wiser course if he had moved to his left, have reached the high road leading from Mons to Bruxelles, and have turned the right of the position of the Allies by Hal.

It is obvious that the Duke was prepared to resist such a movement.

WELLINGTON

VII.

CLAUSEWITZ ON WATERLOO: NAPOLEON AT BAY
by Daniel Moran

Clausewitz wrote his *History of the Campaign of 1815* sometime during what proved to be the last three working years of his life: between July of 1827, when he decided to undertake a thorough revision of the manuscript that would become *On War*, and the spring of 1830, when he left Berlin to take up an operational assignment as inspector of artillery in Breslau. A few months later he was named chief of staff of the Prussian forces that were being assembled to observe, and if necessary to suppress, revolutionary agitation in Poland. It was in the course of the latter assignment that Clausewitz contracted the cholera from which he died the following year, leaving *On War* in the unfinished state in which it has come down to us. The undated manuscript of the *Campaign of 1815* was found among his surviving papers and included among the collected works published under his wife's supervision a few years later.

In contrast to *On War*, which Clausewitz intended to publish someday, the *Campaign of 1815* does not appear to have been destined for anyone's eyes but his own. He suspected, as he wrote to his friend Carl von der Groeben, that most readers would be bored by the historical work with which he was engaged, because it amounted to no more than "a collection of analyses and proofs," and was strictly focused on "the resolution of strategic questions." He had made no attempt to capture "the total impression of external events," so he could not imagine placing such work before the public.[1]

Von der Groeben, who assisted Marie von Clausewitz in the posthumous publication of her husband's works, did not share Clausewitz's sense that people would not be interested in what he had to say about the history of war. Yet it is true that the *Campaign of 1815* does not present a comprehensive account of its subject. Viewed as a freestanding study it

---

1 Clausewitz to Carl von der Groeben, 2 January 1829, in Eberhard Kessel, "Zur Genesis der modernen Kriegslehre: Die Entstehungsgeschichte von Clausewitz' Buch 'Vom Kriege,'" *Wehrwissenschaftliche Rundschau*, volume 3, number 9 (1953): 421.

makes a somewhat odd impression, if for no other reason than because Clausewitz has contrived to drain every trace of fear and exaltation from events that must have included plenty of both. The proportions are also peculiar. Some tactical episodes are analyzed in detail—the Prussian effort to hold onto the village of Saint-Amand outside Ligny, for instance. Others, like the unyielding struggle to control the château of Hougoumont, or the relentless fire that Napoleon's *grande batterie* poured onto Wellington's forces throughout the day at Waterloo, are passed over in a few words or in silence. Overall the climactic struggle at Waterloo gets scarcely more attention than the (admittedly under-rated) Battle of Ligny that preceded it. This imbalance might be interpreted as an expression of Prussian patriotism, were any hints of such patriotism evident, which they aren't. And while Clausewitz makes occasional reference to the limitations of his sources, his personal role in the campaign, as chief of staff to Thielmann's corps, is completely effaced. So too are whatever reminiscences might have been conveyed by his life-long friend and patron Neidthardt von Gneisenau, who was Blücher's chief of staff and must have been privy to all major strategic decisions on the Prussian side; not to mention the memories of any number of brother officers, who were present on the day and were still Clausewitz's colleagues during the years he was working on the manuscript.

The Campaign of 1815 does not include the intimate portraiture that enlivens many of Clausewitz's earlier historical works. There is nothing in it to compare to his incisive survey of the military and political personalities who led Prussia to defeat in 1806,[2] nor to his shrewd portraits of the men who led the armies that expelled Napoleon from Russia in 1812.[3] Such personal excursuses were integral to Clausewitz's analysis of these earlier campaigns. Having declared at the outset of his history of the campaign of 1806 that "Prussia ... was wrecked by its institutions,"[4] it was only right to take account of the personalities, assumptions, and capabilities of the men those institutions had brought to the forefront of Prussian life. And while that account did not absolutely require that the

---

2 Carl von Clausewitz, "Nachrichten über Preussen in seiner grossen Katastrophe," in *Verstreute kleine Schriften*, edited by Werner Hahlweg (Osnabrück: Biblio Verlag, 1979), 301-493, excerpted in *Historical and Political Writings*, 30-84.
3 Carl von Clausewitz, *Feldzug von Russland in 1812*, in *Schriften*, 2: 717-935; excerpted in *Historical and Political Writings*, 110-204.
4 *Historical and Political Writings*, 32.

senior Prussian general at the Battle of Jena be described as a man "suited to carry out the orders of others," it is apparent that such unflinching candor gave Clausewitz's study an explanatory precision that no purely operational analysis could match.[5]

The same can be said of his portrayal, in *The Campaign of 1812 in Russia,* of the ageing Russian field marshal, Mikhail Kutusov, sitting passive and bewildered in his headquarters at Borodino while Napoleon pounded away at his army and his aides ran to and fro with bold proposals for how to set things right. This spectacle compared poorly with the more decisive style of Kutusov's predecessor in supreme command, General Barclay de Tolly, whom Kutusov had relieved only a week before. Clausewitz, an outsider who spoke no Russian, did not feel entitled to challenge the consensus within the Russian army that most of the time Kutusov "counted for nothing" in the course of the battle. And he admits that Kutusov's performance was "anything but brilliant, and far beneath what could have been expected of him in view of his earlier achievements." But even so, Clausewitz was not so sure whether, in the end, Kutusov might not have been the best choice to lead the army though its most bruising confrontation with Napoleon. Kutusov, he concluded:

> would certainly not have fought the battle of Borodino, which he probably did not expect to win, if it had not been pressed upon him by the court, the army, and the whole country. Presumably he regarded it only as a necessary evil. But he knew his Russians and understood how to treat them. With astonishing boldness he presented himself [afterwards] as the victor, announced everywhere the impending destruction of the enemy army, gave the impression, up to the last moment, that he intended to defend Moscow with a second battle, and did not hesitate to bluster and boast. In this way he flattered the vanity of the army and the people; with proclamations and religious addresses he tried to work on their feelings and thus created a new kind of confidence, artificial to be sure, but based on a fact, namely the miserable situation of the French army. The frivolity and hucksterism

---

5 Ibid., 47. Such observations insured that Clausewitz's history of the 1806 campaign could not be included among the ten volumes of the *Werke*. It appeared in print only in 1888, having passed the intervening half-century in the archives of the Prussian general staff.

of the old fox were in fact far more useful than Barclay's honesty would have been.[6]

With the exception of Clausewitz's withering account of Napoleon's behavior at the very end of the Battle of Waterloo, which is discussed below, this sort of rich observation is missing from the *Campaign of 1815*. It has been almost entirely displaced by a single-minded concentration on the logic of events, and specifically on the command decisions that bring the events about. The Waterloo campaign was already world-famous when Clausewitz decided to write about it. Whatever might have drawn his attention to it, it cannot have been a desire for a more thorough acquaintance with the facts. Although Clausewitz's text includes a list of tactical issues on which he would have liked additional information, the truth is that the facts were sufficiently known. It was their authorship, so to speak, that interested him. It is for this reason that his most important source is also the one that is least reliable in factual terms: Napoleon's *Mémoires*. The ultimate subject of Clausewitz's history of 1815 is the minds of the men who commanded the armies that fought it. Clausewitz's approach to the greatest military campaign of his age is not that of a soldier recounting a famous victory, but more in the spirit of a critic engaging a long-familiar text in order to reconstruct the creative process by which it came to exist.

It is natural, considering when it was written, to interpret the *Campaign of 1815* as an exercise that Clausewitz must have undertaken in connection with the proposed revisions of *On War* that he described in his note of July 1827. Yet references to the Waterloo campaign are rare in *On War*—eleven altogether, none terribly interesting.[7] All appear in sections of the book that Clausewitz declares in his note to be in need of complete overhaul, which they evidently did not receive. There is thus no particular reason to believe that writing the *Campaign of 1815* altered the composition of *On War* in any substantial way.[8] It would be more

---

6 Ibid., 140-41.
7 See the index to Werner Hahlweg's critical edition, *Vom Kriege: Hinterlassenes Werk des Generals Carl von Clausewitz*, 19th edition [*Jubiläumsausgabe*] (Bonn: Ferd. Dümmlers Verlag), 1980. Clausewitz's note of July 1827, describing his planned revisions, is in *On War*, ed. and trans. Michael Howard and Peter Paret (Princeton, NJ: Princeton University Press, 1976), 69.
8 Clausewitz's intellectual trajectory during the last years of his life is not easy to reconstruct, owing to the uncertain dating of so many of his manuscripts. It has become especially conten-

accurate to say that the themes and insights that Clausewitz intended to emphasize in revising *On War* are also on display in his account of Napoleon's last campaign. This was written after most, if not all, of the text we know as *On War* was complete.

In the note of 1827, Clausewitz declares his intention to revise *On War* in light of two fundamental principles. The first of these principles is that wars can be of "two kinds": those with limited objectives, intended to bring about negotiations, and those intended to bring about the complete overthrow of the enemy. The second is that "war is nothing but the continuation of policy with other means."[9] Both of these principles make themselves felt in the *Campaign of 1815*, though the influence of the first is perhaps not obvious. If ever there were a clash of arms intended to bring about the complete overthrow of the enemy, one may well feel that Waterloo must be it. But this is true only on the Allied side. Napoleon's political aims in 1815, at least with respect to the Allies (as opposed to the Bourbons, whom he had already displaced), were quite limited. He was fighting to achieve some kind of military result that could serve as a basis for negotiation. This fundamental political fact serves Clausewitz as the touchstone against which Napoleon's military actions had to be judged if they were to be properly understood.

---

tious following the claim, by Azar Gat, that the note of 1827 represented not the crystallization of long-maturing insight into the relationship between war and politics, but an intellectual crisis from which Clausewitz never recovered. Azar Gat, *The Origins of Military Thought: From the Enlightenment to Clausewitz* (Oxford and New York: Oxford University Press, 1989), 213-14. Most specialists accept the claim, in an undated note published by Marie von Clausewitz as part of the front matter to *On War*, that Clausewitz regarded "the first chapter of Book One alone ... as finished" (*On War*, 70). But even this view depends upon accepting that this second note was written immediately prior to Clausewitz's departure for Breslau in 1830, an attribution that Gat has disputed. Ibid., 255-63. Werner Halweg also assigned the undated note to 1827. Carl von Clausewitz, *Schriften–Aufsätze–Studien–Briefe* (Göttingen: Vandenhoeck & Ruprecht, 1990), 625. To the extent that Clausewitz's use of historical arguments and illustrations in *On War* can shed any light on the manner of its composition, there is no question that he relied overwhelmingly on historical studies that he completed before or during the early 1820s—the campaigns of Frederick the Great and those of 1806 and 1812-14—rather than those he worked on during the last years of his life (i.e., the campaigns of 1815 and 1796-99). There is a chronology dating the likely composition of Clausewitz's major works in Peter Paret, *Clausewitz and the State* (New York and London: Oxford University Press, 1976), 330; but cf. Hew Strachan's occasionally diverging analysis in *Clausewitz's* On War: *A Biography* (New York: Atlantic Monthly Press, 2007), 68-105.

9 *On War*, 69.

CLAUSEWITZ ON WATERLOO: NAPOLEON AT BAY

The natural way in which Clausewitz accounts for the political objectives of Napoleon and his adversaries, and integrates this understanding into his analysis of major operations, marks the *Campaign of 1815* as one of his most mature and sophisticated historical works. It also illustrates the general value of reading his historical studies alongside *On War*, in which theoretical insights of great value are often accompanied by historical illustrations that either fail to do them justice or inadvertently limit the point Clausewitz is trying to make. The outstanding example of this is undoubtedly the famous passage, at the end of Book One of *On War*, in which Clausewitz describes war as a "remarkable Trinity" comprising "primordial violence," the "play of chance and probability," and finally "reason," which is the "element of subordination" that defines war's instrumental nature. This striking passage is immediately followed by another, intended to clarify it, in which the three elements of the Trinity are identified respectively with "the people," "the commander and his army," and "the government."[10] As a consequence, any number of readers have concluded that Clausewitz's Trinity—whose true elements are violence, chance, and reason—is instead basically sociological in nature; that its constituent elements are the people, the army, and the government; and that some kind of institutional or moral balance among these is required to achieve strategic success.[11]

This is clearly a misreading, but one that Clausewitz invites by pegging his general theoretical claims to historically contingent social and political conditions. It may be true, as was widely believed after the French Revolution, that the "violence, hatred, and enmity" of war, which make it seem like "a force of nature," will often concern "mainly ... the people." But this is not always the case. It was not the case in the campaigns of Frederick the Great, for instance, and it was not the case in 1815, either. The Waterloo campaign, in Clausewitz's account, is one in which

---

10 Ibid., 89.
11 The most egregious misrepresentation of Clausewitz's famous metaphor must be that of Martin van Creveld, who has declared Clausewitz to be an apostle of "Trinitarian War," by which he means, incomprehensibly, a war of "state against state and army against army," from which the influence of the people is entirely excluded. Martin van Creveld, *The Transformation of War: The Most Radical Reinterpretation of Armed Conflict Since Clausewitz* (New York: The Free Press, 1991), 49. For a thorough discussion of the interpretive difficulties that Clausewitz's Trinity presents, see Christopher Bassford, "The Primacy of Politics and the 'Trinity' in Clausewitz's Mature Thought," in Hew Strachan and Andreas Herberg-Rothe, eds., *Clausewitz in the Twenty-First Century* (Oxford and New York: Oxford University Press, 2007), 74-90.

the armies of France are driven to battle by the primordial passions of their commander, whose hatreds and enmities were merely echoed, and faintly at that, by the nation whose destiny he had seized.

Clausewitz's claim that there are two kinds of war has aroused similar confusion. While the metaphor of the Trinity may be so complex as to elude all but the most attentive reader, the claim that there are two kinds of war is at the very least a misleading oversimplification. As Clausewitz declared elsewhere (and obviously believed), all wars are things of "the *same* nature,"[12] whose shared recourse to violence is the one thing that distinguishes all war categorically and collectively from the other instruments of policy. That Clausewitz should have sought to draw such an emphatic distinction across a phenomenon that he also describes as "diverse" and "chameleon"-like[13] has, at the very least, raised more questions than it has answered. The answers are apparent, however, in *The Campaign of 1815*. There the analytic importance of understanding the political motives that govern war is on display in subtle and convincing form.

Clausewitz's claim that war can be of two kinds is a needlessly unconditional expression of a point that he believed required great emphasis: that the scope and character of a belligerent's political aims matter to the conduct of war, not merely on the margins or at the beginning and the end, but centrally and throughout the entire course of the fighting. One way to illustrate this, as Clausewitz does by implication in his example about the seizure of a province, is to observe that most wars are small because the political stakes are small. But this is an empirical observation rather than a theoretical principle, and if it is mistaken for the latter it implies a rule of proportionality between military means and political ends that is clearly false. Clausewitz himself would have rejected such a rule as one of those unrealistically "algebraic" propositions that so often confound strategic analysis.[14]

Napoleon had limited means and limited objectives in 1815, but nevertheless found himself in a situation that demanded the greatest possible military effort, a common enough predicament of the weaker side in war. His circumstances were complicated by the fact that his objectives

---

12 Ibid., 606; emphasis in the original.
13 Ibid., 87 and 89.
14 Cf. Ibid., 76.

were entirely psychological. There was no way he could inflict sufficient material damage on his opponents to alter their overwhelming military advantage. Instead he needed a victory of sufficient significance to shake the alliance that had assembled against him. When added to his own formidable reputation, such a victory would suggest to his opponents that only a disproportionate amount of additional fighting would suffice to subdue his new regime—disproportionate, that is, compared to the distasteful but easier course of acquiescing in his return to the throne of France. Wellington and Blücher, on the other hand, would have been perfectly satisfied to see him hung from a gibbet—the quintessential "unlimited" objective in Clausewitzian terms—and they enjoyed sufficiently overwhelming superiority of numbers that they did not need to calculate their own costs or risks too closely. If they did not possess the full measure of Napoleon's brilliance, neither did they suffer from his political and material constraints. This is why, in the end, the fortunes of war favored them.

Clausewitz's understanding of the political aims of Napoleon and his opponents is crucial to his tactical analysis. It is a tool by which he can work backwards from the known facts of the campaign to the reasoning and assumptions of the commanders whose decisions, modified as always by the effects of friction, chance, and the interaction of the opposing armies, brought those facts about. Yet there is no avoiding the additional fact that, in political terms, the outcome of the Waterloo campaign was severely over-determined. Napoleon was well and truly at bay, with half a million men and more converging against him and no more than a few weeks to get ready. Under such circumstances it is easy to argue that, realistically, the details of the fighting mattered very little. When all roads lead to defeat, the choice among them makes no difference, except to those seeking purely tactical instruction.

This is a problem that all serious students of Waterloo must confront. Two sorts of answers are available. The first is that there is more than one kind of historical realism, and the most important kind takes full account of contemporary perceptions. The degree to which Napoleon's fate was sealed in 1815 is more apparent in retrospect than it was to those who had to face him. For them he was a figure of near-demonic power, who had escaped certain doom once before in Russia and lived to fight another day. The hand-wave with which he had sent the Bourbons packing confirmed this impression. Napoleon's capacity to wreak havoc could scarcely have been viewed with complacency even if one were confident of the military results. This leads to the second sort of answer, which is that, when fighting Napoleon, one could never be confident of the results until they had actually been achieved. From this perspective, Napoleon's cause is not to be regarded as hopeless at all: A great victory against Wellington and Blücher might indeed have broken the coalition that opposed him and created conditions that would have allowed his reign to continue.

Clausewitz certainly held the first of these two points of view. He believed that historical (and strategic) understanding required him to recapture the way things appeared at the time, rather than to impose retrospective judgments or values upon the past. It is less clear whether Clausewitz believed Napoleon had a real chance of permanent political success. In Chapter 51 of his history, Clausewitz offers what he regards as the maximum military result that Napoleon could have achieved in 1815: a truly crushing victory over Blücher's army, which Clausewitz argues should have been pursued ruthlessly after the Battle of Ligny, without regard for what Wellington might do in the meantime. But while Clausewitz had claimed a few pages before that "Bonaparte was balancing on the tip of his sword not only the crown of France but a number of other crowns as well,"[15] he does not explain why he believes this, nor why the kind of victory he describes would have caused the other Allied armies that were already in motion to come to a halt.

This neglect may simply be owing to the fact that Napoleon did in fact lose everything at Waterloo, so that an analysis of the political weaknesses of the Allies was not necessary. Clausewitz had long been aware of the special problems of coalition warfare and of the cross-purposes that might lurk behind declarations of mutual loyalty.[16] He also suspected, with good reason, that Austria's commitment to Napoleon's destruction was not all that it might have been. Austria's attitude toward France was always moderated by concern that a serious decline of French power would accrue mainly to the benefit of Russia. During the campaign of 1814, which culminated in Napoleon's first abdication, Austria's chan-

---

15 Chapter 48.
16 See the note "On Coalitions" (1803), and the untitled note beginning "I know only two ways to insure that an advantageous alliance leads to advantages in war...." (1805), in *Historical and Political Writings*, 241-3, 245-6.

cellor, Metternich, had sought a negotiated settlement until almost the last moment. This policy was presumably strengthened by the fact that Napoleon was married to an Austrian princess, and that the heir to his throne would have been a grandson of the Habsburg emperor. Napoleon hoped to reawaken Metternich's passion for moderation by beating Wellington and Blücher so badly that the Habsburgs would reconsider their options once more. But since he failed, the issue of Allied cohesion had never emerged in reality. Clausewitz may therefore have felt that no useful purpose could be served by considering it in hypothetical terms.[17]

Overall, Clausewitz's assessment of Napoleon's chances in 1815 might fairly be described as agnostic. For his purpose it is sufficient that neither Napoleon nor his opponents regarded the outcome as having been decided in advance, even if a dispassionate judgment in retrospect might suggest that it had been. Clausewitz's sense of balance seems to have grown more sure with the passage of time, as can be seen if one compares the *Campaign of 1815* with some of his earlier work. The campaigns of 1806 and 1814 present different versions of the same analytic problem posed by Waterloo: how to treat the instrumental reality of war in political circumstances that appear to render merely military decisions inconsequential.

Clausewitz's work on the campaign of 1814 dates from the early 1820s[18] and took the form of two separate manuscripts. These appeared side by side in the seventh volume of his *Hinterlassene Werke*. The first is an "overview" of the campaign, which summarizes the order of battle of the two sides and the course of the fighting.[19] The second, called a "strategic critique," is concerned with "the processes of strategic thought," which Clausewitz believed the fighting of 1814 revealed with exceptional

---

[17] Clausewitz's histories of the campaigns of 1796 and 1799, like that of 1815, date from the last years of his life. In those earlier campaigns the Allies lost, and both of Clausewitz's histories include periodic observations, and concluding summary analyses, of how the military blows that Napoleon delivered were translated into a failure of political nerve by his opponents. See *Der Feldzug von 1796 in Italien*, in *Werke*, 4, especially 330-54; and *Die Feldzüge von 1799 in Italien und der Schweiz*, in *Werke*, 5 and 6, especially 6: 371-97. Paret, *Clausewitz and the State*, 337-8, considers Clausewitz's treatment of these campaigns and includes a long extract in English from the last few pages of the *Feldzug von 1796*, in which the politics of the campaign are summarized.

[18] Paret, *Clausewitz and the State*, 330, places the writing of the *Campaign of 1814* in the period 1816-1818. This may be a little early, since the text refers to one source that was published in 1819. See *Historical and Political Writings*, 205.

[19] "Übersicht des Feldzugs von 1814 in Frankreich," *Werke*, 7: 325-56.

clarity.[20] His primary reason for thinking so, however, is startling. It is that the campaign of 1814 appeared to be relatively "untouched by diplomatic considerations, which like some foreign matter douse the fire of violence," so that "the whole concept of war and of its purpose is not as thoroughly politicized as was the case in most recent wars before the French Revolution."[21]

This is, to say the least, a dramatic simplification, if not an outright dismissal, of the circumstances that had finally brought all of the Powers of Europe together against France. It represents no more than the starting point for Clausewitz's understanding of the analytic relationship of war to politics: politics serves to determine the scale and intensity of the instrumental violence employed to achieve its ends. In this relatively early work, however, Clausewitz does not seem to feel any need to consider second-order political effects, which actually shaped the campaign of 1814 profoundly. It was politics, for instance, that drove Napoleon's need to maneuver so as to keep his army between the Allies and Paris, the loss of which would have meant losing the war. The fact that the "offensive" and "defensive" sides were especially well-defined in 1814[22] is as close as Clausewitz gets to considering what it might mean for someone like Napoleon to be facing certain defeat, much less how the resulting frame of mind might have influenced his choices as a commander. The latter theme predominates in his history of 1815.

While there is no denying the acuity of Clausewitz's operational analysis in his history of 1814, a kind of unreality pervades the whole, because it is not until the end that the true balance of forces in play is fully acknowledged. Realistically, Napoleon could muster perhaps 70,000 men for a final defense of Paris, against an attacking force more than twice as large. This fact inspired the emperor to attempt a vain flanking maneuver, a "march into the blue," which embodied the hopelessness of his cause and sealed his defeat.[23] Such insights were within Clausewitz's

---

20 "Strategische Kritik des Feldzuges von 1814 in Frankreich," Ibid., 357-470, excerpted in *Historical and Political Writings*, 207-19. The quotation is from 207 of the English edition. It is a measure of Clausewitz's increasing sophistication as a historical writer that, in his history of the *Campaign of 1815* (whose subtitle in German is "strategic overview") he dispenses with the intellectual division of labor between objective "overview" and analytic "strategic critique" that he adopted in studying the campaign of 1814. See *Schriften*, 2: 943.
21 *Historical and Political Writings*, 207.
22 Idem.
23 Ibid., 219.

reach throughout his working life, and reveal the essential continuity of his work. In his later years, however, as the *Campaign of 1815* shows, such politically informed analysis was not merely within reach but fully at his command, and available to underpin his analysis of a major campaign.

Clausewitz's treatment of Prussia's defeat in 1806 presents the starkest possible contrast to his account of Napoleon's defeat in 1814. If politics are virtually dismissed from the latter account, they more or less overwhelm the former. Clausewitz felt more strongly about the campaign of 1806 than he did about any other military episode of his life. He fought in the Battle of Auerstädt as a captain, and for a time assumed command of part of the rear guard during the appalling retreat that followed. Afterwards he spent ten months as a prisoner of war in France and Switzerland. That humiliating experience deprived him of the opportunity to distinguish himself when fighting resumed on less disastrous terms in the spring of 1807, culminating in the Peace of Tilsit by which Prussia's survival in France's shadow was secured. When Clausewitz returned to Berlin, he joined the group of military reformers who coalesced around his friend and mentor, Gerhard von Scharnhorst, and sought to build a new base for military resistance to France. When their efforts were cut short by the onset of the campaign of 1812, however, Clausewitz resigned his commission and entered Russian service rather than fight as an ally of Napoleon.

The anger and bitterness that the defeat of 1806 inspired in Clausewitz were suppressed in his first effort to explain it. Early in 1807 he published a series of instructive but, one cannot help but feel, artificially dispassionate articles on "the great military events of 1806." In them he portrayed Prussia's defeat as an honest and courageous effort against a much stronger opponent. He feared, indeed, that Prussia was liable to be judged unfairly by the rest of Europe on account of the martial reputation it had acquired in the previous century.[24] When he returned to the subject some fifteen years later, however, the question foremost in his mind was not how a small but brave state had comported itself against overwhelming odds, but exactly how the odds had become so overwhelming. "Great military events" became Prussia's "great catastrophe."[25] By way

---

24 "Historische Briefe über die großen Kriegsereignisse 1806," *Minerva*, edited by J. W. von Archenholz, volume 1, number 1 (1807), 1-21; volume 1, number 2 (1807), 193-209; and volume 2, number 1 (1807), 1-26; reprinted in *Verstreute Kleine Schriften*, 95-125.

25 See note 3, above. Internal evidence suggests that Clausewitz's "Observations on Prussia"

of explaining the catastrophe, Clausewitz formulated an indictment of Prussia's governing institutions and foreign policy, reaching back to the death of Frederick the Great, that was so scathing as to render his treatment of the campaign itself more or less superfluous.

There is no question that Clausewitz's indictment of Prussia in 1806 goes too far in his scorn for everything from the leading men in Prussia's government to the quality of the rope in Prussia's arsenals. Yet, on balance, Clausewitz sees the politics of 1806 clearly enough, and once that light is allowed to shine bright the effect on the military analysis is searing. In Clausewitz's judgment, Prussia had managed by a series of ill-conceived diplomatic maneuvers to lose the chance of fighting France in 1805 as part of a grand alliance including Austria and Russia. It thus found itself isolated and overmatched a year later. Its response was a swift mobilization of the army, followed by aggressive operations intended to seize the initiative from the enemy—all in accord with Frederician habits and traditions that had been hopelessly overtaken by events.

In Clausewitz's first attempt to come to terms with the disaster that followed, he had claimed that "nothing would appear better suited to multiply our forces, than to seize the advantages of the offensive, by which we might be fortunate enough to surprise the enemy before his preparations were ready."[26] Once the politics of the campaign had been accounted for, however, such a move appeared absurd. It was not simply that Prussia's chances were slim. An army that is already advancing in search of a fight, and led by Napoleon himself, is not likely to be surprised by contact with the enemy, however it may occur. But even that was not the worst of it. The fatal problem, and the ultimate vanity of the whole business, lay in the fact that even an early Prussian success, had it somehow been achieved, would have meant nothing. The most damning of Clausewitz's "Observations on Prussia" is one of the simplest: the army that Napoleon led into Prussia in 1806 was not the only one he had. Even if the Prussians managed to beat it, how would they make good their losses in time to beat the next one?[27]

This is not a question that Clausewitz asks about Waterloo, though he might have done so. The campaigns of 1806 and 1815 are sufficiently

---

was written in the period 1823-25. See *Historical and Political Writings*, 30.
26 "Historische Briefe über die Kriegsereignisse 1806," *Verstreute kleine Schriften*," 97.
27 "Observations on Prussia," *Historical and Political Writings*, 77.

mirror-images of each other that it would have been easy to treat them along parallel lines. Clausewitz does this to some extent early in his text, when he considers the scale of forces that Napoleon was able to mobilize following his return. The resulting army, Clausewitz argues, fell far below the maximum force that a country like France could have mustered, owing to a combination of institutional rigidity and the shortness of time. Prussia had suffered from similar difficulties in 1806. Its defense had been conducted by a regular army that represented a small fraction of potentially available manpower, because the government had failed to provide its people with the kind of military training required to mobilize the civilian population for war. Had it been able to do so, it might then have adopted a posture of defense in depth based on the Vistula.[28] This would have confronted Napoleon with the task of hacking his way across the entire country, with no respite until all of it had been occupied. Because the Prussian monarchy lacked the social and institutional basis for mounting such a defense, it was forced to throw away its only army in a superficially bold but doomed offensive. This is a typical expedient of the weaker side in war, as Clausewitz noted in the article in 1807, but no more likely to succeed on that account.

After 1806, Clausewitz became a strong advocate of a universal, militia-based reserve system known in Prussia as the *Landwehr*. He takes the opportunity, while analyzing Napoleon's problems in 1815, to note that those problems would have been much reduced had France possessed such a system.[29] There is some irony here. As Clausewitz observes, it was

---

28 Idem. The influence of Clausewitz's experience in Russia in 1812 is apparent in his claim that a defense in depth might have served Prussia well in 1806. Such an idea would scarcely have occurred to anyone, including Clausewitz, at the time. There is also no denying that Clausewitz's faith in such a measure is probably misplaced. Prussia was a small country surrounded by states that had already made peace with France. Its defense in depth would not have presented Napoleon with anything like the challenge he confronted in 1812. Clausewitz's advocacy of such measures would appear to be based less upon an analysis of the real military possibilities than on his passionate belief that even a doomed people should be given the chance to succumb heroically. In this connection, see above all his "Political Declaration" [*Bekenntnissdenkschrift*], written shortly before his departure for Russian service in 1812, in *Schriften*, 1: 678-751, excerpted in *Historical and Political Writings*, 285-303.
29 The creation of the *Landwehr* was part of the program put forward by Prussia's military reformers, though effective action was impossible as long as Prussia remained bound to France. The abrogation of the Franco-Prussian alliance after Napoleon's defeat in Russia caused a number of Prussian officers, including Clausewitz, to begin raising *Landwehr* formations in East Prussia on their own authority. Their actions were resented by the crown but were ratified in retrospect, given the general shift in military fortunes that they helped to achieve.

the Revolutionary *levée en masse* of 1793 that had inspired the system of universal military service that helped sustain Prussia's revival.[30] There would be no French *levée en masse* in 1815, however. As a consequence, Napoleon had no choice but to adopt the same kind of speculative offensive strategy that had failed Prussia nine years earlier.

It is here, of course, than any comparison between Prussia in 1806 and France in 1815 must break down. Even by the most uncharitable estimate, France was not "wrecked by its institutions," as Prussia had been. It was wrecked, in Clausewitz's account, by the vanity and ambition of one man. Long before he had grasped the full significance of politics for war, Clausewitz had been acutely sensitive to the role of a commander's personality in shaping military operations. This is apparent, for instance, in his study of the campaigns of Gustavus Adolphus during the Thirty Years' War, which he wrote following his return to Berlin in 1807. There Clausewitz declares that "subjective forces" within the mind of Sweden's great king were the "most decisive" influence upon the actions of his army. Similarly, the failure of his Catholic opponents to concentrate all their forces against him at the crucial Battle of Breitenfeld was a reflection, not of material conditions, but of the fact that they had not yet suffered a defeat sufficiently grave to inspire a maximum effort.[31]

These insights would crystallize in Clausewitz's concept of "military genius." The workings of genius pervade Clausewitz's account of the

---

[30] Prussian conservatives always suspected that Prussia's *Landwehr* might nurture the seeds of revolutionary agitation, because it provided arms and military training to the masses. In 1814 and again in 1819, steps were taken to subordinate the *Landwehr* more formally to the standing army. Clausewitz opposed these moves, because he believed that the *Landwehr*'s character as a civilian militia helped inspire popular loyalty to the government (as opposed to imposing military values upon society). In 1819 he wrote an essay defending the original conception of the *Landwehr* and opposing its amalgamation with regular forces. He was particularly concerned to reject the charge that the *Landwehr* posed a revolutionary risk. Clausewitz, "On the Political Advantages and Disadvantages of the Prussian *Landwehr*," *Historical and Political Writings*, 329-34. The essay remained unpublished, but suspicions that Clausewitz unduly admired the French Revolution's military institutions dogged him throughout the remainder of his career. Paret, *Clausewitz and the State*, 286-98. The *Campaign of 1815*'s explicit links between the Prussian *Landwehr* and the Revolutionary *levée en masse* shows that, at least when writing for himself alone, Clausewitz felt no need to gloss over this association.

[31] "Gustav Adolphs Feldzüge von 1630-1632," *Werke*, 9:8, and 45-46. The significance of psychological factors in Clausewitz's account of Gustavus Adolphus' campaigns was first noted by Hans Rothfels, *Carl von Clausewitz: Politik und Krieg: Eine ideengeschichtliche Studie* (Berlin: F. Dümmler, 1920; reprinted 1980). See also Paret, *Clausewitz and the State*, 85-88, and Gat, *Origins of Military Thought*, 179-80.

CLAUSEWITZ ON WATERLOO: NAPOLEON AT BAY

Campaign of 1815, in which fate contrived to bring the three greatest generals in Europe together on the same battlefield. Clausewitz adapted the concept of genius from the art and literature of his time. He employed it as a means of capturing, for military theory, those qualities of talent, insight, and determination that the best commanders always display, and which cannot be explained with reference to doctrinal norms or abstract strategic principles. Clausewitz's understanding of genius has long been recognized as owing much to the work of Immanuel Kant and to the school of aesthetic philosophy that Kant's ideas inspired. In his *Critique of Judgment*, Kant defined genius as "the innate mental aptitude (*ingenium*) *through which* nature gives the rule to art," and also as "a *talent* for producing that for which no definite rule can be given."[32] These concepts are plainly echoed in *On War*, where Clausewitz describes genius as a natural ability that both "rises above the rules," and, in effect, makes them: "What genius does is the best rule," he wrote, "and theory can do no better than show how and why this should be the case."[33]

Clausewitz's histories of Napoleon's campaigns all reflect his determination to engage with the mind of Napoleon himself, the most terrible embodiment of military genius the world had yet seen. The *Campaign of 1815* is unusual in this regard only by virtue of the intimacy of the encounter. This is made possible by the fact that, in this case, Napoleon himself had provided an explanation of his conduct against which Clausewitz could test his own understanding of the evidence. Napoleon's *Mémoires pour servir à l'histoire de France en 1815* is Clausewitz's most frequently cited source, not because of its factual value but because its misrepresentations could be used as a lens with which to bring the critical events of the battle into sharper focus. In Clausewitz's hands, Napoleon's *Mémoires* do indeed reveal the inner workings of Napoleon's mind, albeit not in the way their author must have hoped.[34]

---

32 Immanuel Kant, *The Critique of Judgement*, translated by James Creed Meredith (Oxford and New York: Oxford University Press, 1978), 168. Emphasis in the original.
33 *On War*, 136.
34 Napoleon's *Mémoires* was published anonymously in Paris in 1820. Its authenticity, which Clausewitz does not question, was initially disputed because the work's initial appearance coincided with that of many forgeries purporting to be his work. There is a reference to its composition in Emmanuel Las Cases' *Mémorial de Sainte-Hélène*, 8 volumes (Paris: no publisher, 1823-24), in an entry dated 26 August 1816 (5:377). Its eventual inclusion in Napoleon's correspondence, in the edition prepared under the auspices of his nephew, Napoleon III, appears to have decided the matter. See *Correspondence de Napoléon Ier, publiée par ordre de l'empereur*

ON WATERLOO

In psychological terms, the fact that Napoleon felt the need to explain what had happened at Waterloo was significant in itself. He had faced apparently final defeat once before, in 1814. On that occasion he had responded by trying to kill himself, using poison that his physician had prepared for him to take into Russia two years before. The poison had lost its potency in the meantime, however, so that it had merely made him ill.[35] Whether Clausewitz would have approved of the attempt, had he known of it, is hard to say. It would at least have conformed to a tragic and heroic ethos that he would have found recognizable.

After Waterloo, however, Napoleon did not take poison. Instead he wrote a book, an unprecedented apologia that invited close scrutiny. Napoleon's *Mémoires* were significant because of their author, and because in Clausewitz's day the death and destruction of war neither required nor received any public explanation by those responsible for it. Napoleon's effort to justify himself was all the more intriguing by virtue of having been written by a famous liar: Napoleon's official bulletins had been notorious for their mendacity since long before Waterloo. Yet these factors did not diminish the value of the source from Clausewitz's perspective. On the contrary, his analysis is informed by the realization that those things that Napoleon wished to conceal were most likely to be of particular significance.

There is no denying the occasionally contemptuous tone with which Clausewitz dismisses Napoleon's attempt to justify himself. Yet the fact of Napoleon's genius shines through. Napoleon wrote his *Mémoires* to shift the blame for France's defeat onto the shoulders of his subordinates, but also, more generally, to suggest that the Waterloo campaign as a whole was not a futile waste of blood and treasure. As with the Duke of Wellington, who famously characterized Waterloo as "a damned nice thing—the nearest run thing you ever saw in your life,"[36] it was important to Napoleon that the campaign of 1815 be recognized as a close call, and specifically as a victory that might have been his but for bad luck and the

---

Napoléon III, 32 volumes (Paris: Impr. Impériale, 1858-69), volume 31. There is an English version, edited and translated by Somerset de Chair, entitled *The Waterloo Campaign* (London: The Folio Society, 1957).
35 Daniel Bell, *The First Total War: Napoleon's Europe and the Birth of Warfare as We Know It* (Boston and New York: Houghton Mifflin, 2007), 300-301.
36 Quoted in Thomas Creevey, *The Creevey Papers: A Selection from the Correspondence & Diaries of the Late Thomas Creevey, M.P.*, edited by Herbert Maxwell (New York: E. P. Dutton, 1904), 236.

bungling of his subordinates. The brilliance of Clausewitz's analysis lies in part in the clarity with which it reveals that this cannot have been how Napoleon saw things at the time. Napoleon fought the campaign of 1815 like a man on the edge of the abyss. As Clausewitz shows repeatedly, Napoleon's *Mémoires* routinely obscured conduct that made perfect sense, or even revealed exceptional insight, once this fact is understood and the true gravity of his circumstances taken into account. But it is that very gravity that Napoleon wished to obscure, rendering his own conduct implausibly naïve in the process.

In Clausewitz's account, it is not Napoleon's genius that fails him in 1815, but his character. Clausewitz would have been the last person to judge the conduct of war in ethical terms. Yet there is something more than tactical judgment at work in his stunning dissection of the climactic moment at Waterloo, when Napoleon, having grasped the finality of the threat posed by the arrival of Prussian forces on his right, nevertheless commits the last of his reserves to a final, pointless attack against Wellington, rather than employing them to cover an orderly retreat.

On other occasions this is the kind of act that Clausewitz had been inclined to defend, on the grounds, as he says, that "there are situations when the greatest prudence can only be sought in the greatest boldness." It is, moreover, a characteristic mark of genius to recognize and seize the opportunity that such situations afford. It was on this basis that Clausewitz justified Napoleon's conduct in 1812, against the commonplace claim that the invasion of Russia was doomed from the start. Clausewitz rejected the idea that Napoleon's defeat could have been anticipated, or that a more incremental approach would have been more promising. "It could not be foreseen with certainty," Clausewitz argued, "it was perhaps not even likely, that the Russians would abandon Moscow, burn it down, and engage in a war of attrition; but once this happened the war was bound to miscarry, regardless of how it was conducted."[37]

Absent a premonition of events without precedent, Clausewitz judged Napoleon's bold attempt to overwhelm Russia in a single campaign to be the proper choice—an example of how rule-book prudence must give way before the dictates of genius. No such defense is possible for Napoleon's conduct at Waterloo, however. In the campaign of 1815, Napoleon is not confronted with anything like the imponderable spectacle of Mos-

---

[37] *Historical and Political Writings*, 201-04; quotation from 202.

cow in flames, a harbinger of people's war, a new "phenomenon of the nineteenth century" that exceeded the boundaries even of Napoleon's genius.[38] At Waterloo, on the contrary, Napoleon's predicament is the foreseeable consequence of his own actions: warfare conducted in a manner that he had perfected, by men only slightly less gifted than himself, and no less determined.

Clausewitz could imagine war as a form of existential violence whose psychological and moral intensity carried it beyond the realm of politics.[39] But he envisioned such conduct as the province of political communities *in extremis*, not of commanders throwing away the last remnants of their army rather than face up to defeat. In the end, Clausewitz deems Napoleon to have acted not "in the manner of a great man but rather in vulgar exasperation, like someone who has broken an instrument and in his anger smashes the parts to pieces on the ground." Even for Clausewitz, genius had its limits. Those limits were reached at Waterloo, where the crushing realities of modern war had piled up so high that even Napoleon could not get past them. Yet he remained bound by war's instrumental nature and by the interests of the political community he purported to serve. Napoleon's ultimate duty was to that community, and to the men under his command, who were its representatives no less than he was. Clausewitz judged that, in the last hours of Waterloo, Napoleon failed in his duty. From one soldier to another, there can be no harsher verdict than that.

---

38 See *On War*, 479.
39 Ibid., 483; cf. "Political Declaration," *Historical and Political Writings*, 290-91.

VIII.

WELLINGTON VERSUS CLAUSEWITZ
by Gregory W. Pedlow

"I am really too hard worked to become an Author and review these lying works called Histories," wrote the Duke of Wellington in September 1842 after reading Lord Liverpool's translation of Clausewitz's account of the Waterloo Campaign. He immediately set to work on a response—his "Memorandum on the Battle of Waterloo"—but when finished he told the editor of his papers, "I don't mean that this paper should be published. I have written it for Lord Francis Egerton's information, to enable him to review Clausewitz's history. I don't propose to give mine enemy the gratification of writing a book!"[1] Wellington's use of terms like "lying works" and "mine enemy" to refer to his critics after he had finished reading Clausewitz's history of the Waterloo Campaign suggests a strong reaction to what was actually a dry, analytical study. Why did the duke react in such a manner? The answer must be sought in his extreme sensitivity to years of criticism of his actions at the start of the campaign—allegations that he was ill-prepared for or surprised by Napoleon's attack, was slow to react when it actually occurred and then failed to fulfill a promise to assist the Prussians, thereby causing their defeat at the Battle of Ligny—and also to his resentment of Prussian claims that they deserved the real credit for the victory at Waterloo. This essay will examine these allegations that first arose in the early 19th century. The main emphasis will be on what Clausewitz wrote about them, how Wellington replied to Clausewitz's criticism, and what the evidence reveals about their differing standpoints.

---

[1] For Wellington's initial hostile reaction to Clausewitz's work see above, pp. 46-47, Wellington to Gurwood, 17 September 1842. The letter forbidding Gurwood to publish the Memorandum was written on 4 October 1842. The Memorandum remained unpublished until 1863, when the Duke's son included it in a new collection of Wellington's papers. Duke of Wellington, *Supplementary Despatches, Correspondence, and Memoranda of Field Marshal Arthur Duke of Wellington, K.G.*, 15 vols. (London: John Murray, 1851-1872), 10:513-531 [hereafter cited as *WSD* for "Wellington Supplementary Despatches"].

WELLINGTON VERSUS CLAUSEWITZ

Wellington's Plans and Preparations

Clausewitz's first criticism of Wellington concerned the very wide deployment of the Anglo-Allied army, which he said stretched across an area 90 miles wide and 65 miles deep and therefore could not be concentrated at its center in less than four or five days—much too long in view of the fact that the line of French fortresses was in many cases only a day's march away. In contrast, Clausewitz claimed, the Prussian army was collected in a much narrower position and could be concentrated at its center in just two days.[2] These calculations led Clausewitz to speculate that Wellington did not intend to assemble his army at a single point and thus may have planned to fight with his forces divided. In Clausewitz's opinion, Wellington was expecting the French to advance "in several columns and on an extended front," which meant that he would have to retain a strong reserve "ready to rush assistance to the point at which the enemy's main force may be found." For such a plan, two days warning would have been sufficient, according to Clausewitz, and he noted that Wellington and Blücher had reached agreement along these lines during their conference at Tirlemont at the beginning of May. Clausewitz added that in evaluating Wellington's promise made at that time to concentrate his army at Quatre Bras and come to the aid of Blücher at Sombreffe, "the term 'army' meant only the greater part thereof, which Wellington himself may have called his main force—his reserve together with his left wing." In Clausewitz's opinion it would have been "completely impossible" to concentrate Wellington's entire army on its extreme left wing in two days.[3]

---

2 As noted previously above (p.75, fn.19), Clausewitz underestimated the extent of the Prussian deployment and overestimated that of Wellington's army. The latter error may have occurred because he was not aware that the units posted on Wellington's far right were never intended for use in the front line. The true nature of Wellington's deployment is shown in a letter written on 15 June 1815 by Lieutenant Ernst-Ludwig von Gerlach of Blücher's staff. After discussing Wellington's dispositions with the British liaison officer to the Prussian headquarters, Lt. Col. Henry Hardinge, Gerlach wrote that "Everything could be quickly concentrated at Braine-le-Comte or Hal; that which stands beyond the Scheldt [River] are troops that Wellington intends to leave in his rear." Hans Joachim Schoeps, ed., *Aus den Jahren Preussischer Not und Erneuerung. Tagebücher und Briefe der Gebrüder Gerlach und Ihres Kreises, 1805-1820* (Berlin: Haude & Spener, 1963), 144-145.

3 See above, pp.76-77. Clausewitz's statement that Wellington had promised, on 3 May 1815 at the Tirlemont meeting, to concentrate his army at Quatre Bras in the event of an attack on the Prussians, should not be taken literally as referring to the tiny crossroads of Quatre Bras,

Clausewitz then rejected the assumption of a divided advance, which he had imputed to Wellington. Napoleon had always preferred to seek an all-encompassing battle, Clausewitz argued, and he certainly needed to do so in this case, since "only an overwhelmingly complete victory, surpassing all his earlier ones, offered him any hope of a better future. The most compelling assumption was therefore that Bonaparte would burst forth with his whole force against a single point." Wellington had never commanded against Napoleon personally and had thus never experienced "such a lightning bolt." Otherwise he "would have carried out quite different arrangements for billeting his forces." Clausewitz therefore argued that no matter where in Belgium the battle occurred, it would have been impossible for Wellington to assemble his entire force and be able to operate together with Blücher.[4]

To Clausewitz, Napoleon's overall goal in 1815 could only have been "a glorious victory over both allied armies." Such a victory would have "electrified" France and greatly strengthened Napoleon's position in the French interior, while slowing the advance of the other Allied forces from Germany. Nevertheless, even a great victory would have given him only "the barest possibility of resistance against the collective power of his enemies." Napoleon had claimed in his memoirs that the results of a French victory would have been decisive: "Belgium rising, its army reinforcing the French army.... the fall of the British government, which would have been replaced by friends of peace, liberty, and the independence of nations; this sole event would have ended the war."[5] Clausewitz

---

which was unknown prior to the battle there, but rather to the far left of Wellington's army. Allied pre-war meetings and plans always made reference to cities or large towns that could easily be found on a map. As for the subjects discussed at this meeting, Blücher's aide-de-camp wrote that these were the rebellion of Blücher's Saxon troops and the future of this contingent, plus the overall campaign for the pending invasion of France. August-Ludwig Ferdinand Graf von Nostiz, *Das Tagebuch des Generals der Kavallerie, Grafen v. Nostitz, Kriegsgeschichtliche Einzelschriften*, vols. 5-6 (Berlin: E.S. Mittler, 1884-5), 6:11. Evidently there was also some discussion of defensive plans, because Wellington wrote that evening that the meeting had been "very satisfactory" in that he had received "the most satisfactory promises of support" from Blücher. Cited in John Hussey, "The Tirlemont Meeting in Context: Wellington and Blücher, 3 May 1815," *First Empire* no. 99 (2008), 16-24. The orders issued by Field Marshal Blücher after Tirlemont suggest that there was also some discussion of possible aid to the Prussians on the part of Wellington. John Hussey, "The Aftermath of Tirlemont: 2-12 May 1815," *First Empire* no. 100 (2008), 23-24.
4 See above, pp.78-79.
5 Napoleon, *Mémoires*, 57-58.

did not think much of these expectations, saying they confirmed how "weak and uncertain" Napoleon considered his position to be.[6] However, given the vital importance of continued British participation in the war, particularly as a major source of funding for the Allied war effort, it does seem hard to accept Clausewitz's evident lack of concern regarding the consequences. He may, however, have doubted that such would be the British response to a battlefield defeat.

As for the specific objective of Napoleon's offensive into Belgium, Clausewitz argued that this could only be "the combined Allied army, not any geographical position such as Brussels or the right bank of the Meuse or even the Rhine." Because a "great, all-encompassing decision" was at stake, geographical points and their connections to the armies could give only "insignificant advantages" in the short term, and any possible long-term impact would have been swept away by the outcome of the great battle. Clausewitz therefore dismissed the idea that Blücher needed to maintain possession of the right bank of the Meuse and that Wellington needed to cover Brussels. Instead, the two Allied commanders "could have united their forces upon one point and been certain that, no matter where this point lay, Bonaparte would seek it out."[7]

Clausewitz's analysis of Wellington's plans and deployment thus appears purely military in character, based upon assumptions about Wellington's intentions derived from an examination of the deployment of the Anglo-Allied army prior to the outbreak of hostilities. Wellington was evidently impressed by the quality of Clausewitz's analysis, for he wrote in the margin of the chapter "Reflections on Wellington's Dispositions" of Lord Liverpool's manuscript translation, "This is an important chapter."[8] In his subsequent Memorandum, however, the duke took a much more critical view, saying that historians such as Clausewitz were "too ready to criticize the acts and operations not only of their own Generals and armies, but likewise those of the best friends and allies of their nations, and even of those acting in co-operation with its armies. This observation must be borne in mind throughout the perusal of Clausewitz's History." In replying to Clausewitz's criticisms, Wellington argued that his deployment was not based solely on military factors, because his

---

6 See above, p.81.
7 See above, p.82.
8 Lord Liverpool's manuscript translation of Clausewitz's history is found in WP 8/1/2.

army's mission was much more than just "the general operations of the war." First and foremost it had to "preserve the communications with England, Holland and Germany." In addition, it had to protect the King of the Netherlands, who had placed his seat of government at Brussels, and French King Louis XVIII, who was residing in Ghent.[9]

Wellington also noted that the initiative rested with the French. Thus the Allied generals had to be "prepared to move in all directions, to wait till it should be seen in what direction the attack should be made, and then to assemble the armies as quickly as possible to resist the attack, or to attack the enemy with the largest force that could be collected." This observation would appear to concede Clausewitz's point that the best course for the Allies would have been to concentrate their forces at the earliest possible moment and then, in effect, wait for Napoleon to make his move. Yet Wellington rejected Clausewitz's assertion that the Allies' sole concern should have been "the early junction of the two Allied armies, with a view to fight a great battle with the enemy." Such a course of action, the duke argued, would have enabled French cavalry and light troops to occupy Brussels, Ghent, and the English lines of communications, while the initiative for fighting a general battle would still have remained with Napoleon, even if his main force remained behind the French frontier. Wellington also thought that Clausewitz was too indifferent to the "moral impression" that would have resulted from the loss of Brussels and Ghent, the flight of the two kings and the loss of his lines of communication without him "making the smallest effort to save any of these objects."[10]

It is on this issue of Wellington's operational plans and priorities that his differences of opinion with Clausewitz are most readily apparent. Wellington's goal, as he said, was to be able to assemble "the largest disposable force at his disposition, after providing for the defense and security of his military communications with England, Holland, and Germany, and of the objects entrusted to his care and protection" by the Congress of Vienna (thus Brussels, Ghent and the two kings). Clausewitz argued that geographic points and lines of communication were less important

---

9 Unless otherwise noted, this and all other quotations from Wellington are taken from his Memorandum of 24 September 1842 (pp. 219-235 above). See pages 221-222.
10 See above, pp.224-225. For the sensitive diplomatic and political situation facing Wellington in 1815, see Gregor Dallas, *1815: The Roads to Waterloo* (London: Richard Cohen, 1996), 331-364.

than the need to concentrate forces for a "great battle." Having stressed the political considerations governing Napoleon's conduct, it is striking that Clausewitz should have argued for the primacy of purely military considerations in the development of Allied strategy, whereas Wellington accounted for his conduct mainly in political terms. Given the fragility of the Allied coalition—its members had nearly come to blows over re-drawing the map of Europe at the Vienna Congress and the loyalty of the Dutch was open to question[11]—Wellington's concerns about the political ramifications of abandoning Brussels without a fight cannot be ignored. Ultimately, however, their disagreement was not about the importance of political concerns but about how quickly they could have an impact. Thus to Clausewitz, if the Allies lost even a symbolically important city like Brussels but then won the "great battle," this would have been like "a mighty river sweeping away such a weak dike." Wellington, in contrast, was not prepared to risk losing Brussels and Ghent under any circumstances. Victory over Napoleon could never be a sure thing, and conceding such psychologically important successes would only amplify the disaster if the great battle were lost.

The greatest obstacle to Clausewitz's call for a rapid union of the two Allied armies was finding provisions for so large a force, which he clearly recognized. Thus, while he stated that it was "very risky" for the Prussians to remain in their extended positions once they knew that Napoleon was assembling troops on the border, he explained that this failure to concentrate in time had resulted to a great extent from "the continual difficulties which the Dutch authorities made with respect to provisioning."[12] These difficulties would of course have been greatly multiplied if both Allied armies had concentrated in a single area.

---

11 Prussian officers and officials frequently expressed concern about the Dutch king's shaky loyalty to the Allied coalition. Thus on 12 June 1815, Prince Blücher's chief of staff, General Neithardt von Gneisenau, wrote to Prussia's chief minister Karl von Hardenberg that "In this country every informed individual has no doubt that if the Allied armies suffered a setback, the King of the Netherlands would immediately attempt to negotiate peace and an alliance with France." Hans von Delbrück, *Das Leben des Feldmarschalls Grafen Neithardt von Gneisenau*, vol. 4, *1814-1815* (Berlin: G. Reimer, 1880), 518-20.

12 See above, p.86. For the difficulties encountered by the Prussian army in receiving sufficient provisions from the Dutch government and the impact this had on its ability to concentrate, see Carl von Damitz, *Geschichte des Feldzuges 1815 in den Niederlanden und Frankreich*, 2 vols. (Berlin, Posen and Bromberg: Siegfried Mittler, 1837), 1:45. Soon after his arrival in Brussels, the new Prussian liaison officer to Wellington's headquarters, General Carl von Müffling, reported that "I have already become convinced that it is best for us to avoid uniting

ON WATERLOO

As for Clausewitz's suggestion that either of the two armies could have ignored its supply line for a time in order to operate together with the other, this would appear to pose major problems in at least one of the two scenarios he proposed: that of Wellington falling back on the Meuse and using Blücher's supply lines. The Prussians already had great difficulty keeping their own army supplied, and it is doubtful that they would have been capable of providing logistical support for both armies, even for a short period of time. In the critical area of ammunition, crossnational supply would have been difficult or even impossible in both scenarios because of the differing calibers of the two armies' firearms.

In addition to logistics, another important reason for the failure of the Allied armies to concentrate prior to the French attack—one not mentioned by either Clausewitz or Wellington—is that until almost the last minute the Allied commanders did not believe Napoleon would attack at all. Thus in an 8 May 1815 letter about plans for an eventual Allied offensive, Wellington remarked, "I say nothing about our defensive operations, because I am inclined to believe that Blücher and I are so well united that the enemy cannot do us much mischief." Three days later the duke wrote to the closest Prussian commander, Lt. Gen. Hans Ernst von Zieten of the 1st Corps, "There is constant talk of an attack, but in view of the strength of the two armies and their close union, this seems hardly likely." Throughout May and even into June, Wellington received a steady stream of intelligence reports describing insurrections in the Vendée and Brittany. These forced Napoleon to take troops away from the frontier and send them to the interior. These reports were intermixed with ones suggesting that Napoleon would indeed attack, but Wellington seems to have discounted the latter reports as overstated or perhaps even part of a French deception plan. As late as 13 June, Wellington was writing, "We have reports of Buonaparte's joining the army and attacking us; but ... I think we are now too strong for him here." Even on the morning of 15 June, when French troops had already begun their offensive (a fact not yet known in Brussels), Wellington told Baron van Reede, the Dutch liaison officer at his headquarters, "I do not believe that they will attack us; we are very strong."[13] Wellington thus did not feel any need to draw

---

completely with the English army, except for battles." Müffling to Gneisenau, 28 May 1815, Geheimes Staatsarchiv, Stiftung Preussischer Kulturbesitz, VI HA Nachlass Gneisenau, Paket 23, Mappe A40, fol. 56.

13 Wellington's statements of 8 May, 11 May, and 13 June are found in J. Gurwood (ed.), *The*

his forces closer together in the weeks prior to the battle, believing he would have adequate time to concentrate once the Allies were ready to take the offensive in early July.

For most of this period, the senior Prussian leadership held similar views. On 3 June the Prussian commander, Field Marshal Prince Blücher, wrote to his wife, "In ten days the shooting will start and we will enter into France. Bonaparte will not attack us. We could stay here for another year, because his situation is far from brilliant." In the same vein, General von Gneisenau, Blücher's chief of staff, wrote on 9 June, "The enemy will not attack us but will instead withdraw back to the Aisne, Somme and Marne in order to concentrate his strength there." Even as late as the 12th, Gneisenau was writing to Prussian Minister of War Hardenberg that "the danger of an attack has almost completely disappeared."[14] It was not until 14 June that the Prussian commanders changed their minds and decided that Napoleon was preparing to attack after all. Their new view was sent to Wellington at 10 p.m. that evening by Lt. Col. Henry Hardinge, the British liaison officer at Blücher's headquarters. He wrote that "The prevalent opinion here seems to be that Buonaparte intends to commence offensive operations."[15] Such an attack was evidently not seen as imminent, however, because Gneisenau had not yet ordered the concentration of the Prussian army. Soon afterward, some new and compelling intelligence must have arrived in Namur, for between 11:30 pm and midnight he hastily wrote and dispatched orders for the army to assemble at Sombreffe. A little more than four hours later, the fighting began.[16]

Dispatches of Field Marshal The Duke of Wellington [hereafter cited as *WD* for "Wellington Dispatches"] (London, 1838), 12:359-360, 373, 462. For reports indicating that Napoleon was unwilling or unable to attack (i.e., French troops being removed from the borders to deal with internal unrest or French defensive preparations along the borders), see *WD*, 12:372, 437; *WSD*, 10:222, 274, 280, 290, 387, 393, 408, 412, 413, 417. For Wellington's statement on the morning of 15 June see John Hussey, "Further Intelligence Reports, 14-15 June 1815," *First Empire* 81 (2004), 31-33.

14 Adolf Saager, ed., *Blüchers Briefe an seine Frau* (Stuttgart: Robert Lutz, n.d.), p. 107; Oskar von Lettow-Vorbeck, *Napoleons Untergang 1815*, 2 vols (Berlin: Ernst Siegfried Mittler, 1904), 1:192; Delbück, *Gneisenau*, 4:518.

15 *WSD*, 10:476.

16 Lettow-Vorbeck, *Napoleons Untergang*, 194-199. General von Lettow-Vorbeck believed that this new intelligence must have come from high-ranking French deserters and noted that it did not seem to have been shared with Wellington.

ON WATERLOO

Wellington's Reaction to the French Attack

In his history, Clausewitz stated that the reports of French concentrations received on 14 June led Blücher to concentrate his forces that evening but that Wellington hesitated to take a comparable decision on committing his forces for another 24 hours. Even after the news of the French attack arrived on the evening of the 15th, Wellington continued to believe that Napoleon would advance via Mons and "considered the clash near Charleroi to be a feint. Thus he was content simply to order his troops to be ready." Clausewitz added that Wellington did not order his reserve to begin its march until midnight on the 15th, after news arrived from Mons that the French had not attacked there and had instead moved to their right. He criticized the duke for losing more time the following morning. He therefore concluded that the duke's hesitation, and the wide deployment of his forces, made it impossible for the Anglo-Allied army to provide any support to Blücher in resisting Napoleon's attack.[17]

Wellington took exception to most of Clausewitz's account. He claimed that on 15 June "The first account received by [me] was from the Prince of Orange, who ... reported that the enemy had attacked the Prussians at Thuin." Wellington added that a second report of the French attack—this time from the Prussians—arrived later that afternoon, brought by General Carl von Müffling, the Prussian liaison officer to the duke's headquarters. Wellington then expressed displeasure with the tardiness of the Prussians in notifying him of the French attack. He noted that, according to Clausewitz, Napoleon attacked Zieten at 4 a.m. on the 15th and forced him back to Charleroi by 10 a.m., yet no news of these events reached Brussels before 3 p.m. (and this report had not come from the Prussians). According to Wellington, once the news did arrive, he reacted immediately: "Orders were forthwith sent for the march of the whole army to its left. The whole moved on that evening and in the night, each division and portion separately, but unmolested.... The reserve ... were ordered to assemble..., which they did on that evening; and they marched in the morning of the 16th upon Quatre Bras, towards which post the march of all the troops consisting of the left and centre of the army, and of the cavalry in particular, was directed." Wellington added

---

17 See above, p.91.

that there was "no evidence" to support Clausewitz's allegations regarding a lengthy pause by the Allied reserve on its march to Quatre Bras.[18]

Wellington's strong reaction to Clausewitz's mild observations must be understood in the context of long-standing criticism of his actions on 15 June. Such criticism included claims that he had been caught by surprise by the French attack or had been slow to react to it.[19] In responding to Clausewitz, however, Wellington made some statements that require closer examination. He claimed in the Memorandum that the earliest report of the French attack on the Prussians arrived in Brussels at 3 p.m. This differs from what he wrote in his report on the battle to Earl Bathurst on 19 June 1815. There he stated that this news arrived "in the evening" of 15 June. The issue of what time this news actually reached Brussels has long been the subject of considerable controversy, with some Prussian accounts claiming that Wellington had learned of the French attack much earlier—at 9 a.m. on 15 June—through a message sent by General Carl von Zieten, commander of the Prussian 1st Corps at Charleroi.[20] The evidence to support such an early message is

---

18 See above, pp.229-230.

19 Wellington and his circle were particularly upset by the frequent allegations that he had been caught by surprise when Napoleon attacked. This was one of the main reasons why he provided the July 1842 version of the Memorandum to Lord Francis Egerton for use in the *Quarterly Review* article attacking the British historian Archibald Alison. Alison had claimed that Wellington had been surprised because he was waiting for information that French Interior Minister Joseph Fouché had promised but then deliberately delayed sending. See above, p.43, Gurwood to Wellington, 6 September 1842.

20 In 1848 Prussian diplomats and officers sent a series of letters to Captain William Siborne arguing that Zieten's message to Wellington had arrived at 9 a.m. Siborne revised the third (1848) edition of his *History of the Waterloo Campaign* to reflect this allegation despite the weak evidence provided by the Prussians. This evidence included a letter written by Zieten in 1819 claiming that he had sent his message about the French attack to Wellington at 3:45 a.m. (This is not very credible in view of the fact that his own first message to Field Marshal Blücher that morning clearly stated that hostilities did not start until 4:30 a.m.). It also included an ambiguous letter written by Wellington to the Duc de Feltre in French at 10 p.m. on 15 June 1815 [*WD*, 12:473] saying "I have received the news that the enemy attacked the Prussian outposts at Thuin on the Sambre this morning and appears to be threatening Charleroi. I have received nothing from Charleroi since 9 a.m." As most historians of Waterloo campaign have recognized, this statement has two possible meanings—either nothing since a report that <u>arrived</u> at 9 a.m. or nothing since one that had been <u>sent</u> at that hour—and thus cannot be taken as firm evidence for either view. The Prussian correspondence with Siborne is found in Gareth Glover, *Letters from the Battle of Waterloo: Unpublished Correspondence by Allied Officers from the Siborne Papers* (London: Greenhill Books, 2004), 311-319. Renewed claims for a 9 a.m. arrival time based upon the same evidence offered in 1848 are found in Peter Hofschröer, *1815: The Waterloo Campaign*, 2 vols. (London: Greenhill Books, 1998, 1999) [hereafter cited

very weak, however. Most historians now believe that Zieten did not send a message to Wellington based solely on the initial sounds of firing at 4:30 a.m., but instead waited until reports from the front arrived at his headquarters. Thus his message did not leave Charleroi until around 9 a.m.[21] At any rate, the key issue here is not when Zieten <u>sent</u> the message, but when Wellington <u>received</u> it.

The 33-mile distance from Charleroi to Brussels could normally have been covered in approximately six hours.[22] Some unknown source of "friction"—of which there were many examples in the transmission of messages in June 1815—delayed Zieten's courier. He did not arrive in Brussels until after 5 p.m., as two letters written that evening show. Thus the Württemberg liaison officer to Wellington's headquarters, General Ernst von Hügel, described the arrival of Zieten's message in Brussels in a report to his king written at 6 p.m.:

> Just now a Prussian hussar has ridden up to General v. Müffling, who lives very close to me, and has brought him news that Müffling immediately passed on to me: Napoleon attacked the Prussian Army at Thuin on the Sambre this morning. The results are not yet known. Müffling has just now returned from the Duke. The Prince of Orange had reported that strong canon

---

as Hofschröer, *1815*, followed by the volume and page number]; 1:194, 334, 339-40; 2:329-330.

21 The head of the Prussian military archives prior to World War I, Professor Julius von Pflugk-Harttung, reached this conclusion after studying all the available evidence, including that provided to Siborne in 1848. "Die Preußische Berichterstattung an Wellington vor der Schlacht bei Ligny," *Historisches Jahrbuch* 24 (1903), 54-55; idem., *Vorgeschichte der Schlacht bei Belle-Alliance—Wellington* (Berlin: Richard Schröder, 1903), 49-50. Two recent studies of this issue agree and have demonstrated that postwar statements made by Zieten about his message to Wellington are not credible because their alleged times of dispatch took place before the start of hostilities at 4:30 a.m. (In addition to the above-mentioned 1819 letter, Zieten claimed a dispatch time of 2:15 a.m. in his error-ridden 1839 autobiography that Peter Hofschröer mistakenly identified as an 1815 journal in *1815*, 1:170, 193.) John Hussey, "At What Time on 15 June 1815 Did Wellington Learn of Napoleon's Attack on the Prussians," *War in History* 6 (1999), 88-116; Gregory W. Pedlow, "Back to the Sources: General Zieten's Message to the Duke of Wellington on 15 June 1815," *First Empire* no. 82 (2005), 30-36. [This article is available on the internet at *http://firstempire.net/sample82.pdf*.]

22 The Prussian General Staff's history of the Waterloo campaign stated that messages in 1815 were carried at speeds between 6 and 7 minutes per kilometer (5¼-6¼ m.p.h.). Lettow-Vorbeck, *Napoleons Untergang*, 199. John Hussey's analysis of the transmission times for messages sent on 15 June 1815 reached the same conclusion (5-6 miles per hour). Hussey, "What Time," 96-97. Both studies note that some messages took much longer than expected to arrive.

fire has been heard on our left flank. Wellington at once ordered all his Corps to march through the whole night and concentrate. Müffling allowed me to read Zieten's report: in the face of considerable enemy superiority he must withdraw his advanced posts towards Fleurus. By the evening of the 17th we will know whether the campaign has begun favorably or unfavorably for the Allies. But this much I can assure Your Majesty with complete certainty: the best understanding exists between the Duke of Wellington and Prince Blücher, and both are acting in complete agreement."[23]

One hour later, at 7 p.m., General Müffling wrote to Field Marshal Blücher that "The news has just arrived that Lt. Gen. v. Zieten has been attacked."[24] While both letters contain phrases like "just now" and "just arrived," these should not be taken too literally. Hügel's letter described a number of actions that happened after Zieten's message arrived—Müffling taking the letter to Wellington, then returning, then discussing the contents with Hügel—so the most likely arrival time is between 5 and 5:30 p.m.[25]

As General Hügel's letter shows, Zieten's message was not the first news of the French attack to arrive in Brussels. The duke had already been told about the attack by the Prince of Orange. The prince, in turn, had learned of it during his visit to the Dutch outpost at Saint Symphorien southeast of Mons early in the morning and had then decided to ride to Brussels to bring the news himself.[26] In his 1842 Memorandum

---

23 Maj. Gen. A. Pfister, *Aus dem Lager der Verbündeten, 1814 and 1815* (Stuttgart: Deutsche Verlagsanstalt, 1897), 366. See also Hussey, "What Time," 112. General Hügel's statement that the results of the French attack were not yet known must refer to the overall situation rather than simply to the fate of the outpost at Thuin, because the village's fall was already known by the time Zieten wrote to Wellington. (It was mentioned in a message sent by Zieten to Blücher at 8:15 a.m.)
24 Lettow-Vorbeck, *Napoleons Untergang*, 287-288.
25 Peter Hofschröer has argued ["Reply to John Hussey: At What Time on 15 June 1815 Did Wellington *Really* Learn of Napoleon's Attack on the Prussians?," *War in History* 6 (1999), 474] that the Prussian letter that arrived in Brussels at 5 p.m. was the one sent by Blücher from Namur at noon. This cannot be correct, however, because that letter from Blücher was based on Zieten's very sketchy initial report that shots had been heard. It therefore contained no mention of an attack on Thuin or Zieten's withdrawal plans. Furthermore, Hügel quite specifically mentioned reading "Zieten's report," not "Blücher's letter."
26 Two Dutch historians are currently publishing extensively researched histories of the Wa-

ON WATERLOO

Wellington recalled that the prince arrived in Brussels at around 3 p.m. It is possible, however, that his arrival time was somewhat later. General von Müffling wrote in his history of the Waterloo Campaign, published in 1816, that the news of the French attack arrived in Brussels at 4:30 p.m.[27] Lord Fitzroy Somerset, Wellington's Military Secretary at Waterloo, recalled in a memoir written sometime between 1815 and 1820 that "about five o'clock in the afternoon the Duke of Wellington while at dinner received from the Prince of Orange, who was up at Braine-le-Comte, a report sent to his Royal Highness from his advanced posts" [about the French attack].[28] Such an arrival time would also be more in keeping with Wellington's dispatch to Earl Bathurst immediately after the battle, in which he stated that the news first arrived in the "evening," a term that had a much broader meaning in 1815 than it does today.[29] As for Clausewitz, he wrote that "on the evening of the 15th [Wellington] received the report that General Zieten had been attacked and driven back by the main French army at Charleroi." He thus accepted Wellington's statement in the Waterloo Dispatch concerning the arrival time for news of the French attack, but incorrectly assumed that this news included the fact that Charleroi had fallen.[30]

---

terloo Campaign on the internet, drawing from a wide range of sources including many previously unpublished Dutch sources. For the Prince of Orange's discovery of the French attack while visiting St. Symphorien, see Pierre de Wit, "15 June 1815, Observations Part 3, The Sector of the Army of the Netherlands: Communication Toward Braine-le Comte and Brussels," in "The Campaign of 1815: A Study" (a manuscript published on the internet at http://www.waterloo-campaign.nl), and Erwin Muilwijk, "15 June 1815, Events During the Morning Concerning I. Anglo-Allied Corps," in "Waterloo Campaign 1815: The Contribution of the Netherlands Mobile Army," a manuscript previously available on the internet but currently withdrawn while being prepared for publication on the website www.1815.ltd.uk.
27 ["C. de M."], *History of the British, Dutch, Hanoverian, and Brunswick Armies, under the Command of the Duke of Wellington, and of the Prussians, under that of Prince Blucher of Wahlstadt, in the Year 1815* (1816; reprinted London: Ken Trotman, 1983), 1. Müffling's 1816 history is considered by most historians to be far more accurate than his much later memoirs.
28 "Lord Fitzroy Somerset's Account of the Events from 15-18 June 1815," in Edward Owen, ed., *The Waterloo Papers: 1815 and Beyond* (Tavistock: AQ & DJ Publications, 1997), 7. Owen dated the manuscript containing Somerset's account and other letters and accounts relating to the battle at around 1820, while Somerset's biographer, John Sweetman, who published this same account in *Raglan: From the Crimea to the Peninsula* (London: Arms & Armour Press, 1993), 48-69, thought it was written in the autumn or winter of 1815. John Hussey, "Toward a Better Chronology of the Waterloo Campaign," *War in History* 7 (2000), 477.
29 John Hussey, "'Evening' and the Waterloo Dispatch," *Journal of the Society for Army Historical Research* 79 (2001), 336-338.
30 Clausewitz's statement is on pp.90-91 above.

WELLINGTON VERSUS CLAUSEWITZ

The arrival of Zieten's message, which confirmed the initial report brought previously by the Prince of Orange, led Wellington to begin issuing orders to his troops shortly before 6 p.m. These were not, however, orders "for the march of the whole army to its left," as the duke claimed in his Memorandum. Rather, they simply directed units to assemble and be ready to move. The actual movement orders (the so-called "After Orders") did not go out until after 10 p.m. These directed the army, including units already located farther to the east at the crossroads of Quatre-Bras on the highway from Charleroi to Brussels, to concentrate in the vicinity of Nivelles.[31] Wellington's emphasis on Nivelles in his movement orders is understandable. It was the most significant town behind his troops on the front lines of the left flank, and the Prussian commander under attack by the French, General Zieten, had requested that Wellington concentrate there when he reported the news of the French attack.[32] Furthermore, the Prussians had previously announced their intention to defend the Sambre crossings and—if a retreat from Charleroi became necessary—to concentrate at Gosselies. This meant that they would be covering the portion of the Allied line in front of Quatre-Bras.[33]

The actual situation of the Allies was quite different, however. The Prussians had abandoned Gosselies and moved eastward toward Sombreffe—leaving the road to Quatre-Bras uncovered—without notifying Wellington. Wellington therefore continued to assume that this approach to Brussels was protected by Zieten. The lack of any reports from the Prussians, beyond the fact that their outposts had been attacked, led Wellington to write at 10 p.m. that the French were "threatening" Charleroi, when in fact they had captured it 11 hours earlier.[34] This lack of current information, combined with Zieten's request, led to Wellington's con-

---

31 Wellington's initial orders to the Prince of Orange stated that he should "collect at Nivelles the 2nd and 3rd divisions of the army of the Low Countries; and, should that point have been attacked this day, to move the 3rd division of British infantry upon Nivelles as soon as collected. This movement is not to take place until it is quite certain that the enemy's attack is upon the right of the Prussian army and the left of the British army." WD, 12:472-473.
32 At 8:15 a.m. on 15 June 1815, Zieten wrote to Field Marshal Blücher informing him that the French had captured Thuin, pushed back his outposts, and were now advancing on both banks of the Sambre. He added, "I have informed the Duke of Wellington of this and have entreated him to concentrate his troops without delay near Nivelles." Lettow-Vorbeck, *Napoleons Untergang*, 253.
33 Pflugk-Harttung, *Vorgeschichte*, 54, 76-77.
34 WD 12:473.

centration orders, which—if carried out to the letter—would have led to the abandonment of Quatre-Bras on the vital approach road to Brussels. Fortunately for the Allies, the Prince of Orange's able chief of staff, Baron Jean de Constant Rebeque, possessed more recent information about the growing French threat in this sector. He therefore ignored the portion of Wellington's movement orders that no longer corresponded to the actual situation. Instead, Constant ordered General Perponcher's 2nd Netherlands Division to concentrate at Quatre-Bras.[35]

Wellington first became aware of the seriousness of the situation when a courier, bearing General Constant's report of the French advance up to Quatre-Bras, arrived around 12:30 a.m. at the famous "Waterloo Ball" held by the Duchess of Richmond in Brussels. After issuing orders to hasten the departure time of the reserve from Brussels, Wellington continued to consider the entire situation before getting a few hours of sleep. When General Wilhelm von Dörnberg—commander of the frontier outpost and intelligence-gathering centre at Mons—arrived between 4 and 5 a.m., Wellington quickly got up. He told Dörnberg to ride to Waterloo and order General Picton to march immediately with his division to Quatre-Bras.[36]

Clausewitz was critical of Wellington's actions on the morning of 16 June, saying that "much time was lost" while the duke reconnoitered the enemy at Frasnes and then went to meet with Prince Blücher at Sombreffe at 1 p.m. During that time, "the reserve appears to have waited for further orders at the edge of the Soignies Forest, where the road divides in the directions of Nivelles and Quatre Bras." Wellington's Memorandum rejected this last claim outright, saying "he can have no proof of this fact, of which there is no evidence." In reality, there is. The reserve did indeed pause at the edge of the Forest of Soignies. This is confirmed by the accounts of several officers involved in the march. But this pause was to give the troops a chance to rest and cook a meal in the shade (important on a hot summer day), while allowing missing units to catch up. Its purpose was not to await further orders from Wellington, as these had

---

35 For a full discussion of Constant Rebeque's role in saving the vital crossroads of Quatre Bras, see F. de Bas and J. de t'Serclaes de Wommersom, *La campagne de 1815 aux Pays-Bas d'après les rapports officiels néerlandais*, 2 vols. plus atlas (Brussels: Librairie Albert Dewit, 1908), 1:436-441.
36 From a manuscript by Dörnberg formerly in the Prussian Military Archives, cited by Pflugk-Harttung, *Vorgeschichte*, 292.

already been brought by General von Dörnberg. Furthermore, the pause did not last until Wellington returned from his meeting with Field Marshal Blücher, as Clausewitz suggests. It had already ended at noon for most of the units.[37] In all this, it is worth recalling that, owing to poor reporting on the Prussian side, no one on Wellington's staff had any reason to believe that major fighting was imminent. The lack of urgency in the procedures adopted for the march to Quatre-Bras was entirely consistent with the expectation that contact with the enemy would not take place until the following day, 17 June.[38] And had the Prussian 1st Corps carried out its previously announced intention to defend the Sambre River crossings, thus delaying the French advance, it does seem likely that no major battles could have taken place on 16 June.[39]

The lack of urgency in Wellington's concentration orders was an important reason why much of his army arrived late or not at all at the Battle of Quatre Bras. The ultimate cause, however, was his long delay in recognizing the true location of Napoleon's main attack and then in issuing orders to counter it. Wellington's Memorandum is essential for understanding the reasons for this delay, because it shows the preconceptions under which he was acting: that a French attack was unlikely, but that if it did occur, it would be against his center or right wing. The duke wrote that he "did not at first give credit to the reports of the intention of the enemy to attack by the valley of the Sambre and the Meuse" (thus against Zieten's 1st Corps) because "the enemy had destroyed the roads leading through those valleys." Wellington therefore believed that Napoleon could have made his attack "by other lines with more advantage,"[40] meaning an attack along the road from Mons to Brussels, or an even

---

37 Pflugk-Harttung, *Vorgeschichte*, 89-90. For accounts of the pause at Waterloo by officers in the Reserve, see Hofschröer, *1815*, 1:223-224. While these accounts show that the Reserve did indeed pause at Waterloo, they do not necessarily agree with Clausewitz's statement that this pause lasted until Wellington returned from his meeting with Blücher after 2 p.m.
38 This expectation was clearly reflected in General Müffling's 7 p.m. letter to the Prussian headquarters on 15 June, in which he expressed the hope that "we can shoot [guns to celebrate] victory on the 17th." General Hügel's previously cited 6 p.m. letter also expressed the belief that the decisive battle would be fought on the 17th, a belief that he certainly picked up in Wellington's headquarters.
39 Pflugk-Harttung (*Vorgeschichte*, 64-65) noted that the War Diary of the Prussian 1st Corps showed that all of the plans that the corps had made to defend against a French attack had called for the Sambre River crossings to be defended. He commented that Wellington was aware of this and was counting on it.
40 See above, p.230.

greater turning movement around the Anglo-Allied right. In the days and weeks preceding the attack, a large flow of often-contradictory intelligence reports had reached Wellington, some suggesting that the French were preparing defenses, others suggesting a French attack on the Prussians, and still others providing support for Wellington's strongly-held notion of a French attack against his right.[41] Some intelligence reports arriving in Brussels in early June even suggested that Napoleon would attempt to deceive the Allies by launching a feint or a diversionary attack against the Prussians, to be followed by the real attack against the Anglo-Allied army.[42] As such reports fit right in with Wellington's preconceptions, he may have given them more weight than others. Ultimately, however, he was not expecting Napoleon to attack at all.

Wellington's comments in the Memorandum about the dangers of making a "false movement" reflect considerable anxiety about being deceived by Napoleon. The duke noted that "whatever may be thought of Buonaparte as a leader of troops in other respects, there certainly never existed a man in that situation, in any times, in whose presence it was so little safe to make what is called a false movement."[43] A key eyewitness has confirmed that such concerns were paramount for Wellington. In an account written within a few years of the battle, Lord Fitzroy Somerset, Wellington's Military Secretary, recalled that at about 10 p.m. on the evening of 15 June he said to the duke, "No doubt we shall be able to manage these fellows [the French]." Wellington replied that "there was little doubt of that provided he did not make a false movement."[44] Many

---

[41] A wide range of often contradictory reports about French movements and intentions can be found in *WSD*, 10:212-481.

[42] See the 6 June report from General Dörnberg, passing on intelligence of a possible forthcoming "false attack on the Prussians and a real one on the English army," and another report on the same day from the Dutch General Behr containing intelligence that "the Emperor will be going in person to Avesnes to conduct a false attack on the Allies by Maubeuge with the principle attack coming from Flanders between Lille and Tournai, toward Mons." *WSD*, 10:423-424. The Prussian General Staff's 1825 history of the campaign concluded that "the prevailing opinion in Brussels seems to have been that the enemy wanted to attract the allies toward Charleroi by means of a feint and then attack somewhere else with the main force. It is said Wellington was expecting to be attacked via Mons." Johann Christian August Wagner, *Pläne der Schlachten und Treffen, welche von der preussischen Armee in den Feldzügen 1813, 1814 und 1815 geliefert worden sind*, 4 vols. (Berlin, 1821-1832), 4:21. Wagner was a captain attached to Blücher's headquarters during the campaign of 1815.

[43] See above, p.224.

[44] "Somerset's Account" in Owen, ed., *Waterloo Papers*, 7.

years later, Wellington summarized his overall philosophy on this issue when commenting on the strange movements of d'Erlon's corps between the battlefields of Quatre Bras and Ligny on 16 June: "I wonder what they would have said of me if I had done such a thing as that. I have always avoided a false move. I preferred being late in my movement to having to alter it."[45]

Given this mindset, it is not surprising that Wellington failed to react strongly to the initial reports of a French attack on the Prussian army. Those reports offered no proof that this was the main attack rather than an "affair of outposts" or, even worse, a deception designed to inspire a "false movement" away from the real French threat elsewhere. Such a feint had been suggested in several intelligence reports from France.[46] Vague initial reports of cannon and small arms fire, whenever they may have arrived, would not have been sufficient evidence of the true direction of the main French attack to cause Wellington to order his entire army to concentrate on its extreme left, thus virtually abandoning the other main approaches to Brussels. It was not until the initial hours of 16 June that Wellington received firm proof that Napoleon's main advance was via Charleroi.

Wellington's unwillingness to commit his forces prematurely in response to something that might turn out to be a mere feint by the French is understandable. Yet he can be criticized for neglecting some basic preparatory measures that could have hastened such a march once sufficient intelligence concerning Napoleon's true intentions had been received. Even the duke's personal secretary, Colonel John Gurwood, editor of the Wellington Papers and a cavalry officer at Waterloo, felt that more could have been done on 15 June. In an 1842 letter to Wellington, Gurwood wrote, that "It is clear that the regiments of cavalry were not in hand, as they ought to have been by order of their Brigadiers and that

---

45 Herbert Maxwell, *The Life of Wellington: The Restoration of the Martial Power of Great Britain*, 3rd edition (London: Sampson, Low, Marston and Co., 1900), 2:23.

46 See above, p.273, fn.42. Wellington's concern that the French attack on the Prussians might be merely a feint is also confirmed by Constant Rebeque's journal of the Waterloo campaign. He wrote that the Prince of Orange returned from Brussels at 3 a.m. on 16 June and "informed me that the Duke had at first believed the attack upon Charleroi to be a feint, but my report concerning the appearance of the enemy at Frasnes had finally made him decide to send all his forces to Quatre Bras." Constant Rebeque's account is found in John Franklin, ed., *Waterloo: Netherlands Correspondence*, vol. 1, *Letters and Reports from Manuscript Sources* (Dorchester: Dorset Press, 2010), 9.

under the circumstances they ought to have been assembled daily after daylight in their respective alarm posts. In consequence of this want of arrangement nearly four hours were lost in the assembly of the brigades, and the brigade to which I belonged made several very long halts, waiting for orders."[47] Gurwood's suggestion that the units should have been assembled daily after daylight would have been quite practicable in June 1815. This is shown by the fact that the Dutch Army had actually issued such an order to its units.[48] An experienced commander such as Wellington should not have omitted such an elementary precaution. One can only conclude, as his correspondence prior to the battle reveals, that he was not expecting to be attacked. Surprise in war is a matter of degree. Wellington, like Blücher and, for that matter, Napoleon, was looking for a fight in June of 1815. He just found it a little sooner than he expected and—contrary to his expectations—was now defending Belgium rather than invading France.

Prussian Allegations That Wellington Caused Their Defeat at Ligny

On the morning of 16 June, Wellington's army was still scattered across the Belgian countryside, while the Prussian army was concentrating around the villages of Sombreffe and Ligny. Wellington then sent a letter to Blücher from the most forward Allied position at Frasnes, describing the intended movements of his army. That letter gave the impression that the Anglo-Allied army was more concentrated than it actually was. Soon

---

47 Gurwood to Wellington, 24 September 1842, WP 8/3/15. See also Gurwood's 16 September 1842 letter to Lord Greenock [WP 8/3/8], in which he described how he returned from the Duchess of Richmond's ball at midnight and slept until 3 a.m. at his own lodgings in Brussels. Afterward he went to the 10th Hussars, whose troops had not yet turned out at 6 a.m. on the 16th. He noted that "had they started at 7 o'clock even, 3 hours after daylight, three or four brigades might have been at Nivelle[s] before 3 o'clock."

48 Andrew Uffindell, *The Eagle's Last Triumph: Napoleon's Victory at Ligny, June 1815* (London: Greenhill Books, 1994), 56. Pflugk-Harttung commented (*Vorgeschichte*, 73) that "one must recognize that the English commander could scarcely do anything during the day [15 June]. There was just one thing that he could have done and thus should have done—to assemble his troops in their cantonments, possibly even in their brigade areas. This would not have led him into any false movement, thus not risked anything, but it would have made his army ready to march immediately after receiving further orders, thus ready to act, which was not the case now."

afterward, he rode over to the Prussian army to discuss strategy with the Prussian leadership. This meeting at the Mill of Brye, behind the Prussian right flank, has become the center of a major controversy. There are Prussian claims that Wellington made a firm promise to support them but then failed to do so, thereby causing their defeat at the Battle of Ligny.[49] While Clausewitz himself never made such an extreme allegation against Wellington, his book does shed some light on this important issue.

The first such Prussian criticism of Wellington came before the Battle of Waterloo had even been fought. When Blücher sent his report on Ligny to King Frederick William on 17 June, it contained Gneisenau's complaint that "the army of the Duke of Wellington was unexpectedly, and in contrast to his promise, not yet concentrated sufficiently to be able to operate together against the enemy." That same evening, Gneisenau wrote to his wife that "because promised help did not come and misunderstandings had occurred, we were forced to retreat." Shortly after Waterloo, Gneisenau wrote that "The Duke of Wellington had promised to attack the enemy in the rear, but he also did not come, because his army—for who knows what reason—could not be concentrated." In August 1815, Gneisenau again claimed that Wellington "did not keep his promises to be ready to help us on the 16th [of June]," and mentioned the "defeat we had suffered because of him."[50]

In his Memorandum of 1842, Wellington gave no details of the discussions with the Prussians at Brye beyond simply mentioning that the meeting took place. His only other remarks on the meeting were made to friends in conversations that focused on his criticism of the Prussian positions at Ligny rather than on any promise of support.[51] While

---

49 The official Prussian historian of the campaign of 1815, General Oskar von Lettow-Vorbeck, wrote in 1904 that "The course of the battle of Ligny clearly reveals that the assistance that was promised [by Wellington] but did not arrive had a very unfavorable impact on the battle and was a major cause of the defeat." *Napoleons Untergang*, 312. More recent claims that the Prussians would not have stood and fought at Ligny had Wellington not deceived them by promising support he knew he could not deliver are found in Hofschröer, *1815*, 1:212-215, 232-242, 331-351 and *idem.*, "Did the Duke of Wellington Deceive His Prussian Allies in the Campaign of 1815?," *War in History* 5 (1998), 185.

50 Julius von Pflugk-Harttung, "Zu Blüchers Brief an den König von Preußen vom 17. Juni 1815," *Jahrbücher für die deutsche Armee und Marine* (1904), 219-221. Gneisenau to his wife, 17 June 1815; Gneisenau to Hardenberg, 22 June 1815; Gneisenau to Arndt, 17 August 1815; in Karl Griewank, *Gneisenau: Ein Leben in Briefen* (Leipzig: Koehler & Amelang, 1939), 323, 325, 332.

51 In 1827 Wellington said that the Prussians at Ligny had "persisted contrary to the Duke's

ON WATERLOO

he was not a participant at the meeting at Brye, Clausewitz's account nevertheless deserves close attention, because he certainly had close contact with senior Prussian leaders who were there, Gneisenau in particular. Clausewitz wrote that "the Duke told the Field Marshal that his army was at that moment assembling at Quatre Bras, and in a few hours he would hasten with it to assist Blücher." Clausewitz then added that, when Wellington spurred his horse to ride away, his parting words were supposedly, "At four o'clock I will be here."[52] Since much of Wellington's army was still on the march across the Belgian countryside, Clausewitz's account suggests that Wellington was promising much more than he could deliver.

Two other participants at the meeting at Brye recalled a much more conditional statement by Wellington. General von Dörnberg wrote that Wellington had said to Gneisenau, "I will see what is opposing me and how much of my army has arrived and then act accordingly." Genera von Müffling stated in his memoirs that Wellington had promised to come to the Prussians' aid "provided I am not attacked myself."[53]

---

advice in exposing their whole line to cannon-shot." Francis Egerton, Earl of Ellesmere, *Personal Reminiscences of the Duke of Wellington* (London: John Murray, 1904), 127. The Earl of Stanhope recounted an 1837 conversation in which Colonel Hardinge recalled Wellington saying to him at Brye, "If they fight here, they will be damnably mauled." (*Conversations*, 108-109.) Wellington then told Stanhope that the Prussian troops were posted "along the slope of a hill, so that no cannon-ball missed its effect upon them." Considerable doubt about the accuracy of such "war stories" told by Wellington long after the event is found in Hofschröer, *1815*, 1:239-242, 343-344, but Clausewitz also offered some criticism of the Prussian positions at Ligny (pp.120-122 above). Several contemporary accounts also support Wellington's views on the Prussian deployment. Captain Robert Batty commented on pages 58-59 of his *An Historical Sketch of the Campaign of 1815*, 2nd. ed. (London: Bodwell, Martin & Clark, 1820) that "the French batteries were posted on the heights behind the villages of St. Amand and Ligny, and, owing to the long slope of ground on which the Prussian columns were posted, the fire of the French artillery was very destructive, the shot bounding en ricochet in to the Prussian reserves on the heights." Similarly a French eyewitness wrote in 1815 that "the cannonade did not slow down for an instant, and our artillery, from what one could see, played havoc with the Prussian columns which—posted in mass on the slopes that formed the amphitheatre [of the Prussian position at Ligny] and on the plateau that terminated it—presented themselves without cover and received all the shots fired by the numerous batteries established along our line. [René de Bourgeois], *Relation Fidéle et détaillée de la dernière campagne de Buonaparte, terminée par la Bataille de Mont-Saint-Jean dite de Waterloo ou de la Belle Alliance par un témoin oculaire*, 2nd ed. (Paris: P.J. De Mat, 1815), 25-26.
52 See above, p.104.
53 Carl von Müffling, *Passages from My Life, together with Memoirs of the Campaign of 1813 and 1814*, 2nd ed. (London: Richard Bentley, 1853), 233-237. Dörnberg's account is in Pflugk-Harttung, *Vorgeschichte*, 293. Pflugk-Harttung analyzed the various accounts of the meeting

Placing such reservations on possible support to the Prussians does seem very much in character for the cautious Wellington. But even if this were not the case, and he actually had made the definite promise reported by Clausewitz, such a promise would have been based upon the assumption under which both Allied commanders were operating at the time of their meeting—i.e., that virtually all of the French army of about 130,000 men was opposing the Prussians. Clausewitz noted that the Allies thought Blücher had about 80,000 men on the field, so if Wellington could bring another 40-50,000 (his left wing plus the Reserve), the two sides would be about equal. Once the additional 35,000 men of the Prussian 4th Corps arrived, Blücher thought, victory would be "pretty certain." To Clausewitz, these odds were no guarantee of success against Napoleon, but they were still sufficient to make Blücher decide to give battle. The Prussian commander was reluctant to consider retreating, because doing so would move his army further from Wellington's and make a bad impression on the troops and the nations.[54] And it was certainly in keeping with Blücher's fiery character for him to decide to stand and give battle no matter what the odds rather than start the campaign with a retreat.

Clausewitz's account suggests that the Prussians were not expecting the entire Anglo-Allied army to participate in the battle. Rather, they were counting on the appearance of a substantial portion of it in the course of the day. Given the long delays in concentrating Wellington's army, however, it is doubtful that even the expected 40-50,000 men could have arrived in time.[55]

---

at Brye and concluded that Wellington had not made any unconditional promises of support. "Die Verhandlungen Wellingtons und Blüchers auf der Windmühle bei Brye (16. Juni 1815)," *Historisches Jahrbuch* 23 (1902), 80-97.

54 See above, p.104. Pflugk-Harttung suggested (*Vorgeschichte*, 65-66) that Blücher and Gneisenau actually preferred taking on Napoleon alone and therefore did not initially ask directly for Wellington's assistance but merely inquired as to his intentions. They wanted Wellington's forces in the vicinity in case the battle did not go their way, but hoped that an unaided Prussian victory would give their country increased prestige—and thus greater bargaining power—at the Congress of Vienna. Only when it became clear that the Prussian 4th Corps would not arrive in time did they begin to seek definite promises of support from Wellington. General von Lettow-Vorbeck strongly disagreed with this suggestion that the Prussians initially wished to try to defeat Napoleon by themselves. *Napoleons Untergang*, 273 fn.

55 Neil Carey has calculated that if Wellington had not been attacked, he would have been able to send a column of at least 20,000 men from Quatre Bras to the Prussian right flank by 4:30-5:15 p.m. "Quatre Bras and Ligny: Did Wellington Really Deceive the Prussians at Brye

In any case, the situation upon which any promise of support by Wellington would have been based was not what the commanders had assumed during their meeting at Brye. Napoleon had not massed his whole army against Blücher. He had instead divided it, sending 45,000 men toward Quatre Bras under Marshal Ney to prevent Wellington from interfering with the battle that Napoleon and the rest of the army were going to fight against Blücher. Another 10,000 men of Lobau's 6th Corps had been left behind and then forgotten at Charleroi, leaving the force that Napoleon led on 16 June at only 63,000 men. As a result, the 83,000 Prussian troops waiting to receive Napoleon's assault at Ligny actually enjoyed considerable superiority in numbers, although Gneisenau either did not realize this fact or was unwilling to admit it.[56] The Prussians also benefited greatly from the strong stand of Wellington's army at Quatre Bras. Wellington was unable to provide assistance on the battlefield of Ligny itself, but his stubborn defense and subsequent strong counterattack generated such heavy pressure that Ney recalled d'Erlon's corps just when it was about to intervene at Ligny. If the two neighboring battles of Quatre Bras and Ligny are considered as one large engagement, as they should be, then Wellington did provide considerable assistance to Blücher. Prussian complaints that their defeat was due to Wellington's failure to provide support therefore sound like a search for a scapegoat outside their own ranks to explain their defeat in a defensive position of their own choosing by a numerically smaller force. To his credit, Clausewitz—although critical of Wellington's delays in concentrating his forces—never went so far as Gneisenau in blaming Wellington for the Prussian defeat at Ligny.

Controversy Over Who Won Waterloo

Another area of Anglo-Prussian controversy in the 19th century was the issue of who deserved the lion's share of credit for the final victory over

---

on 16th June 1815?" *First Empire* no. 43 (1998), 33.

56 Gneisenau's letter to his king on 17 June 1815 claimed that 80,000 Prussians had fought 120,000 Frenchmen at Ligny, while his letter of 22 June spoke of the Prussians' three corps being "such disproportionately small forces against the overwhelming numerical superiority of the enemy." Griewank, *Gneisenau*, 319, 322. Andrew Uffindell has concluded that 83,000 Prussians with 224 guns faced 63,000 Frenchmen with 230 guns. *Eagle's Last Triumph*, 79.

Napoleon on the 18th of June. This debate began almost immediately after the battle's end. The first Prussian claim that they had struck the decisive blow came in General Gneisenau's post-battle report to his king:

> It was half an hour past seven, and the issue of the battle was still uncertain.... The French troops fought with desperate fury: however, some uncertainty was perceived in their movements, and it was observed that some pieces of canon were retreating. At this moment the first columns of the corps of General Zieten arrived on the points of attack, near the village of Smohain, on the enemy's right flank, and instantly charged. This moment determined the defeat of the enemy. His right wing was broken in three places; he abandoned his positions. Our troops rushed forward at the *pas de charge*, and attacked him on all sides, while, at the same time, the whole English line advanced.[57]

Such Prussian claims soon became public. In July 1815 the British Foreign Secretary, Viscount Castlereagh, recommended that Field Marshal Blücher not be the only Allied field marshal to receive the Prince Regent's prestigious Military Order, because the Prussians "rather assume more than their fair share of credit for the battle of Waterloo."[58]

Clausewitz's history also attributed the collapse of Napoleon's army to the actions of the Prussians. He concluded that after many hours of very heavy fighting, Wellington's and Napoleon's armies were like fighters "who had been driven to such a state of exhaustion that a decisive blow would be all the more decisive, such that the defeated side would not be able to rally again. This decisive blow resulted from the attack of the Prussians." In Clausewitz's account, the village of Plancenoit had been captured and Zieten's corps had broken through the right side of the French line before Wellington defeated the final assault of the Imperial Guard and ordered the general advance of his army. But Clausewitz admitted that he was not completely certain of the timing of events on the French right flank. He commented in his next chapter, "It would be interesting to know if the Prussians were already firmly in possession of

---

57 Gneisenau's report on the battle of Waterloo was published in English in Christopher Kelly, *The Memorable Battle of Waterloo* (London: Thomas Kelly, 1818), 61.
58 Viscount Castlereagh to Earl Bathurst, [1] July 1815, in *WSD*, 10:638.

Plancenoit when Bonaparte marched off with these last reserves [the Imperial Guard battalions used to attack Wellington], throwing them into the very jaws of destruction."[59]

The issue of how much of a role the Prussians played in the collapse of Napoleon's army remains controversial to this day. Two recent books have restated the old Prussian claim that their attacks on the French right were the main cause of Napoleon's defeat.[60] But these claims—and thus also Clausewitz's account—are not supported by key Prussian accounts of the fighting on this side of the battlefield. The War Diary of the Prussian 1st Corps, which was written shortly after the end of the battle, described how the advance guard of the corps' 1st Brigade attacked and captured the hamlet of Smohain and continued on to attack the French right wing. But then, "because our forces were too weak, they were forced back to Smohain. In the meantime the rest of the brigade's infantry arrived. The enemy, who were already being attacked in the rear and the flank by the 4th Corps from Plancenoit and now also by us and also by the entire English army in the front, fell back, offering only slight resistance, which soon ended and turned into flight and the complete dissolution of their entire army."[61] The War Diary thus shows that the 1st Corps suffered an initial setback when advancing from Smohain, and succeeded in pushing back the French right wing only after the English general advance took place. The casualty returns for Zieten's corps on 18 June also show that it did not undergo much heavy fighting that day, as would have been the case had it attacked and broken through a deployed French force, rather than simply advancing against disordered enemy units that were already in the process of disintegration due to events elsewhere on the battlefield.[62]

---

59 See above, pp.144, 150.
60 David Hamilton-Williams argues for the decisive impact of Zieten's attack in *Waterloo: New Perspectives, The Great Battle Reconsidered* (London: John Wiley and Sons, 1994), 344-345. Hofschröer, *1815*, 2:138-145, emphasizes Zieten's attack but considers the Prussians' capture of Plancenoit, which he depicts as coming before Wellington ordered a general advance of his army in the wake of the Imperial Guard's repulse, to be the decisive blow against Napoleon.
61 Julius von Pflugk-Harttung, "Das I. Korps Zieten bei Belle-Alliance und Wavre," *Jahrbücher für die deutsche Armee und Marine* (1908), 200-201.
62 The Prussian 1st Brigade, which led the advance of the 1st Corps, suffered only 31 killed, 158 wounded and 111 missing on 18 June 1815. The accompanying 1st Cavalry Brigade, alleged by some accounts to have slashed its way through the French right wing, lost only 2 killed and 11 wounded. Barry Van Danzig, *Who Won Waterloo? The Trial of Captain Siborne* (St. Leonards-on-Sea: UPSO Limited, 2006), 266-267.

WELLINGTON VERSUS CLAUSEWITZ

The other event mentioned by Clausewitz as a cause for the dissolution of Napoleon's army—the final capture of Plancenoit by the Prussians—did not occur until after the defeat of the Imperial Guard's attack. This prompted Prussian historian Julius von Pflugk-Harttung to write, "The main problem of the Prussians was their lack of success at Plancenoit.... Because the enemy Guard battalions unswervingly held this village until Wellington's line had achieved the final victory, they also kept the Prussians from gaining the laurels of the day.... If Bülow had captured Plancenoit an hour earlier, he would have achieved the decisive results in the flank and rear, which Wellington now won at the front."[63] Clausewitz and Wellington, each from their different perspectives, would doubtless have smiled at this sort of perfectly legitimate but ultimately empty speculation. There were any number of occasions in the campaign of 1815 in which an hour one way or another might have made all the difference.

Ultimately any attempt to give complete credit for the victory over Napoleon to either Wellington or Blücher is meaningless. This was neither a British victory nor a Prussian victory; it was an Allied victory. The tenacious stand of Wellington's army against a series of heavy French attacks throughout the day was the essential precondition for the final Allied victory, for if he had been forced to retreat, the late arrival of the Prussians could have left them exposed to great danger. The arrival of the Prussians and their subsequent attack contributed to Wellington's successful defense by diverting Napoleon's attention and a considerable portion of his reserve at critical junctions in the battle. And at the end of the battle, the complete dissolution of Napoleon's army occurred as a result of a combination of near-simultaneous actions by both armies that shattered French morale: Wellington's forces defeated the supposedly invincible Imperial Guard and began a general advance; the leading elements of General Zieten's corps attacked French right-wing troops who had been told to expect reinforcements under Marshal Grouchy; and General Bülow's and General Pirch I's corps renewed their heavy attacks on Plancenoit, leading finally to its capture.

Wellington's Memorandum clearly supports such an "Allied victory" viewpoint because, while he wrote that the battle was terminated by the attack of his own army, he gave great credit to the contribution of the

---

63 Pflugk-Harttung, "I. Korps Zieten," 239.

Prussians by noting that the French troops had retired from their final attack "in great confusion" due in part to the fact that the "march of General Bülow's corps by Frischermont upon Plancenoit and La Belle Alliance had begun to take effect." He also stated that the arrival of the Prussians on the left of the Anglo-Allied line had led him to decide to undertake the final assault that destroyed the French army. Quoting from his 1815 Waterloo Dispatch, Wellington called the attack of the Prussians against Napoleon's right flank "a most decisive one," and he concluded that "even if I had not found myself in a situation to make the attack which produced the final result, [the Prussian assault] would have forced the enemy to retire if his attacks should have failed, and would have prevented him from taking advantage of them if they should unfortunately have succeeded."

Can We Still Benefit from Reading Clausewitz and Wellington on Waterloo Today?

Now that so much time has passed since Clausewitz wrote his history and Wellington his reply, are these two accounts still useful for today's historians? The answer is yes, very much so. Their value lies not so much in providing tactical details as in the insights they provide about the thinking of the key participants. Clausewitz's history is generally quite accurate, particularly where the Prussians are concerned. His analysis of Napoleon's attempts to rewrite history via his memoirs written in exile on St. Helena provides a very valuable corrective to the many accounts of Waterloo that accept Napoleon's statements without question. Clausewitz's descriptions of the Anglo-Allied army's plans and actions are less authoritative, due to the lack of information available to him, a fact of which he was well aware. Still, the obligation to think things through using all the available evidence remained, and Clausewitz did not shrink from criticizing anyone, even his own commander in the campaign. His criticisms never had the object of judging them as individuals, however. Rather, they were made in order to understand the commanders' actions, and he therefore stressed the need for analysts and critics to put themselves "precisely into the position of the individual who had to take action."

WELLINGTON VERSUS CLAUSEWITZ

Clausewitz's analysis of the overall strategic situation prior to the start of the campaign also offers a valuable perspective that is often ignored by historians anxious to begin right away with a description of the fighting. And at the tactical level, Clausewitz was careful not to expect unrealistic feats of movement—unlike many armchair critics of the Waterloo campaign, who lacked practical experience leading troops under similar conditions.

Wellington's Memorandum, written specifically in reply to Clausewitz's account of the duke's actions during the opening stages of the campaign, is therefore a much less comprehensive account of the campaign of 1815, but it represents the most detailed statement ever made by Wellington about his decision-making process in 1815, breaking his decades of silence on this subject. Wellington's description of the complex political-military situation at the start of the campaign is a significant contribution in itself. This does not mean that everything in the Memorandum should be accepted as gospel. It was written 27 years after the events by a 73-year-old man no longer at the height of his powers. Wellington was also clearly trying to put his actions in a favorable light in response to decades of criticism far less measured than Clausewitz's. In doing so, however, the duke made statements about the timing of orders and troop movements that are not in accord with the available documentation. Since much of this information was readily available to Wellington in the form of the published dispatches, and was in fact consulted by him as he wrote his Memorandum, these errors cannot be blamed simply on the faulty memory of an old man.[64]

Wellington's inaccurate statements about his orders and the movements of his troops at the start of the campaign have led some historians to question the value of the Memorandum. Colonel Charles Chesney complained in 1868 that "Wellington clearly gives his own impression, in 1842, of what he ought to have done in 1815."[65] The American historian John Codman Ropes went even farther, writing in 1893 that, "We are

---

[64] I share Peter Hofschröer's view (*1815*, 2:332-333) that Wellington's 1842 account of the orders he issued prior to Quatre Bras is far less accurate than Clausewitz's history. And it cannot be claimed that the passage of years had dimmed the duke's recollection of the events, because he definitely consulted volume 12 of his dispatches containing his correspondence and orders for June 1815 prior to writing his Memorandum. This is shown by a letter from Arbuthnot to Egerton, 22 July 1842, pp.34-35 above.

[65] Charles Chesney, *The Waterloo Lectures* (1907; reprinted London: Greenhill Books, 1997), 79, 95-96.

quite within bounds when we say that this Memorandum adds nothing to our knowledge of the facts. We may add that it is a pity that this is so.... It is a pity, we repeat, that he did not set himself to the task of drawing up an exhaustive and accurate narrative of the facts of the campaign."[66]

Ropes' statement goes too far. The importance of the Memorandum lies not in details about orders and movements but in its revelation of Wellington's overall state of mind and his strategic concept at the start of the campaign. Wellington clearly demonstrated the primacy of his instructions to defend Brussels at all times. He also noted his concerns about being fooled by Napoleon into making a "false movement"—concentrating his army in the wrong area against a threat that turned out to be a feint. And his continued insistence that Napoleon would have been better advised to attack "by other lines rather than by the valleys of the Sambre and the Meuse" show why the duke remained preoccupied with this possibility, even to the extent of leaving a considerable force to guard his flank at Hal prior to the Battle of Waterloo. There is no question that some of the caution that Wellington displayed in his encounter with Napoleon was rooted in his personality and in the engrained habits of a long and successful military career. Clausewitz regarded such influences as natural and characteristic of all great commanders. These personal qualities and habits in turn provided the lens through which Wellington evaluated what was for him the outstanding fact of his situation when the fighting began on the 15th of June: that he did not know much of anything about events on the Prussians' front and thus was reluctant to abandon his own beliefs about what Napoleon was likely to do.

In closing, it is worth recalling what both men thought about trying to analyze a battle such as Waterloo. Clausewitz remained very cautious as both a historian and theorist of war:

> With battle plans and all sorts of retrospective accounts before us, and with the events behind us, it is very easy to discover the actual causes of failure and, after thoroughly considering all the complexities of events, to highlight those that can be deemed mistakes. But all this cannot be done so easily at the time of action. The conduct of war is like movement in a resistant medi-

---

66 John Codman Ropes, *The Campaign of Waterloo: A Military History* (1893; reprinted Tyne & Wear: Worley Publications, 1995), 90-91.

um, in which uncommon qualities are required to achieve even mediocre results. It is for this reason that in war, more than in any other area, critical analysis exists only to discover the truth, not to sit in judgment.[67]

Wellington, for his part, doubted that it would ever be possible or even desirable to write an accurate history of the battle:

> The history of a battle is not unlike the history of a ball. Some individuals may recollect all the little events of which the great result is the battle won or lost; but no individual can recollect the order in which, or the exact moment at which, they occurred, which makes all the difference as to their value or importance.
>
> Then the faults of the misbehavior of some gave occasion for the distinction of others, and perhaps were the cause of material losses; and you cannot write a true history of a battle without including the faults and misbehavior of part at least of those engaged.
>
> Believe me that every man you see in a military uniform is not a hero; and that, although in the account given of a general action, such as that of Waterloo, many instances of individual heroism must be passed over unrelated, it is better for the general interests to leave those parts of the story untold, than to tell the whole truth.[68]

Wellington obviously believed that a true history of the Waterloo Campaign could tarnish some glittering reputations, and the inaccurate statements he made in the Memorandum about his initial orders and troop movements suggest that one of the reputations he was trying to protect was his own. Such defensiveness was actually unnecessary, because his performance in command of the Anglo-Allied army at the battles of Quatre Bras and Waterloo more than made up for his initial cautious response to the French attack. And it is the Memorandum that best helps us understand the reasons for this caution by showing the situation in June 1815 from Wellington's perspective, thus enabling

---

67 See above, p.123.
68 *WD*, 12:590.

us to fulfill Clausewitz's criteria for strategic criticism by placing ourselves precisely in Wellington's shoes. Historians should be grateful that Clausewitz's carefully reasoned analysis of the campaign of 1815 finally provoked Wellington into breaking his long-held silence on the subject and revealing his mindset at the start of the campaign. Clausewitz's history and Wellington's Memorandum therefore remain essential reading for everyone interested in the Waterloo Campaign.

INDEX

Alexander I, Czar of Russia (1777-1825, r.1801-1825), 20, 68, 231

Alexander III (the Great) of Macedonia (356-323B.C., r.336-323B.C.), 68

Alison, Sir Archibald (1792-1867), British historian, 2, 35, 36, 37, 40, 47, 49, 266

Alten, Karl August von, Count (Hannoverian general, 1764-1840), 16, 19, 72, 98, 99, 129

Anderlues (pl.), 197

Anthing, Carl Heinrich Wilhelm (Dutch general, 1766-1823), 72, 98

Arbuthnot, Charles (British diplomat and Tory politician, 1767-1850), 12, 34, 35, 37, 42, 47, 50, 54, 284

Argenson, Marc-René-Marie, Marquis (French statesman, 1771-1842), 211

Argenteuil (pl.), 26, 207, 214

Aubervillers (pl.), 202, 206, 213

Aunay (pl.), 202

Austerlitz, Battle of (1805), 7, 31, 172

Avesne (pl.), 26, 27, 88, 158, 189, 193, 196, 197, 198, 201, 202, 203, 273

Bachelu, Gilbert-Désiré-Joseph, Baron (French general, 1777-1849), 144

Barclay de Tolly, Michael Andreas, Prince (Russian field marshal and statesman, 1761-1818), 217, 239, 240

Beaulieu, Jean-Pierre de, Baron (Austrian general, 1725-1819), 186

Beaumont (pl.), 27, 88, 94, 158, 193, 196, 197, 200, 201, 202

Becker, Léonard-Nicolas, Count of Mons (French general, 1770-1840), 212

Belle Alliance (pl.), 18, 25, 65, 137, 138, 140, 146, 149, 152, 157, 176, 178, 180, 182, 185, 187, 189, 191, 192, 195, 234, 267, 276, 281, 283

Bernonville (pl.), 202

Berton, Jean-Baptiste (French officer, 1769-1822), 150

Binche (pl.), 95, 193, 197, 201

Bonaparte, Jérôme, Marshal of France (1784-1860), 128, 142, 188, 189

Bonaparte, Joseph, King of Naples and Sicily, King of Spain and the Indies, Comte de Survilliers (1768-1844), elder brother of Napoleon, 159, 180, 210, 266

Bonaparte, Lucien, Prince of Canino (1775-1840), 210

Borcke, Karl August Ferdinand von (Prussian general, 1776-1830), 25, 154

Bossu Woods, 128, 129

Bourbons, French royal family overthrown in French Revolution, restored in 1814, deposed by Napoleon and restored in 1815, 209, 210

Bourguet (pl.), 202

Breitenfeld, Battle of (1631), 251

Britain, 1, 9, 12, 43, 274

Brune, Guillaume-Marie-Anne, Marshal of France (1763-1815), 60, 217

289

INDEX

Brunswick, Friedrich Wilhelm, Duke (1771-1815), 16, 17, 70, 73, 91, 98, 269

Brussels, also Bruxelles (pl.), 15, 16, 23, 44, 45, 53, 73, 75, 76, 77, 81, 82, 83, 84, 86, 92, 98, 99, 100, 102, 106, 108, 111, 118, 126, 131, 134, 138, 143, 149, 152, 153, 158, 163, 164, 167, 168, 175, 185, 186, 220, 221, 224, 225, 228, 229, 230, 233, 235, 260, 261, 262, 263, 265, 266, 267, 268, 269, 270, 271, 272, 273, 274, 275, 285

Brye, also Bry (pl.), 101, 104, 109, 110, 113, 122, 127, 128, 275, 276, 277, 278, 279

Bubna and Littitz, Ferdinand, Count (Austrian field marshal, 1768-1825), 218

Bülow, Friedrich Wilhelm von, Baron, Count of Dennewitz (Prussian general, 1755-1816), 16, 18, 20, 73, 85, 89, 90, 98, 100, 104, 106, 118, 120, 126, 142, 143, 144, 145, 147, 148, 149, 163, 169, 170, 176, 177, 230, 233, 234, 282, 283

Bunzelwitz (pl.), 68

Cambrai (pl.), 202, 203

Carnot, Lazare-Nicolas-Marguerite (French general and statesman, 1753-1823), 210, 215

Caulaincourt, Armand-Augustin-Louis de, Duke of Vicenza (French general and diplomat, 1773-1827), 210

Cerisi (pl.), 202

Charleroi (pl.), 15, 17, 27, 54, 73, 75, 76, 83, 85, 86, 88, 91, 92, 93, 94, 95, 96, 97, 99, 107, 108, 124, 128, 157, 158, 185, 188, 193, 196, 197, 198, 201, 227, 229, 265, 266, 267, 269, 270, 273, 274, 279

Chassée [Chasse], Henri, Baron (Dutch general, 1765-1849), 72, 74, 98, 99, 137, 145

Chaunay (pl.), 202

Clausewitz, Marie von, née von Brühl, Prussian countess (1779-1836), wife to Carl von Clausewitz from 1810 and editor of his collected works, 5, 23, 27, 28, 29, 237, 240

Clauzel, Bertrand, Count (French general, 1772-1842), 60

Clinton, Sir Henry (British general, 1771-1829), 19, 72, 77, 86, 98, 137

Colbert, Louis-Pierre-Alphonse de, Count (French general, 1776-1843), 188

Collaert, Jean Alphonse de, Baron (Dutch general, 1761-1816), 72, 74, 145

Colleret (pl.), 197, 201

Colloredo-Mansfeld, Hieronymus von, Count (Austrian field marshal, 1775-1822), 217

Colville, Sir Charles (British general, 1770-1843), 72, 74, 98, 137

Compiègne (pl.), 26, 28, 29, 199, 202, 203, 204, 205, 206

Cooke, George (British general), 2, 16, 19, 72, 98

Creil (pl.), 202, 203, 204, 206

Dammartin (pl.), 26, 28, 202, 207

Daun, Leopold Josef von, Count, Prince of Thiano (Austrian field marshal, 1705-1766), 62

Davout, Louis-Nicolas (1770-1823), Duke of Auerstedt, Prince of Eckmühl, Marshal of France, French minister of war in 1815, 215

Davout, Louis-Nicolas (1770-1823), Duke of Auerstedt, Prince of Eckmühl, Marshal of France, French minister of war in 1815, 211, 212, 214, 215

Decaen, Charles-Mathieu-Isidore, Count (French general, 1769-1832), 60

Decken, Johann Friedrich von der (British/Hanoverian general, 1769-1840), 73, 74

DeLancey (or De Lancey), Colonel Lord William Howe (1778-1815), Wellington's chief of staff at Waterloo, 20

Dendre river, 76

Dinant (pl.), 158, 159, 185, 198, 201

Dohna, Karl Friedrich Emil zu Dohna-Schlobitten (1784-1859), Prussian regimental commander in 1815, later field-marshal, 26

Domon, Jean-Simon, Viscount (French general, 1774-1830), 137, 142, 143, 148

Dörnberg, Wilhelm Kaspar Ferdinand Freiherr von (Hanoverian general, 1768-1850), 19, 91, 271, 272, 273, 277

Duhesme, Guillaume-Philibert, Count (French general 1766-1815), 115

Dumouriez, French General Charles-François (1739-1823), 43

Dyle River, 24, 34, 132, 135, 147, 148, 152, 153, 154, 155, 167, 168, 179, 180, 181, 182, 185, 193

Egerton, Francis (1800-1857), born Lord Francis Leveson-Gower (his name until 1833), 1st Earl of Ellesmere and Viscount Brackley after 1846, 2, 7, 8, 9, 12, 34, 35, 39, 40, 42, 43, 44, 45, 47, 53, 54, 231, 257, 266, 276, 284

Elizabeth I, Czarina of Russia (1709-62), 68

Ellesmere. See Egerton.

Estorff, Baron von (Hanoverian officer), 98

Etrouenge (pl.), 202

Eugene, Prince of Savoy (1663-1736), great captain, 176

Exelmans, Remi-Joseph-Isidore (French general, 1775-1852), 133, 135, 150, 157, 166, 180, 181, 207

Eylau, Battle of (1807), 172

Fesmey (pl.), 202

Flahaut de la Billarderie, August-Charles-Joseph, Count (French general, 1785-1870), 127

Fleurus (pl.), 15, 23, 85, 92, 95, 96, 97, 100, 104, 105, 106, 108, 109, 110, 125, 135, 150, 165, 229, 268

Fontaine l'Evèque (pl.), 196, 197

Fouché, Joseph, Duke of Otranto (French statesman, 1763-1820), 43, 210, 211, 212, 266

Foy, Maximilian-Sebastian (French general, 1775-1825), 142

France, 1, 3, 4, 15, 47, 55, 56, 57, 58, 60, 67, 68, 69, 70, 74, 80, 81, 109, 177, 191, 209, 210, 217, 218, 219, 220, 221, 226, 227, 243, 244, 245, 247, 248, 249, 250, 251, 252, 253, 258, 259, 262, 264, 274, 275

Frasne (pl.), 16, 110

Frederick II (the Great), King of Prussia (1712-86, r.1740-1786), 62, 68, 174, 176, 242, 249

Frederick William III, King of Prussia (1770-1840, r.1797-1840), 276

Frederick, Prince of the Netherlands [Willem Frederik Karel, Prince of

INDEX

Orange-Nassau] (1797-1881), 72, 77, 80, 137, 204, 218

Frimont, Johann Maria Philipp, Count (Austrian field marshal, 1759-1831), 217

Frischermont (pl.), 18, 138, 142, 148, 149, 175, 176, 234, 283

Gelicourt (pl.), 202, 204

Gembloux (pl.), 24, 90, 100, 132, 133, 134, 135, 150, 151, 156, 157, 158, 162, 168, 169, 179, 180, 181, 197, 201

Genappe (pl.), 17, 19, 193, 196

Gérard, Étienne-Maurice, Count (French general, 1773-1855), 72, 105, 106, 115, 121, 133, 155, 165, 166, 180, 181, 205

German Legion, 18

Girard, Jean-Baptiste, Baron (French general, 1775-1815), 97, 105, 113, 114, 115, 137, 138, 161, 193

Glabbaix la Hutte (pl.), 196

Gneisenau, August Wilhelm Anton Neithardt von, Count (Prussian general, 1760-1831), Blücher's chief of staff, Clausewitz's patron, 5, 26, 28, 89, 193, 194, 238, 262, 264, 276, 277, 278, 279, 280

Gonesse (pl.), 28, 202, 203, 207

Gosselies (pl.), 95, 97, 105, 107, 111, 127, 193, 196, 197, 229, 270

Grenier, Paul, Count (French general and statesman, 1768-1827), 210, 215

Grouchy, Emmanuel de, Marshal of France (1766-1847), 5, 7, 25, 33, 34, 35, 37, 105, 108, 109, 117, 121, 133, 134, 135, 141, 150-157, 158, 159, 161-170, 175, 177, 179, 180, 181, 182, 186, 189, 194, 195, 196, 197, 198, 200, 201, 203, 205, 206, 211, 212, 215, 232, 233, 282

Guise (pl.), 202, 203

Gurwood, John, Captain (later Colonel) British army (1790-1845), in later years, Wellington's private secretary and editor of the Wellington Dispatches, 2, 7, 8, 15, 31, 32, 33, 34, 35, 36, 37, 39, 40, 41, 43, 44, 45, 46, 48, 49, 50, 51, 52, 53, 229, 235, 257, 263, 266, 274, 275

Gustavus Adolphus, King of Sweden (1594-1632, r.1611-1632), great captain and military innovator, Protestant hero, 251

Guyot, Claude-Étienne (French general, 1768-1837), 140, 144

Hacke, Albrecht Georg Ernst Karl von (Prussian general, 1768-1835), 73

Ham (pl.), 26, 27, 95

Hannut (pl.), 85, 87, 89, 90

Hesse-Homburg, Ludwig Wilhelm Friedrich, Prince (Hessian general, 1770-1839), 218

Hill, Sir Rowland Baronet of Almaraz and Hawkstone (British general, 1772-1842), 19, 72, 76, 77, 137

Homblieres (pl.), 202

Hougoumont (pl.), 17, 18, 139, 142, 171, 176, 238

Hulot de Mazarny, Baron (French general), 155

Huy (pl.), 74, 185

Imperial Guard, 15, 19, 59, 72, 87, 88, 97, 105, 108, 111, 113, 173, 188, 220, 280, 281, 282

Jagow, Friedrich Wilhelm Christian Ludwig von (Prussian general, 1771-1857), 116, 123

Jena, Battle of, often Jena-Auerstedt or Jena-Auerstädt, 1806, 4, 111, 151, 187, 239

Jomini, Antoine-Henri, baron (Swiss national, French—later Russian—general, military historian and theorist, 1779-1869), 2

Jürgass or Wahlen-Jürgass, Alexander Georg Ludwig Moritz Konstantin Maximilian von (Prussian general, 1758-1833), 113, 116, 122

Kellerman, François-Etienne, Marquis, second Duke of Valmy, French general (1770-1835), 128, 129, 140, 144

Kleist von Nollendorf, Friedrich Heinrich Ferdinand Emil, Count (Prussian general, 1762-1823), 64, 65, 201

Knesebeck, Karl Friedrich von dem (Prussian Field Marshal, 1768-1848), 5

La Bavette (pl.), 24, 152, 154

La Fère (pl.), 202, 203

La Forest, Antoine-René de, Count (French statesman, 1756-1846), 211

La Haye Sainte (pl.), 17, 18, 47, 138, 139, 142, 143, 144, 145

Lafayette, Marie-Joseph-Paul-Rochyves-Gilbert de Mortier, Marquis de (French general and statesman, 1757-1834), 209, 211

Lamarque, Jean-Maximilien, Baron (French general, 1770-1832), 60

Lambert, Sir John (British general), 19, 73, 98, 148, 175

Lambusart Woods, 96

Landrecy (pl.), 198, 201, 218

Landwehr, Prussian militia or national guard, 56, 57, 73, 74, 123, 250, 251

Laon (pl.), 29, 72, 88, 159, 188, 189, 193, 197, 198, 199, 200

Lassigny (pl.), 202

Laurent (French officer), 127

Le Menil (pl.), 202, 207

Lecourbe, Claude-Jacques (French general, 1759-1815) or Claude-Joseph, Count (French general, 1760-1815), 60, 217

Lefebvre, François-Joseph, Duke of Danzig, Marshal of France (1755-1820), 215

Lefebvre-Desnouettes, Charles, Count (French general, 1773-1822), 144

Lefol, Etienne-Nicolas, Baron (1764-1840), 113

Leipzig, Battle of (1813), 56, 276

Levée en masse, radical innovation of mass conscription during French Revolution, esp. in 1793, 56, 251

Liége (pl.), 73, 74, 85, 89, 90, 126, 163

Ligny (pl.), 4, 9, 12, 15, 23, 48, 83, 89, 90, 99, 101, 102, 103, 105, 106, 112, 115, 116, 117, 118, 119, 120, 121, 122, 123, 124, 125, 128, 130, 131, 133, 135, 138, 141, 147, 152, 161, 170, 175, 191, 192, 229, 230, 231, 233, 238, 245, 257, 267, 274, 275, 276, 278, 279

Lille (pl.), 42, 72, 75, 76, 77, 84, 87, 88, 219, 228, 273

Limale (pl.), 151, 153, 155, 156, 168, 181

Lobbes (pl.), 15, 196

Lockhart, John Gibson (1794-1854) editor, Quarterly Review 1825-1853, 40, 45

London, 1, 2, 9, 11, 12, 15, 31, 35, 36, 40, 42, 43, 47, 48, 52, 91, 159, 240, 252, 257, 261, 263, 266, 269, 274, 275, 276, 277, 280, 281, 284

Louis XVIII Bourbon (1755-1824), King of France 1814-1824, 55, 217, 218, 219, 220, 221, 225, 235, 261

Louvres (pl.), 202

INDEX

Malmaison (pl.), 207, 211, 212
Malplacquet (pl.), 201
Marchiennes-au-pont (pl.), 196
Marie Louise, Habsburg princess, Duchess of Parma (1791–1847), second wife of Napoleon Bonaparte (married 1810) and Empress of the French, 28
Marli (also Marle, Marly, Marlis, pl.), 198, 202, 207
Marwitz, Friedrich August Ludwig von der (1777-1837), Prussian officer, later general, politician, and reactionary, 113, 114, 116
Masséna, André, Duke of Rivoli, Prince of Esslingen, Marshal of France (1758-1817), 215
Maubeuge (pl.), 76, 93, 174, 197, 201, 218, 273
Maurin, Antoine, Baron (French general, 1771-1830), 157
Meaux (pl.), 201, 202, 203, 205, 206
Mechelen (pl.), 73, 82
Meillereaux (pl.), 196, 197
Merbe le Chateau (pl.), 197
Merke Braine (pl.), 17
Metz (pl.), 87, 88
Meuse river, 15, 23, 38, 54, 69, 70, 74, 75, 81, 82, 84, 87, 92, 93, 102, 120, 126, 134, 135, 158, 159, 179, 182, 184, 185, 195, 220, 226, 230, 235, 260, 263, 272, 285
Milhaud, Edouard-Jean-Baptiste (French general, 1766-1833), 137, 140, 144
Mitchell (British officer), 19, 98
Mons (pl.), 42, 53, 54, 73, 75, 76, 84, 91, 174, 196, 198, 227, 228, 233, 235, 265, 268, 271, 272, 273
Mont St. Jean (pl.), 65, 137, 138, 163, 168, 169, 172, 173, 196, 276

Montenotte, Battle of (1796), 186
Mont-Saint-Guibert (pl.), 179, 180
Morand, Charles-Antoine-Louis-Alexis de, Count (French general, 1771-1835), 188
Morfontaine (pl.), 202
Mortier, Édouard-Adolphe-Casimir-Joseph, Duke of Trévise, Marshal of France (1768-1835), 72, 201
Moscow, 4, 68, 239, 254, 255
Müffling, Friedrich Karl Ferdinand von, Baron (Prussian general, 1775-1851), Prussian liaison to Wellington's headquarters during the Waterloo campaign, 20, 91, 229, 262, 265, 267, 268, 269, 272, 277
Murat, Joachim-Napoléon (1767-1815), Marshal of France, 1st Prince Murat, King of Naples from 1808 to 1815, Napoleon's brother-in-law due to marriage to Caroline Bonaparte, 220, 221
Namur (pl.), 23, 24, 26, 27, 54, 73, 74, 75, 76, 79, 83, 85, 89, 90, 92, 106, 108, 124, 128, 131, 132, 133, 134, 135, 137, 138, 144, 157, 158, 159, 164, 165, 166, 167, 179, 195, 197, 200, 227, 232, 264, 268
Nanteuil (pl.), 202, 205, 206
Nassau, 16, 20, 70, 73, 98
Nesle (pl.), 202
Netherlands, 15, 20, 38, 55, 60, 62, 63, 65, 69, 70, 72, 74, 80, 81, 137, 142, 204, 217, 218, 219, 220, 221, 223, 225, 226, 227, 229, 230, 261, 262, 268, 271, 274
Ney, Michel, Duke of Elchingen, Prince of Moskova, Marshal of France (1769-1815), 96, 97, 99, 105, 106, 107, 110, 111, 112, 124, 125, 126, 127, 128, 129, 130, 131, 132,

133, 135, 137, 138, 141, 144, 161, 164, 173, 184, 185, 230, 231, 279
Nivelles (pl.), 16, 17, 19, 72, 77, 87, 91, 98, 99, 137, 138, 193, 197, 231, 233, 235, 270, 271
Nogelle (pl.), 198
Nouvion (pl.), 27, 202
Noyon (pl.), 202
Ohain (pl.), 17, 18, 147, 233, 234
Oise River, 28, 189, 199, 200, 203, 204, 205
Orange, William Frederick George Louis, Prince of (1792-1849), Dutch general and political leader, 16, 19, 64, 72, 74, 76, 77, 80, 91, 129, 137, 220, 229, 265, 267, 268, 269, 270, 271, 274
Orville (pl.), 202
Pack, Sir Dennis (British general), 16, 19, 98
Paget, Henry William, Earl of Uxbridge, Marquess of Anglesey (British general, 1768-1854), 17, 19, 73, 98
Pajol, Claude-Pierre, Count (French general, 1772-1844), 133, 135, 137, 150, 151, 155, 165, 166
Papelotte (pl.), 138, 142
Paris, 5, 23, 26, 27, 28, 29, 55, 57, 59, 66, 67, 72, 87, 88, 92, 107, 134, 150, 167, 180, 182, 185, 189, 190, 191, 192, 198, 199, 200, 201, 202, 203, 204, 205, 206, 207, 209, 210, 211, 212, 213, 214, 215, 216, 219, 220, 247, 252, 276
Paris Woods, 144
Péronne (pl.), 193, 202, 203
Perponcher-Sedlnitzky, Hendrick George, Count (Dutch general, 1741-1819), 16, 72, 74, 97, 98, 127, 128, 130, 132, 142, 143, 178, 271

Petit, Jean-Martin, Baron (French general, 1772-1856), 188
Picton, Sir Thomas (British general, 1758-1815), 16, 19, 72, 98, 128, 129, 271
Pirch, Georg Dubislaw Ludwig von [Pirch I] (Prussian general, 1763-1838), 96, 282
Pirch, Otto Karl Lorenz von [Pirch II] (Prussian general, 1765-1824), 96, 113
Piré de Ronovinene, Hipployte-Marie-Guillaume, Count (French general, 1778-1850), 129
Plancenoit (various spellings, pl.), 18, 138, 145, 147, 149, 150, 164, 196, 234, 280, 281, 282, 283
Plessis-Piquet (pl.), 23, 27, 207, 208, 216
Pochhammer (Prussian officer), 24
Ponsonby of Imokilly, Sir William Brabazon, Baron (British general, 1744-1815), 18, 19, 20, 143
Pont St. Maxence (pl.), 199, 202, 203, 204, 206
Poret de Morvan, Paul Jean-Baptiste, Baron (French general, 1777-1834), 188
Quatre Bras (also Quatre-Bras, Les-Quatre-Bras, pl.), 16, 17, 39, 77, 86, 91, 97, 98, 99, 104, 105, 106, 108, 110, 111, 120, 124, 127, 128, 129, 130, 131, 132, 137, 138, 166, 167, 169, 193, 228, 229, 230, 231, 232, 233, 258, 265, 266, 270, 271, 272, 274, 277, 278, 279, 284, 286
Quinette, Nicolas-Marie, Baron of Rochemont (French statesman, 1762-1821), 210
Rapp, Jean de, Count (French general, 1771-1821), 57, 60, 62, 63, 80, 217

INDEX

Reede, Major-General W.F. van, Dutch liaison to Wellington's headquarters, 263

Regnauld de Saint-Jean d'Angély, Michel-Louis-Étienne, Count (French statesman, 1762-1819), 210

Reille, Honoré-Charles-Michel-Joseph, Marshal of France (1775-1860), 72, 97, 108, 127, 140, 142, 212, 230, 231

Rocroy (pl.), 202, 218

Russia, 4, 7, 9, 31, 42, 56, 68, 220, 238, 239, 244, 245, 249, 250, 253, 254

Sambre River, 15, 27, 75, 83, 85, 95, 105, 159, 184, 187, 193, 195, 196, 198, 203, 230, 235, 266, 267, 270, 272, 285

Saxe-Weimar, Karl Bernhard von, Duke (Dutch officer, 1792-1862), 97

Scharnhorst, Gerhard Johann David von (Prussian general, 1755-1813), 3, 4, 7, 248

Schwarzenberg, Karl Philipp von, Prince (Austrian field marshal, 1771-1820), 62, 69, 187, 217

Sebastiani, François-Horace-Bastine de, Count (French statesman, 1772-1851), 211

Senlis (pl.), 202, 205

Sèvres (pl.), 29, 202, 208

Siborne, William, British Army captain and historian (1797-1849), 2, 47, 51, 52, 266, 267, 281

Smohain (pl.), 138, 142, 149, 280, 281

Sohr, Friedrich Georg Ludwig von (Prussian lieutenant-colonel, 1775-1845), 28, 158, 200, 207, 208

Soignies, Forest of, 91, 128, 137, 138, 147, 162, 163, 171, 175, 178, 230, 271

Soissons (pl.), 28, 189, 199, 200, 201, 202, 203, 204, 205, 206

Solre-sur-Sambre (pl.), 88, 94

Sombreffe (pl.), 15, 17, 23, 77, 83, 84, 85, 86, 89, 90, 91, 96, 98, 99, 100, 101, 102, 105, 108, 109, 116, 117, 118, 120, 125, 230, 232, 258, 264, 270, 271, 275

Soult, Nicolas-Jean-de-Dieu, Duke of Dalmatia, Marshal of France (1769-1851), 108, 109, 110, 111, 135, 157, 161, 162, 163, 164, 166, 188, 211, 213, 215, 233

St. Achtenrode (pl.), 156, 157, 197, 201

St. Amand (pl.), 15, 23, 96, 100, 101, 102, 105, 106, 109, 111, 112, 113, 114, 115, 116, 118, 119, 121, 122, 125, 126, 133, 137, 165, 230, 231, 238, 276

St. Balâtre (pl.), 83, 100, 117, 118, 120

St. Cloud (pl.), 28, 29, 208, 216

St. Denis (pl.), 202, 207

St. Germain (pl.), 26, 28, 29, 202

St. Lambert (pl.), 147, 148, 152, 156, 163, 164, 169, 170, 174, 175, 176, 182

St. Quentin (pl.), 26, 27, 202

Stedman, J. A. (Dutch general), 72

Steinmetz, Karl Friedrich Franziskus von (Prussian general, 1768-1837), 105

Stengel, Rudolf Anton Wenzislaus von (Prussian officer, 1772-1828), 153, 155, 156

Stülpnagel, Wolf Wilhelm Ferdinand von (Prussian colonel, 1781-1839), 25, 155, 156

Subervie, Jacques-Gervais, Baron (French general, 1776-1856), 142, 143, 148

Suchet, Louis-Gabriel, Duke of Albufera, Marshal of France (1770-1826), 60, 63, 217, 218

Tauroggen, Convention of (1812), 4
Teste, François-Antoine (French general, 1775-1862), 133, 135, 150, 155
Thielmann, Johann Adolf, Baron (Prussian general, 1765-1824), commander of Prussian 3rd Corps in 1815, Clausewitz's immediate commander, 4, 34, 73, 106, 116, 117, 119, 120, 121, 126, 134, 152, 153, 154, 155, 156, 157, 158, 181, 182, 195, 208, 238
Thuin (pl.), 15, 94, 95, 196, 198, 229, 265, 266, 267, 268, 270
Tiedemann, Karl von (Prussian officer), 25
Tirlemont, conference at, 77, 258
Tournai (also Tournay, pl.), 54, 75, 84, 227, 228, 273
Turenne, Henri-de-La-Tour-d'Auvergne, Viscount, Marshal of France (1611-75), 174, 176, 177
Valenciennes (pl.), 54, 72, 76, 77, 84, 88, 174, 198, 228
Vandamme, Dominique-Joseph (French general, 1770-1830), 25, 72, 96, 105, 126, 130, 133, 166, 181, 205, 206, 208
Vandeleur, Sir John Ormsby (British general, 1763-1849), 19, 143
Versailles (pl.), 28, 29, 202, 207, 208
Vichery, Louis-Joseph, Baron (French general, 1767-1831), 150, 155

Uxbridge. See Paget.
Wagnelée (pl.), 101, 105, 113, 119, 122, 124, 125, 126
Wagram, Battle of (1809), 172
Wavre (pl.), 5, 17, 23, 24, 25, 132, 134, 135, 136, 139, 147, 148, 150-157, 162, 163, 167, 168, 169, 170, 179-181, 185, 186, 196, 197, 201, 203, 231, 232, 233
Wellesley, Richard Colley Marquis of (1760-1842), Wellington's older brother, 2, 48
Wrede, Karl Philipp von, Prince (Bavarian field marshal, 1767-1838), 217
Württemberg, William Friedrich Karl, Crown Prince (1781-1864), 217
Yorck, Johann David Ludwig, Graf (Count) von Wartenburg, Prussian general, later field-marshal (1759-1830), 4, 7, 28, 31, 201
Zepelin, Konstantin von (Prussian officer, 1771-1848), 155, 156
Zieten (also Ziethen), Hans Ernst Karl, Count (Prussian general, 1770-1848), corps commander in 1815, 15, 27, 73, 85, 88, 89, 90, 92, 94, 95, 96, 100, 104, 142, 145, 150, 177, 198, 206, 208, 228, 229, 230, 231, 232, 263, 265, 266, 267, 268, 269, 270, 272, 280, 281, 282

Printed in Great Britain
by Amazon.co.uk, Ltd.,
Marston Gate.